Sources for Local Historians

PRINCIPAL CHANGES IN RATES OF WAGES REPORTED DURING JULY, 1927 (*continued*).

Industry.	Locality.	Date from which change took effect.	Classes of Workpeople.	Particulars of change. (*Decreases in italics.*)
			MINING AND QUARRYING—(*continued*).	
Coal Mining (*contd.*)	Cannock Chase ...	1 July	Workpeople employed in or about coal mines, other than those whose wages are regulated by movements in other industries.	*Decrease of 33·44 per cent. on basis rates of 1911, leaving wages at the minimum of 42 per cent. above basis rates.**
	Leicestershire ...	1 July		*Decrease† of 8·75 per cent. on basis rates of 1911, leaving wages 51·25 per cent. above basis rates, subject to a minimum gross daily wage, inclusive of subsistence allowance, of 7s. 2d. and 7s. 6d. for day-wage surface and underground workers respectively.**
	Bristol	1 July		*Decrease† of 7½ per cent. on basis rates, leaving wages at the minimum of 22 per cent. above basis rates for pieceworkers and 24 per cent. above basis rates for other workers.‡*
	North Wales ...	1 July		*Decrease† of 10 per cent. on standard basis rates of 1911, leaving wages at the minimum of 22 per cent. above standard, subject to a minimum gross daily wage of 6s. for lower-paid day-wage men.§*
Iron Mining	Cleveland	25 July	Ironstone miners	*Decrease of 5 per cent. on standard rates, leaving wages 64·3 per cent. above the standard. Rates after change for labourers: underground, 3s. 4d. to 3s. 8d. per shift; surface, 3s. 4d. to 3s. 6d., plus 64·3 per cent., plus amounts varying, according to base rates, from 5d. to 1d. per shift.*
	Cumberland... ...	18 July	Workpeople employed at iron ore mines.	*Decrease‖ of 2d. per shift in the bargain price (8s. 9d. to 8s. 7d.), of 2d. per shift in the minimum wage (7s. 3d. to 7s. 1d.), of 2d. per shift for other underground and surface workers, and of 1d. per shift for youths under 18 years of age. Rates after change: shift men, 8s. 7d.; leading labourers, 7s. 5d.; winding enginemen, joiners and blacksmiths, 8s. 7d.; pumping enginemen, loco drivers and crane drivers, 8s. 1d.*
	Furness and District	11 July	Iron ore miners and surfacemen (except blacksmiths and fitters whose wages are not regulated by sliding-scale arrangements).	*Decrease‖ of 2d. per shift in the bargain price (7s. 8d. to 7s. 6d.), of 2d. per shift in the minimum wage (6s. 11d. to 6s. 9d.), of 1½d. per shift for surfacemen, and of ¾d. per shift for boys.*
	Northamptonshire ...	20 July	Ironstone miners and limestone quarrymen.	*Decrease of 3 per cent. on standard rates, leaving wages 42¾ per cent.¶ above the standard of 1920.*
	Banbury	27 July	Ironstone miners and quarrymen...	*Decrease of 3 per cent. on standard rates, leaving wages 42¾ per cent.¶ above the standard.*
Quarrying	West Cumberland ...	11 July	Limestone quarrymen	*Decrease‖ of 1½d. per shift for men, and of ¾d. per shift for boys under 16 years. Rates after change: haulage enginemen, 7s. 1½d.; blacksmiths and joiners, 7s. 10¾d.; day borers (1st class), 6s. 11¼d.; day labourers, 6s. 3¼d.; plus, in each case, a temporary bonus of 1s. per shift; ruddmen, 5s. 9¼d., plus a temporary bonus of 1s. 6d. per shift.*
	South and West Durham.	25 July	Limestone quarrymen	*Decrease of 5 per cent. on standard rates, leaving wages 64·3 per cent. above the standard.***
	Portland	1 July	Limestone quarryworkers (excluding labourers and workpeople in sawmills and masons' yards).	*Decrease†† of ½d. in the 1s. on earnings, of 6d. per day in the minimum wage for pieceworkers, and of 6d. per day for timeworkers. Rates after change: timeworkers, 12s. 1d. per day; minimum wage for pieceworkers, 11s. 9d. per day.*
			Limestone quarry labourers ...	*Decrease of 5d. per day (10s. 1d. to 9s. 8d.).*
			IRON AND STEEL INDUSTRIES.	
Pig Iron Manufacture.	Cleveland and Durham; Tees-side	3 July	Blastfurnacemen ... ...; Cokemen and by-product workers	*Decrease‖ of 3½ per cent. on standard rates, leaving wages 20½ per cent. above the standard of 1919 (plus, in some cases, an output or input bonus). Minimum rate after change for scale labourers, 6s. per shift, plus 20½ per cent.*
	West Cumberland and North Lancashire.	2nd full pay in July.	Workpeople (excluding skilled craftsmen and bricklayers on maintenance work, and also labourers) employed at blastfurnaces.	*Decreases in bonuses†† of amounts varying, according to base rates, from 1·3d. to 3·5d. per week, leaving total amount of bonuses varying from 1s. 6·6d. to 3s. 9d. per week.*
			Keepers, slaggers, fillers, enginemen, etc., employed at blastfurnaces.	*Decrease‖ of 2 per cent. on output bonus earnings, leaving the percentage payable 51¼ in the Workington area and 46¼ in the Furness area.*
	North Staffordshire	1st making-up day in July.	Tonnage men employed at blast furnaces.	*Decrease‖ of 6½ per cent. on standard rates, leaving wages 54½ per cent. above the standard.*
	Northamptonshire ...	20 July	Blastfurnacemen	*Decrease of 3 per cent. on standard rates, leaving wages 42¾ per cent.¶ above the standard of 1920. Minimum rate for labourers, 4s. 1d. and 4s. 3d. per shift, plus 42¾ per cent.*
	West of Scotland ...	31 July‡‡	Workpeople (excluding lower-paid day-wage men) employed at blastfurnaces.	*Decrease‖ of 2 per cent. on standard rates, leaving wages 16 per cent. above the standard.*
			ENGINEERING, SHIPBUILDING AND OTHER METAL INDUSTRIES.	
Ship-repairing	Hull (certain firms)...	1st pay day in July.	Blacksmiths, fitters, brass finishers, turners, smiths' strikers and machinists.	Increase of 3s. per week for smiths' strikers and machinists, and of 4s. per week for other classes.§§
Electrical Cable Manufacture.	Greater London ...	1 July	Jointers and jointers' mates ...	*Decrease†† of 3s. 11d. per week. Rates after change: jointers, 74s. 3d.; jointers' mates, 64s. 10d.*
	Other Districts in Great Britain (except North-East Coast).	1 July	Plumber-jointers, jointers and jointers' mates.	*Decrease†† of 3s. 11d. per week.*
Bobbin and Shuttle Manufacture.	England and Wales	1st pay day in July.	Workpeople employed in the bobbin-making industry; also shuttlemakers employed by certain firms at Garston and Blackburn:— Males 21 years and over ...	*Decrease†† of 2s. per week. Rates after change: higher-skilled, 61s. 6d.; lesser-skilled, 52s.; labourers, 42s.*
			Females 18 years and over ...	*Decrease†† of 1s. per week (25s. 6d. to 24s. 6d.).*
			Youths and girls	*Decrease†† of amounts varying, according to age, from 4d. to 8d. per week.*
	Yorkshire		Journeymen shuttlemakers ...	*Addition to base rate reduced†† from 54 to 46 per cent. Minimum daywork rate after change, 10½d. per hour, plus 46 per cent. (1s. 3·33d. per hour).*
	Lancashire (excluding Garston and Blackburn).		Journeymen shuttlemakers ...	*Addition to base rate reduced†† from 51 to 43 per cent. Minimum daywork rate after change, 1s. per hour, plus 43 per cent. (1s. 5·16d. per hour).*
	Lancashire		Apprentices to shuttlemakers ...	*Addition to base rate reduced†† from 33½ to 25½ per cent.*

* In the case of adult day-wage workmen whose gross wages are less than 8s. 9d. per shift, a subsistence allowance is granted sufficient to bring wages up to 8s. 9d. per shift, provided that the maximum addition in any instance does not exceed 6d. per shift.

† The above change in wages is based on the proceeds of the industry, and is the first change to take effect in this district under the revised arrangement made for determining wages by the proceeds, following the stoppage of work in 1926.

‡ The above decrease applied to the majority of workpeople in the coalfield, excluding one colliery which makes independent agreements. A subsistence allowance is payable as previously to married men in receipt of a total wage less than 6s. 9d. per day to make wages up to that sum, subject to the allowance not exceeding 6d. per day for underground workers and 1s. per day for surface workers.

§ At one colliery, under an independent agreement, the decrease took effect from 16th July and left wages at 28 per cent. above basis rates, subject to a minimum daily wage of 6s. 9d. or 7s. for underground men and 6s. or 6s. 5d. for surfacemen.

‖ Under selling-price sliding-scale arrangements.

¶ This percentage is arrived at by adding to the selling-price sliding-scale percentage a subsistence allowance calculated on varying proportions of the difference between the sliding-scale percentage and the average cost-of-living figure for the period covered by the prices ascertainment.

** A flat-rate increase of 5d. to 1d. per shift, varying according to base rate, is paid in addition to the percentage quoted.

†† Under cost-of-living sliding-scale arrangements.

‡‡ The change took effect from the pay starting nearest 1st August—in most cases this was 31st July.

§§ These increases were granted as the result of an agreement between the Hull Fishing Vessel Owners' Association Limited, the Amalgamated Engineering Union, and the Associated Blacksmiths, Forge and Smithy Workers' Society.

Principal changes in rates of wages reported during July 1927 in The Ministry of Labour Gazette, *volume 35, 1927, p.309*. (TNA: ZPER 45/13.)

SOURCES FOR LOCAL HISTORIANS

Paul Carter and Kate Thompson

PHILLIMORE

2005

Published by
PHILLIMORE & CO. LTD
Shopwyke Manor Barn, Chichester, West Sussex, England

ISBN 1 86077 358 3

Printed and bound in Great Britain by
CAMBRIDGE PRINTING

Contents

Preface

Local historians are a diverse group and thus there are many reasons for people to want to spend time researching the history of a particular place and its past inhabitants. It may be general interest in the place of their birth, the place where they currently live, or indeed, for the non-migrant, both. They may be pursuing their studies as part of an undergraduate or post-graduate degree, undertaking a local history diploma/certificate or taking advantage of the numerous single-term local studies courses which colleges and universities now offer. They may be taking part in a group study undertaken by a local history society, or working free from the constraints of any formal structure (and the attendant deadlines). Therefore, the authors' initial problem was: who are the people at whom this volume should be aimed? Should they be professional historians with a wealth of research skills, enthusiastic amateurs with detailed knowledge of a relatively small number of particular records, or newcomers to local history with little or no experience of primary source material? Should we run the risk of ignoring both the experts and new researchers, falling between two stools and satisfying no-one? We eventually decided to give ourselves the more adventurous target of reaching out to everyone interested in local and community research. The reason for this decision was, in the end, a very simple one. Those records that are of use for local studies research are valuable to the paid professional, the newcomer, and of course everyone in between, and they are not exclusive to any specific segment within this diverse group.

Much can be gleaned from published works, including selections or full transcripts of original material, but at some point local historians will almost certainly need to consult primary sources. They may then encounter some practical problems: unfamiliar handwriting; a document written in Latin or Anglo-Norman French (or other language); or a document may be difficult to interpret. Documents were created for specific purposes – none of them with particular historical research questions in mind! Therefore the researcher needs to understand the document's background: who wrote it, why, what was its function and will it answer questions fully or adequately? Our task is to introduce, explain and illustrate sources that the local historian will use while keeping in mind their relevance.

W.B. Stephens' pioneering work, *Sources for English Local History*, was first published in 1973 and most recently revised in 1994. This book is not intended to be a substitute for Stephens; rather it supplements and updates sections of it. Our backgrounds, working in The National Archives (TNA) and county record offices respectively, gives us a different slant from professional historians and we believe that our experience qualifies us to interpret the records and their organisation – which is sometimes complex and esoteric – for the benefit of readers.

Today, there are many branches of history including political, social, economic, urban, industrial (including industrial archaeology), local and family. The list is potentially endless and can be mixed-and-matched to the researchers' interests and inclinations. Arguably the most popular form is family history, the second most popular topic for internet searches; there are many excellent books describing sources for family history and it is not our intention to replicate this information. However, many (perhaps all) of the sources we describe for local historians are equally relevant for family historians; after all, family history is about people whereas local history is about places – but you cannot really talk about one without the other.

History has become increasingly popular as a subject for television and radio producers, and the explosion of non-terrestrial channels has added to the number of historical programmes. As a result, the number of useful secondary sources has increased; these include books, videos, audio tapes and computer software. Of the initiatives to make archive catalogues and an increasing selection of their contents available remotely in a digitised form, led by TNA, perhaps the most useful are TNAs own electronic catalogue, the NRA (National Register of Archives), A2A (Access to Archives), the emerging ANW (Archive Network Wales) and SCAN (Scottish Archives Network), which are described in more detail in appendix 3/2. Comm@NET is a community archives network designed to build links between record repositories and local communities; projects have been started in West Yorkshire and Swindon by, respectively, the West Yorkshire Archive Service and the National Monuments Record (part of English Heritage).[1]

The creation of regional archive councils and a branch of the Department for Media Culture and Sport [DCMS] devoted to archives, libraries and museums – formerly called *Re*:source, now the Council for Museums, Libraries and Archives [MLA] – has created a higher profile for archives and related 'heritage' services. MLA was invited by government in 2002 to set up a Task Force to review the state of the UK's archives. *Listening to the Past, Speaking to the Future: The Report of the Archives Task Force* is the culmination of a detailed investigation and analysis of the state of the UK's archives, published in 2004. The Heritage Lottery Fund has enabled local and other archives to improve their facilities, undertake specialist conservation, or purchase documents which may otherwise have left the country. Major grants have partly funded new record office buildings for Essex, Surrey and others and there are dozens of other projects which have benefited from HLF funding. TNA and the Society of Archivists (the main professional body) have jointly funded a post of Heritage Lottery Adviser.

There are hundreds of local history societies: national bodies include the British Association for Local History and the Historical Association, and some specialist societies such as the Agricultural History Society, the Association for Industrial Archaeology and the Society for the Study of Labour History. There are some county local history societies and many more at the town or village level. Most produce a journal (see chapter 1), hold regular meetings and organise visits to places of historical interest; some undertake co-operative research projects, many of which lead to publication.

There are differences between the four countries which make up the United Kingdom. Most of the sources we describe relate primarily to England and Wales. Although Scottish and Irish material is mentioned, researchers will need to consult the National Archives of Scotland (NAS), the National Library of Scotland (NLS), the Public Record Office of Northern Ireland (PRONI) and the National Archives of Ireland (NAI). Because legal and other systems differ in the constituent parts of the United Kingdom, we have been unable to give as much detail for Scotland and Ireland as we have for England and Wales, but there are plenty of sources which will help.[2] In Wales there is a system of county and other local record offices similar to that in England and there are some local authority archives in Scotland, either at the old county or city level or covering the modern regions. PRONI covers the whole of Northern Ireland; as well as the NAI there are some local repositories. *British Archives* gives full details of all publicly funded archive repositories, as well as many private organisations that give access to their records.[3]

We have placed more emphasis on records from the early modern period onwards, when most documents are written in English, as these are the sources which most local historians will be using. Those wishing to use medieval records will already have obtained the necessary skills and will perhaps have little need for a volume such as this. Apart from manorial and estate records, most medieval documents will be found in TNA (which has produced excellent guides to the records in its care) and other major repositories described more fully in chapter 1. We hope that this book will be of value to local historians in the United Kingdom and our main intention is to provide a pathway to the documents that local historians need for their research.

We believe that we are 'standing on the shoulders of others' and wish to pay tribute to those who have trodden this road before. This is illustrated by the way we have extracted information from published and unpublished guides and the hundreds of information sheets/research guides that you can find produced by record offices the length and breadth of the United Kingdom. These unpublished (and regularly updated) research guides can be excellent. Furthermore you will see that we have regularly footnoted the work of other local historians. Partly to give credit where it is due; and also to provide researchers with references to those 'who have done it' – that is to say 'here is an article written by someone using the records' – we can all learn from example! We are also grateful to colleagues in various record repositories in the United Kingdom, in particular TNA, the NAS, the British Library, and the county record offices in Hertfordshire and Leicestershire, who have freely shared their knowledge with us.

PAUL CARTER AND KATE THOMPSON

Acknowledgements

We would like to thank Dr A. Bevan, Mr N.G. Halsey, TD, DL, FRICS, Mrs J.A. Giddings and Mrs A. Morton for their freely given help and advice during the writing of this book. Also the Hertford Town Council, Hertfordshire Archives and Local Studies, The National Archives and The Record Office for Leicestershire, Leicester and Rutland for permission to reproduce the illustrations. We also want to thank Andrew Illes of Phillimore for his good humour and practical assistance during the several proof stages of this book.

Any omissions, mistakes and lack of clarity rest (by right and tradition) on the shoulders of the authors.

I

Introduction to Sources

Once anyone decides to undertake some form of local history study,[1] a journey begins which will at some point lead to the archives; this may be the appropriate Local Studies Centre, County Record Office (CRO), a specialist subject archive (such as the Rural History Centre at Reading), or a major archive which holds significant collections across subject and geographical locations such as the Bodleian Library, British Library, the National Library of Wales (NLW) and The National Archives (TNA) at Kew. It may take the researcher to organisations that are not in themselves archive repositories, but which hold archival records (for example, a local trades council which has retained all of its records back to the 19th century). Some of the work can be a lonely experience and frustration may be a companion for the historical researcher until it is overcome by the discovery of the archival 'gold dust' that provides the sought-after answers.

It is difficult to make clear and unambiguous statements about the location of some types of records. The local borough, town or county archives are recommended for subjects such as local government, parish, business, education, crime, religion and so on. However, material on a similar range of subjects for most areas of England and Wales will be found in TNA, as will become clear in the following chapters. Moreover, subject-specific archives are important for a study of, say, working-class organisations (Labour History Archive and Study Centre at Manchester), maritime history (National Maritime Museum at London), or rural life in any of its manifestations (Rural History Centre at Reading). Records may turn up in apparently unlikely places and just one example demonstrates this: the Herrick MSS (Record Office for Leicestershire, Leicester and Rutland) contains material relating to the Wolverhampton Orphan Asylum and Wolverhampton Grammar School, presumably because a member of the family had some connection with these institutions. In addition, museums should not be overlooked as many of them hold considerable amounts of archive material.[2]

The world of historical research (in particular local and family history) has changed beyond recognition in the last two decades. Arguably the largest impact has been the internet and the World Wide Web. Like any other source, web sites are created by individuals and are therefore subject to the frailties of human nature, and are more ephemeral than other, more traditional avenues.

Despite the advantages of new technology, nothing can match the excitement of using original archives, although some heavily-used sources, such as the census returns, can only be consulted in facsimile. Original manuscripts and rare printed material will be found in a variety of repositories, some of which are described below. Appendix 1 gives contact details for principal national record offices and libraries but a complete listing can be found in the ARCHON directory, by going to 'Search other archives' on TNA's web site. All the national institutions and most other archive repositories now have web sites and many of them are digitising the catalogues of their collections; the list in appendix 2 gives some relevant sites but this can never be exhaustive. The speed at which this medium changes renders most paper-published advice inaccurate between writing and publication.

TNA is a one-off in the local history archives community. It is one of the most important and complete archives in the world. Although holding some early (10th-century) deeds, the material really begins with Domesday Book (1086) and runs up to the present day. It holds the records created or collected by central government departments of the United Kingdom, primarily England and Wales (as both Scotland and Northern Ireland have their own central record offices), and the central law courts of England and Wales. The archive, therefore, holds an enormous amount of material appropriate for local historians and has great potential for a wide range of subjects in domestic history. The list of subject areas for which local historians have used records at TNA is almost endless. Historical studies concerning gender, agriculture, labour, education, public health, poverty, policing, transport, wages (the list goes on) can all benefit from the records held there.

Of lesser importance to the local historian is the fact that Britain's trading, military and imperial past has ensured that TNA is seen as an archive of international importance. Its vast holdings also contain records concerning former British colonies and foreign relations over eight centuries. Although such records may not at first sight seem important, it can depend on the questions local historians ask about their locality – what effect did international trade have on urbanisation, did groups of people from a particular place emigrate during economic downturns, etc?[3] These are the kinds of question which the records of the foreign and colonial offices may help to answer. In short, the records held at TNA are of immense importance to local historians and the collection of domestic material held there may be summed up as a national collection of local history sources.

Along with TNA local historians cannot afford to miss out on material at the British Library, Bodleian Library and the NLW. The manuscript collections of the British Library form part of the national repository of manuscripts, private papers and archives, and contain material of outstanding research importance for all periods, countries and disciplines. There is a separate manuscripts reading room on the second floor of the British Library, and the collections are divided into three areas: medieval and earlier manuscripts (*c.*300 BC to 1603), modern historical collections (1603 to the present), and literary and theatrical collections. The manuscripts comprise a series of named collections that have been acquired over the history of the British Museum and Library, from the Foundation Collections (Cotton, Harley and Sloane) to the series of Additional Manuscripts, which make up the largest collection. Manuscripts are rarely arranged thematically, as most recent acquisitions are simply added to the continuing additional series, and closed collections, assembled by collectors before being acquired by the British Library, and which naturally encompass a wide variety of material. The Bodleian Library in Oxford is the main research library of the university; its Department of Special Collections and Western Manuscripts is divided into: western manuscripts, rare books and printed ephemera, maps, and music. The western manuscripts section holds the second largest collection in Britain, with items ranging in date from papyri of the third century BC to correspondence and papers of the present. Its particular strengths are medieval manuscripts, 17th-century literary and historical collections, antiquarian and topographical manuscripts, and modern scholarly, literary, and political papers. Other universities have important collections for local historians. The Archives Hub[4] is the point of access to (at present) nearly 19,000 descriptions of archives held at over 80 UK universities. These are not only archives relating to the universities but business records, private and family papers and a host of other miscellaneous material.

The Parliamentary Archives (House of Lords Record Office) holds several million historical records relating to Parliament, dating from 1497. It is located in the Palace of Westminster and proof of identity is required for access to its collections; researchers are strongly advised to make an appointment (see chapter 13 for details of collections). The holdings include some important series, covering a wide variety of subjects of interest to local historians. Printed sessional papers, also known as Parliamentary Papers or 'Blue Books', were papers laid before Parliament; they include bills, Parliamentary committee reports and proceedings, and non-Parliamentary papers printed 'by Command' (Command Papers). As well as the records at the HoLRO, sets of sessional papers are also available in many research libraries throughout Britain. The BOPCRIS (British Official Publications Collaborative Reader Information Service) web site contains an online catalogue to many important sessional papers and a searchable list of libraries which hold them. They are not the easiest source to use but should not be overlooked for the wealth of detail they contain; details of particularly valuable books will be found in the following chapters. House of Lords and House of Commons Journals are original manuscript journals of the proceedings of the two houses, dating from 1510 (Lords) and 1547 (Commons), which are now printed; sets of the printed Journals may also be found in large research libraries. Acts of Parliament survive from 1497; they are in roll form up to 1849 and book form thereafter, printed on vellum. Most public Acts and many private and local Acts are printed and there is an online catalogue of them on the A2A web site; printed Acts are also widely available in public libraries. There are other series of useful records in the HoLRO and a short guide can be found on its web site. Due to the 1834 fire which burnt down the Houses of Parliament, there are no records of the House of Commons before that date, apart from the manuscript journals and minutes, and printed journals of the House. Everything else created by the House of Commons prior to 1834 was destroyed by the fire. There are a few records of MPs and peers, mostly very prominent politicians. The medieval records of Parliament (pre-1497) are to be found among the Chancery records at TNA. The NLW at Aberystwyth has a large collection of works regarding Wales in book, pamphlet, magazine and newspaper form as well as thousands of manuscripts and archives which are essential to Welsh local historical study. These are all large institutions which are essential for local history research, holding records which are not available elsewhere. All have their own web sites and all will be referred to later in this book.

Local record offices vary enormously in their facilities. It is fair to say that many are under-resourced and struggle to maintain a level of service that they consider adequate. Despite new funding opportunities provided by the Heritage Lottery Fund and other sources, many collections remain unlisted and uncatalogued, or with minimal finding aids. It is not a statutory requirement to provide an archive service and many local authority record offices have seen drastic staff and budget reductions, leading in extreme cases to closure on one or more days a week; some single-manned offices have to close completely if the member of staff is ill or on holiday. It is inadvisable to visit any record office, especially one at a distance, without checking in advance about opening hours and any other restrictions. Traditionally county and city record offices were located in the county or town hall but outgrew their premises as their holdings multiplied. A number of new record offices have been built in the last twenty years, usually but not always in the county town. It is not normally necessary to make an appointment but a reader's ticket is required for access to original archives; documents have become financially valuable and some well-publicised cases of theft and damage have led rightly to restrictions on the amount of material that can be consulted at any one time. In order to minimise the number of tickets a researcher using more than one office would need, the County Archive Research Network (CARN) was set up, whereby a ticket issued in one participating office is valid in all the others. A form of identification bearing name and address is required for the issuing of a CARN ticket.

Using original documents can be exciting and frustrating. There is nothing to equal the thrill of reading something which has been barely touched since it was created, but at the same time not everything has survived and a key source for a particular piece of research may not be available. Good examples are the losses of sections of central government department records (Valuation Office, Ministry of Health etc.) during the Second World War, which account for some of the gaps in TNA material, and the Four Courts in Dublin in 1922. Original manuscripts are the most reliable source available but even here there may be evidence of bias or selective use of information. As indicated in the preface, the language and handwriting may present problems; there is no easy way round reading Latin documents, if they have not been transcribed, but there are books to help the researcher, such as Eileen Gooder, *Latin for Local History* (1961, 1978) and Denis Stuart, *Latin for Local and Family Historians* (1995, 2000). Palaeography is a relatively easy skill to master and there is no substitute for practice. There are a number of helpful books, such as Lionel Munby, Steve Hobbs and Alan Crosby, *Reading Tudor and Stuart Handwriting* (2002) and Hilary Marshall, *Palaeography for Family and Local Historians* (2004), and there may be adult classes available locally run by the WEA, university or record office. Early hands are actually easier to read than later ones, as those few people who could write did so in the same style. A palaeography tutorial is available on the TNA website. Another potential problem is dating documents if they are undated; in the medieval period documents were dated by reference to a feast day and regnal years; C.R. Cheney's *A Handbook of Dates for students of British history*, first published in 1945 and revised by Michael Jones in 2000, gives dates of all the reigns, feast days and other useful information. A calendar for every year from AD 400 gives the date of Easter and shows what day of the week a particular date falls on.

Any researcher would be well advised to find out what has been done already.[5] It is unlikely that the place being studied has never been looked at by someone undertaking a local study and the following paragraphs are really just a series of hints to find some of the previous studies. Someone may have done a little (or much) of the work. A number of articles or books may have been published with the area already as the focus. Perhaps some of the records have been transcribed (copied) and published, thus making the task easier. A particular town, village or hamlet may have been the subject of a previous local historian's pamphlet or someone's university thesis. For England the parish may have been the subject of one of the *Victoria County History* volumes (*VCH*).[6] The *VCH* was founded in 1899 and dedicated to Queen Victoria (from whom it takes its name). As stated on the VCH website, it was set up to produce an 'encyclopaedic national history in a series of volumes which cover, county by county, and parish by parish, the general and detailed history of England from earliest times to the present.' Some of the volumes are now available on the *VCH* web site. It would be frustrating indeed to have put in a great deal of time and effort preparing a piece of work only to find someone was there first and that many of your conclusions were simply the rewording of another researcher's published work.[7] Tracking down all earlier pieces of research is not easy as they can take many forms. So how might the researcher begin to explore what has already been done?

There are a number of general publications from the 18th century onwards which will greatly assist the local historian. The *Gentleman's Magazine*, published from 1731 to 1868, contains a miscellany of topographical, historical and genealogical information. There are some indexes to its contents and at least one county has produced a book based on the magazine – *Hertfordshire 1731-1800 as recorded in the Gentleman's Magazine*, edited by Arthur Jones in 1993. Facsimile copies of the magazines and their indexes are being produced by Midlands Historical Data on CD-Rom. *The Annual Register* is an invaluable year-by-year record of British and world events from 1758 to the present day. There is a printed index and an online version, which enables cross-searching of volumes and the ability to perform full-text searches.[8] There is a demonstration of it via the 'History online' web site. *Notes and Queries* dates from 1849; as the name suggests, it deals with the asking and answering of readers' questions. It is devoted principally to English language and literature, lexicography, history, and scholarly antiquarianism. Each issue focuses on the works of a particular period, with an emphasis on the factual rather than the speculative. The journal comprises notes, book reviews, readers' queries and replies, and is published by the Oxford University Press. There are also county sets of the same title. The

Internet Library of Early Journals provides sections of the above publications (and others) and was a joint project by the Universities of Birmingham, Leeds, Manchester and Oxford, conducted under the auspices of the Electronic Libraries Programme. The project finished in 1999 and no additional material will be added.[9] A superb source for researchers working on the late 18th and early 19th centuries is the reports of the first Board of Agriculture. These are often referred to as the General Views and cover a multitude of local social and economic issues such as poor rates, roads, labour etc as well as agricultural practices; see appendix 3.9 for details.

There is a dazzling array of local history journals produced by societies. Just how local these societies and journals are can differ enormously in terms of a parish, a town, a city, a county or a defined region. The journals may or may not be of assistance but researchers should find out if there is or has been a published local history journal concerning their area. The major difficulty is that such journals come and go depending upon the level of interest and enthusiasm of local historians. A local society that published a journal for a decade or more may cease publication for several reasons: general apathy, the loss of a number of key members or a drop in the society's revenue. There are a number of places the interested researcher can look to find out if a journal for the area is (or has been) in publication. Check with the local studies library/ centre if there is one. This is the most likely place to have information on whether a local history society has published, or continues to publish, a journal. The appropriate local studies centre will be likely to have its own copies. This would also be the case for the appropriate CRO.

There are also national local history organisations which may also have information on local history journals. The first is the British Association for Local History (BALH). BALH produces its own quarterly journal, *The Local Historian*, and regularly lists around 30 to 40 current local history titles in its reviews section. The Local History Press publishes *The Local History Magazine* every two months and again the reviews section carries details of around 30 to 40 current local journals. *The Local History Magazine* also occasionally includes a list of local history societies. These societies are usually based on the county, and names, contact addresses and numbers are supplied; if the locality is smaller than the county the appropriate county organisation should have information about smaller societies within its boundaries. Both of these organisations have their own web sites and series of useful links.

In addition to journals, local history societies can provide other assistance. Firstly, they can give the local historian an opportunity to talk to someone who may have spent many years researching the area of interest. Secondly, the society may also have a collection of papers from a number of its past and current researchers who have transcribed, or made notes on, primary material which may be consulted. Thirdly, the society may have original primary material which may not be well-known, and this point should not be underestimated. There are vestry minutes, overseers' accounts, enclosure commissioners' notebooks – and undoubtedly much more – in the hands of local history societies. It is excellent practice to deposit a copy of any research with the local society (and any local studies centre); resources for future local history are thus increased and future local historians will be able to benefit.

Other journals, less well used by non-academic local historians, are the regular history titles produced through the academic press, which good reference libraries will hold.[10] Journals such as *The Economic History Review, History Workshop* and *Past and Present* regularly contain local or regional studies, such as:

> W.A. Armstrong, 'The Trend of Mortality in Carlisle Between the 1790s and the 1840s: A Demographic Contribution to the Standard of Living Debate', *Economic History Review* (1981) Vol. XXXIV/I, pp 94-114;
>
> P. Horn, 'Pauper Apprenticeship and the Grimsby Fishing Industry, 1870-1914', *Labour History Review* (1996) Vol. 61/1, pp 173-94;
>
> J.M. Neeson, 'The Opponents of Enclosure in Eighteenth-Century Northamptonshire', *Past & Present* (1984) Vol. 105, pp 114-39;
>
> J.A. Sheppard, 'Small Farms in a Sussex Weald Parish, 1800-1860', *Agricultural History Review* (1992), Vol. 40/2, pp 127-41. [Study of the parish of Chiddingly].

Such articles will provide numerous insights (and of course a collection of useful footnotes) that may greatly assist further research. Many of these journals now publish consolidated indexes, and, rather than searching through each volume on the library shelf for something relevant, the librarian should be consulted to find out if there are indexes to relevant journals. Some journals (or their publishers) have now begun to invest in web sites and their indexes are available on-line, where key word searches can be undertaken.

There is a union index, *Historical Abstracts*, that brings together articles in journals serving the humanities sector of academia. Articles on history and the related social sciences are included (chronologically these begin from 1450). Although not all publications are included, some 2,110 journals have their articles listed and abstracted, and around 20,000 new entries are added every year. Many reference libraries hold paper copies of *Historical Abstracts* (it began publication in the early 1950s) and this is an excellent place to start searching for appropriate articles. Recently it has become available as a subscription-based web resource, so it would be useful to find out if the nearest reference library is a subscriber. Although this can appear to be a time-consuming exercise it will mean that the researcher can begin with a clear idea of what earlier historians have said about the area under investigation. Reading through such material usually generates questions about the place which may not have been considered; they will indicate historical sources and ultimately bring local historians, and their research, into the debates, arguments and disagreements within historical study.

Many counties have a series of published Record Society volumes; these are usually published annually and consist of a transcript of a document, or series of documents, prefaced by an introductory essay that places the transcribed material in context. It may be a full or edited transcript or a calendar to a series of records thought of as too large to be transcribed in full. It may be a diary, a set of vestry minutes, overseers' accounts, early company minutes, quarter sessions records, settlement examinations; indeed this type of published volume can refer to almost any record, any period and any subject. They have the obvious added bonus of being printed, sometimes translated (from Latin to English), and usually fully indexed by name, place and subject. As such these volumes are of primary importance to local historians and a quick example will demonstrate the point. A local historian interested in issues surrounding poverty or poor relief in Surrey would find *Mitcham Settlement Examinations, 1784-1814* of obvious importance.[11] Indeed, a brief glance through the index of this volume also makes it valuable for those interested in people who served in the militia, pre-1834 workhouses and apprenticeships. The index also gives a list of occupations and trades referred to in the text. The moral is that, where local historians in the past have transcribed and indexed material, their successors should do the decent thing – take advantage of their many years of toil. Published volumes have been indexed in two volumes published by the Royal Historical Society in its 'Guides and Handbooks' series: E.L.C. Mullins, *Texts and Calendars: an Analytical Guide to Serial Publications* (1958, reprinted with corrections 1978) and *Texts and Calendars II: an Analytical Guide to Serial Publications, 1957-1982* (1983). These indexes will shortly be continued on the Royal Historical Society's web site. Researchers should not just look for a designated record society; all manner of organisations may have published material of interest, such as archaeological, antiquarian, architectural or natural history societies. In some counties a well-known local historian's name is used for the name of the society: the purpose of the Surtees Society is to publish manuscripts relating to the north of England and south of Scotland and the Thoroton Society has the same purpose in Nottinghamshire.

The British Record Society was founded in 1889, taking over from the Index Library, which published indexes to public records. Initially it was concerned with probate material, but it also published indexes to other records, notably chancery proceedings and inquisitions post mortem. With the creation of an official series of Lists and Indexes in 1892 the need for private publication of indexes to records in the Public Record Office was reduced, and the Society turned its attention to records held elsewhere. It now concentrates on probate records and 17th-century hearth tax returns. Two further sets of useful record publications are the British Academy's Records of Social and Economic History and the Royal Historical Society's Camden series.

Antiquarianism as opposed to history is usually defined in terms of 'facts' versus 'facts and explanation'. This is not a debate for a source guidebook; however, it is essential that local historians are aware of the work of antiquarian journals, i.e., those that sprang up with the increased interest in history and archaeology in the middle of the 19th century. They may be the forerunners of current local history and archaeology journals and perhaps have retained their names without any formal restructuring, but they may now focus more on explaining the past as well as presenting facts. It is this presentation of facts in isolation of any explanation that has earned antiquarianism its current bad press. Nevertheless, 18th- and early 19th-century antiquarians spent a great deal of their time reading the records and may have provided many 'facts' which can be incorporated into later work. Indeed some of the antiquarian journals provide early examples of the transcripts now published annually in record society volumes.

The British Newspaper Library at Colindale, north London (part of the British Library) holds enormous collections of British and Irish newspapers, magazines and similar material, including some foreign titles, and its web site allows a search of its holdings by place-name, title of newspaper, etc. Its holdings include some unlikely publications, such as football club programmes. Newspaper holdings include English provincial, Welsh, Scottish, and Irish newspapers (as well as those from the Channel Islands and the Isle of Man) dating back to 1699 in their original, hard-copy format, although they are far from comprehensive in the early years. British national and provincial papers from the mid-19th century have few gaps. About 2,600 UK and Irish newspaper and weekly/fortnightly periodical titles are received, which represents about 90 per cent of acquisitions; this includes the main London edition of the national daily and Sunday newspapers, and free newspapers, with the exception of those consisting entirely of advertising. Many newspapers can now be accessed online and there is a useful list of sites on the British Library web site. There are a number of publications concerned with newspapers (see bibliography) and most local libraries will have sets of the major local titles. NEWSPLAN is a co-operative programme for the microfilming and preservation of local newspapers and for making them accessible to users, which has benefited from a £5m HLF grant.

Oral history uses the reminiscences of people and was first conducted in Britain in the 19th century; the term is now invariably used for recorded interviews with individuals but can include printed or written sources. The Oral History Society, based at Essex University, has published its journal *Oral History* since 1971. The British Library's Sound Archive holds over a million discs, 185,000 tapes, and many other sound and video recordings; the collections come from all over the world and cover the entire range of recorded sound from music, drama and literature, to oral history and wildlife sounds. They range from cylinders made in the late 19th century to the latest CD, DVD and minidisc recordings. It keeps copies of commercial recordings issued in the United Kingdom, together with selected commercial recordings from overseas, radio broadcasts and many privately-made recordings. A number of local archives have begun to build up collections of oral history material, which will undoubtedly begin to inform much late 19th- and early 20th-century local history research.

There are a number of illustrative sources. Photography was invented in England and France in the early to mid-19th century but it was some time before it became available to ordinary people. One of the pioneers in England was William Henry Fox Talbot (1800–77), who invented the negative/positive process; his descendants gave his family home, Lacock Abbey in Wiltshire, to the National Trust in 1944, and there is a photographic museum there which commemorates his achievements. Other museums include the National Museum of Photography, Film and Television in Bradford and the Royal

Photographic Society's headquarters in Bath. Most local libraries, museums and record offices have large collections of photographs which are an invaluable but often frustrating source, as they may give no details of place, date or other important information. There are many published books of photographs, both national and local, such as the series published by Phillimore and Batsford.

Before the age of photography the only visual source comes from prints and drawings. These will be found in record offices, libraries and museums and will vary enormously in quality and value. More recently, film and video have become available; moving film rarely survives before the middle of the 20th century but occasionally earlier material can be found. The BBC has recently shown some black and white film taken mainly in the industrial north-west around 1900. This was 'The Lost World of Mitchell and Kenyon'; two early film makers working in the late 19th and early 20th centuries. These film have now been conserved and is now located at the British Film Institute, National Film and Television Archive at Berkhamsted, Hertfordshire. The collections held by the British Film Institute were started over sixty years ago and comprise more than 275,000 feature, non-fiction and short films (dating from 1894) and 210,000 television programmes. Other custodians of film and video include the BBC and commercial television stations.

Many record offices provide talks, exhibitions and other sources of help. TNA has a special exhibition area at Kew with a changing programme of exhibitions, as well as the permanent display of Domesday Book. CROs often have an interesting programme of special events, such as lunchtime talks on particular sources; for example, in early 2005 the Norfolk Record Office staff gave half-hour talks on workhouse records, the farm labourer, enclosure maps, shipping registers, probate records and the suffragette movement.

2

THE LAND

One of the starting points for local historical study is that of the topography of the area being studied. The basic documents for such a study are maps, plans and surveys of all descriptions, but there are many other sets of records relating to land use and rural society. Many of the first series of records referred to in this chapter are not 'rural records' *per se* but simply refer to a nation which had a predominantly agricultural economy and a rural population; by definition the vast majority of records generated in such a society will illuminate rural issues.

Perhaps the most well known of central government surveys is the Domesday Survey of 1086 carried out under the instruction of William the Conqueror. Its function was to assist in the assessment of land tax and other dues to the government, ascertain the value of crown lands, and allow the king to make some estimation of the power of his vassal barons. The survey falls short of full national coverage. Northumberland and Durham were not surveyed, neither were London, Winchester and a substantial part of the North-West.[1]

Domesday Book has always comprised two separate volumes, Great and Little Domesday, because of their respective sizes and contents. It is unnecessary to consult the original volumes at TNA (indeed Domesday Book is now produced only under the severest of restrictions) as modern published and fully indexed translations are available on a county-by-county basis.[2] Most local archives and CROs have copies for their own area, but there are copies of these modern published translations, as well as excellent facsimiles, available at TNA if they cannot be found locally.

From 1086 until the early 18th century there were no comparable surveys, with anything like a near-national coverage undertaken by central government. However, there are several series of records that provide information on agriculture and rural society covering much of England and Wales. Their creation is due to locally instigated surveys undertaken at varying times (over many decades and centuries) which together had the cumulative effect of creating a set of local records of national coverage and significance, and central government instructions for local surveys for national reasons (usually for tax purposes).

Feet of fines (sometimes referred to as final concords) are copies of agreements reached in a court of law, usually the Court of Common Pleas, and usually refer to fictitious disputes concerning land. The agreement would be written three times on a single piece of parchment; once on the left-hand side, once on the right and once along the bottom or foot. The parchment would then be cut into three indented parts. The two parties involved in the action were given the left- and right-hand copies with the foot being retained as the official court record of the action. The records begin in 1185 and continue until 1834. Although the original purpose was to resolve conflict concerning the ownership of land it quickly became a simple method of recording the transfer of land from one party to another. It should be remembered that there was no legal requirement to undertake this process so nothing like all land is covered. The records are held in two TNA series; CP 25/1 contains feet of fines from 1185 to 1509 while CP 25/2 contains those from 1509 to 1834. The feet are arranged mainly by county in a rough chronological order. However, some fines that cover more than a single county, and are termed 'diver fines', are kept within the county files and so are easily missed by local historians. Researchers will also need to examine the material in 'Unknown Counties' and 'Various Counties' files as for some fines the county is not obvious, or they were missed out from the main county sequence.

The records can be used to illustrate changes in land use and values, corrodies (exchanges of land for the right to claim free board and lodgings), open field systems, urbanisation, mills and mill rights, and periodic references to local occupations.[3] Published calendars and abstracts of the feet of fines are extensive. Various local history and county record societies continue to transcribe and index these records. Feet of fines are essentially deeds; for a thorough explanation of deeds in their entirety (and variety) see N.W. Alcock's *Old Title Deeds*.[4]

The manor was both a legal and geographical entity. Taken together, the vast collection of manorial documents provides a huge archive for local historians. It would be useful to begin by discussing what a manor was before moving on to explain the documents created by manorial officials, the information contained in such documents and the prevalence of these records.

Following the Norman Conquest the new rulers introduced a system referred to as the feudal system. This meant that all land was held by the king, who rewarded his followers through a grant, or grants, of lands. This group of superior tenants then granted land to their supporters, and so on, creating a pyramid structure of landholding that eventually covered England and most of Wales (northern Wales did not develop in this way). Land was organised into units called manors, but it would be a mistake to view manors as always being discrete units of land. This was certainly true in many cases, but they could be spread or intermixed amongst the lands that made up other manors. It was the bonds of allegiance though various land tenures to a specific lord of the manor (evidenced by the lord's right to hold a manor court) that defined the manor as a unit.

For local historians the local manor court records can provide a great deal of information. Until the late 18th and early 19th centuries a large number of people held their lands as freehold or customary tenants; initially the relationships within a medieval manor were based on the fact that land was given by the lord in return for services. These could be a mixture of money rent, military obligations or work on the lord's land. The general rules of each manor (setting out these services and obligations) were known as the customs of the manor. The word custom in this sense has a much stronger meaning than we usually attach to it today. Customs of the manor were local laws; customs were regulated through the manor courts that had the power to fine people who transgressed the local regulations and were enforceable in the national courts. The type of information found in the court rolls or minute books varies but includes details of landholding, agricultural practices, disputes over the conditions of the fields, which people (and how many) had rights to any common lands within the manor, as well as the revenue collected by the courts and generated by feudal ties.

Those who lived and worked the lands of the manor fell into different social groups, often based on the way in which they held land from the lord of the manor. The lord was usually the key person in the locality and the records of his court show that the rules of agricultural practice were laid down there, together with the recording of incoming and outgoing tenants. In addition, the court records refer to freeholders, copyholders, leaseholders, tenants at will, cottagers and squatters who lived on and by the manor.[5]

Manorial records can be found in huge numbers and in many repositories. These records were private possessions and could be retained by the lord of the manor and later family members. Some lords owned several manors across the country and often resided in only one of them, or perhaps lived in a town or city some miles from any of the manors; this could lead to all the records being deposited in a single local archive. Therefore, finding manorial records is not an easy task. To help identify which manorial documents survive, and where they are held, the Manorial Documents Register (MDR) was set up; it is now held at TNA. Some counties have their part of the register online but for others the paper indexes still need to be used as this is very much at an early stage; at the time of writing only Wales, the Isle of Wight, Hampshire, Middlesex, Norfolk, Surrey and the three Ridings of Yorkshire are online. An extremely useful source for identifying manorial records is the published *Victoria County History* volumes.

One of the most useful series of manorial documents is the manor court rolls of the court baron. They are quite formulaic and begin by giving the name of the manor, the type of court and the names of the lord and that of his steward (who would often manage the proceedings). The rolls (physically these later sometimes became bound volumes) are arranged chronologically and act as minutes to the court session recording the names of the court jurors, tenants and the administration of copyhold land. A copy of the formal admittance of a tenant entered on the roll would be handed over as proof of title. Surrenders to the uses of a will, to bypass the descent of land via manorial custom, as well as sales and mortgages of land, were also recorded in the rolls. However, it is the earlier sections of the rolls for each court which are potentially most valuable for the local historian, where the various 'presentments' of matters dealt with by the court are found. These may on first examination appear to be minor matters, for example, disputes between tenants over boundaries, stocking of cattle on the commons, the right to take brushwood for firing etc – but to the tenant these were things of great concern. As the court rolls were written

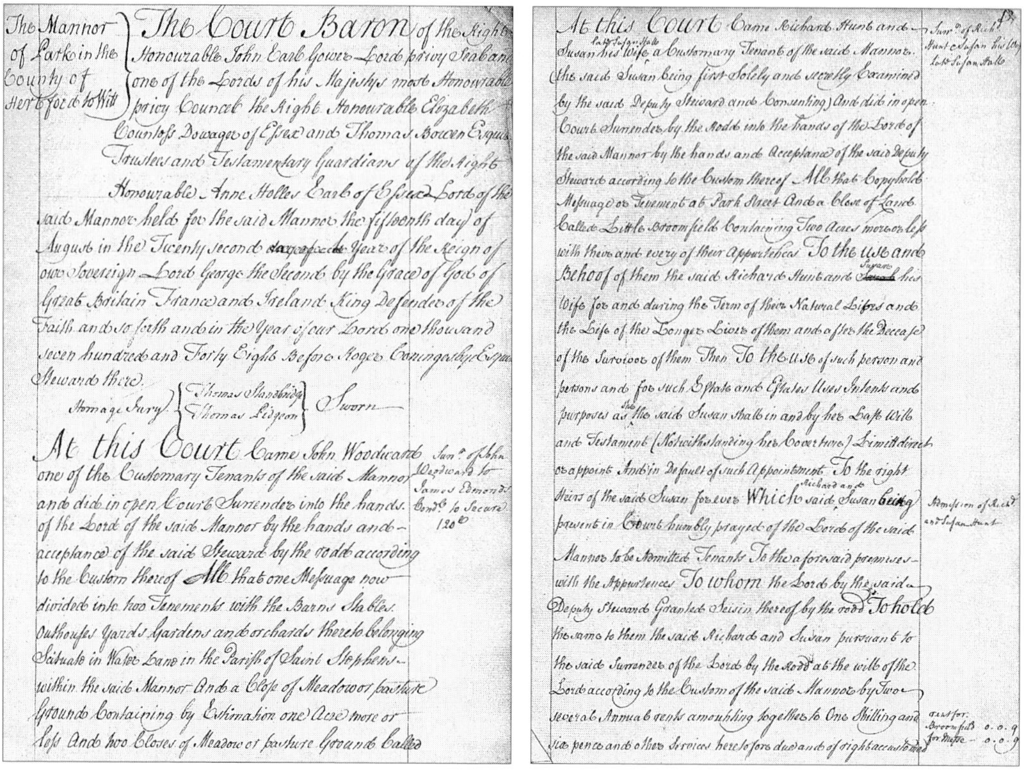

The Mannor of Park in the County of Hertford to Witt } The Court Baron of the Right Honourable John Earl Gower Lord privy Seal and one of the Lords of his Majestys most Honourable privy Councell the Right Honourable Elizabeth Countess Dowager of Essex and Thomas Bowen Esquire Trustees and Testamentary guardians of the Right Honourable Anne Holles Earl of Essex Lord of the said Mannor held for the said Mannor the fifteenth day of August in the Twenty second Year of the Reign of our Sovereign Lord George the Second by the Grace of God of Great Britain France and Ireland King Defender of the Faith and so forth and in the Year of our Lord one thousand seven hundred and Forty Eight Before Roger Coningsby Esquire Steward there.

Homage Jury { Thomas Standbridge / Thomas Lidgeon } Sworn

At this Court Came John Woodward one of the Customary Tenants of the said Mannor and did in open Court Surrender into the hands of the Lord of the said Mannor by the hands and acceptance of the said Steward by the rodd according to the Custom thereof All that one Messuage now divided into two Tenements with the Barns Stables Outhouses Yards Gardens and orchards thereto belonging Scituate in Water Lane in the Parish of Saint Stephens within the said Mannor And a Close of Meadow or pasture Ground Containing by Estimation one Acre more or less And two Closes of Meadow or pasture Ground Called

Surr. of John Woodward to James Edmonds Cond. to Secure 120£

At this Court Came Richard Hunt and Susan his Wife late Susan Stallo a Customary Tenant of the said Mannor the said Susan being first Solely and secretly Examined by the said Deputy Steward and Consenting) And did in open Court Surrender by the Rodd into the hands of the Lord of the said Mannor by the hands and Acceptance of the said Deputy Steward according to the Custom thereof All that Copyhold Messuage or Tenement at Park Street And a Close of Land Called Little Broomfield Containing Two Acres more or less with their and every of their Appurtenances To the use and behoof of them the said Richard Hunt and Susan his Wife for and during the Term of their Natural Lives and the Life of the Longer Liver of them and after the Decease of the Survivor of them Then To the use of such person and persons and for such Estate and Estates Uses Intents and purposes as she the said Susan shall in and by her Last Will and Testament (Notwithstanding her Coverture) Limitt direct or appoint And in Default of such Appointment To the right Heirs of the said Susan for ever Which said Richard and Susan being present in Court humbly prayed of the Lord of the said Mannor to be Admitted Tenants To the aforesaid premises with the Appurtenances To whom the Lord by the said Deputy Steward Granted Seisin thereof by the rodd To hold the same to them the said Richard and Susan pursuant to the said Surrender of the Lord by the Rodd at the will of the Lord according to the Custom of the said Mannor by Two several Annual rents amounting together to One Shilling and six pence and other Services heretofore due and of right accustomed

Surr. of Richd Hunt & Susan his Wife late Susan Stallo

Admission of Richd and Susan Hunt

rent for Broomfield 0.0.9 / for Messe 0.0.9

1 *Manorial court rolls survive in large quantities for most of the country but are not always found in the county record office. Oxbridge colleges, for example, were substantial landowners and manorial records relating to their property are still kept in their archives. This example, for the manor of Park in Hertfordshire shows typical entries in 1748.* (Hertfordshire Archives and Local Studies, DE/CP/M22.)

up by the steward they were usually, in some way, a biased record of events. In the introduction to the published 17th-century Hornsey court rolls the Marchams observed that:

> These records are legal. Herein lies a certain danger unless it be fully recognised that such records did not always mean what they say. Truth is indeed many sided, and truth as presented by the legal mind requires careful examination. Unfortunately most of the material for local history has this defect. The lawyers who held courts and wrote these records were actuated by a single-minded devotion to the material interests of their clients, their own being usually identical. Much of the legal theory and so-called manorial law embodied in the old text books is simply a reflection of the landlord's point of view.[6]

Along with the court rolls may be several sets of associated drafts or minute books which can be used as substitutes if the rolls themselves do not survive. Additionally, there may be other collections of records created by the steward to manage the business of the manor, such as estreat rolls (in which various amercements or fines were recorded) and the suit rolls and call books comprising the names of tenants owing suit to the court.

Rentals and surveys[7] date from the 12th century, although the vast majority are from the 16th and 17th centuries. The purpose of these documents was to set out the various revenues and services owed to the lord. Some may only relate to a single manor while others cover two or more properties. Initially in Latin, they are increasingly in English by the 16th century, but significant numbers remain in Latin until the 18th century. The early basic survey is known as a custumal and dates from the 12th and 13th centuries. It sets out the names of the tenants, with details of the land they held along with money, labour services and any payments in kind they owed the lord. In addition to this a short recital of the customs of the manor may be given. One of the most important types of manorial survey was the extent. It typically lists all the tenants for the manor regardless of tenure, and so freeholders and leaseholders are recorded, as well as the copyhold tenants who appear in the court rolls. The documents also list the date the extent was made and describe the land and its rent value to the lord, assigning the type of land to the name of a tenant with a brief description of the property. They also include some details of the demesne land of the manor (land held by the lord and not let to a tenant). These records were less popular by the 15th century.

Extents were gradually replaced by rentals, which tend to be less detailed but still cover all types of manorial tenants; there may also be evidence of labour services having been commuted to monetary payments. This period also saw the development of accounts which are documents based on a charge (the money which should be gathered from rents, fines and any other profits) and discharge (any outgoings). These would include money paid out in wages to various tradesmen and farm labour when required. The balance was the amount paid to the lord of the manor. On large estates the money was collected by the lord's receiver and the records are known as receivers' accounts. Ministers' and receivers' accounts at TNA are listed in *Lists and Indexes V*, *VIII* and *XXXIV* and *Supplementary Series II*. Most of the records are in series SC6 and DL29, although records in E315 and E36 are covered as well. Other records can be identified in series LR7-LR9. They are difficult to use and the researcher should first look at some of the printed material; P.D.A. Harvey's *Manorial Records of Cuxham, Oxfordshire, c.*1200-1359 has extensive explanations on accounting as well as transcripts for the Cuxham accounts.[8] Rent rolls (sometimes referred to as rentals) will list all tenants who held property in the manor, plus a note of the actual rent they paid. Maps were occasionally produced to accompany survey documents and sometimes contain a separate reference book listing all the tenants for each holding. Relevant maps at TNA are scattered across a wide range of series, and the extracted map catalogue is the best place to begin. Two distinct and significant record series are DL31 and LRRO1.[9]

Enfranchisement of copyhold to freehold was introduced in 1841 with compensation for disputed loss of manorial income arbitrated by the Ministry of Agriculture. Deeds for awards, from 1841 to 1921, are at TNA in record series MAF 9. The medieval tenure of copyhold was finally abolished under the 1922 and 1924 Law of Property Acts; all outstanding copyhold land was made freehold from 1 January 1936. Certificates of determination for compensation are in MAF 27.

Private estate records are invaluable to the local historian in several ways, but may still be in private hands. Subjects as varied as landholding patterns, rents, reports on farms and building within the manor as well as general social and economic matters (crime, wages, leases, etc) can be found within such papers. Large numbers have been deposited in CROs. As estate owners may have owned lands in several counties it is not enough to search only the CRO applicable to the place of interest. All of the papers for a particular family may be deposited in the CRO serving the area in which the principal family home was located.[10] Many private estate records are also deposited in TNA, NLW, British Library and the Bodleian Library.

One of the largest landowners in England and Wales is the Crown which generated huge amounts of administrative records for crown lands and manors. The importance of these records for local studies cannot be overestimated. Records of the Crown Estate will principally be found at TNA; predecessors and associated bodies include the Surveyor General of Crown Lands, the Surveyor General of Woods and Forests, Office of the Auditors of Land Revenue, Office of Woods, Forests and Land Revenues, Works and Buildings and the Commissioners of Crown Lands, relating to the management of crown estates. All of these departments will contain specific and general information on the management of crown estates, and contain leases, papers and various correspondence. A relatively quick way to find out if a particular area was a part of a crown estate is to consult CRES 2/1613 which includes a list of crown manors in 1827, and CRES 60 comprises annual reports of crown estates administration between 1797-1942. For 1786 to 1830 the best source is the published *Crown Land Returns,* 1831.[11]

Parliament produced a series of 17th-century surveys of crown lands and estates to assess their potential revenue value. The records are listed in series E317 in county and then parish order. For the 17th and 18th centuries another useful source is the FEC record series, relating to forfeited estates after the Jacobite risings. In FEC 1 there is a large collection of deeds and other documents which were produced for the Commissioners of the Forfeited Estates; although they relate to the estates of people attainted in the 1715 rising some of the records go much further back, as far as the 16th century. They include: original claims on the several estates forfeited, proceedings of the commissioners, including correspondence, minutes and memoranda, accounts, lists and schedules, and inventories of documents. Similar material can be found for other particular jurisdictions; these will be found in CHES for the Palatinate of Cheshire, DURH for the Palatinate of Durham, and DL for the Duchy of Lancaster.

An inquisition post mortem was a local enquiry into the lands held by people of high social and economic status in order to discover and set down any and all incomes and rights due to the Crown and consequently the records are held at TNA. All have been indexed and many are now published in English. They provide the details of lands held, by what tenure, and from whom. They will also give the date of death as well as the name and age of the heir. They are formulaic in outline but in Latin. They were usually returned to Chancery, which had ordered them in the first place or, if one had been held under the escheator's own authority, it would only be returned to the Exchequer. The Exchequer also received duplicates of those ordered by Chancery. This was done to support the escheator's accounts (in E 136) of his administration of land falling into the king's hands (for however brief a period). After 1540 another copy was sent into the Court of Wards and Liveries (WARD 7). Quite often the Exchequer and Wards inquisitions are easier to read, because they have been less used. The records are held in record series C 132, E 149, and (after 1540) in WARD 7. Many are now published in the relevant volume of the *Calendar of Inquisitions Post Mortem* (for the period 1236-1418). A full set is available at TNA but some reference and university libraries may have copies. There is a gap in the published records but these begin again for 1485-1509. The palatine counties of Cheshire, Durham and Lancashire and the Duchy of Lancaster also had inquisitions *post mortem* and can be found in CHES 3, DURH 3, PL 4 and DL 7. Many of these records have been published by record societies.

Enclosure of common fields, wastes, meadows and other lands took place under several mechanisms. Depending on the way in which a particular enclosure was undertaken will determine what (if any) documents were created.[12] A well-known division is between non-Parliamentary and Parliamentary enclosure. Parliamentary enclosure refers to enclosure by Act of Parliament (after 1845 by referring cases to commissioners and requiring the consent of parliament). Non-Parliamentary enclosure refers to a wide variety of processes such as approval, agreement, or purchase. Parliamentary enclosure became popular from the middle of the 18th century, peaking in the 1770s and again during the French Wars (1793-1815). Enclosure is a historical perennial and there is much secondary material; there are a few extremely good county-based guides such as Barbara English's *Yorkshire Enclosure Awards* and John Chapman and Sylvia Seeliger's *A Guide to Enclosure in Hampshire*.[13]

Medieval agreements to enclose land could be undertaken locally and with little necessity to provide any central record. However, by the 16th and 17th centuries a greater degree of legal certainty was achieved by having the enclosure recorded in one of the central courts. This would mitigate against an enclosure agreement being disputed (or ignored) by future generations, who may have calculated that as they had had no say in the original agreement they had no commitment to its continuation. One way in which this was obtained was to have the enclosure recorded in the Decree and Order Books of the Court of Chancery. Chancery was a court of civil law and as such an enclosure needed to be disputed before any record could be made.[14] The initial pleadings are held at TNA in record series C1-10 and C11-13 (from Richard II to 1842). The pleadings of the various cases resulted in a variety of decrees and orders by the court in C33. From 1597 it was determined that enrolling the decrees in Chancery gave decisions a further degree of legality. An enclosure contained within a Chancery enrolled decree would need to be appealed against through the House of Lords. Chancery enrolments are in class C 78,[15] with a supplementary series in C 79.

Grants to enclose by the Crown can be found in the Close Rolls in record series C 66. An English calendar of the patent rolls from 1232 to 1582

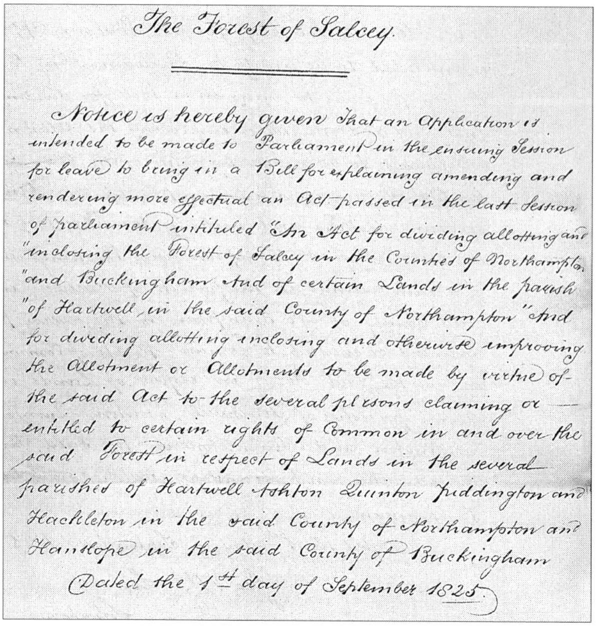
The Forest of Salcey.

Notice is hereby given That an Application is intended to be made to Parliament in the ensuing Session for leave to bring in a Bill for explaining amending and rendering more effectual an Act passed in the last Session of parliament intituled "An Act for dividing allotting and inclosing the Forest of Salcey in the Counties of Northampton and Buckingham And of certain Lands in the parish of Hartwell in the said County of Northampton" And for dividing allotting inclosing and otherwise improving the Allotment or Allotments to be made by virtue of the said Act to the several persons claiming or entitled to certain rights of Common in and over the said Forest in respect of Lands in the several parishes of Hartwell Ashton Quinton Piddington and Hackleton in the said County of Northampton and Hanslope in the said County of Buckingham

Dated the 1st day of September 1825.

2 *Salcey Forest, Northamptonshire: Enclosure: papers of the enclosure act commissioners, 1826-29. Copy of the notice to enclose the Forest of Salcey. TNA CRES 2/1019.*

was published as *Calendar of the Patent Rolls*[16] while those for Henry VIII are calendared in *Letters and Papers*. A vast amount of references to enclosure can be found in the various State Papers Domestic record series; these are essential for local historical studies and are particularly rich for investigating any subject concerning land.[17] Enclosure by agreement or because of the wishes of an individual landowner predated and ran alongside Parliamentary enclosure and was more common in some parts of the country than others.

A comprehensive listing of English parliamentary enclosure has been published as *A Domesday of English Parliamentary Enclosure Acts and Awards*,[18] which also indicates the place of repository for the awards. A similar publication, *A Guide to Parliamentary Enclosures in Wales*, performs the same function for Welsh enclosures[19] but also lists associated material such as enclosure commissioners' notebooks, letters, accounts, etc which had come to the author's attention. In addition to indicating the repository where the material is located, Chapman provides the full document reference. Most acts, awards, maps, statements of claims, general correspondence and any associated papers listed are now to be found in the appropriate CRO.

There is a published list of enclosure commissioners' working papers in *Archives* which is arranged by county, of locations of minute books, account books and other associated documents.[20] Undoubtedly many others are yet to be found in CROs and other local archives as well as smaller amounts in larger archives such as the British Library. It is difficult to make generalisations concerning parliamentary enclosure working papers. There are substantial collections at TNA including commissioners' minutes, solicitors' accounts, statements of claims and holdings in the pre-enclosure common fields, sale particulars (post-enclosure),[21] correspondence concerning exchanges and sales of lands, fuel allotments, disputes and a host of records which defy a succinct summary. Alongside these records, often in the same bundles, are the various bills, acts, awards, maps and plans.[22] Perhaps the biggest difference between the papers listed by Chapman, Turner and Wray concerns the bureaucratic management of lands of the Crown Estate and central government departments. In many ways it is useful to think of the crown records as simply estate records, as in a strict sense this is exactly what they are. However, the surviving records are influenced by their bureaucratic origin. For the local historian concerned with an area which was in the possession of the Crown at the time of enclosure this takes on particular significance. The Crown required a body of full-time administrators who worked, accounted for, planned, surveyed and exploited the crown lands. In the process an archive of amazing diversity and immense size was created. Local officials wrote to the Commissioners of Woods, Forests and Land Revenues, the Commissioners wrote to the Surveyor General, the Surveyor General to the Treasury. During enclosure local inhabitants and landowners would write to the Commissioners of their concerns, plans, desires or unease at the changes being undertaken. Some of these concerns became a topic of correspondence between the network of local and central government officials and those who owned and occupied the affected lands. This opens up the possibility of tracing material which may have crossed to (or have been created by) other government departments. Appreciating the bureaucratic nature of central government will help to account for the wide variety of material found in individual cases. An example would be the sale particulars of freehold land and the detailed *Statement of the Quantity of Common Field Lands, Downs and Other Commonable Lands* in East Hendred, Berkshire. Enclosed by Act in 1801, the parish included a crown manor and therefore a number of records concerning the enclosure are among the records of the Commissioners of Woods, Forests and Land Revenues.[23] There were also disputes amongst landowners such as that between the Crown and the Duke of Bedford at Campton cum Shefford,[24] lists of tithe owners and proprietors in the common fields at Westmanside in East Hendred,[25] and the complaints against the agents of one of the lords of the manor involved in the enclosure of White Waltham and Shottesbrooke.[26] Those overseeing the enclosure of Teddington (Middlesex) at the close of the 18th century saw fit to compile a list of inhabitants opposed to the scheme, including those residing in the parish poor house.[27] The records provide a great deal of information concerning the central debates surrounding enclosure. The issue of waged work being created for labourers during enclosure is illustrated at Delamere forest. In 1815 the map of the first allotment to the Crown is accompanied with the advice to wait until the corn harvest is complete 'when Labourers may be had probably at a cheaper rate'.[28] The importance of commons as building plots for the poor is evidenced by the memorial of Edward Hawkins and Anne Cooke who complained in 1790 that 'divers new encroachments ... [had been] lately made on the Waste and Commons ...' at Macclesfield, and goes on to identify these as being very small and in the possession of the very poor.[29] A case of professional tension is highlighted by the complaints of the Windsor Forest enclosure surveyors who wrote to William Huskisson in

1817 complaining that their bills for supplying the several surveys, maps and plans had been ignored, held up and ultimately altered.[30]

There are other classes of records which can be essential to local historians interested in enclosure. The legal courts provide much information and the historian has reason to be grateful to those who provided the courts of Chancery and Exchequer with exhibits (correspondence, accounts and other miscellaneous papers) to illustrate their claims and counter-claims, and subsequently refrained from collecting them. Examples, taken from the Court of Chancery, include the several books of enclosure award extracts at Bampton at Oxfordshire in 1838,[31] and the printed statement of claims of landowners and others interested in the enclosure of Wymondham, Norfolk in 1806.[32] A less obvious place to look for enclosure records is amongst the Admiralty archive; an example is the bound volume which contains both a copy of the Act for the enclosure of Langley South Common in the parish of Warden (Northumberland) and the commissioners' minutes. This item is contained in the Admiralty records as the lords of the manor were the governors of the Royal Hospital for Seamen at Greenwich.[33] The more obvious connection between railways and the land they were built upon has resulted in some very interesting papers in the records of a number of railway companies. Several useful and enlightening printed items can be found in the bound volume of papers once belonging to Francis Mewburn, a solicitor involved with a number of railway ventures in the first half of the 19th century which are now held in the large Great Western Railway collection at TNA. It seems that he (or his office) was concerned with a number of enclosures, as relevant papers relating to Givendale (Yorkshire ER) and Oakington (Cambridgeshire) in 1833 are included in the volume, as well as several papers referring to the regulation of common pasture at Beverley (Yorkshire ER) in 1836.[34]

From the establishment of the Enclosure Commission in 1845 more centralised record keeping was instituted. The Enclosure Commissioners' *Annual Reports to Parliament* list the enclosures for specific years (although individual Acts could still be passed) and copies of awards and enclosure papers are now at TNA in MAF 1 and MAF 25 respectively. Less comprehensive collections of material will still be found at CROs.

At the time of the wars with Revolutionary France there was a fear that agricultural production would be unable to provide for the population. A series of poor harvests and the difficulties of securing agricultural imports led to food shortages and food riots. The government decided to undertake a 'crop census' and chart agricultural production. The returns for 1795, 1800 and 1801 are the result of this investigation. The responsibility for the 1795 returns rested with local magistrates and the high constables of the hundreds. The efficiency of this work varied, and this is reflected in the returns themselves; there are summaries for hundreds, other districts or whole counties. A usual return reported the yield for 1794 and 1795 in quarters (or local measures) and may include the acreage from which the yield was taken. Some of the returns are qualitative rather then quantitative; the return for the Rape of Arundel, Lower Division, Sussex describes the wheat as 'partial and in some districts blighted. Many farmers have better crops than usual and more productive than in 1794. Others find their crops deficient and not so productive as in 1794. On the whole it is not a fair crop as in common years and the produce not equal to 1794'.[35]

The returns for 1795 can be found in HO 42/36-37. They are not indexed and researchers will have to spend some time to find material relating to their locality, if it is covered at all. In late October 1800 another investigation was initiated to determine that year's harvest. Specific questions were presented to the Bishops who passed these down to the local parish clergy. The investigation centred on the produce of the last harvest, to be estimated in bushels, and specifying wheat, barley, oats, potatoes, comparative crops of hay, beans and turnips; prices of the above crops comparing October 1800 with the same month in 1799 and 1798; whether the produce of the late harvest had been consumed and the quantity of wheat in store, what quantity of foreign wheat and flour had been brought in, and what use was made of rice, barley or oats as substitutes. These returns were made either directly to the Home Office, or to the Bishops who forwarded them to the Home Office, and are in HO 42/52-55. Like the earlier 1795 returns the surviving documents display a variety of precision and coverage. Many are on a parish-by-parish basis, although only summaries exist for Herefordshire, Norfolk, Suffolk, Durham and Northumberland.

The 1801 crop census was easily the most organised and standardised enquiry the government had made up to that time; this is reflected in the subsequent returns. The Home Office circulated a letter to the Bishops and included sets of pre-printed forms for distribution to the local clergy. These forms were to be filled in by the clergy for areas under arable production; there are no requests for acreage under hay production or use for pasture. On occasion the individual compiling the return annotated the form with a crop not included as part of the form. The column for 'general remarks' can provide much unexpected information. Many of the local clergy were happy to provide general comments on many aspects of early 19th-century England and Wales; for example, the curate of Wibsey in Bradford, West Yorkshire (see colour plate XIV), commented on the loyalty of the country during the 1790s against the spread of seditious revolutionary pamphlets, but warned that 'strenuous efforts have been made to cause civil disturbance by dint of starvation; and, if the wise and powerful hand of Government be not stretched out to our rescue, those efforts, it is to be feared, will involve us all in one common ruin'.[36] The compiler for Bruntingthorpe in Leicestershire considered that the high price of provisions was the result of 'farmers and graziers, corn factors, corn jobbers, millers, mealmen, butchers, bakers etc ...' running a 'most nefarious system of monopoly and speculation ...'. He claimed that local farmers were unwilling to provide figures for production to avoid any 'check on their rapacity'.[37] Complaints of refusal to comply (partially or fully) were common. At Kempston in Bedfordshire the compiler stated he had much trouble in ascertaining the various acreages from the occupiers – 'some were not able, and others unwilling to give account of their crops'.[38] The compiler for Amersham in Buckinghamshire reported that 'I have used my utmost endeavours to obtain the information your Lordship wished, but I am sorry to be under the necessity of adding that I find the farmers so universally averse to the measure, though wholly without reason, that I cannot, with any degree of accuracy at least, get at it'.[39] Reasons for both under and over estimating the crop size were deemed complex. The estimated return for Lanivet in Cornwall, it was thought, did

> not contain one-third of the produce of this parish, the farmers have been extremely backward and shy in giving their return, the produce was uniformly great. Some apprehend the return is in order to new taxes, others for my private advantage (as they are conscious the composition they pay me is not equal to the value of one quarter of their tithes if taken in kind) in some parishes they think it their interest to make the return as large as possible, hoping to stop the importation.[40]

The coverage of the returns varies from county to county; a little over 85 per cent of the Isle of Wight can be compared with 0 per cent for Nottinghamshire; the average for England comes out at 46.7 per cent. However, if we accept that around 10 per cent of most counties was used for buildings, and standing and running water, then it is reasonable to suppose that over 50 per cent of the land available for agricultural use is covered in these returns. They have been transcribed and in many cases researchers may find they have no need to view the originals. The Welsh material was transcribed in the 1950s by D. Williams and D. Thomas, and the English returns by Michael Turner. While the Welsh transcriptions contain only the crop and acreage data, the English returns are fully transcribed, including the general remarks.[41] The harvest of 1801 produced a good crop and government decided against undertaking such an investigation on an annual basis. More detailed crop returns were instituted in the 1860s and these are described below.

Tithe payments were originally extracted from the inhabitants of a parish for the maintenance of the church and its incumbent. The history of tithes shows that it had been accepted as law by 855. The extraction of produce for the maintenance of the clergy had undoubtedly been in place for some time before this as the legislation referred to above mentions tithes being already a system of much antiquity. Tithes were the right of the established church to a tenth of the annual production of each farm or holding, originally payable in kind. For example the incumbent of a parish would have the right to the tenth pig, sheep and cow, tenth sheaf of corn, the tenth fleece of wool, even the tenth pail of milk. However, from the point of view of the incumbent, it was no easy feat to collect tithes in kind. After the Reformation the right to tithes often passed into the hands of private individuals; thus tithes were paid to the church and the laity. In many areas tithes were commuted to money payments or 'moduses', that is to say a local agreement was entered into by which agricultural producers paid an agreed money payment to the church rather than a tenth part of the physical produce. Nevertheless, tithes remained a contentious issue well into the modern period. Dissenters argued they should not pay towards the finances of the established church while those interested in improving the output of agricultural produce claimed that tithes were a hindrance to enterprising farmers.

In 1836 the Tithe Commutation Act established a Tithe Commission to solve the various problems. Based on the administrative structure of the Poor Law Commission (1834) there were to be three Tithe Commissioners in

London, a full-time secretariat and a number of assistant commissioners who would be the commissioners' representative in each locality. It was the job of the assistants to supervise the voluntary or compulsory commutation of tithes in the 12,275 tithe districts in England and Wales, setting up meetings, offering advice, settling petty disputes and seeking agreements where possible.

Tithe payments under the Act were calculated to raise a money payment to the church based on crop prices over a seven-year average instead of any payment in kind. However, it should be remembered that not all localities were paying tithe in kind by 1836, or indeed that all lands were titheable. Local agreements for commutation may already have been reached before the 1836 Act, or the local church may have been awarded land in lieu of tithes during enclosure. Where lands were titheable and a map and apportionment was produced, the local historian will find, regardless of problems of inaccuracy and incompleteness, an excellent source for land ownership, holding and usage.[42] The main series of tithe records are maps and the apportionments. The apportionments provide the names of owners, occupiers, description of land and buildings, land use and acreage. Each entry is given a number, which corresponds to the map; this is a generalisation and the quality of information contained in these records varies. For example, some of the maps contain a great deal of topographical information such as railway lines, factories and other buildings, urban centres, etc. On the other hand some may be little more than sketches providing the basic information required to identify lands mentioned in the apportionment. There were plans to have all of the tithe maps made to a single standard but unfortunately this was rejected on financial grounds. A key was produced to represent topographical features such as toll roads, private roads, woods, pasture grounds and so on, and a colour copy can be found on the open shelves in the Map and Large Document Reading Room at TNA and this will be useful where surveyors used the key.

The use of centrally printed forms has meant that the apportionments conform to a more standardised format than the maps. The preamble of the apportionment gives the extent and use of the acreage liable to tithe, the names of the tithe owners and any customary payments in lieu of tithe. However, even here the information may vary; for example, many of the Welsh apportionments are silent on the state of cultivation of individual plots. Copies of the maps and apportionments can be found in CROs and some can still be found at the parish church. TNA has sets separated into two series: apportionments are in record series IR 29 and the maps in IR 30. Maps that had fallen into disrepair by the early 20th century were copied by the Ministry of Agriculture and Fisheries and these copies are now in IR 30 with the originals now in IR 77. The quickest way to track down the appropriate map and apportionment is to consult Kain and Oliver's *Tithe Maps and Apportionments of England and Wales*.[43] This book lists the maps and apportionments and is arranged in county and then place (usually township or parish) order. Because earlier agreements may have rendered the mapping of a parish unnecessary it should be noted that the maps and apportionments resulting from the 1836 Act cover around 79 per cent of the area of England and Wales. An excellent guide to the records is R.J.P. Kain and H.C. Prince's *Tithe Surveys for Historians*.[44]

The assistant commissioners' questions, records of meetings and correspondence with the Commission and various local landowners were kept in individual place-specific files; in effect these 'tithe files' are the working papers of the assistant commissioners and are at TNA. Such files were created regardless of the tithe status of the locality and the files therefore cover the whole of England and Wales, but unfortunately they were heavily weeded in the early 20th century. The surviving material may include only a notice of any voluntary agreements and the report of the assistant commissioner on the fairness of that agreement, or simply a confirmation that tithes were commuted under an earlier specified enclosure act. However, many of the files contain detailed sets of printed questions, and the annotated answers, concerning the land, soil fertility, farming methods, levels of rent, etc, and so provide a snap-shot of mid-19th-century agricultural society. The files are held in record series IR 18 and are arranged in county and place order thus making searching relatively easy.[45] Kain has also produced a published list referenced to subjects covered in the files.[46]

From 1866 central government began collecting agricultural information on each parish, which were always anticipated to be a continuing investigation undertaken annually. The individual returns from each agricultural holding were used to compile a 'parish summary' which, as the phrase makes obvious, simply summarised the returns on a parish basis. The records for the period 1866 to 1988 are held at TNA in record series MAF 68 and are arranged by county with each parish listed alphabetically in the first column on the sheet.[47] The summaries provide such information as number and size of holdings, numbers and types of animals and crop acreage. Once the summary was created the individual farm returns were destroyed and it is not possible to chart the fortunes of individual farms from these records. Until 1917 the returns were made on a voluntary basis, but after that date they became compulsory. The records from 1989 are held electronically at the University of London.[48] (For records of individual farms see chapter 5.)

The returns of the owners of land in 1873 are useful for a snap-shot of landownership and are available in Parliamentary Papers (*Return of Owners of Land*, 1873, 1874, LXXII, c1097) or more recently on CD-Rom. The unequal ownership of land was considered by some to be a major social and economic concern in the early 20th century. Government response was to seek to tax the increase of the value of property in the United Kingdom and private owners were required to give to the government a part of the increase in the site value that may have occurred through public expenditure on roads, drainage, building of nearby parks, etc. The Valuation Office Survey records, *c*.1910-15, are the result of this initiative. The Valuation Office itself was set up to assess and record the value of each property from a base line figure or datum line. The result was a nationwide survey of all workshops, houses, farms, etc, which recorded details such as the owner, occupier, value and the number of rooms of each property. The surveyors used Ordnance Survey maps to identify each property and then enter the detailed information into Field Books. This is not a survey of agricultural land *per se*, as it was taken irrespective of use. The archive provides a snapshot of farm size, ownership, occupancy and land values, but does not say anything directly or systematically about land use, agricultural labour or other intimate details of farming. However, local historians have been imaginative in using these records, as Paul Anderton's work on researching Cheshire dairy farming through the descriptions of the various rooms and outbuildings in the field books demonstrates.[49]

When each property (field, house, factory, etc) was valued it was allocated a hereditament number. Details of each property were then entered into a Field Book (under the appropriate hereditament number) and each hereditament number was then recorded on an Ordnance Survey map to record its location. The vast amount of information contained in the Field Books makes these records a key source for local studies. For England and Wales the Valuation Office maps at TNA are in IR 121 and IR 124 to IR 145; the Field Books are in IR 58. The maps are the best way of locating specific properties, before looking at the relevant Field Book for more details. Not all of these maps and books have survived, but the Valuation Office's working maps and Valuation Books may be in the appropriate CRO. The Field Books for Basildon, Birkenhead and most of the Wirral, Chelmsford, Chichester, Coventry, Liverpool, Portsmouth, Southampton and Winchester do not survive.[50] The amount of information entered in the Field Books varies considerably, but usually includes: name of owner, name of occupier, owner's interest (freehold, copyhold), details of tenancy (term and rent), area covered by the property. However, other details were occasionally recorded and may include: date of erection, number of rooms, state of repair, liability for rates, insurance and repairs, date(s) of previous sale(s), and some of the early work includes a sketch-plan of the property. Figures entered for the purpose of valuation normally included the market value of the whole property and the market value of the site alone, with no structures. Some large properties were too big to be entered into the books and were recorded on separate forms. Unfortunately these were not preserved. The tax was eventually deemed too complex to continue as a permanent system and discontinued in 1920. Material for Scotland is held at the NAS.

From the start of the Second World War the government realised that Britain faced serious problems concerning food production and supply, and farms had rapidly to increase their output. The records of the National Farm Survey tell the story of this initiative in great detail. The Ministry of Agriculture and Fisheries sought to increase production through County Agricultural War Committees, and in order to do so they could reclaim derelict land, redirect labour, order how much or what crops were to be grown, inspect property and farming practices and ultimately had the right to evict farmers.[51] During the early part of 1941 British farms were assessed to determine their ability to produce the required foodstuffs for the duration of the war. Overall the documents produced for the National Farm Survey give much detailed information of mid-20th-century rural England and Wales and provide a concise inventory of farming at the time. There are four sections: a return dated 4 June 1941 giving details of fruit, vegetables and stocks of straw and hay; a return dated 4 June 1941 giving details of crops and grass, livestock and labour employed; the primary farm record and finally a return with additional questions on labour, motive power and tractors, rents and the length of occupancy. The answers to the several returns provide local researchers with a wealth of information including: numbers and size of farms, labour employed in farming, the standard of farming, the facilities (electricity and water) available at local farms, acreage farmed and numbers of animals. The records are held at TNA and the main series are the survey maps (Ordnance Survey maps marked with farm boundaries and other annotations) in MAF 73 and the textual records (completed forms) in MAF 32. The minutes of the County War Agricultural War Committees and their various sub-committees are in MAF 80. Three of the sets of documents here are prime 'record linkage' sources where the researcher may examine a place of interest based around tithe, valuation office and farm survey material.[52] The NAS has the records of the Scottish Agricultural Executive Committees and the farm boundary maps.

The first manuscript map of the British Isles was drawn by Matthew Paris in about 1250 and the well-known Mappa Mundi, housed in Hereford Cathedral, has been dated to about 1290. By the beginning of the 15th century the principles of cartography were sufficiently understood for the making of maps to accompany local surveys, although they were not very accurate, and they are the earliest maps found in local record offices.

Somewhat surprisingly, TNA holds the earliest local map in existence, of Inclesmoor, Yorkshire, made in 1406-7; there is a huge collection of local maps under various record series, and a good starting point for TNA research is *Maps and Plans of the British Isles*.[53] The Map Team at TNA are currently working towards making the card index and various other finding aids to extracted maps redundant by inserting the descriptions and document references into the electronic catalogue. Most county record offices have considerable examples of estate maps which vary in size, accuracy and aestheticism. They were concerned primarily with establishing ownership, boundaries, field names and sometimes land use. Paul Hindle's *Maps for Historians* is perhaps the best general guide to the variety of maps the researcher should expect to find, what they were designed to show and where they will be found.[54]

There are many printed maps which the local historian can use. The Italians were the first to excel at the surveying and engraving of maps and the drawing of architectural plans; from 1473 they published printed maps from engraved copper plates. They were overtaken in the 16th century by Dutch and Flemish cartographers and in 1564 Gerard Mercator published a wall-map of the British Isles; at about the same time an Englishmen, Lawrence Nowell, engraved a map of the country. Interest in mapping the whole of the British Isles began in the 1540s, due to the improved skills and techniques of military engineers and by the 1570s some English surveyors understood the principles of triangulation and were using surveying instruments made by London craftsmen. Elizabethan London became a centre of map-making and publishing and during the 1570s Christopher Saxton produced county maps for England and Wales. His achievement provided the framework in which other topographers could work and there were many maps produced thereafter. They vary in accuracy and attractiveness but are of limited practical use. John Ogilby pioneered a new approach by publishing 100 strip maps of the main roads in the country in 1675 and others, such as Emanuel Bowen and John Cary, produced similar maps. The 17th-century cartographer, John Speed, included one or two town plans in his county maps and the production of town maps became very popular; most towns have at least one from at least the 18th century.

The Ordnance Survey was founded in 1791 although military maps were produced before this date; the first was one of the Highlands of Scotland, surveyed between 1747 and 1755 after the battle of Culloden brought the Stuart rebellion to an end. The engineer responsible, William Roy, did not live to see his vision of a national military survey but the threat of invasion from France at the end of the 18th century led the Board of Ordnance to map the south coast of England at a scale of one inch to the mile. The first map, of Kent, was published in 1801 and within twenty years about a third of England and Wales had been mapped at the one-inch scale. In 1824 Parliament ordered the Ordnance Survey to produce a six-inch to the mile valuation survey of Ireland; the first maps began to appear in the mid-1830s, leading to calls for similar surveys in England and Wales. The one-inch map was virtually useless for the newly emerging railway engineers and mapping of England and Scotland remained incomplete; in 1840 the Treasury agreed that the remaining areas should be surveyed at the six-inch scale. There was no consistency of scale until 1863 when it was agreed that the six-inch scale should be the standard for mountain and moorland areas and 25 inches for rural areas; detailed plans as large as ten feet to the mile were introduced for built-up areas. The 25-inch survey was complete by 1895. After the Second World War metric maps began to appear and are now the standard scale; in 1973 the Ordnance Survey began to digitise its maps and this process was completed in 1995, making Britain the first country in the world to complete a programme of large-scale electronic mapping. Its maps are arguably the best in the world and no local historian can do without them. Historic maps will be found in record offices and libraries, and the most complete set is in the British Library.

In the 1830s and '40s there was greater awareness of the link between public health and the condition of buildings. Under the 1848 Public Health Act councils were allowed, rather than compelled, to take action on building control; some did so but the majority did not. Where the new system was adopted developers were required to submit plans for approval to a committee of the local authority and a copy retained by it for future reference. There are large quantities of such maps for some towns, which vary in quality and condition; the best sets of plans tend to be for large and important new buildings, which would probably have been drawn by leading local architects. Their survival rate also varies considerably and even those towns with substantial collections have gaps in coverage; the plan for the 19th-century town hall in Leicester, for example, cannot be found. Because of the sheer quantities involved decisions have had to be made about 'culling' and plans for structures such as small extensions, garages and the like are unlikely to be kept. Many of the plans are fragile and therefore may only be available in a microform or digitised form.

From 1793 private canals or waterworks bills submitted to Parliament, involving new works or compulsory acquisition of land, had to be accompanied by a plan; this requirement was extended to railway bills from 1803 and in 1836 elaborate new procedures were introduced for railway bills. Plans of river improvements, waggonways and the like which preceded canals and railways are much scarcer. Once Parliamentary sanction was granted detailed engineering plans were prepared for construction and maintenance. They delineate the proposed route and land about a quarter of a mile on either side in some detail;

each plot of land was numbered and described in the accompanying book of reference. Any alterations to the line in the future also required a plan and book of reference. The records will be found in the House of Lords Record Office and in local record offices; copies had to be deposited with the Clerk of the Peace for the local Court of Quarter Sessions and plans of docks, tramways, turnpike roads and public utilities may also be found.

Many early travellers left descriptions of their journeys and many of these are well known, such as Celia Fiennes and Daniel Defoe; Defoe's *A Tour Through the Whole Island of Great Britain* (1724-6) was a compilation of observances made on journeys undertaken over many years, with additional information taken from other writers. Diaries and other descriptions will be found in local record offices and some of them have been published by record societies or similar organisations. Robin Gard's *The Observant Traveller* includes a catalogue of 608 diaries found in record offices;[55] although it is no longer in print copies can be found in local record offices and libraries. Heather Creaton has listed diaries in her *Unpublished London Diaries*, 2003. Samuel Lewis published *A Topographical Dictionary of England* in seven editions between 1831 and 1849, and similar volumes for Wales, Scotland and Ireland. Topographical guides to particular areas were first published in the late 18th century to cater for the increasing number of visitors to the Lake District, Snowdonia and the Highlands of Scotland. John Murray's *Handbooks for Travellers* began with Devon and Cornwall in 1851 and eventually covered every English county, as well as single volumes for Scotland and Ireland.

Antiquarian histories are invariably illustrated with local views and it became fashionable in the 17th century to commission drawings of country houses and views of London. Libraries and record offices have holdings of topographical drawings dating from the 18th century. Photographs are a very common and useful source for evidence of how a place used to look and these probably exist in greater quantities than any other material and will include aerial shots and postcards. The great garden designer, Humphry Repton (1752-1818) produced 'red books' for work he undertook, which showed the estate before and after he had remodelled it; they are comparatively rare but where they exist are a charming and unusual source for the topography of a landed estate. During the late 16th and 17th centuries landowners often employed a land surveyor to make a survey of their estate, showing the extent of each property, the form of tenure by which it was held and often the use to which it was put; some also describe the buildings. Glebe terriers are surveys of the endowments of benefices compiled by incumbents and churchwardens and will be found in parish, archdeaconry and diocesan records.

Place- and field-names are also sources for topographical information, as they can indicate features on the ground or the nature of the land; for example 'slough' means marshy ground and 'frith' indicates a wood. The systematic study of English place names began in the late 19th century and in 1923 the English Place-Name Society was founded; it began a county-by-county study of place-names which is still ongoing. It is now housed in the School of English Studies of Nottingham University. W.G. Hoskins introduced the idea of 'reading the landscape' and a new genre of landscape history has grown up in the last half-century or so. It is now accepted that documents, while of immense importance for a study of local and family history, are not the only source.

3
THE PEOPLE

The best-known source for demography is the decennial census, first taken in 1801; before that date local and family historians need to rely on a variety of sources, none of them without problems. An explanation of these records and where they can be found is on pp.34-6. Before 1801 citizens were counted in different ways for a variety of purposes, many of them linked with new ways of raising income for the Crown and therefore the subject of much fear and distrust. According to Stephens, until 1538 the sources for the study of population and social structure in England are largely feudal or fiscal in nature and from 1538 to 1801 mainly ecclesiastical;[1] 1538 was the year in which records of baptisms, marriages and burials were first kept by the Church of England. There are two problems with early 'censuses' or name lists: firstly, the reliability of the document contents and, secondly, how they can be used to answer questions they were never designed to address. Weak, corrupt and inefficient administrators, linked with tax avoidance or evasion, can make early sources somewhat suspect, and the percentage of the population whose names are recorded is disappointingly low. There are many studies of population and demography, a specialist journal and at least one major research organisation.[2]

There are a number of pre-1801 census or 'people lists' produced. Perhaps the most well known is the Compton census of 1676, named after Henry Compton, Bishop of London, which was an ecclesiastical enquiry into the number of Anglicans, Papists and Nonconformists in each parish. Its interpretation is subject to debate, as with any similar records, but it is seen as a major source for estimating the size of the population and of fundamental importance in assessing the strength of Roman Catholicism and nonconformity in the reign of Charles II. The principal documents are at the William Salt Library in Stafford (Salt 33) and the Bodleian Library (Tanner 144 and 150), although there is other relevant material in Lambeth Palace Library and CROs.[3] It is always worth checking to see if any early censuses (including pre-1801) were produced and survive for a given area.[4] Episcopal visitations are also useful as they may give an estimate of local population size.

The memory of the 1745-6 Jacobite rebellion and the threat of invasion from France led to the re-establishment of the local militia; an Act of 1757 required parish constables to compile lists of able-bodied men between the ages of 18 and 50 (reduced to 45 in 1762), giving their rank, occupation and any incapacity. They were sent to the Lord Lieutenant of the county and a ballot was held to determine who was to serve. Certain categories were exempt, such as peers, clergymen, apprentices, seamen and soldiers, and there was also exemption from service on the grounds of infirmity or poverty in order to limit pressure on the poor rates. An Act of 1802 divided the able-bodied into four classes, who could be called on in order: men under 30 without children, men over 30 without children, men aged between 18 and 45 with no children under 14, and men between 18 and 45 with children under 14 years old. The returns do not cover the entire adult male work-force but they are a useful source where they survive; some counties have good sets, such as Hertfordshire and Northamptonshire, many of which have been published. The returns will usually be found with other records of quarter sessions and elsewhere.[5]

As the name suggests, poll books were drawn up after an election had taken place and record which person each elector voted for. An Act of 1696, designed to prevent fraud by returning officers, authorised the publication of copies of the poll, and returning officers allowed local printers to publish the details as a commercial venture. They continued to be published until the introduction of the secret ballot in 1872. As each printer decided what to include, poll books vary in their detail; some included addresses and occupations, others one or the other, and some neither. Several thousand books are still extant and will be found in local libraries and record offices, as well as the British Library, Guildhall Library and Bodleian Library. Electoral registers, on the other hand, are lists of those eligible to vote and were required under the Parliamentary Reform Act of 1832. They list electors by ward and street so can be difficult to use if personal names are sought. Most libraries and record offices have good sets but with gaps during the two world wars. Until recently electoral registers were freely available but the problems associated with identity fraud have led to access being restricted (to the more modern registers); advice should be sought from the library or record office.[6] It must be remembered that the franchise was heavily restricted until the end of the 19th century and women were not allowed to vote in Parliamentary elections until 1918 and even then only women over 30; only with the 1928 Equal Franchise Act was the age qualification for women brought into line with men.

There are a number of specialist directories covering well-known people, particular occupations and members of certain organisations. The *New Dictionary of National Biography* was published by Oxford University Press in September 2004; it consists of over 50,000 detailed biographical entries describing the notable men and women who have helped shape British history, culture, and attitudes, from the fourth century BC to the present day. The dictionary includes: artists, scientists, doctors, business people, writers, performers, reformers, criminals, eccentrics, politicians, church leaders, military leaders, and scholars. It is available as a 60-volume print edition and as an online subscription service, and major libraries should have one or the other, as well as the older set of books. Other listings include the various printed registers of those who attended Oxford and Cambridge, the clergy and members of the military. A further collection of biographical data stems from the idea of G.D.H. Cole for a *Dictionary of Labour Biography*. Under the editorship of Professor John Saville and Dr Joyce Bellamy, both based at the University of Hull, 11 volumes of the dictionary appeared between 1971 and 2003. As well as being available in print the project has its own web site and search facilities.[7]

Apart from published lists the most usual place to find people in the medieval or early modern period is through records relating to rates. A rate is a levy for local purposes, usually based on an assessment of the yearly value of property; they were levied spasmodically in different parts of the country from at least the 14th century, for purposes such as drainage and bridge maintenance. Compulsory rating (at least in theory) throughout the country began with the 1601 Act for the Relief of the Poor although earlier acts had gradually introduced an element of compulsion into the Christian duty of almsgiving; for example, an Act of 1552 ordered the regular weekly collection of alms in each parish and the entry of such payments in a book, and one of 1562-3 ordered that those who refused to contribute voluntarily should be assessed by the Justices of the Peace to pay a regular weekly sum. Once the principle of compulsory rating had been established it was used for a variety of purposes, such as the repair of highways and gaols, and remained in use until the late 20th century. Rate books will normally be found with other parish records, but also with borough records and similar series. Their survival varies, due to the size and quantity of the books and their limited historical value; it is rare to find complete sets and where they have been kept they have sometimes been sampled. Early books are unlikely to survive except as isolated examples. They list occupiers and owners of properties, sometimes with the address of the property and the amount of money levied on it.

The earliest source to list names, with which everyone will be familiar, is the Domesday survey of 1086; it gives details of the holders and value of land in England and covers most parts of the country. It is a difficult source to use and only lists the principal landowners, but is one of the archival treasures of the country and essential for medieval local history studies (see chapter 2).

A major, and varied, series of taxation records is held at TNA in record series E 179; it contains the detailed records which survive among the public records of taxation of lay people in England from *c.*1190 to 1690, in Wales from 1543 to *c.*1690, and the taxation of clerics in England and Wales from 1269 to 1663. They are described in detail in M. Jurkowski, C. Smith and D. Crook, *Lay Taxes in England and Wales, 1188-1688*.[8] Briefly, the earliest records relate to carucages, a land tax, levied on several occasions between 1194 and 1224. Taxes imposed on the income and moveable property of more prosperous individuals, lay subsidies, survive from 1225 and are supplemented and later replaced by income derived by the Crown from such as tallages and scutages (which were old customary and feudal taxes); some material relates to these levies for the late 13th and early 14th centuries. Lay subsidies ceased to be assessed directly on individuals in 1334 and were replaced by fixed quotas paid by individual tax units. From 1291 there were occasional taxes levied in Wales. Experimental taxation was developed as subsidies on parishes in 1371 and the initiation of poll taxes in 1377. These were discontinued after being a major contributor to the Peasants' Revolt of 1381 (but were revived in the 17th century). Further 15th-century taxation experiments in 1404, 1411, 1435 and 1449, and a number of levies on aliens from 1439 to 1487, continued. Revised Tudor versions of the lay subsidy were created between 1512 and 1515 and a tax known as the fifteenth[9] disappeared after 1623. The experimental taxes associated with the Civil War and Interregnum, weekly or monthly assessments, and some records of the decimation tax of 1655, are also in this series. From 1660 a variety of taxes was introduced but the principal one was the hearth tax, based on the number of hearths in a property. It was collected periodically between 1662 and 1689 (however, most surviving records relate to 1662-6 and 1670-4); it was abolished in 1689. Many returns have been printed by record societies. Royal taxation of the clergy is also found in this series, including some returns of the 'taxatio' – a new assessment of the English church decreed by Pope Nicholas IV in 1291-2. Other early sources include the hundred rolls. In the late 13th century enquiries were made by central government into local royal rights and privileges; the documents created are known as the hundred rolls and are at TNA in records series SC 5. Some similar records (also often regarded as hundred rolls) in SC 11 and E 164, were published in full by the HMC during the early part of the 19th century as *Rotuli Hundredorum*.[10] Both the rolls and HMC publications are in Latin and there are also several county record society publications of the records. They are less extensive than Domesday and cover Bedfordshire, Buckinghamshire, Cambridgeshire, Huntingdonshire, Leicestershire, Oxfordshire and Warwickshire in varying degrees of detail. The records are popularly known as hundred rolls as most of the returns were made by hundreds, the principal subdivision of the county.

There is further useful material for linking names to places in land tax and other assessed taxes such as the window tax. Further (and more detailed) land tax records are in IR 20-5. Income tax was first levied in 1798 and the surviving returns can be found in E 182 although these lack individual assessments. Under the Marriage Duty Act, 1695, a rather curious tax was levied between 1695 and 1706, a product of the government's desperate need for money in the 1690s. It had two parts: charges on 'vital events' (births, marriages and burials) as and when they occurred, and annual payments by bachelors aged over 25 and childless widowers, the latter essentially a poll tax on single independent men. Collection of the tax was organised through magistrates and any surviving records will be found in CROs. The Institute of Heraldic and Genealogical Studies in Canterbury has a list of surviving returns.

Freemen's rolls and registers will be found with other borough records (see chapter 13). Admission to the freedom of a corporate city enabled a man to practise his trade and vote at elections, and was a jealously guarded right. It was normally gained by serving an apprenticeship to a trade or following a father's occupation. The names of freemen were registered annually and some have been published; they usually include the name of the freeman and his father, their occupation, or the name and occupation of his master. The records should be used with caution in estimating population, as they exclude servants, apprentices and casual labourers, as well as women and children. There are also examples of freemen being created for other purposes as happened in Leicester in the 1820s. In 1822 the Tory Corporation began to enrol honorary freemen on an unprecedented scale and 800 were created in two years; nearly a third of them lived outside the county, most from Nottingham, and the exercise was a blatant attempt to win the next election for the Tories.

Before 1858 the proving of wills was a function of the church courts and the records can be found in a number of record offices depending on where the will was proved. The location of the testator's property will partly determine whether the will would be proved at the archdeaconry, diocesan or archbishop's court; the wills of major landowners who owned property in both provinces (Canterbury and York) would be proved at the Prerogative Court of Canterbury (PCC), which took precedence. PCC wills to 1858 are held at TNA in PROB 11 (with the index in PROB 12); these are now available online at TNA's web site. Those for the Prerogative Court of York are held at the Borthwick Institute. Some testators chose to have their wills proved at the PCC as it was seen to be more prestigious. From 1858 the records can be found at the Probate Search Room, First Avenue House, 42-49 High Holborn, London, WC1V 6NP. In some dioceses there are wills of people with modest incomes but the practice was not widely adopted by farmers and urban craftsmen until the 16th century; labourers and other poor people rarely made wills. Even those who had property to leave sometimes made arrangements before their death and did not make a will. The whole system is complex but there are a number of books which provide information on the boundaries of the various courts.[11] The British Record Society (see chapter 1) has published many indexes to wills and other probate material.

Wills in Scotland were proved at a commissary court or sheriff's court and the records are in the NAS; the Scottish Record Society has published indexes up to 1800. The Scottish Documents web site, part of the Scottish Archive Network (SCAN), has a fully searchable index to more than 52,000 wills and testaments from 1500 to 1901; there is free access to the index but a charge is made for images. The system in Ireland was similar to that in England and Wales until 1858, when responsibility for proving wills passed to a new Principal Registry in Dublin; the records were destroyed by fire in 1922, although the indexes survived, and there are few wills before 1780. PRONI has a large collection of wills from 1900 to 1984 and some records will be found in other repositories. Before the original wills were sent to Dublin each local registry had copied them into books which are available at PRONI on microfilm. In all parts of the British Isles wills may be found in other collections, especially family and estate, and solicitors' records. Bundles of title deeds to property often contain wills. More information on inventories will be found in chapter 10.

In 1642 Parliament ordered all males in England and Wales over the age of 18 to take an oath 'to live and die for the true Protestant religion, the liberties and rights of subjects, and the privilege of Parliaments'. Lists were made by churchwardens and constables of all who signed and those who refused. The records are in the House of Lords Record Office and surviving returns are listed in the appendix to the *5th Report of the Historical Manuscripts Commission* (1876); some lists were entered into parish registers and some have been published by local or family history societies.[12]

The first suggestion for a national census in the modern sense came in 1753 when a Cornish MP, Thomas Potter, introduced the idea. Opposition to the suggestion centred around its expense, that it was impracticable, would infringe liberty, be used for taxation and conscription and by our enemies. It was supported by the government and went through the Parliamentary stages only to lapse because the session came to an end. A second Bill was introduced by another Cornish MP, Charles Abbot; its aims were to discover the number of people in the country and their occupations, and whether the population was increasing or declining. It succeeded because of the fear that a rising population would outgrow the available resources; the most famous proponent of this theory was a clergyman, Thomas Malthus, who in his book *Essay on the Principle of Population*, published in 1798, argued that the natural tendency of population was to increase faster than the means of subsistence.

Census Enumerators Books (CEBs) are a key government source.[13] From 1801 onwards, information about the population has been collected every ten years by means of a census or population count. Original census material for 1801, 1811, 1821 and 1831 has not been preserved[14] but local population totals which make some differentiation in terms of trade can be found published in Parliamentary Papers. From 1841 the CEBs have been kept.[15] They provide personal information and include more data than previous censuses. As the original material is closed for 100 years local historians will only have recourse to the Parliamentary Papers published abstracts for 1911 onwards. The overriding concerns of the Second World War meant suspension of the census in 1941.

Many borough and CROs have some original copies of early (pre-1841) censuses. The details contained within them and the reasons for their preservation will vary. For example, there is 'An Account of the Population of the Parish of Hitchin, Herts taken in the Month of Jan 1807'.[16] There is no explanation why this document was compiled but it gives the numbers in each family, the number of boys and girls and the occupation of the head of household. As well as the usual occupations there are two toymakers, and some interesting notes in the 'Observations' column: one child is subject to fits, another child classed as a cripple and a husband enlisted as a soldier. These documents will usually be found in parish records but in theory almost any archive can contain material of interest, and the Hitchin example referred to was transferred to the CRO as part of a 'magpie' collection from the local museum. Michael Barke concluded that a part census for North Shields dating from 1811 survived as it was 'an economical re-using of an old but only partially filled manuscript [which] passed into the ownership of the new guardians of the poor after the passing of the 1834 Poor Law Amendment Act because the township overseers had not only previously managed the poor law but were also one of the agencies charged with collecting census data' for the earlier census.[17]

The first four censuses were organised by John Rickman, a clerk of the House of Commons, by asking parish clergy and overseers of the poor a number of questions; these included the number of individuals and families, the number of baptisms, marriages and burials and the numbers involved in agriculture, trade or crafts. Some lists of names survive in local record offices for these early censuses. More details on ages were included in 1821 and on occupations in 1831.

Rickman died in 1840 and the organisation of the census was taken over by the General Register Office. It was based on poor law unions established in the wake of the 1834 Poor Law Amendment Act, which also became registration districts set up to record births, marriages and deaths from 1837; each district was divided into enumeration districts of about 250 houses and some 35,000 temporary enumerators were appointed. The 1841 census, taken on Sunday 6 June, marked a transitional stage between the first four censuses and what Higgs describes as the 'mature' Victorian censuses from 1851 onwards.[18] Pressure was building up during the late 1830s for a much more ambitious census and one of the bodies pressing for change was the London (later Royal) Statistical Society. The first Census Act for the 1841 census contained many of its recommendations but retained some similarities with Rickman's work. Initially it was proposed that the enumerators would gather the information themselves by house-to-house enquiries but a trial run showed how many officials would be needed. A supplementary Act was passed only two months before census day, authorising the use of household schedules.

The registrar general, Thomas Henry Lister, was anxious to have as simple a household schedule as possible and the information recorded in 1841 was limited to name, age (rounded down to the nearest five years for those over 15), sex, occupation, whether born in the same county or not or whether born in Scotland, Ireland or 'foreign parts'. The 1841 census is therefore much less useful than those from 1851 onwards; the limitation of only knowing whether someone was born in the same county is particularly frustrating for the historian of population movement. In 1851 the scope of the census was extended to include the relationship of each member of the household with its head, marital status and if someone was blind, deaf or dumb; exact ages and place of birth were given. Farmers had to state how many acres they farmed and how many labourers they employed, and other employers had to state the number of their employees. Vessels in harbour or on rivers, ships at sea, soldiers and British subjects abroad were all counted, and there were special forms for institutions such as workhouses and prisons. From 1861 there was only a requirement to record those in institutions by their initials which is not as helpful; the practice varied though, with workhouse inmates (but not prisoners) usually having their full name recorded. Census day in 1851 was Sunday 30 March and for the rest of the 19th century the census was taken on a Sunday at the end of March or beginning of April, in order to avoid the distortion caused by seasonal movements of some workers which occurred later in the year, and which it was felt had distorted the figures in 1841.

Local registrars were responsible for finding enumerators and the basic requirements were:

> He must be a person of intelligence and activity; he must read and write well, and have some knowledge of arithmetic; he must not be infirm or of such weak health as may render him unable to undergo the requisite exertion; he should not be younger than 18 years of age or older than 65;

> he must be temperate, orderly and respectable, and be such a person as is likely to conduct himself with strict propriety, and to deserve the goodwill of the inhabitants of his district.[19]

The general register office was mainly interested in census data for medical and actuarial purposes; it believed that the incidence of disease was directly related to density of population and the materials with which people worked. In 1891, for example, there was a requirement to state the number of rooms occupied by a household if less than five – this was quite clearly an attempt to find out the extent of overcrowding and insanitary conditions. The census returns are closed for 100 years because of undertakings given when they were compiled that the information would only be used for the preparation and publication of statistical data. The only censuses currently available to consult cover 1841 to 1901; the 1911 returns will be released at the begining of January 2012.

Census analysis is a popular activity for local historians, and evening class groups studying the 1851 census in particular have been held in different parts of the country for several years; the work sometimes leads to publication.[20] It is also a popular topic for school pupils undertaking a local study, often in conjunction with other statistical or pictorial sources like maps and photographs. The statistical data in the census lends itself to analysis by computer database and the source is one of the most popular with university history departments. With all its drawbacks, the census provides an unrivalled picture of a particular community at a single point in time.

The available records for England and Wales are to be found at the Family Records Centre (FRC), in Myddelton Street, London, EC1R IUW, and most CROs and many local history libraries have purchased microfilm copies of the returns for their area. TNA class reference for the 1841 and 1851 censuses is HO 107, and for 1861 to 1891 is RG 9-12, and these references will be used to locate a particular entry in the returns. The 1901 census in TNA series RG13 was released in digital format in 2002 and is available in that format either at TNA/FRC or remotely. Those unfamiliar with the census may need a little help at first to find their way around the class lists, but there are details of the places included in each enumeration district and for large towns there may be a street listing; however, house numbers should be used with caution as they frequently changed over time, and street names also changed, sometimes more than once. The household schedules for the 1841 to 1901 censuses were destroyed once they had been checked against the enumerators' books and it is these books which survive; from 1911 the household schedules were kept. There are problems with the census and these are dealt with in some detail in Edward Higgs' three books on the subject. At the time of writing the 1861 to 1901 censuses are available online via the TNA web site and it is only a matter of time before the full 1841 to 1901 material is available in this way. Scottish census material is held by the NAS and like England and Wales the returns are from the period 1841 onwards.

Most of the personal records available for consultation for the various branches of the military can be found at TNA. England had no regular standing army until the outbreak of the Civil War in 1642; prior to that regiments took the names of the colonels who raised them. At the restoration in 1660 a Secretary at War with responsibility for army administration was appointed. Limited information about officers can be found in the published *Army List*, which is available from 1754 in larger libraries. The regimental registers of births from 1761 to 1924 are indexed, giving the regiment and place of birth of children born to the wives of serving soldiers, if they were attached to the regiment. The index can be seen at TNA and at the FRC, but the records are held by the Office of National Statistics and are not on open access. There are also indexes of marriages and deaths of soldiers stationed in the United Kingdom. The Army Register Book (1881-1959) gives details of births, marriages and deaths of those serving overseas, and the index is at FRC. Similar books exist for the other services: the Royal Navy Register Book (1837-1959) and the Royal Air Force Register Book (1918-1959); from 1959 there is one register covering all the armed forces overseas. The National Army Museum tells the story of the army as a whole and there is a regimental museum for most of the major regiments. The systematic recording of naval service began in the 1660s when Samuel Pepys reorganised its administration. The official *Navy List* has been published quarterly since 1814 and was preceded by Steele's *Navy List* from 1782. The National Maritime Museum is another useful source of information on naval matters.

The Royal Air Force was formed in 1918 by combining the Royal Flying Corps and the Royal Navy Air Service; the *Air Force List* has been published since 1918. The RAF museum is at Hendon, north London, with a branch at Cosford, Shropshire. The Imperial War Museum's main site is in London but it also has branches at Duxford, Cambridgeshire and Manchester, and is responsible for the Cabinet War Rooms and HMS *Belfast*. In addition to these major museums, there are further specialist ones, such as the Tank Museum in Bovington, Dorset and the Fleet Air Arm Museum in Yeovilton, Somerset.

4
Transport, Communications and Trade

Good transport links were essential for local and regional economies to reach and develop any specialist agricultural and industrial production. Before adequate roads, heavy and bulky goods were transported by water and even in the medieval period rivers were often navigable far inland. The navigability of the major rivers was improved by companies authorised by private Acts of Parliament in the 17th and early 18th centuries, the period before the great age of canals, often by digging 'cuts'. If copies of bills and acts do not survive locally (and this is the same for canals and turnpike trust roads below) they can be found at the House of Lords Record Office, as well as references in the House of Commons Journals. By about 1730 some 1,160 miles of English rivers were navigable for light craft. The following example of material on this subject is held at the Flintshire Record Office and relates to the construction of a navigable cut from Chester to Connah's Quay, empowered by an Act of Parliament in 1732 to replace the old deep-water channel to the north of the estuary. In 1740 the River Dee Company was established in order to maintain the navigation. Several administrative changes over the next two and half centuries saw the creation of various minutes (several sets of) enclosure records, plans and other documents. Some of the records pre-date the River Dee Company by many years and go back as far as the mid-16th century.[1] Survival rates of large river archives will vary but references to individual rivers and their importance for local communications, trade and commerce will be much more common, as with the example here, where a decree had been made for stopping the

> 'auncient and navigable river of Rother' near Thorney Wall; this the inhabitants of Rye and Tenderden [*sic*] consider will 'utterly decaye' the haven of Rye and impoverish the ports of Rye and Tenderden [*sic*]. The Lord Warden asks that Commissioners of Sewers forbear the execution of that decree until further enquiry was made.[2]

The construction of artificial canals to link industrial districts with markets and navigable rivers was the next logical step and the first important British canal to be cut ran from the Duke of Bridgewater's mines at Worsley in Lancashire to Manchester, authorised by an Act of Parliament in 1758 and completed by 1761;

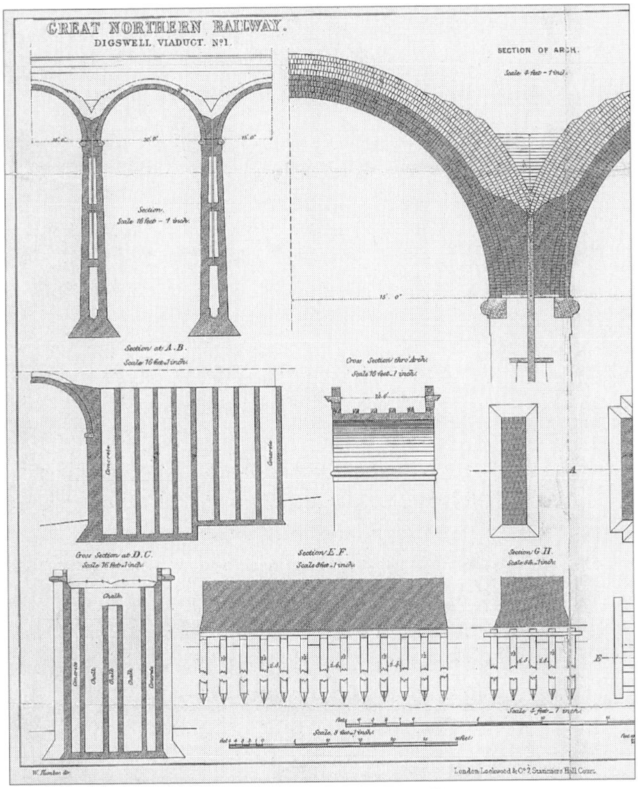

3 *Digswell Viaduct was built between 1848 and 1850 to cross the Mimram valley and was designed by William Cubitt. It has 40 arches of an average span of 40 feet, the highest being 97 feet above the river. The first train crossed the viaduct on 5 August 1850 but Queen Victoria refused to travel across it; it is still part of the East Coast main line. This plan dates from 1864.* (Hertfordshire Archives and Local Studies DE/Gr/z7.)

by 1780 the Duke was selling 400 tons of coal a week in Manchester. Within two generations the industrial districts of Britain were connected by a system of canals that involved some amazing technical achievements, such as locks and aqueducts. A number of canal ports developed, such as Ellesmere Port and Stourbridge. The importance of canals for practical purposes diminished with the coming of the railways and they are now largely used for leisure purposes. Some interesting canal structures survive, such as museums (Ellesmere Port in Cheshire, the National Waterways Museum in Gloucestershire and Stoke Bruerne in Northamptonshire, which have amalgamated under The Waterways Trust), warehouses, boat lifts and flights of locks.

Anyone wishing to build a canal had to obtain a private Act of Parliament and so, after exhausting local CROs and other record offices for relevant material (including the records of canal companies), researchers may need to consult the House of Lords Record Office.[3] Many thousands of plans for canals, as well as roads, railways and other public works, were deposited in the Houses of Parliament in connection with private bills from 1794. Often associated papers are also preserved, including books of reference, lists of owners and occupiers, and estimates of expenses. Details also had to be deposited with the court of quarter sessions; they usually comprise a book of reference, plans and other documents. Barges, wherries, and similar craft on navigable rivers and canals had to be registered with the court from 1795 to 1871. Canal records can also be found in other national and local archives, such

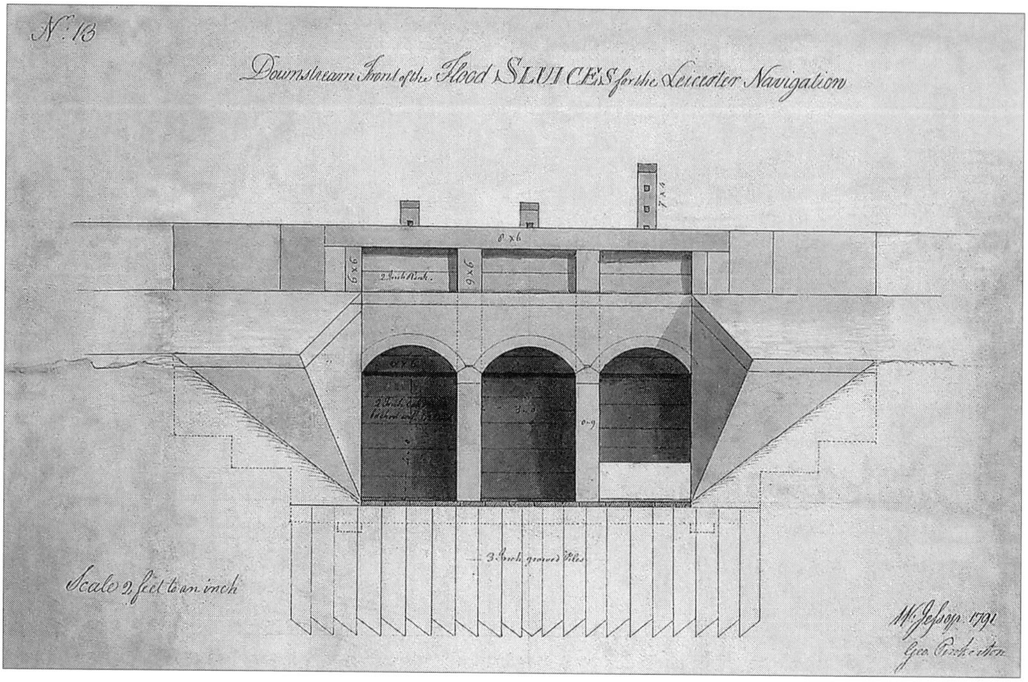

4 *William Jessop was a leading canal engineer and was responsible for the Leicester Navigation, which gained its Act of Parliament after two failed attempts. Jessop's drawings of various canal features date from 1791; they are part of a major solicitors' collection (Salusbury & Woodhouse) the firm which acted for the canal company.* (Record Office for Leicestershire, Leicester and Rutland, 3D42/M37/6/13.)

as the British Waterways Archive and the Institution of Civil Engineers. The Railway and Canal Historical Society is a good starting point for advice on the location of relevant material and information on its activities can be found on the Bodleian Library web site. The British Library has canal plans, including those for structures that were never built. TNA has an impressive number of canal company and canal-related records, mainly from the 17th through to the 20th centuries, and many (although not all) which were carried over, as companies moved from canals to railway enterprises. The following example is an unusually early reference to a canal, taken from the TNA catalogue and believed to date from 1319:

> The petitioners state that the transportation of goods and merchandise by water from Cambridge to Boston, Boston to Lincoln, and Lincoln to the River Trent, is being prevented by the weir (gorce) at Saxilby, where the people have blocked the course of the river, and where goods have to be unloaded and carried by land to Torksey. In the reign of the late King money was given for the repair of a canal there, but nothing has been done about this. They request a remedy, for the repair of this canal.[4]

The records of canal companies may survive in local record offices and can include minutes, accounts, reports, plans, and so on. They may be found in solicitors' collections, where the firm acted for the canal company, as in the Record Office for Leicestershire, Leicester and Rutland, which has drawings of lock gates by the canal engineer William Jessop.[5] George Bradshaw is best known for his railway maps but he also drew canal maps; in 1830 he produced one showing the canals of Lancashire and Yorkshire and this was followed by similar maps for other parts of the country. The British Library holds a large collection of canal maps. The 'Viewfinder' online picture resource[6] includes a collection of photographs by the celebrated architectural photographer, Eric de Maré, including canals and waterways.

Road transport was slow and dangerous until the late 18th and early 19th centuries as Britain continued to depend on roads left by the Romans.[7] Most existing routes were maintained by individual parishes and the records of the surveyors of the highways may be found with other parish records in CROs or other local archives. An Act of 1555 required the annual appointment of one or more surveyors and the most common records to survive are annual accounts, although even these are not plentiful. The surveyors were responsible for the supervision of statute labour whereby local people were required to maintain their roads. The 1835 Highways Act enabled two or more parishes to apply to the magistrates to be united in highway districts. The supposed advantages were the employment of a more skilled person to supervise repairs, greater uniformity of method and greater efficiency in management. Where parishes had a population of more than 5,000 the rights and duties of the surveyor of the highways could be assumed by a board of between five and twenty people, who might appoint a salaried assistant surveyor to supervise the work. The 1862 Highways Act enabled magistrates to form compulsory unions of parishes for highway purposes. These highway districts were to be managed by a board consisting of the magistrates resident in the district and waywardens elected annually by each parish in the place of surveyors. Other Acts between 1878 and 1894 affected the operation of Highway Boards, which came to an end under the 1888 and 1894 Acts which created county, urban district and rural district councils (see chapter 13).

By the 18th century the amount of road traffic was increasing to the extent that the parish-based system was no longer adequate.[8] Many roads were criticised for their quality, lack of upkeep or even their setting:

> ... the road between Barnstable and Clumleigh, which, instead of being constructed through the valley of the Taw, is carried over the highest brows of the river hills, where the traveller is unceasingly compelled to ascend and descend the sharpest hills in the country.[9]

Turnpike trusts were formed and empowered to levy tolls for the upkeep and improvement of named stretches of highway. The first one was established by Act of Parliament in 1663 to repair and maintain a particularly badly-worn stretch of the Great North Road (the modern A10) between Wadesmill and Royston in Hertfordshire. No further trusts were established until 1696, after which the number rose steadily. By 1750 most of the major through routes in England had been turnpiked apart from parts of the west country. The other three home countries only had limited numbers of turnpike trusts. The most active period for the formation of trusts was between 1751 and 1772, when 389 new Acts were passed; by 1820 over 1,000 trusts controlled about 22,000 miles of British roads. The last turnpike was created in 1836 and the last trust ended in 1895, by which time turnpike roads had largely been overtaken by railways. In Scotland turnpike trusts were created later than in England but were efficient and systematic in carrying out their responsibilities. During the 1820s and '30s a network of new roads was created in Fife and they are still distinguished by attractive tollhouses and a particularly fine series of cast-iron milestones, many now scheduled as ancient monuments.[10]

Turnpike roads were maintained more regularly and widened to allow the passage of wheeled vehicles; this often involved building new bridges to replace existing packhorse bridges. By the late 18th century new routes were being created and improved methods of construction introduced. The existence of a turnpike road should not be assumed to have brought road engineering to an acceptable local level, as this complaint from Devon demonstrates:

> the turnpikes have by no means that width prescribed by law, and required for the accommodation of the public – so essential to the giving a proper form, and afterwards keeping them in sufficient repair ... these narrow ways are raised so high in the middle, that ... they are ... forced out upon their sides, when the only passage remaining is confined to a narrow ridge on the top of the road ... very much to endanger the knees of the horse, and the neck of its rider.[11]

The greatest road engineers of the late 18th and early 19th centuries were John Metcalf, Thomas Telford and John McAdam. Sometimes there was local opposition to turnpike roads, notably the ferocious 'Rebecca riots' in Wales, *c.*1839-44.

Large numbers of turnpike records can be found in CROs and include acts, minutes, accounts, deeds, correspondence, etc and large numbers of them can be found through A2A, ANW and SCAN. Local long-established firms of solicitors, who acted for the trust, may also still retain relevant material. The archives of prominent local estates can also reveal material, and plans and accounts may be found in quarter sessions records. Physical evidence of turnpikes often remains in features such as toll houses and noticeboards listing the tolls due. By the 1630s public stagecoaches provided links with London within 30 miles of the capital and by 1658 places as far north as Yorkshire could be reached by coach in four days. Many more routes were introduced as roads improved and coaching inns opened to cater for the new trade; many of them still exist all over the country and are easily recognised. Records of coaching firms are rare but evidence of their routes can be found in local newspapers and trade directories.

In Scotland General Wade, Commander-in-Chief of the British Army in the Highlands, built a number of new roads after the Jacobite rebellion of 1715, to help suppress the clans supporting the Stuarts, and some of them can still be seen. The records will be found in TNA,[12] and in the NAS which holds General Wade's papers on the military roads in the Highlands.[13]

As well as roads there is a network of other routes across the country, many of which are defined as public rights of way. Although footpaths and bridlepaths

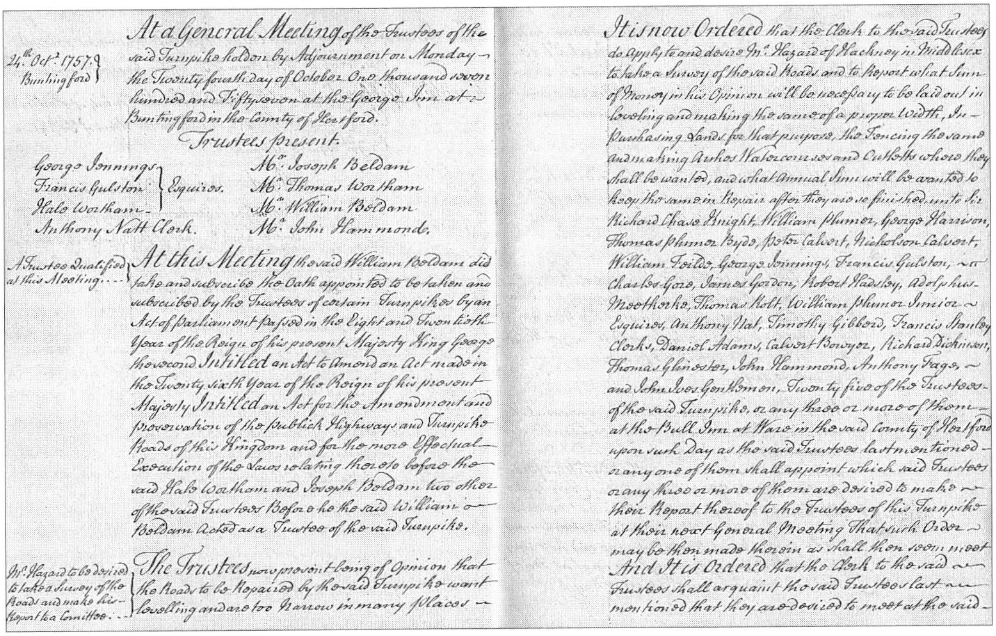

24th Octr 1757. Buntingford

At a General Meeting of the Trustees of the said Turnpike holden by Adjournment on Monday the Twenty fourth day of October One thousand seven hundred and Fiftyseven at the George Inn at Buntingford in the County of Hertford.

Trustees present.

George Jennings, Francis Gulston, Hale Wortham — Esquires. Anthony Natt Clerk.

Mr. Joseph Beldam, Mr. Thomas Wortham, Mr. William Beldam, Mr. John Hammond.

A Trustee Qualified at this Meeting...

At this Meeting the said William Beldam did take and subscribe the Oath appointed to be taken and subscribed by the Trustees of certain Turnpikes by an Act of Parliament passed in the Eight and Twentieth Year of the Reign of his present Majesty King George the second Intitled an Act to Amend an Act made in the Twenty sixth Year of the Reign of his present Majesty Intitled an Act for the Amendment and preservation of the publick Highways and Turnpike Roads of this Kingdom and for the more Effectual Execution of the Laws relating thereto before the said Hale Wortham and Joseph Beldam two other of the said Trustees Before he the said William Beldam Acted as a Trustee of the said Turnpike.

Mr. Hazard to be desired to take a Survey of the Roads and make his Report to a Comittee...

The Trustees now present being of Opinion that the Roads to be Repaired by the said Turnpike want levelling and are too Narrow in many Places —

It is now Ordered that the Clerk to the said Trustees do apply to and desire Mr. Hazard of Hackney in Middlesex to take a Survey of the said Roads and to Report what Sum of Money in his Opinion will be necessary to be laid out in leveling and making the same of a proper Width, In Purchasing Lands for that purpose, the Fencing the same and making Arches Watercourses and Outletts where they shall be wanted, and what Annual Sum will be wanted to keep the same in Repair after they are so finished unto Sir Richard Chase Knight, William Plumer, George Harrison, Thomas Plumer Byde, Peter Calvert, Nicholson Calvert, William Feilde, George Jennings, Francis Gulston, Charles Gore, James Gordon, Robert Hadsley, Adolphus Moothorke, Thomas Holt, William Plumer Junior Esquires, Anthony Nat, Timothy Gibbord, Francis Stanley Clerks, Daniel Adams, Calvert Bowyer, Richard Dickinson, Thomas Glinoster, John Hammond, Anthony Fage, and John Ives Gentlemen, Twenty five of the Trustees of the said Turnpike, or any three or more of them at the Bull Inn at Ware in the said County of Hertford upon such Day as the said Trustees last mentioned or any one of them shall appoint which said Trustees or any three or more of them are desired to make their Report thereof to the Trustees of this Turnpike at their next General Meeting That such Order may be then made therein as shall then seem meet And It is Ordered that the Clerk to the said Trustees shall acquaint the said Trustees last mentioned that they are desired to meet at the said

5 *The first turnpike trust was established by Act of Parliament to repair and maintain a badly-worn stretch of the Great North Road between Wadesmill and Royston. This minute book relates to the same turnpike road, although from a century later (1757).* (Hertfordshire Archives and Local Studies, TP7/2.)

were originally used for access to church, work, etc their use today is almost entirely for leisure purposes. Some routes have been defined as byways and can be used by vehicular traffic. Responsibility for determining and maintaining rights of way lies with county and unitary authorities who are required to maintain a definitive map and settle disputes, some of which end in legislation. Researchers have used many sources for determining a right of way such as enclosure and tithe maps and the 1910 Finance Act maps and books, and these records are dealt with in detail in chapter 2.

Wooden waggonways for horse-drawn waggons were used in the Northumberland and Durham coalfield in the 17th and 18th centuries to carry coal from the pits to wharves on the navigable rivers and an elaborate system was in operation by the late 18th century. The Cornish engineer, Richard Trevithick, built the first steam locomotive for a railway in 1804 and George Stephenson built *Locomotion* for the Stockton & Darlington railway, which opened for passengers as well as goods in 1825. The Manchester to Liverpool railway of 1830 was the first to convey passengers and goods by mechanical traction and Stephenson's *Rocket* was the first steam locomotive designed to pull passenger traffic quickly. Thereafter railways were built all over the country in the 'railway mania' period of the late 1830s and 1840s. The first important amalgamation came in 1844 when the Midland Railway Company was formed by Act of Parliament, and by 1852 nearly all the main lines of the modern system in England were authorised or completed; there was slower progress in Wales, Scotland and Ireland. The last main line to London, the Great

6 *Horse-drawn trams were introduced into towns at the end of the 18th century and from 1895 were replaced by electric vehicles. Leicester's electric trams were brought into service in 1904 and this photograph records the laying of the lines in Granby Street, one of the principal thoroughfares of the town, in 1903-4.* (Record Office for Leicestershire, Leicester and Rutland, Henton 1796.)

Central, was opened in 1899. Details of all the lines which once existed will be found in the *Pre-grouping atlas*.[14] The first underground railway in the world was the Metropolitan Railway, which began to run between Paddington and Farringdon Street and then on to Moorgate in 1865. Most of the other lines in London were finished before the First World War, apart from the Victoria and Jubilee lines. In the last decade the latter has been extended eastwards to serve the growing population in the former docklands area. Other cities in Britain, such as Newcastle upon Tyne and Glasgow, have underground systems. The records for London form part of the London Transport archive and will be found at the London Metropolitan Archives, part of the Corporation of London Joint Archive Service. For other cities enquiries should be made at the relevant local library or record office. Light railways, trams and trolley buses have all been used in major cities since the 19th century; many of them were replaced by buses after the Second World War but trams have been reintroduced in cities and boroughs such as Sheffield, Manchester and Croydon with varying success. Horse-drawn trams were an American invention and were introduced into London in 1870. They were cheaper than trains and could carry more passengers than buses, and were soon replaced by electric trams. The first horse-drawn omnibus service was started by George Shillibeer in 1829 and by the 1850s buses were providing services into central London from the northern and western suburbs; similar services were soon established in provincial towns. Trolley buses took their power from overhead lines but did not run on rails, and were introduced into some towns. The growth of trams, trolley buses and motor buses enabled workers to live in suburbs some distance from their places of work and were used to take them to various leisure facilities. The largest museum devoted to trams can be found in Crich in Derbyshire. There will be material in CROs and other local archives relating to local transport.

For much of its history the railway was a privately run industry although largely taken over by government during two world wars. The government enforced amalgamation in the 1920s and nationalised the railways in the late 1940s; they were denationalised at the end of the 20th century and once again the number of private companies proliferated. Railway history is one of the most popular local history topics and the literature is vast. This is largely because much 19th-century expansion was dependent upon improved transport links and this usually included some local railway development. The impact which the railways had on the lives of ordinary people cannot be over-estimated, enabling them to live further from their place of work, take holidays by the sea or in the country and ultimately to assist travel abroad. Pioneers such as Thomas Cook took vast numbers of passengers to undreamt of destinations (see chapter 14).

Like the canal builders, railway entrepreneurs had to submit details to the court of quarter sessions of their undertakings, as described above. Surviving railway records include plans and surveys, minutes and other policy materials, staff registers, various photographs, trade newspapers and journals as well as timetables, posters and other ephemera. There is no single point of entry to finding the records but one of the best recent guides is Cliff Edwards, *Railway Records: A Guide to Sources*.[15] The amount of material relating to railways is huge and, although the inevitability of archive loss will have taken its toll, much has survived. A small number of key places for railway material and a larger number of smaller archives may require a visit. In general terms TNA is the best place for administrative records such as minutes, financial and business records, staff registers and pay material, records about the lines themselves, bridges, buildings, embankments, and cuttings. The technical records on the locomotives and rolling stock largely went to the National Railway Museum (NRM) in York which also has the largest collection of photographs. Both administrative and technical material relating to Scotland are now with the NAS and, as mentioned above, the London Transport archive is at the London Metropolitan Archives. Although in the main this is a true reflection of the distribution of most of the records there is some intermixing, whereby (for example) Scottish material is at TNA or administrative records are at the NRM. The Institution of Civil Engineers holds the papers of the great engineers of the past, such as James Brindley, John Smeaton, Thomas Telford and the Rennies, and engineering wonders like Marc Brunel's Thames Tunnel, Robert Stephenson's Britannia Bridge and the Forth Railway Bridge.

There are also an enormous number of Parliamentary Papers on canals, roads and railways. The most useful for the researcher will depend on the mode of transport, the specific place and period of interests but the following are generally useful: for roads the 1818 report on highways and turnpike roads and the 1836 report on turnpike trusts and tolls; for canals the 1883 report on canals and the 1906 Royal Commission report on canals; for railways the 1839 report on railroads and turnpike trusts, 1840 report on railways and the regular (every ten years) railway returns from 1841 onwards giving annual details of traffic, capital, working stock, accidents, etc.[16]

The most important port in the country was the Pool of London; by the late 18th century it accounted for 75 per cent of all British imports and exports. By 1828 London had the largest dock system in the world but most of this has now gone and many of the dock warehouses have been converted into luxury flats. Liverpool and Bristol began to grow in the 18th century and were joined by other ports with the coming of the railways. There were also inland ports on the major rivers. Records of overseas trade will be found in TNA but material will also be found locally in quarter sessions records, harbour authorities' records, borough council minutes and accounts.[17] Stephens refers to local vice-admiralty courts as being particularly useful where their records survive.[18] Similar information to the records of the vice-admiralty courts can be found in TNA in HCA 15-20, HCA 23, HCA 24 and HCA 30.

The most important and systematic sources are the TNA Port Books in record series E 190. These records were the result of an Exchequer Order from 1564 requiring all customs officials in English and Welsh ports to record details of their work in blank books issued by the Exchequer. There are three types of books; firstly the entry books of the collectors and other officials; secondly, the entry books of searchers and other officials concerned with shipping movements and inspection of cargoes; and thirdly, the coasting books, recording the issuing and returning of certificates for the movement of goods by coast from one domestic port to another. Information will usually be found on the ship, master and relevant merchants' names, a description of the goods, and the amount of duties paid (in the collectors entry books). In some of the early books it is not clear to which place the data refers, but from the early 17th century there are only a few omissions of this nature. Earlier (and similar) material can be found in TNA record series E 122 from Edward I to 1565 which contains detailed information on the collection of customs in English and Welsh ports as well as details of the seizure in the ports of money and goods intended for illegal export. Two documents from the British Library Addn MSS series contain useful statistical information: 11255 has tables of tonnage of ships from British ports to foreign parts, or used for fishing (1709-82), and 11256 consists of tables of the tonnage of shipping employed in the foreign trade at each British port (1709-79).[19]

Aeroplanes are essentially a 20th-century form of transport, originally developed for military or leisure purposes; the Royal Flying Corps was created during the First World War. For many years air travel was a luxury for the wealthy but during the course of the last century it has become the chosen form of international transport for most people. Records of military operations will be found at TNA,[20] with additional research material at the Royal Air Force Museum;[21] information on local airfields may be found in CROs. The Royal Aircraft Establishment began in 1878 when the War Office set up the Balloon Equipment Store at Woolwich before moving to Aldershot in 1892 as the renamed Balloon Factory. The Factory became interested in aeroplanes and, once they had moved to Farnborough, was renamed the Royal Aircraft Factory. It was involved in the design and building of many types of aircraft and related products. In 1916 the war-time government transferred this work to industry, with Farnborough dedicated to research and development. In 1918 it was renamed the Royal Aircraft Establishment (RAE). Early reports can be found in TNA record series AIR 1 and AIR 5, plans and drawings of aircraft in AVIA 14; reports by the RAE from 1924 in AVIA 6 with various files in AVIA 13. The AVIA record series is extensive and very useful for research in areas where the various airship, aeroplane, radar and other establishments are based. Most airlines are run by private companies which will probably still hold early records.

The office of Postmaster of England was created by James I in 1609 and by the middle of the 17th century towns throughout England and Wales were connected by a postal service; the service was later extended to Scotland and Ireland. Letters were carried along main roads by horses; mail coaches were used from 1784 until superseded by railways. In 1840 a standard charge of 1d was introduced. Records of the Post Office, dating from 1672, are located at the main London sorting office in Mount Pleasant,[22] but there may also be material kept locally. In times of political upheaval letters were extracted from the system (sometimes to copy and return them to the system) and passed on to central government; much of this material now survives in various Privy Council and Home Office series at TNA (see chapter 11).

Telephones became widely available at the end of the 19th century and the first exchange was installed in Britain in 1879; in 1896 the Post Office acquired the monopoly of telephone and telegraphic communication and the first public phone boxes were installed in 1921. Telephone directories date from 1879 and a full set can be found at the BT Archives in High Holborn; smaller collections may be found in local libraries and record offices relating to their area. The Marconi archive, dealing with early wireless telegraphy, is now at the Bodleian Library.

5
Working Life

This chapter covers a multitude of interests, such as occupations, wages, health and safety, staff records, trade unions and friendly societies. Some of the records will provide systematic information about how people earned their living and their working lives, whereas others (while no less significant) are more fragmentary. The records also relate to the growth in trade unions from the 18th century (and earlier 'combinations' in their many guises); further information on trade unions can be found in chapter 11. This chapter will also look at prices; examining and understanding wages without doing the same for prices is of little value and it is essential that prices are considered when making any evaluation of local standards of living.

For information on wages and prices researchers should, before examining any of the manuscript material, look at how historians have interpreted them. Examples are numerous but the classic works are still Thorold Roger's *History of Agriculture and Prices in England* and Thomas Tooke's *A History of Prices ... from 1793 to 1856*. Lord Beveridge's *Prices and Wages in England: Vol 1: The Mercantilist Era* is very good for the 16th century onwards while Elizabeth Gilboy's *Wages in 18th Century England* provides tabular data from across the country.[1]

Any researcher interested in the 19th and 20th centuries should begin by investigating government published reports. Government interest in the various aspects of working life grew throughout the 19th century, and much of this material is to be found in various Parliamentary Papers.[2] Of particular use are the reports of Parliamentary Committees and Commissioners, including government departments, boards, councils and non-parliamentary committees. Although researchers should of course search the Parliamentary Papers index under wages, working conditions, etc, material will also be found in reports concerning poor laws, railways, agriculture and similar subjects.

In 1886 the House of Commons resolved that 'immediate steps should be taken to ensure in this country the full and accurate collection and publications of Labour statistics'. The result was an ongoing process of data collection and publication, initially the responsibility of the Board of Trade, in the *Labour Gazette* (the name sometimes changed but is usually referred to as *The Gazette*) and a number of *Abstracts* presented to Parliament. The *British Labour Statistics: Historical Abstract, 1886-1968* provides a mixture of local, national and industry pay rates from the late 18th through to the 20th centuries, mainly taken from these *Gazettes* and *Abstracts*.[3] More recently R. Floud and D.N. McCloskey's *The Economic History of Britain Since 1700* has brought together work on the calculation of wages and prices and how historians might use this type of data.[4]

Many modern historians looking at work and occupations begin with the Census Enumerators Books (CEBs) as these are perhaps the best used sources for determining occupational structures at a local level (census records are described in more detail in chapter 3). There was never a central series of registers listing the occupation of each individual and showing changes over time; it would be difficult to envisage how this could work in practice because of the seasonal nature of much work in the past. People could have several occupations throughout their lives; indeed it would not be uncommon to have more than one occupation in any one year. It is easy to imagine someone engaged as an agricultural labourer during the hay harvest in northern Middlesex, turning later to general carrying work on the Thames docks before securing a little work carrying a very different cargo across London by sedan chairs (the taxi cabs of their time). As CEBs are arranged by place they can be used as a basis for determining which type of jobs were important to the local economy as long as the problem of multiple occupations is addressed. Different historians have criticised the CEBs for confusing agricultural labourers with general labourers, omitting the respective occupations of many women, or under-reporting craftsmen and traders.[5] Catherine Crompton has looked at linking CEBs and local trade directories (see below) in 19th-century Hertfordshire to establish new and different figures for local craft and trade structures,[6] while Dennis and Joan Mills, in their work on 19th-century rural Lincolnshire, accept the problems of description but still describe the CEBs as 'a valuable and essential tool for the understanding of the rural social structure ... if for no other reason [than] that they list the whole population of the countryside at given dates'.[7]

Trade and commercial directories are a major source of work-related information from the late 18th century onwards (although the first London work was published as early as 1677). Most major towns produced a number of directories, but inevitably they contain limited information; generally the earlier volumes are less informative than later ones. In the late 18th century directories covering a wider area began to appear; the first national series was produced by James Pigot between 1814 and 1853. The firm was taken over by Francis Kelly, still the name most associated with trade directories. Tradespeople were listed alphabetically under their occupation and, although there was sometimes a full alphabetical list by surname, most directories require knowledge of the address or occupation of an individual. Inevitably labourers, servants and the like are not included. Trade directories grew in both size and coverage during the 19th century. Individually they are rather static (being published for a specific year) although many were updated sporadically; for example, White's 19th-century directories for Devon were published in 1850, 1878 and 1890. As well as the early London directories the Post Office directories began from the start of the 19th century. From the early decades of the 19th century a style of local directories began to emerge;

an introduction to the county, an entry for each place, some details of coaches, carrying services, railways and perhaps some information on population figures. More important are the lists of craftsmen, traders, shopkeepers and merchants. Most CROs have sets of published directories for their areas although there are important collections at the Guildhall Library, the Institute of Historical Research and the Society of Genealogists. J.E. Norton's *Guide to the Provincial Directories of England and Wales, Excluding London, Published Before* 1856 and C.W.F Goss's *The London Directories, 1677-1855* are good starting points. Some of this material is now on the internet;[8] there is no single way into this source but a useful entry is through the pages of the excellent Genuki web site where a lot of this material has been transcribed.[9] There are some problems with accuracy and descriptions in trade directories and anyone using them would be advised to read some of the published literature.[10] Some local historians have begun to survey the material to test the descriptions; see Neil Raven's work on North Essex on the relationship between the size of the business and the directory descriptions where he found 'manufacturer' applied to larger concerns.[11]

Apprenticeship was a period of training in which skills and knowledge would be passed down from a skilled master. The resulting skilled worker (often referred to as a journeyman) would seek eventually to form the next generation of future masters. The details of each apprenticeship were set down in writing (an indenture) and specified the names of the parties involved, the nature of the trade in which the apprentice would be instructed and the number of years during which training would take place. Originally apprenticeship was regulated by the gild to which the master belonged. Even though the structure of gilds broke down after the 16th century, apprenticeship was still managed through legally enforceable indentures. The process was essentially a private one and so there is no single national regular run of apprenticeship material across time, although where an organisation like the Sheffield Cutlers' Company has the bureaucracy to organise and protect its own records they can be impressive.[12] Wages of apprentices were often included in the appropriate general wage registers and business records described below.

Between 1710 and 1804 the state levied a tax on apprenticeship indentures and the resulting tax records, 1710-1811, can be found in TNA in record series IR 1.[13] The registers give the dates at which the apprenticeship began and when the tax was received. The master's name and residence are entered as well as the title of the trade being taught. This is followed by the name of the apprentice and details of the cost of apprenticeship and the subsequent tax payment. There are two general points to be aware of when undertaking a study of local apprenticeship. Firstly, in cases where the parish vestry apprenticed poor children there was no requirement to pay the tax – and subsequently there will be no records of those apprenticeships in the tax registers. The best place to start looking for this material is in the records of the vestry. Some vestries will have specific separate records of apprenticeship while others may simply enter details of apprenticeship in other more general sets of records such as vestry minutes or overseers accounts (see chapter 8). The second point is that many disputes concerning apprenticeship (such as runaways, cruelty,

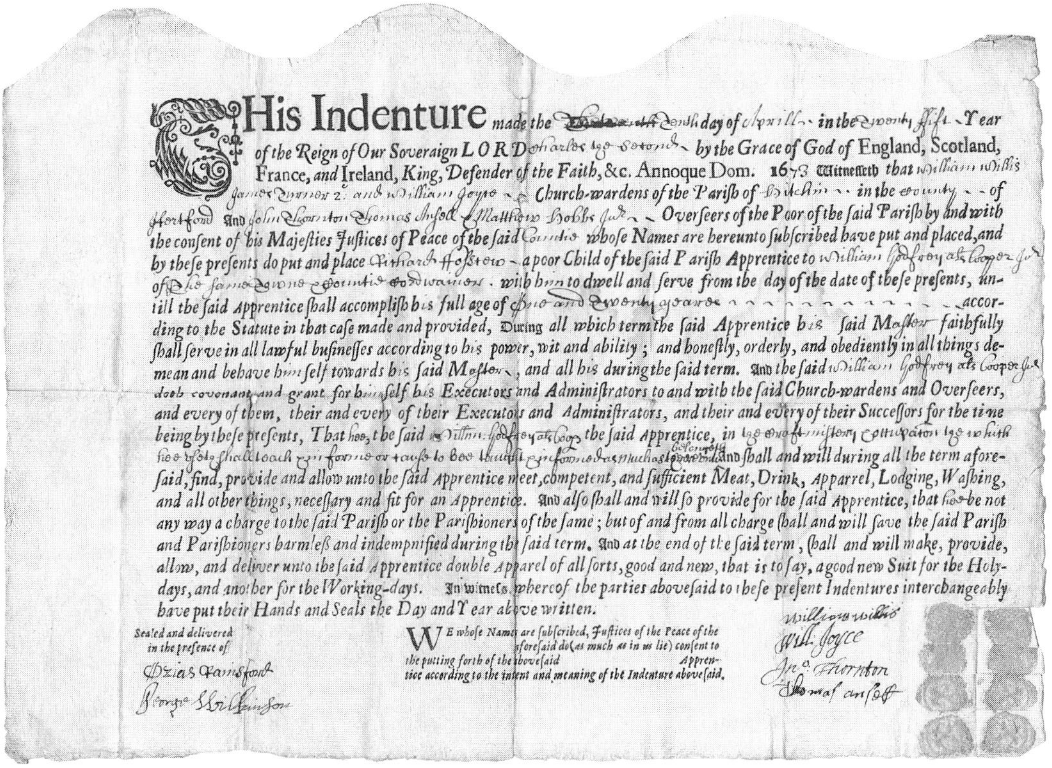

THis Indenture made the twentieth day of Aprill in the twenty fift Year of the Reign of Our Soveraign LORD Charles the Second by the Grace of God of England, Scotland, France, and Ireland, King, Defender of the Faith, &c. Annoque Dom. 1673 Witnesseth that William Willis James Turner 2 and William Joyce Church-wardens of the Parish of Hitchin in the county of Hertford And John Thornton Thomas Ansell Matthew Hobbs [illegible] Overseers of the Poor of the said Parish by and with the consent of his Majesties Justices of Peace of the said County whose Names are hereunto subscribed have put and placed, and by these presents do put and place Richard Fosstew a poor Child of the said Parish Apprentice to William Godfrey als Cooper [illegible] of the same towne & countie Cordwainer with him to dwell and serve from the day of the date of these presents, until the said Apprentice shall accomplish his full age of One and Twenty yeares according to the Statute in that case made and provided, During all which term the said Apprentice his said Master faithfully shall serve in all lawful businesses according to his power, wit and ability; and honestly, orderly, and obediently in all things demean and behave himself towards his said Master, and all his during the said term. And the said William Godfrey als Cooper [illegible] doth covenant and grant for himself his Executors and Administrators to and with the said Church-wardens and Overseers, and every of them, their and every of their Executors and Administrators, and their and every of their Successors for the time being by these presents, That hee, the said William Godfrey als Cooper the said Apprentice, in the arte mistery & occupacon he now useth [illegible] shall teach [illegible] And shall and will during all the term aforesaid, find, provide and allow unto the said Apprentice meet, competent, and sufficient Meat, Drink, Apparrel, Lodging, Washing, and all other things, necessary and fit for an Apprentice. And also shall and will so provide for the said Apprentice, that hee be not any way a charge to the said Parish or the Parishioners of the same; but of and from all charge shall and will save the said Parish and Parishioners harmless and indempnified during the said term. And at the end of the said term, shall and will make, provide, allow, and deliver unto the said Apprentice double Apparel of all sorts, good and new, that is to say, a good new Suit for the Holy-days, and another for the Working-days. In witness whereof the parties abovesaid to these present Indentures interchangeably have put their Hands and Seals the Day and Year above written.

Sealed and delivered in the presence of
Ozias [illegible]
George Wilkinson

WE whose Names are subscribed, Justices of the Peace of the foresaid do (as much as in us lie) consent to the putting forth of the abovesaid Apprentice according to the intent and meaning of the Indenture abovesaid.

William Willis
Will. Joyce
Jn° Thornton
Thomas Ansell

7 *Pauper apprenticeship indentures, such as this one, will be found with other poor law documents in parish records, but there are non-pauper indentures elsewhere, especially in borough records. In pauper apprenticeships the churchwardens and overseers of the poor acted 'in loco parentis': this document records the apprenticeship of Richard Fosstew to William Godfrey, alias Cooper, a cordwainer of Hitchin in 1673.* (Hertfordshire Archives and Local Studies, DE/R/Z2.)

abuse, etc) were heard by county magistrates and the records should be found in quarter sessions records. Searching may be time intensive but using the A2A and ANW databases can reduce the scale of the problem, as there are thousands of references to apprenticeship across the contributing record offices. Other specialist repositories such as the Modern Records Centre, Warwick University, and the Labour History Archive and Study Centre will also have varied material on apprenticeship.[14] Medieval craft gilds protected their financial position by regulating the number of members of particular trades, and payments for apprenticeship would be listed in the various accounts of the gild. Surviving records of individual firms may have some references to, or registers of, apprenticed labour.

Central records on apprenticeship held at TNA are quite patchy but still significant and useful, particularly with regard to the military and merchant marine. The general apprenticeship tax registers in IR 1 contain records of merchant seamen apprentices. In addition a register of apprentices from various counties across England to south-east fishermen survives for 1639-1664 in HCA 30/897, and a list of children apprenticed to the sea from Christ's Hospital for the single year 1766 can be found in T 64/311. There is a single volume of apprentices' indentures for the port of Colchester covering 1704-1757 and 1804-1844 in BT 167/103. There are also indexes of apprentices registered in the merchant fleet, 1824-1953, in BT 150. The earlier material is less useful for local studies. However, the later records include the port where the apprentice signed on. The specimen copies of indentures (taken at five-year intervals), 1845-1950, in BT 151; and apprentices' indentures for fishing, 1895-1935, in BT 152, provide a wealth of seamen's apprenticeship material for the second half of the 19th and the first half of the 20th centuries. Apprenticeship registers of merchant seamen at Scarborough for 1884-1894 have survived amongst Customs records in CUST 91/121. Further examples of such records may yet be found in other Customs records.

Records concerning naval apprenticeships can be found in the various ADM record series. These include ADM 1: Admiralty: Correspondence and Papers, 1660-1976, and ADM 106: Navy Board: Records, 1659-1837. In the series ADM 12: Admiralty: Digests and Indexes, 1660-1952, researchers should begin by looking under the heading 'Apprentices in Dockyards'. From 1876 the examination results for some dockyard employees can be found amongst CSC 10. There are further apprenticeship registers for children from the Greenwich Hospital School, 1808-1838, in ADM 73/421-448. There are some military apprenticeship records relating to the army. A register for the period 1806-35, of those who enlisted for the army but were required to return to their masters until the completion of the time specified by their indentures, can be found in WO 25/2962. TNA also holds the records of the Royal Military Asylum (RMA). In 1892 the RMA was renamed the Duke of York's Military School. Registers of admission and discharge, covering the period 1803-1923, are arranged by date of admission and can be found in WO 143/17-26. The equivalent for soldiers on the Irish establishment, the Royal Hibernian Military School (RHMS), was founded in Dublin in 1769. Most of the records of the RHMS were destroyed during the Second World War and only one register *c.*1863-1919 survives in WO 143/27.

Government investigations in the late 18th and 19th centuries into matters relating to apprenticeship reflects growing industrialisation and waged labour. Thus references to apprenticeship can be found in growing numbers of Parliamentary Papers investigating wages, specific sectors of employment (women and children, railways, textile workers) as well as poor law reports (see chapter 8 for details).[15]

Only periodically were wages between private employers and their employees of any concern to central government. Following the Black Death of 1348-9 lords of the manor and other employers found that the subsequent labour shortage proved problematic in terms of paying their workforce pre-Black Death wages. Workers demanded more money and more flexible working conditions which would allow them to take up better offers of work when and where they appeared. The Statute of Labourers (1351) was an attempt to reduce wage rates (by providing maximum levels) and standardise working conditions to those of 1346. It is the infringements of statute that are recorded in the assize and ancient indictments in TNA record series JUST 1 and KB 9.[16]

Presentments were also made at quarter sessions; the following example comes from Lincolnshire in 1374:

> The jurors ... declare that John Gale, dwelling with Thomas of Talous, on the Thursday after Whitsuntide in the forty-eighth year [25 May 1374] enticed John Donney, servant of Walter Hardegray of Edlyngton away from Walter's service; and he admitted and retained him in his own service at Edlyngton, giving him for his yearly wage one mark and his food as well as other goods, against the form of the ordinance of labourers, etc.[17]

There has been considerable work done on medieval wage regulation and it is advisable to check what is available. For example, Simon Peen has done some statistical work on a surviving labourers' roll for Somerset for 1358-60, which provides the names of 466 offenders, the amount they were fined and the occupational activity they were engaged in.[18]

Local magistrates were able to regulate wages at minimum levels under the Statute of Labourers (1563) and, although the legislation was not repealed until 1813, it is believed to have largely fallen into disuse by the mid-18th century. There will therefore be some local wage regulation material in the records of county, town and borough sessions.[19] Further detailed information on wages, earnings and payments can be found for specific places and trades in published reports such as Parliamentary Papers.[20] Examples would include *Minutes of Evidence on the State of Their Trade, and on Disputes Concerning the Rate of Wages* [calico printers], 1803-4; *Report from the Select Committee on the Petition of the Cotton Weavers of Manchester, etc*, 1810-11, *Abstract of Returns Respecting Labourers' Wages*, 1825, and *Returns of Wages Published Between 1830 and 1886*, 1887. The material can be very detailed and give much social as well as economic information concerning particular trades. *The Report from the Select Committee on Petitions of Several Cotton Manufacturers and Journeymen Cotton Weavers, &c*, 1808 provides much information on the state of the trade and the inadequacy of wages. One of the main features discussed in the evidence is the fixing of a minimum wage.

Central government became more interested in wage rates when they were a source of conflict such as in times of high inflation or mass unemployment. It should also be noted that wages were only one element of income. Small farmers in the 17th and 18th centuries would have been working their smallholdings, supplemented with access to large commons, primarily to provide for their own subsistence. They may have worked for wages to supplement their own produce or for money to pay rent. Waged labour was, therefore, a part of their working lives and did not reflect the totality of their labour. Long-established perks were also important in making up a customary income essential to maintaining a recognised and acceptable 'standard of living'. These were regarded as rights and were applied to many trades.[21]

Borough or CROs have a great deal of wage books or accounts of local businesses. There is much scattered information concerning local wages and payments and these can be found across a variety of archives and can be located by consulting the NRA, A2A, ANW or SCAN.[22] Often they will be included in a general archive for a specific firm or set of firms (in case of amalgamation).

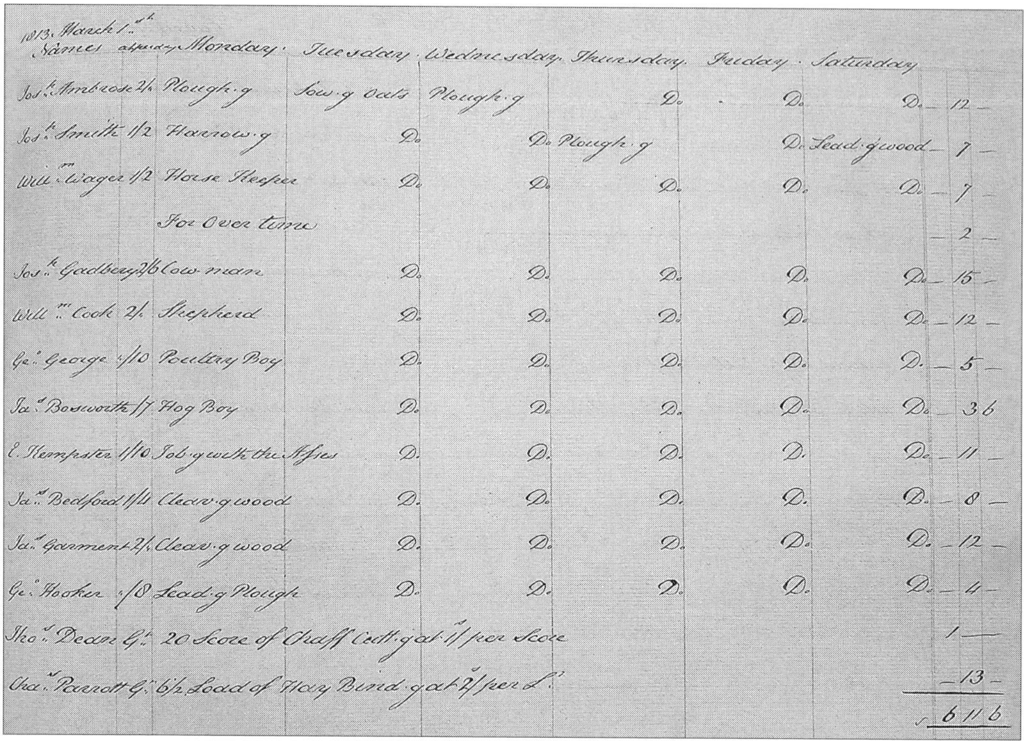

1813. March 1st

Names & Employ		Monday	Tuesday	Wednesday	Thursday	Friday	Saturday	
Josh. Ambrose 2/-	Plough·g		Sow·g Oats	Plough·g	D.	D.	D.	12 —
Josh. Smith 1/2	Harrow·g		D.	D. Plough·g		D. Lead·g wood		7 —
Wm. Wager 1/2	Horse Keeper		D.	D.	D.	D.	D.	7 —
	For Over time							2 —
Josh. Gadbury 2/6	Cow man		D.	D.	D.	D.	D.	15 —
Wm. Cook 2/-	Shepherd		D.	D.	D.	D.	D.	12 —
Geo. George -/10	Poultry Boy		D.	D.	D.	D.	D.	5 —
Jas. Bosworth -/7	Hog Boy		D.	D.	D.	D.	D.	3 6
E. Kempster 1/10	Job·g with the [illegible]		D.	D.	D.	D.	D.	11 —
Jas. Bedford 1/4	Clear·g wood		D.	D.	D.	D.	D.	8 —
Jas. Garment 2/-	Clear·g wood		D.	D.	D.	D.	D.	12 —
Geo. Hooker -/8	Lead·g Plough		D.	D.	D.	D.	D.	4 —
Thos. Dean Gt.	20 Score of Chaff Cutt·g at 1d per Score							1 —
Chas. Parrott Gt.	6½ Load of Hay Bind·g at 2d per Ld.							13 —
								£ 6 11 6

8 *Few wages books and other employee records survive, but where they do they provide a fascinating glimpse into working life for many people, especially those employed on large, usually rural, estates. This example, from Great Gaddesden in 1813, shows the type of work each man undertook.* (Hertfordshire Archives and Local Studies, DE/HL/E3.)

The records of William Baird and Co, coal and iron masters at Coatbridge in North Lanarkshire, include material from 1805 to 1971, with board papers, accounts, various correspondence and ledgers, journals, stock, share and asset records as well as wage books.[23]

Many of these records, especially for the earlier period, may only record wages or payments for short periods of time, for specific areas and in particular occupations. Specialist archives will also hold records concerning wages of specific groups; the Rural History Centre[24] at Reading holds significant collections of wage-related material regarding agricultural labourers' wages (and related trades) from across the country and the Modern Records Centre at Warwick and Labour History Archive and Study Centre at Manchester will also hold relevant material. Medieval and early labour was, of course, essentially rural (if not always agricultural). In the various manorial and ministers' accounts there will be references to the agricultural day labourer employed in weeding and threshing alongside payments for smiths, masons, carpenters and other craftsmen. Examples of this can be seen in John Fletcher and Christopher Upton's work on the Merton College (Oxford) domestic accounts where there are references to work done by named carpenters, brewers, stonemasons, a coal merchant and 'undercook and handyman'[25] (see also chapter 2). A further consideration for those interested in rural wage labour is the many relevant scattered records to be found in estate papers. The type of information will vary from recorded wages rates to simply comments or references to wages. For example, the account book listing wage payments to labourers employed during the enclosure of Delamere Forest provides wage data of some detail. This bundle also includes correspondence we have referred to earlier, containing advice to wait until the corn harvest is complete 'when Labourers may be had probably at a cheaper rate' and thus tells a little about the strategies of those who employed wage labour.[26] In contrast the rather acrimonious parting of the ways of Edward Wood and his groom William Hobbs at Littleton in Middlesex in 1663 reminds us that this was not a period with any easily initiated regulations or mechanisms for enforcing severance pay. Their conversation ends with a threat and demand; Hobbs informed Wood he 'would see my neck as long as his arm & ... he bids me give his wages'.[27]

Borough, town and vestry minute books and accounts will often give details of payments paid for jobs done under their orders. In urban centres the various records of the craft gilds will refer to social and economic activities.[28] Furthermore, as urban authorities regulated the gilds their own minutes and accounts will contain much information on specific local gilds. For some occupations the records relating to wages are easier to track down. Records of railway companies and their wage-rate payments are relatively extensive – there are literally hundreds of wage-related railway company records from all over the country held at TNA. Many of these are individual files or registers that span several years or decades.[29] However, they are not all drawn together into one record series and researchers will need to search by individual company and then tie these records to specific places. The types of records vary enormously from company staff and apprentice wages registers through various petitions from labourers and carpenters for wage increases, notification of strike action relating to wages disputes, requests for weekly payment of wages and adjustments to overtime rates. The fact that some of the railway companies trace their own transport roots back into earlier canal companies has ensured the survival of a few early 19th-century canal records. The variety of wage-related material in the RAIL classes is immense and greatly supplements the material held at the National Railway Museum Library at York, as well as any surviving material in CROs.[30]

A further strong series of wage material at TNA survives for Royal Dockyard workers. The main collection of yard-paybooks for 1660 to 1853 is in ADM 42, with records of the minor yards in ADM 32, ADM 36 and ADM 37. Another source of long-term wage information, covering both England and Wales, is the workhouse staff books in MH 9. These records cover the period from 1837 to 1921 and provide data on the workhouse masters, mistresses, nurses and other staff employed by each poor law union. Additional information (such as application forms and employment or wage issues) can sometimes be found in the poor law union correspondence papers in MH 12 from 1833 to 1909.[31] This type of employment (by local authorities) is, of course, extended as the 19th century progressed and there will be employment and wage material at

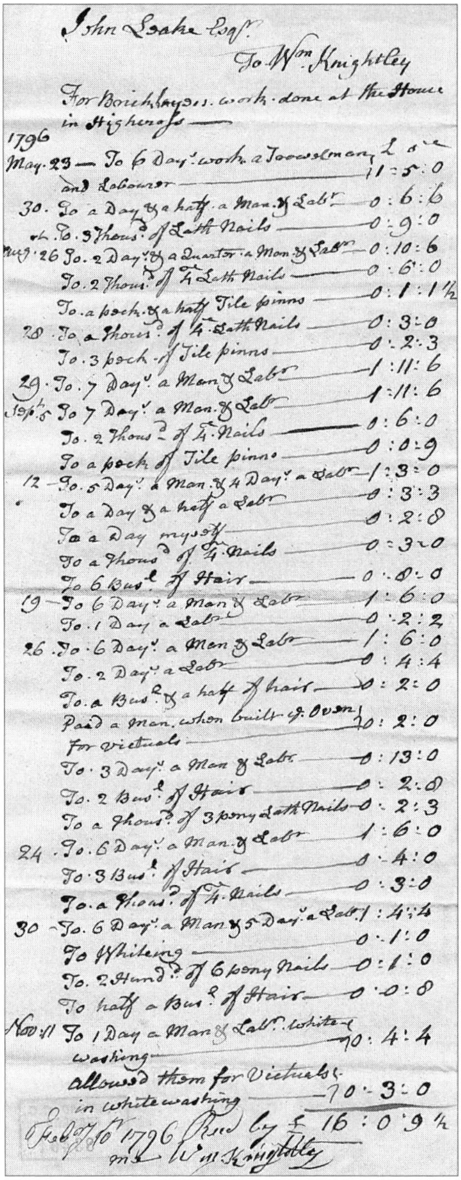

John Leake Esqr.

To Wm. Knightley

For Brickclayers work done at the House in Highcross —

		£ s d
1796 May 23	To 6 Days work a Troweleman and Labourer	1 : 5 : 0
30	To a Day & a half a Man & Labr	0 : 6 : 6
	To 3 Thous. of Lath Nails	0 : 9 : 0
Aug 26	To 2 Days & a Quarter a Man & Labr	0 : 10 : 6
	To 2 Thous. of 4d Lath Nails	0 : 6 : 0
	To a peck & a half Tile pinns	0 : 1 : 1½
28	To a Thous. of 4d Lath Nails	0 : 3 : 0
	To 3 peck of Tile pinns	0 : 2 : 3
29	To 7 Days a Man & Labr	1 : 11 : 6
Sept 5	To 7 Days a Man & Labr	1 : 11 : 6
	To 2 Thous. of 4d Nails	0 : 6 : 0
	To a peck of Tile pinns	0 : 0 : 9
12	To 5 Days a Man & 4 Days a Labr	1 : 3 : 0
	To a Day & a half a Labr	0 : 3 : 3
	To a Day myself	0 : 2 : 8
	To a Thous. of 4d Nails	0 : 3 : 0
	To 6 Bush. of Hair	0 : 8 : 0
19	To 6 Days a Man & Labr	1 : 6 : 0
	To 1 Day a Labr	0 : 2 : 2
26	To 6 Days a Man & Labr	1 : 6 : 0
	To 2 Days a Labr	0 : 4 : 4
	To a Bush. & a half of hair	0 : 2 : 0
	Paid a man when built ye Oven for victuals	0 : 2 : 0
	To 3 Days a Man & Labr	0 : 13 : 0
	To 2 Bush. of Hair	0 : 2 : 8
	To a Thous. of 3 peny Lath Nails	0 : 2 : 3
24	To 6 Days a Man & Labr	1 : 6 : 0
	To 3 Bush. of Hair	0 : 4 : 0
	To a Thous. of 4d Nails	0 : 3 : 0
30	To 6 Days a Man & 5 Days a Labr	1 : 4 : 4
	To Whiteing	0 : 1 : 0
	To 2 Hund. of 6 peny Nails	0 : 1 : 0
	To half a Bush. of Hair	0 : 0 : 8
Nov 11	To 1 Day a Man & Labr whitewashing	0 : 4 : 4
	allowed them for Victuals in whitewashing	0 : 3 : 0
		£ 16 : 0 : 9½

Feb 7 1796 Recd by me Wm Knightley

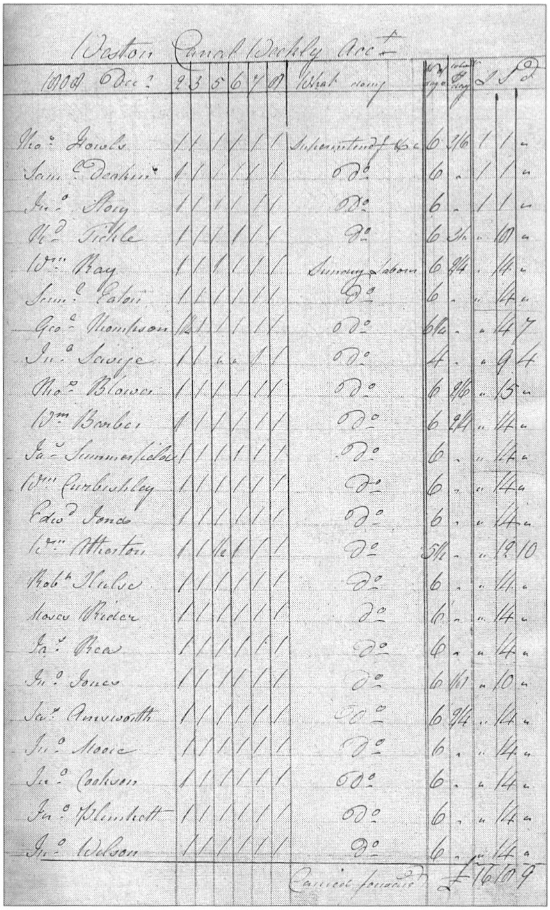

Weston Canal Weekly Acct.

1808 Decr	9	3	5	6	7	8	What doing	No. of days	Wages per day	£	s	d
Thos. Fowls	/	/	/	/	/	/	Superintending &c	6	3/6	1	1	..
Saml. Deakin	/	/	/	/	/	/	Do.	6	..	1	1	..
Jno. Story	/	/	/	/	/	/	Do.	6	..	1	1	..
Richd. Tickle	/	/	/	/	/	/	Do.	6	3/-	..	18	..
Wm. Ray	/	/	/	/	/	/	Surveying Labour	6	2/4	..	14	..
Saml. Eaton	/	/	/	/	/	/	Do.	6	..	..	14	..
Geo. Thompson	½	/	/	/	/	/	Do.	6¼	..	..	14	7
Jno. Savige	/	/	..	..	/	/	Do.	4	..	..	9	4
Thos. Blower	/	/	/	/	/	/	Do.	6	2/6	..	15	..
Wm. Barber	/	/	/	/	/	/	Do.	6	2/4	..	14	..
Jas. Summerfield	/	/	/	/	/	/	Do.	6	..	..	14	..
Wm. Curbishley	/	/	/	/	/	/	Do.	6	..	..	14	..
Edwd. Jones	/	/	/	/	/	/	Do.	6	..	..	14	..
Wm. Atherton	/	/	½	/	/	/	Do.	5½	..	..	12	10
Robt. Hulse	/	/	/	/	/	/	Do.	6	..	..	14	..
Moses Rider	/	/	/	/	/	/	Do.	6	..	..	14	..
Jas. Rea	/	/	/	/	/	/	Do.	6	..	..	14	..
Jno. Jones	/	/	/	/	/	/	Do.	6	1/8	..	10	..
Jas. Ainsworth	/	/	/	/	/	/	Do.	6	2/4	..	14	..
Jno. Moore	/	/	/	/	/	/	Do.	6	..	..	14	..
Jno. Cookson	/	/	/	/	/	/	Do.	6	..	..	14	..
Jno. Plumkett	/	/	/	/	/	/	Do.	6	..	..	14	..
Jno. Wilson	/	/	/	/	/	/	Do.	6	..	..	14	..
							Carried forward			£16	10	9

9 *A page from the Weston Canal weekly account (wages book). December 1808.* (TNA, RAIL 883/36.)

10 *Like wages books, records of an individual's work are rare; this bill, dating from 1796, relates to work done for John Leake at his house in High Cross, by William Knightly.* (Hertfordshire Archives and Local Studies, 83404.)

the relevant CROs. Other similar institutions, such as the Asylum Districts and Boards from 1845-1930, will have wages and employment records for their officers and workforce. These records are distributed; some are at TNA while others are held locally.[32]

Speculative searches can uncover real gems in the various non-local repositories; for example, there are workmen's bills for 1710-15 in the Marlborough House accounts at the British Library,[33] farm account books for Tilton and Tugby in Leicestershire, 1849-57 (which include daily employment records for each farm labourer and weekly accounts of their wages) at the

Bodleian Library,[34] early 20th-century wages books in the records of the Broom Hall Estate, Caernarfonshire at the NLW,[35] and a few early 19th-century wages books and ledgers for Hopwood and Hathershaw collieries, Lancashire, at TNA.[36]

As well as archival material there is a huge number of printed parliamentary reports on labour in general and wages in particular. For example the *Report from the Select Committee on Labourers Wages* in 1824, the *Report from the Select Committee on the State of the Coal Trade* in 1830, the *Reports of Special Assistant Poor Law Commissioners on the Employment of Women and Children in Agriculture* in 1843, *Return of Rates of Wages in the Minor Textile Trades of the United Kingdom with Report Thereon* in 1890 and the *Report of an Enquiry by the Board of Trade into Working-Class Rents and Retails Prices Together with the Rates of Wages in Certain Occupations in Industrial Towns of the United Kingdom in 1912* in 1913.[37]

Where a researcher is looking to examine a particular industry, trade or profession within a specific locality then the different experience of workers would be of immense benefit. Obviously CROs and other local repositories would be the first places to search as such records can be found in surviving business records.[38] For some occupational records there are genealogical guides and advisory articles that will list the material from local, national and specialist repositories. So some staff records on coalminers, seamen, policemen, railwaymen, postal workers, etc can, where they have survived, be relatively easy to find while others are not so.[39] Some local historians have used local school records to examine the development of teacher training and the development of professionalisation.[40]

There are of course other specific employment records that may be held centrally. Searching for the relevant records of railway (RAIL), coastguards and royal dockyard workers (ADM), Customs and Excise Officers (C, CUST, PRO and T), workhouse staff (MH) and metropolitan police staff[41] (MEPO) records at TNA is made easy by the appropriate record research guides and through searches on the electronic catalogue. The information contained in the various employee staff records can range from simple lists of names to quite detailed registers which may provide information on someone's full service, including salary, promotions and general comments. Depending on the nature of information contained in the records used, local historians may be able to analyse the length of employment in particular trades or jobs, wage levels, disciplinary action by managers and staffing numbers. For information on other employment not mentioned here (such as attorneys, barristers, doctors, lawyers, judges, nurses and midwives etc) see Amanda Bevan's *Tracing Your Ancestors*.[42]

A less obvious place to look for information concerning local wages and payments is in the records of the civil courts of Chancery and Exchequer. Disputes over wages or payments may constitute part of a civil case, which may have been prompted by a disagreement over the rate of the wage or payment, or through the death of the employer. Records lodged with the court as evidence (referred to as Masters' Exhibits) in specific cases provide a further collection of local wage material, but searching for cases concerning wage dispute material can be difficult and time consuming. A similar process

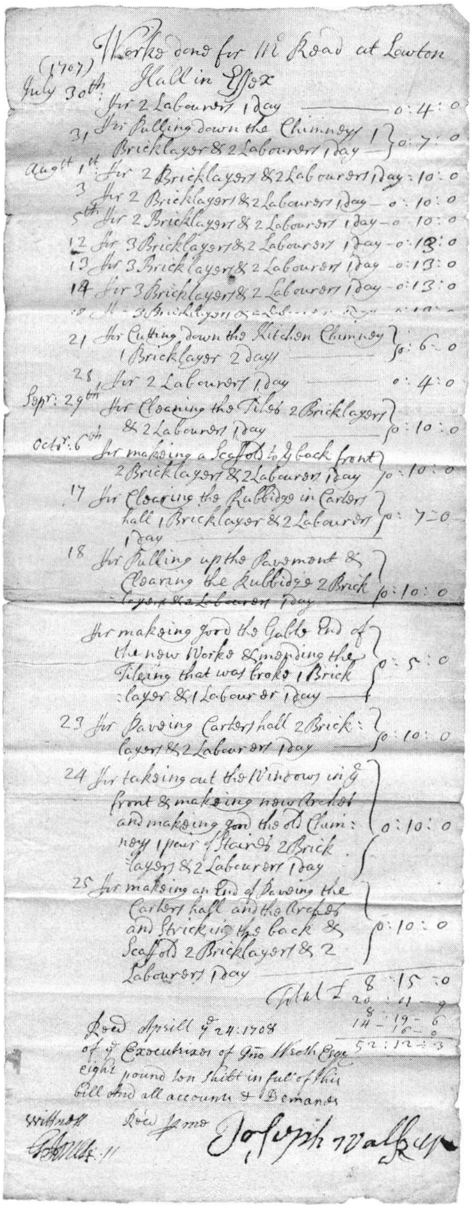
(1707) Works done for Mr Road at Lowton Hall in Essex
July 30th For 2 Labourers 1 day — 0:4:0
31 For Pulling down the Chimneys 1 Bricklayer & 2 Labourers 1 day — 0:7:0
Augst 1st For 2 Bricklayers & 2 Labourers 1 day : 10 : 0
3 For 2 Bricklayers & 2 Labourers 1 day — 0 : 10 : 0
5th For 2 Bricklayers & 2 Labourers 1 day — 0 : 10 : 0
12 For 3 Bricklayers & 2 Labourers 1 day — 0 : 13 : 0
13 For 3 Bricklayers & 2 Labourers 1 day — 0 : 13 : 0
14 For 3 Bricklayers & 2 Labourers 1 day — 0 : 13 : 0
[illegible]
21 For Cutting down the Kitchen Chimney 1 Bricklayer 2 days — 0 : 6 : 0
28 For 2 Labourers 1 day — 0 : 4 : 0
Sepr: 29th For Cleaning the Tiles 2 Bricklayers & 2 Labourers 1 day — 0 : 10 : 0
Octr: 6th For making a Scaffold to ye back front 2 Bricklayers & 2 Labourers 1 day 0 : 10 : 0
17 For Clearing the Rubbidge in Carters hall 1 Bricklayer & 2 Labourers 1 day 0 : 7 : 0
18 For Pulling up the Pavement & Clearing the Rubbidge 2 Bricklayers & 2 Labourers 1 day 0 : 10 : 0
For making good the Gable End of the new Works & mending the Tiling that was broke 1 Bricklayer & 1 Labourer 1 day 0 : 5 : 0
23 For Paving Carters hall 2 Bricklayers & 2 Labourers 1 day 0 : 10 : 0
24 For taking out the Windows in ye front & making new Arches and making good the old Chimney 1 pair of Stairs 2 Bricklayers & 2 Labourers 1 day 0 : 10 : 0
25 For making an End of Paving the Carters hall and the Arches and Striking the back & Scaffold 2 Bricklayers & 2 Labourers 1 day 0 : 10 : 0
Total £ 8 : 15 : 0
20 : 11 : 9
8 : 19 : 6
14 : 19 : 6
: 16 : 0
52 : 12 : 3
Recd April ye 24: 1708 of ye Exceutrixes of Jno Wroth Esqr eight pound ten shill in full of this bill and all accounts & Demands
Witness Recd p me Joseph Walker

11 *An account for work done at Lowton Hall, Essex. April 28th 1708.* (TNA, C 104/264 [part 1, bundle 23, no 61].)

(and record material) can be found in the records of the Court of Exchequer.[43]

An extremely useful guide to regional wages from 1893 to 1952 is the annual *Labour Gazettes*. These volumes begin as the Board of Trade, *Labour Department Gazette* 1893 until 1919 when they became the *Ministry of Labour Gazette*, from 1920 to 1952. Bound copies are held by TNA in record series ZPER 45. Although quite poorly indexed for local historians, the layout of the *Gazettes* is easy to follow and provides essential information, broken down by region with regard to industry and wages.

From the early 20th century the state itself became far more important as a direct employer and also as a regulator of wages. Various mechanisms were established and minimum wage rates for particular industries were set down. The resulting records are more systematic in their coverage and subject matter, but also extremely bureaucratic in their creation and organisation. The Trade Boards Act (1909) set up the machinery required to provide a statutory minimum wage in certain 'sweated trades'.[44] Initial responsibility lay with the Board of Trade although this was later (1917) transferred to the Ministry of Labour. During the inter-war period the Trade Boards developed as a self-contained unit within the Ministry of Labour and were replaced in 1945 by Wages Councils. However, two industries developed independent schemes outside the inter-war Trade Boards; these related to haulage (Road Haulage Wages Act 1938) and catering (Catering Wages Act 1943). These Acts saw the respective establishment of the (haulage) Central Wages Board and the Catering Wages Commission. The Central Wages Board became a Wages Council in 1948 and the Catering Wages Commission established four Wage Boards which eventually became four Wages Councils in 1959. The minutes of Trade Boards and Wages Councils are in LAB 35, with those of the Central Wages Board and the Catering Wages Board in LAB 11 and LAB 35. There are some of the

LONDON TRADES' COUNCIL.

Official Programme.

GREAT LABOUR DEMONSTRATION
HYDE PARK
SUNDAY, MAY 4th, 1890,

In favour of Reducing the Hours of Labour.

The various Organized Bodies will assemble on the Thames Embankment at 2.30 o'Clock, and fall into Procession **SIX ABREAST**, will march from thence at 3 o'Clock precisely to Hyde Park, where resolutions will be submitted for adoption, regarding the

EIGHT HOURS' MOVEMENT.

SUPERINTENDENT--IN--CHIEF - - - - - - - - GEORGE SHIPTON.

GENERAL ORDERS.

1. No Reporter or other person will be admitted to the Platforms unless provided with a Ticket signed by the Secretary of the Trades' Council.
2. The Procession will be formed under the direction of the Superintendent above named, and the Delegates who may be appointed to assist him. These Delegates will be distinguished by blue rosettes.
3. The Organizing Committee will wear a small star on the left breast.
4. The head of the Procession will be formed at the extreme end of the Embankment (River-side) opposite the Clock Tower.
5. The Societies will be formed into Sections or Divisions. Section I. will take up its position at the Westminster Bridge end (River-side) of the Embankment, and the other Sections will follow in order along the same side towards the Blackfriars Bridge end.
6. Each Society will, where convenient, be accompanied by its Banners and Emblems.
7. The Band at the head of the Procession will be provided by the London Trades' Council, and all others must be provided by any Society desiring one to head its special Section.
8. The Committees of Local Bodies and Districts will so time the leaving of the Procession, in their respective localities, as to ensure their arrival on the Embankment by 2.30 o'clock. The Members of each District Procession, immediately on its arrival, will attach themselves to the Industry to which they belong, where such Industry is represented, the position of which may be ascertained by referring to the published Programme. Each Industry, on coming on the Embankment, will proceed at once to the point where the Section to which it is attached is situated, under the direction of appointed Delegates.
9. Workmen, generally, will attach themselves to the Society in the Procession representing the Trade to which they may respectively belong.
10. The Bugle will sound the fall-in at 2.45 o'clock, when the Societies and Members will take up position, six a-breast, until moved off the ground by order of the Delegate of the Section.
11. The Bugle will sound the departure precisely at Three o'clock, when the head of the Procession will at once move off the ground, followed by the various Sections, with their Bands playing.

ORDER OF PROCESSION.

BAND.

SECTION I.—LEATHER TRADES.
No. 1. Skinners.
,, 2. Saddle and Harness Makers.
,, 3. Fancy Leather Workers.
,, 4. Fellmongers.
,, 5. Portmanteau and Trunk Makers.
,, 6. Tanners.
,, 7. Curriers.

SECTION II.—METAL TRADES.
No. 1. Brass Workers.
,, 2. Wheelwrights and Blacksmiths.
,, 3. Smiths.
,, 4. Engineers.
,, 5. Pattern Makers.
,, 6. Gas Meter Makers.
,, 7. Electro Plate Workers.
,, 8. Wire Weavers.
,, 9. Boiler Makers and Iron Ship Builders.
,, 10. Iron Founders.
,, 11. Zinc Workers.
,, 12. Tin Plate Workers.
,, 13. Silver Workers.
,, 14. Steam Engine Makers.
,, 15. Coppersmiths.
,, 16. Wire Workers.
,, 17. Whitesmiths and Bell-hangers.

SECTION III.—CABINET & FANCY TRADES.
No. 1. Cabinet Makers.
,, 2. Upholsterers.
,, 3. Organ Builders.
,, 4. French Polishers.
,, 5. Basket Makers.
,, 6. Gold Beaters.

SECTION IV.—GENERAL TRADES.
No. 1. Tobacco Strippers.
,, 2. Glass Blowers.
,, 3. Farriers.
,, 4. Rope Makers.
,, 5. Cigar Makers.
,, 6. Coach Makers.
,, 7. Gas Workers.
,, 8. Bass Dressers.
,, 9. Coal Porters.
,, 10. Bakers.
,, 11. Potters.
,, 12. Glass Cutters.
,, 13. Millers.
,, 14. Coopers.
,, 15. Tobacco Pipe Makers.
,, 16. Cocoa Fibre Mat Makers.
,, 17. Railway Servants.

SECTION V.—SHIPPING TRADES.
No. 1. Ship Scrapers.
,, 2. Boat Builders.
,, 3. Sailors and Firemen.
,, 4. Ship Caulkers.
,, 5. Mast and Block Makers.
,, 6. Barge Builders.
,, 7. Shipwrights.
,, 8. Stevedores.
,, 9. Dock Workers.
,, 10. Sail Makers.
,, 11. Riverside and General Labourers.

SECTION VI.—CLOTHING TRADES.
No. 1. Boot Closers.
,, 2. Clothiers' Cutters.
,, 3. Tailors.
,, 4. Boot Rivetters and Finishers.
,, 5. Hatters.
,, 6. Boot and Shoe Makers.

SECTION VII.—PRINTING & PAPER TRADES.
No. 1. Pressmen.
,, 2. Lithographers.
,, 3. Paper Makers.
,, 4. Machine Rulers.
,, 5. Bookbinders.
,, 6. Machine Managers.
,, 7. Compositors.
,, 8. Vellum Binders.

SECTION VIII.—BUILDING TRADES.
No. 1. Plumbers and Gasfitters.
,, 2. Stonemasons.
,, 3. Plasterers.
,, 4. Bricklayers.
,, 5. Carpenters and Joiners.
,, 6. Gilders.
,, 7. Stone Carvers.

12 *Poster advertising the 'Great Labour Demonstration' called by the London Trades Council. 4 May 1890.* (TNA, HO 45/9816.)

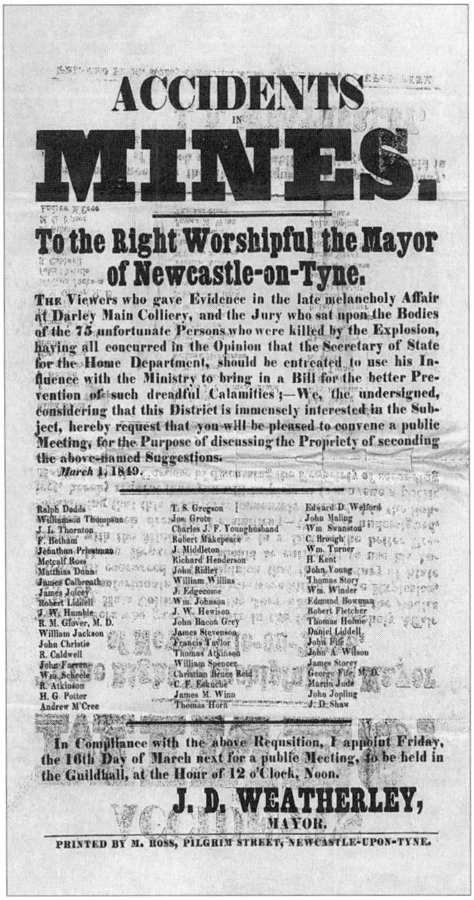

ACCIDENTS IN MINES.

To the Right Worshipful the Mayor of Newcastle-on-Tyne.

THE Viewers who gave Evidence in the late melancholy Affair at Darley Main Colliery, and the Jury who sat upon the Bodies of the 75 unfortunate Persons who were killed by the Explosion, having all concurred in the Opinion that the Secretary of State for the Home Department, should be entreated to use his Influence with the Ministry to bring in a Bill for the better Prevention of such dreadful Calamities;—We, the undersigned, considering that this District is immensely interested in the Subject, hereby request that you will be pleased to convene a public Meeting, for the Purpose of discussing the Propriety of seconding the above-named Suggestions.

March 1, 1849.

Ralph Dodds	T. S. Gregson	Edward D. Welford
Williamson Thompson	Jos. Grote	John Maling
J. L. Thornton	Charles J. F. Younghusband	Wm. Swanston
F. Betham	Robert Makepeace	C. Brough
Jonathan Priestman	J. Middleton	Wm. Turner
Metcalf Ross	Richard Henderson	H. Kent
Matthias Dunn	John Ridley	John Young
James Calbreath	William Willins	Thomas Story
James Joicey	J. Edgecome	Wm. Winder
Robert Liddell	Wm. Johnson	Edmund Bowman
J. W. Humble	J. W. Hewison	Robert Fletcher
R. M. Glover, M. D.	John Bacon Grey	Thomas Holme
William Jackson	James Stevenson	Daniel Liddell
John Christie	Francis Taylor	John Fife
R. Caldwell	Thomas Atkinson	John A. Wilson
John Farren	William Spencer	James Storey
Wm. Scheele	Christian Bruce Reid	George Fife, M. D.
R. Atkinson	C. F. Eskuche	Martin Jude
H. G. Potter	James M. Winn	John Jopling
Andrew M'Cree	Thomas Horn	J. D. Shaw

In Compliance with the above Requsition, I appoint Friday, the 16th Day of March next for a public Meeting, to be held in the Guildhall, at the Hour of 12 o'Clock, Noon.

J. D. WEATHERLEY,
MAYOR.

PRINTED BY M. ROSS, PILGRIM STREET, NEWCASTLE-UPON-TYNE.

13 *As mining technology improved mines became deeper, more dangerous and deadly. Agitation for regulation and better safety measures were on going throughout the 19th and 20th centuries.* (HO 44/39f 139.)

Catering Wages Commission records in LAB 2 and others in LAB 30. Agriculture remained outside the system described above and retained its own independent statutory wage regulation under the Agricultural Wages Board and its various district committees. Of particular interest to local historians are the minutes of the district committees which negotiated and set down local minimum wage rates under the Agricultural Wages (Regulations) Act 1924 in TNA record series MAF 64. These records should be treated with care and used to supplement local material; they are records of minimum not actual wages. As well as national government agreements and records there is also local government material. As councils became direct employers in the late 19th and early 20th centuries, wage rates and hours of work were drawn up and these records (if deposited) would be held in CROs.[45]

Low wages have often been cited as contributing to crime, riots and other forms of unrest. This means that researchers need to cast a wide net, as disputes over wages may have led to criminal activities. For example, Adam Mash was tried at the Old Bailey for setting fire to farm buildings belonging to William Newman of Harrow in 1729; Newman deposed that Mash had set fire to his sheep house and stables because 'I did not give him Money enough for Reaping some Wheat'. A second deposition stated that Mash had threatened to return after transportation (if that had been the sentence) and do Newman some further mischief. Although Mash admitted to saying these things he denied firing the farm buildings, but was found guilty and sentenced to death. Further examples may be found on the Old Bailey Online web site and the NLW Crime and Punishment database.[46]

Poor conditions and accidents at work did not begin with industrialisation. However, the concentration of people into larger workplaces, the increased use of machinery and the new dangers of deep mining saw the numbers involved in accidents rise. Agitation by workers alongside demands by some middle-class public opinion to introduce safer equipment and work practices saw 19th-century governments increasingly involved in setting minimum safety

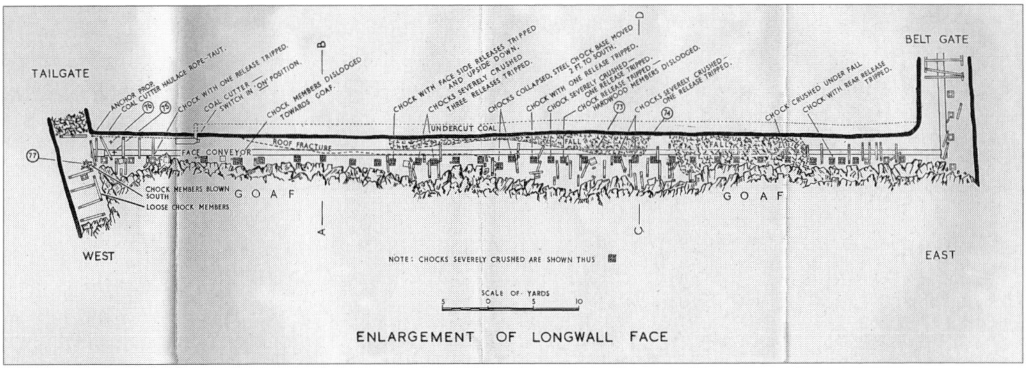

14 *Part of the plans of Easington Colliery, Durham. Taken from the report into the Easington disaster in 1951 where 81 men were killed.* (TNA, EF 2/7.)

standards in various industries. The increased legislation, and particularly the monitoring of employers to ensure the legislation was adhered to (Factory Inspectors after 1833 and Inspectorate of Coal Mines from 1850 being the two obvious examples) saw the collection of a great deal of information regarding working conditions, accidents at work and the development of safety rules and regulations. This information is distributed across a wide number of repositories. Much information was collected, collated and published in various Parliamentary Papers.[47] However, there is a significant series of manuscript material that is of great importance. Coroners records are perhaps the best in terms of coverage. Some material survives for most parts of England and Wales but for specific areas and periods the records are patchy. Records are held locally and nationally with much material still left unlisted. Gibson and Rogers *Coroners' Records* is the starting point for identifying surviving material on a county-by-county basis (and then within constituent districts).[48] There are several published indexes or calendars of coroners; in particular Roy Hunnisett's series of three published calendars for Sussex coroners' inquests covering 1485 to 1688 is particularly impressive for their introductions as well as giving examples of the cases such records would cover.[49] Examples of work-related accidents in the Sussex calendars include the death of Richard Fynall in 1561 who was killed when working in 'a stone delve' [quarry] at Slaugham when the soil above him fell in, and William Benskin, a labourer employed at Beckley in harrowing a field in April 1576, when the horse drew the harrow over his left side piercing it with one of its tines; Benskin died of the wound several days later.[50]

Home Office correspondence in TNA in record series HO 44 and HO 45 includes in-letters concerning the workings of the various 'factory acts' legislation, reports of private individuals' ideas concerning improving industrial safety, a small collection of manuscript and printed safety rules and a wide variety of ephemeral material relating to health and safety. Some of this material refers to specific places while other records refer to particular industries. Key central government records relating to health and safety will be found in various Board of Trade (BT), Coal Board (COAL) and Explosives Directorate

(EF) record series. Some will be continuous and regular runs of material (such as HO 87: Factory and Mines Entry Books, 1836-1921), while others will concern particular accidents, such as the investigation of the Valleyfield Colliery Explosion of 1939 in BT 103/105-8. This is a major unexplored area of local history.

When searching for this type of material, local historians can search under specific industries, such as RAIL and AN (railway workers) and COAL, as well as the more general record series such as Ministry of Labour (LAB), Ministry of Power (POWE), Home Office (HO) and the Health and Safety Executive (EF), where local information on particular work-related risks and specific localised accidents can be found. The following are a few examples which indicate the range of material available:

> RAIL 227/431. Stratford. Great Eastern Railway, various dates. Photographs of accidents, employees, engines etc.;
>
> COAL 75/2141. Durham Division No. 1 Area, 1959-60. Special Safety Committee (Accidents) Formation: Durham Division;
>
> POWE 6/7. New Glynen Colliery, Llanelly, 1919. Inspector's report of explosion and papers regarding the prosecution of colliery manager;
>
> HO 44/39 f 179. Manuscript set of safety rules for a small mine at Shelly in Kirkburton (Yorkshire W.R.). 1856;
>
> EF 2/7. Easington Colliery, Durham. Report, papers and plans relating to the Easington explosion. 1951.

The legal position of trade unions or 'combinations' (as opposed to friendly societies) changed during the 18th and 19th centuries. In the 18th century it was common for individual trade unions and their members to find themselves prosecuted for trade union activities. The Combination Acts of 1799-1800 banned all workers' combinations from taking industrial action (as organisations in restraint of trade) and although these Acts were repealed in 1824 the activities of trade unions were still severely legally limited. By the second half of the 19th century trade unions were accepted as a permanent feature of modern Britain. In 1868 the first meeting of the Trades Union Congress (TUC) took place and in 1871 the TUC Parliamentary Committee was formed (later to become the General Council of the TUC) to report on parliament's handling of the Trade Union Bill. With the passing of the Trade Union Act 1871 unions became legal organisations with full protection of union funds. From this time the government began collecting detailed routine information on trade unions and their members, such as numbers of trade unions, numbers in individual unions and industrial disputes.

The continuing interest in trade unions by central government is reflected in the mass of union information found in Parliamentary Papers.[51] In part this is due to the fluctuating legal status of trade unions and trade union activity as outlined above. At the beginning of the 1870s unions were still dominated by skilled craft trades and it was not until the late 1880s that trade unions were established for unskilled workers in any great numbers. An example of this

15 *The plaiting of straw for hats was a major occupation in much of Bedfordshire and Hertfordshire in the 19th century, but because it was a home-based trade there are few records. Plaiters took their work to local centres to sell, such as the one in Hitchin shown in this photograph, dating from 1907.* (Hertfordshire Archives and Local Studies LRR:Library Reference Room.)

'new unionism' can be seen in the 1889 London Dock strike. The workforce, from all the sections of the docks, struck over wages and poor employment conditions. Not only did they win the strike, but they established the Dock, Wharf and Riverside Labourers Union. The establishment of large general unions had a profound effect on the numbers of trade union members.

Friendly Societies, where members subscribed towards financial benefits in times of sickness, old age, unemployment etc, became increasingly popular in the 18th century. In 1793 they were granted certain privileges and their rules confirmed at quarter sessions (but not all societies registered). Copies of friendly societies' rules are held at TNA and are indexed by place-name. The major series of rules (1784-1912) can be found in classes FS 1 and FS 3 with the indexes in FS 2 and FS 4. There is a series for branches, rules and amendments, etc, Series I for 1855 to 1912 in FS 5 with Series II, for 1848-1970, in FS 11. Because these societies were local, copies will be scattered across local archives;[52] correspondence and any minutes or account books would be held locally rather that in any national collection (although there is a small collection of such material at the Modern Records Centre). The

'Self-Help in Edinburgh, Lothian and Fife' digitisation project has some good material on friendly societies available through the web.[53] Early trade union material (up to *c.*1850) in TNA can be mainly found in the Home Office[54] and Treasury Solicitors Office records (see chapter 11). Due to the illegal status of much trade union activity during this period there is also information in legal criminal records (see chapter 12). There are hundreds of Parliamentary Papers for which friendly societies or trade unions are the principal and subsidiary subject.[55]

Major record classes for trade union activity at TNA, for the late 18th through to the 20th centuries, can be found in HO 40, 41, HO 42, HO 43, HO 44, HO 45 and HO 144. There is also a significant collection of material in the Metropolitan Police record series MEPO 1 and MEPO 2. Information on union activities in particular industries or services will be also found in their appropriate classes, such as railways (RAIL) and mining (COAL) with a wider variety of material held in the various Ministry of Labour (LAB) classes. Of particular interest are the recently listed LAB 2 Ministry of Labour and Predecessors' correspondence for 1886 to 1955. The series contains over 30,000 files and covers a wide range of labour and employment subjects including conciliation machinery, arbitration awards, wages agreements, the Industrial Court and similar subjects.

A principal class of records providing information on particular trade unions is FS 12 (1872-1958). These are annual returns for registered trade unions and give information such as the name of the individual union, numbers in the union (and any change during the previous year), branch status (whether it is a branch of a regional/national union), political affiliation, names/addresses of individual union officers, income and financial position, comments on disputes or short working. These records are listed by place-name and can be easily searched.

Many local (branch) or trade council records can be found in the appropriate CROs such as the Kirkintilloch Trades Council records for 1930-75.[56] However, many of these branches and councils still have significant sets of their own historical records, sometimes in the homes of lay officials. These are supplemented with material from specialist record repositories such as the Rural History Centre (for agricultural labourers) and the National Union of Mine Workers Archives (for mineworkers). The British Library has a scattered but important collection of trade union material,[57] but a key national repository for trade union material is the Modern Records Centre at Warwick, which holds the national records of trade unions, as well as those of the TUC. Although the centre advises local branches to deposit their records at a local level, it has significant collections of early local trade union records such as the Bradford Tin-Plate Workers' Society, 1864-1913, Birmingham and Midland Sheet Metal Workers' Society, 1825-1972 and the London Society of Compositors, 1785-1955.[58] A really useful collection of working-class autobiographies was gathered together by three academics when they were compiling their three-volume annotated bibliography;[59] the material covers 1790 to 1945, includes photocopies of over 230 autobiographies and is kept at the Uxbridge Campus Library in west London.[60] General information on trade unions and some strike activity can be found in newspaper reports as well as industry related papers such as the *Railway Gazette* (later the *Railway Review*).[61]

Records relating to prices can be difficult to track down and to interpret, but is essential for many social and economic studies.[62] Before looking for archival material the various reports in the parliamentary journals and reports should be consulted. Some of these will be specific, such as the *Report on the High Price of Coals. Means to Lower and Prevent Excessive Prices for the Future* 1702-3. Others, such as the *Third Report from the House of Commons Select Committee on the State of Agriculture* (which includes data on the average prices of wool in Norfolk and Suffolk for 1815-35 and crops and prices of wheat in the U.K for 1815-35) are not so obviously relevant but will provide a great deal of information on prices, price movements and the problems these cause; they will be picked up by BOPCRIS.[63]

Early material can be found at TNA in the Pipe Rolls, and various borough records for the assize of bread and ale which regulated their relative prices to that of wheat, barley and oats. With the increase in customs laws it became necessary to publish *Books of Rates* to guide both customs officers and merchants. These *Books*[64] can be used to approximate the value of imported and exported goods. Other material is the registers of weekly and monthly returns from the Board of Trade, Ministry of Agriculture, etc with regard to the average price of corn in several markets of England and Wales (with some separate material for Scotland) for the period 1791-1959 in record series MAF 10, and the returns of markets prices in MAF 15. There is a great deal of further food-price material in various other MAF record series such as the average meat prices at the Metropolitan Meat Market for 1864 to 1882 at MAF 7/3; speculative searches on the TNA electronic catalogue are encouraged.

For the late 18th and 19th centuries *The London Gazette* will provide average weekly prices for various foodstuffs across regions and counties and by the 1830s for some specific towns. Other searches can be made through publications such as *The State of the Poor* and *The Case of Labourers in Husbandry Stated and Considered*,[65] as well as journals such as the *Gentleman's Magazine*, *Annual Register*, *Annals of Agriculture* and *Journal of the Royal Agricultural Society*; John Houghton's *A Collection of Letters for the Improvement of Husbandry and Trade* (1681-1683), is considered to be the first agricultural periodical. The Rural History Centre has many of these and similar titles.

6

Religion

Until 1534 England was a catholic country; Henry VIII renounced papal supremacy and became head of the Church of England when the pope would not grant him a divorce from Catherine of Aragon. Records of the period before 1534 will be found in TNA and other major national repositories and it is unlikely that much material will survive elsewhere. There are a number of relevant printed works: D. Knowles and R.N. Hadcock, *Medieval Religious Houses, England and Wales* (2nd edn, 1971) lists all monasteries, friaries, nunneries, hospitals and colleges together with their dates of foundation and dissolution, an outline of their history and further bibliographical information; D. Knowles, C.N.L. Brooke and V.C. London, *The Heads of Religious Houses, England and Wales*, 940-1216 (1972) gives information about abbots and priors; and for England the *Victoria County History* contains detailed histories of religious houses county by county, and its footnotes are often a useful way of finding primary sources. Sir William Dugdale's *Monasticon Anglicanum*, ed. J. Caley, H. Ellis and B. Bandinel, 6 vols (Record Commission, 1817-30) prints a selection of charters and includes engravings of monastic buildings. Original foundation charters for monasteries rarely survive and most of the texts have been transmitted in later copies. Kings, as well as founding monasteries themselves, often confirmed the foundation charters of others.[1]

Chancery records at TNA contain considerable material for monastic history. C 1 (equity pleadings) are searchable online and there are over 3,000 suits involving religious houses between about 1377 and 1558. From King John's reign, royal charters of foundation and confirmation were enrolled in the Chancery rolls and the Crown issued many *inspeximuses* validating much earlier grants, some of which are the sole source for the original texts. Record classes which will yield material include the Close Rolls in C 54, Patent Rolls in C 66, Charter Rolls in C 53, Confirmation Rolls in C 56 and *Cartae Antiquae* Rolls in 52.[2] There is also material in the Exchequer records. Royal charters and monastic cartularies provide information about royal grants of lands, rights, pensions etc, and royal pensions to the religious orders paid out by the sheriffs are noted county by county in the *elemosina constituta* section of the Pipe Rolls in E 372. Alms dispensed by kings and queens on their travels are noted in the wardrobe books in E 101, Exchequer Various Accounts. Cartularies (registers of charters and deeds) are invaluable; TNA has a substantial holding but they are also widely scattered in other public and private archives and collections.[3] Miscellaneous collections of deeds at TNA are in classes E 40-43, 210-3, 326-9, 354-5, C 146-8, LR 14-15, WALE 29-30, DURH 21, PL 29, DL 25-7; rentals and surveys contain rent rolls, registers and valuations of the lands of many religious houses and can be found in SC 11 and C 12. Court rolls and related documents of manors owned by monastic houses are in SC 2; similar material can be found in WARD 2, C 103-116 and manorial accounts and related documents in SC 6.[4]

Most religious houses were liable for taxation and some of the larger ones made valuable contributions to the Exchequer. A useful list of quotas in 1166 is provided in the *cartae baronum* in the Red Book of the Exchequer (E 164/2) with a few original returns in E 198;[5] material about their later contributions is to be found in the King's Remembrance Subsidy Rolls etc in E 179, and in the *Testa de Nevill* (E 164/5-6).[6] In 1253 the clergy, including the religious orders, first paid a subsidy to the Crown on the annual values of their benefices; this was repeated in 1288-91 with the co-operation of Pope Nicholas IV. A record of the levy has been preserved in the 'taxation of Pope Nicholas' (E 164/13-14, printed by the Record Commission in 1801), with another copy in C 270/16 and subsidiary documents in E 179. From 1294 clerical subsidies became a regular levy, and were raised on the basis of the 1291 figures. Records of payments – normally tenths – are preserved in the clerical series of E 179, and are listed by diocese; enrolled accounts of subsidies are in E 359.[7] A survey of the possessions of the Knights Templar in England, together with other records, can be found in E 164/16;[8] other records of the order are in E 142, E 358/18-20 and IND 1/7029.

The Dissolution of the Monasteries and other monastic houses by Henry VIII generated enormous quantities of records; the TNA have produced a research guide on the subject. The State Papers series at TNA are a key source and have been calendared; copies can be found in many good reference libraries. Surrenders of religious houses from 1536 to 1540 are in E 322; copies of the Acts authorising the dissolution were entered into the register of the Court of Augmentations (E 315/2). Several monks were tried as traitors for taking part in the Pilgrimage of Grace in 1536-7; the trial records are in KB 8. In 1547 chantries were appropriated by the Crown, except for Oxford and Cambridge colleges, and relevant records are in E 117, 301, 315, LR 2, DL 14, 38 and SC 11. There are records relating to monastic lands confiscated because of their abbots' treason and these records are in E 315, LR 1-2 and DL 41.[9]

The Church of England was created by a series of Acts, culminating in the Elizabethan Settlement of 1559. The Anglican church was run on similar lines to its predecessor, with two archbishops and 24 bishops. The two provinces were Canterbury and York, with the former taking precedence. There were 17 medieval dioceses and Henry VIII created six new ones in the 1540s after the Dissolution of the Monasteries, although Westminster only lasted a decade. No further dioceses were created until 1836 when 20 more were founded to serve a growing population. Dioceses were sub-divided into archdeaconries, rural deaneries and parishes. Dioceses did not follow county boundaries and their extent was complex (see J.S.W. Gibson's *Wills and Where to Find Them*, 1997). Diocesan records will usually be found in the diocesan record office, usually the local county or unitary record office, although many records from dioceses north of the Trent will be found in the Borthwick Institute in York. Those for the four medieval Welsh dioceses are in the NLW.

Diocesan records are complex and difficult to use but many of the more important documents, such as bishops' registers, have been published and are therefore more accessible in every sense of the word. Bishops' registers are the single most important series of records created by episcopal administration in the Middle Ages. They vary in form and content from diocese to diocese and in some dioceses from bishop to bishop, but their central feature is the institution of clergy to benefices. They may also include ordination lists, licences and dispensations for clergy and laity, visitation records, royal writs and copies of any documents issued or received by the bishop and judged worthy of permanent preservation. The earliest surviving registers are those of Hugh of Wells, bishop of Lincoln (*c.* 1214-15) and Walter de Grey, archbishop of York (1225). Good series of medieval registers have survived for most dioceses; they decline in their range of contents in the 16th century when other series of records began to be kept. The registers are usually in Latin, but sometimes Anglo-Norman French or English was used for some entries; they are often heavily abbreviated.[10]

The dioceses of the medieval church covered enormous areas of the country, especially the diocese of Lincoln which stretched from the Humber to the Thames, and were therefore divided into smaller units for administrative purposes. A bishop delegated administrative authority over parts of his diocese to a number of archdeacons; the number of archdeaconries in each diocese varied according to the size of the area covered: Canterbury, Rochester, Ely and Carlisle each had only one archdeaconry whereas Lincoln had eight and York had five. The archdeacon was charged with visiting each of his parishes from time to time to ensure that churches were kept in good repair, services conducted along approved lines and scandalous behaviour punished. The autonomy and responsibility of archdeacons varied, usually depending on the size of their parent diocese; in large dioceses the archdeacon would exercise more power simply because it was necessary to split the responsibility into smaller units and, for example, to have archdeaconry as well as episcopal courts.

Archdeaconry records include visitation books, court registers, inductions, admissions and licences for staff, church briefs, returns of dissenters and recusants, glebe terriers and marriage bonds and allegations – in addition to wills, inventories and other probate records. They will be found in the relevant diocesan record office. The records of archdeacons' visitations are valuable sources for information on church buildings as well as other details. The complex system of probate administration prior to 1858, when responsibility was transferred from church to state, is explained by Karen Grannum and Nigel Taylor in *Wills and Other Probate Records*. Subscription books record the names of schoolmasters, midwives and doctors, who had to testify their allegiance to the church.

Church court records are potentially invaluable but are virtually unexplored, due to their complexity, use of Latin and the lack of indexes. Church courts maintained spiritual discipline and dealt with a variety of offences including defamation, matrimonial and tithe disputes, and arguments over wills and legacies. To quote Anne Tarver, 'Sometimes scandalous (the bawdy courts), sometimes serious, the causes can provide much local background material, through which we can hear people actually talking about their daily lives and problems. More importantly, the papers furnish specific facts – of relationships, of property, of chronology – which are pure gold to the researcher'.[11] The Leicester archdeaconry court records are a good example of the type of material contained in them; they are divided into three types of business – instance, correction and visitation, and non-contentious cases. Instance business dealt with disputes between individuals, mostly relating to tithes, defamation, marriage and testaments. The main series of records – act books – date from 1524 to 1828 and run to 84 volumes. As well as the formal records there are some 25,000 other documents relating to the cases heard, dating from 1526 to 1621, including interesting and potentially valuable material on excommunications. The second part of the records dealt with visitation and correction business, in which matters discovered during the archdeacon's visitation were 'corrected'; most of the cases were brought by churchwardens against those who failed to attend church or had committed any of a wide range of offences against canon law. Examples of the latter include failure to receive the sacrament, hindering preaching, brawling, clandestine marriage and untimely ringing of bells. The Leicester act books date from 1522 to 1718 in 83 volumes and there are separate churchwardens' presentments, dating from 1608/9 to 1832, although incomplete. A small but interesting group of documents relates to the guardianship of children between 1745 and 1810.[12]

Parish registers are one of the best-known sources held by local record offices. In 1538 Thomas Cromwell ordered each parish in England and Wales to keep a record of baptisms, marriages and burials. At first they were kept on loose pieces of parchment but in 1597 it was ruled that these entries should be bound into a register kept for the purpose, and the older records should be entered into it; this explains why the first 60 or so years of many early registers are all written in the same hand. Some larger parishes had separate books for each event but most smaller ones used a single volume for all the entries; they vary enormously in the care with which they were compiled. Not all registers survive and some indeed have been lost since the Church of Latter-Day Saints began its programme of microfilming English parish registers. Many registers have been published and family history societies have been involved in indexing them. Registers are almost always held at the appropriate CRO.

There was no change in the format of parish registers until Hardwicke's Marriage Act of 1753, designed to prevent clandestine marriages, which led to a new form of marriage register. Rose's Act of 1812 brought in new, standardised, registers for baptisms and burials. The 1597 Act also required that a copy of each year's entries should be sent to the bishop's office, and these bishop's transcripts sometimes survive where the original registers are lost. Some banns books survive and may be useful in the absence of marriage registers. Marriage by licence was used when the three-week period for banns to be read was too long, and the bonds and allegations required before the issue of a licence should be found in the diocesan record office. In 1978 the Church of England

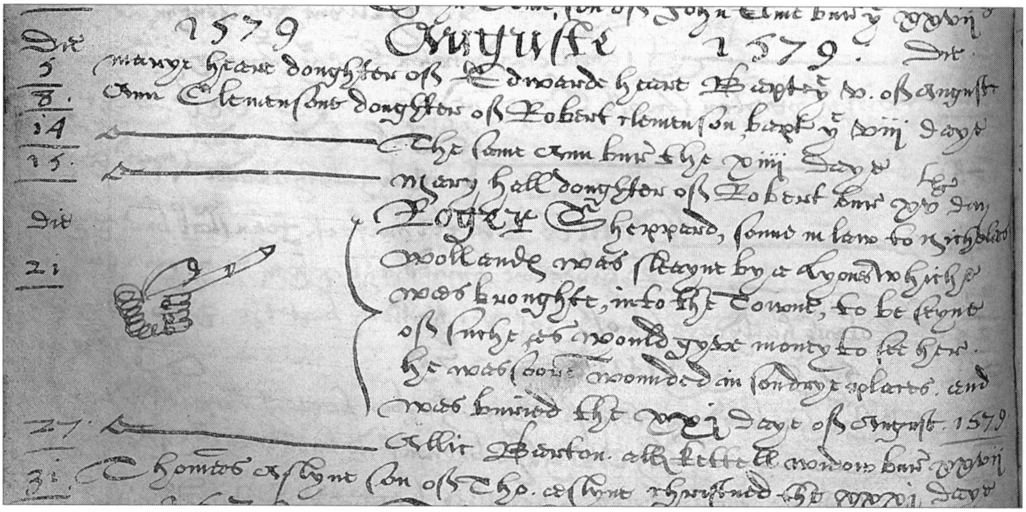

16 *Parish registers are used by family historians and by statisticians, and generally conform to a set pattern. However, some clergymen added incidental details, such as this unusual death in Loughborough in 1579. Particularly interesting entries are indicated by a pointing finger.* (Record Office for Leicestershire, Leicester and Rutland, DE667/1.)

brought in the *Parochial Registers and Records Measure* which stated that certain records must be deposited with the diocesan record office unless a church has adequate facilities to look after them; these include environmental conditions and other safeguards, so that in practice very few parish records are now kept in churches.

Records relating to the liturgical aspect of the Church of England are underused; they include service registers (detailing the form of each church service), faculties (required before any alterations could be made to a church), notices, glebe terriers and tithe records. Records of church charities may also be found. Churchwardens were responsible for the maintenance, cleaning and decoration of the church, and provision for services. Until 1868 all parishioners had to pay church rates, a cause of great annoyance to nonconformists. Churchwardens' accounts can be a wonderful source of information and, as well as payments towards the upkeep of the church, may also record money paid for dead birds and vermin, relief to itinerant poor and payments to bell-ringers. A few accounts survive from the 14th century and those from the next two centuries are an important source of information about changes associated with the Reformation, such as the removal of rood screens and gilded images. Many early accounts have been published by national and local record societies, such as the Hertfordshire Record Society's first publication on Tudor accounts, covering 16th-century documents for five parishes. The parish was a civil unit of administration, as well as ecclesiastical, and details of other records relating to this area of responsibility will be found in chapters 8 and 12.

Lambeth Palace Library, founded in 1610, houses many of the documents of the Archbishopric of Canterbury, such as enquiries about benefices, tithes, buildings, etc, the marriage licences of the Faculty Office and Vicar General's

Office, and the probate records of the Court of Arches and certain peculiar jurisdictions in London (peculiars were areas outside the jurisdiction of the bishop and archdeacon for the place in which they were located); it is now administered by the Church Commissioners, 1 Millbank, London, SWIP 3JZ. There is also material in the British Library and a search in its integrated online catalogue should yield relevant sources.[13]

A nonconformist or dissenter was originally one who refused to conform to the Acts of the 'Clarendon Code', passed after the restoration of the monarchy, especially the Act of Uniformity of 1662; it required all English and Welsh clergy to consent to the entire contents of the Book of Common Prayer. Over 2,000 clergymen, about a fifth of the total, refused and were ejected from their livings. In 1689, after the 'Glorious Revolution', protestant nonconformists were allowed to license their meeting houses for public worship at the quarter sessions (see below), but they were still banned from holding public office and excluded from the universities. Fears of a Catholic revival led to more restrictions on Roman Catholics, until the Catholic Emancipation Act of 1829, although many Anglican ministers turned a blind eye to the presence of Catholic families who worshipped privately; Catholic places of worship had to be registered at quarter sessions from 1791.

Nonconformity covers a wide variety of beliefs and doctrines, and it is a difficult task to differentiate between different sects over time. Researchers should, at least initially, refer to secondary sources for information on this subject; although Gwenith Jones's *The Descent of Dissent* is long out of print, it is a very useful and accessible guide, and may be found in a library. The main denominations are Methodist, Baptist, Independent, Presbyterian, Congregational, United Reform Church, Unitarian and Quaker. There were divisions within them: Methodists encompassed primitive, Wesleyan, the Countess of Huntingdon's connexion, etc.; Baptists were split into particular and general. Congregationalists and Presbyterians joined together in 1972 to form the United Reformed Church. In the last half-century many immigrants to Britain have followed other religions, such as Islam, but few if any of their records have been deposited in a record office.

The quantity and quality of records also varies, with some sects – such as Quakers – having excellent records, but others are disappointing. The earliest known register dates from 1644; many nonconformists recorded baptisms, but still used the Church of England for marriages and burials. When civil registration of births, marriage and deaths began in 1837 the rule requiring Anglican baptism for the holding of public office was relaxed and nonconformist registers were allowed as legal evidence by the Non-Parochial Registers Act of 1840. This involved the Registrar-General calling in the registers, which are now in TNA in record series RG 4, 6–8; birth certificates from the Presbyterian, Independent and Baptist Registry and also from the Wesleyan Methodist Metropolitan Registry are in RG 5. RG 4, 1567–1858, consists of registers of births, baptisms, deaths, burials and marriages; the majority of the series are unofficial registers but there are a few official Anglican registers which had been kept by institutions outside the normal Church of England structure. The unofficial registers are usually of nonconformist and Roman Catholic congregations in England and Wales but include a few Scottish churches in England. RG 6, 1578-1841, is registers of births, deaths, burials and marriages of congregations of the Religious Society of Friends (Quakers) in England and Wales. RG 7 is registers of clandestine marriages and of baptisms in the Fleet Prison, King's Bench Prison, the Mint and the May Fair Chapel. RG 8, 1646-1970, is registers of births, marriages and deaths surrendered to the Non-Parochial Registers Commission of 1857, and other registers and church records. Many libraries and record offices have microfilm copies of these registers; some were overlooked and may now be found in local record offices or in the relevant chapel.

The Methodist Archives and Research Centre is located at the John Rylands University Library of Manchester; it has the world's largest collection of manuscripts relating to the founders of Methodism, John and Charles Wesley, and other members of their family. In all, the collection comprises approximately 5,000 letters, notebooks and associated papers for the period 1700-1865. Prominent 18th-century Evangelicals, other than the Wesleys, whose personal papers are represented in the collections include George Whitefield (1714-70), the Countess of Huntingdon (1707-91), Howell Harris (1714-73) and Benjamin Ingham (1712-72). In addition, there is a very large collection of manuscript material relating to John Fletcher (1729-85) of Madeley and his wife Mary Bosanquet (1739-1815). The Archives also include extensive small collections of personal papers of approximately 4,000 ministers and lay-Methodists from the 18th century to the present. These include Thomas Coke (1747-1814), Adam Clarke (1760-1832), Hugh Bourne (1772-1852), Jabez Bunting (1779-1858), John Ernest Rattenbury (1870-1963) and Dr Rupert Davies (1909-94). The institutional records of Methodism include the records of the Methodist Conference and its several committees and large collections deposited by the administrative divisions of the Church, and there is material relating to all the major pre-union Methodist denominations.

The Angus Library, at Regent's Park College, holds the greatest quantity of printed and manuscript sources for the Baptist Church; this includes: the archives of the Baptist Missionary Society; Baptist Church minute books and other records from the 17th century onwards; letters, diaries and notebooks of many prominent Baptists, such as William Carey, Andrew Fuller, John Rippon, John Ryland (both father and son), Joshua Thomas, Benjamin Beddome, Abraham Booth, Samuel Pearce, John Saffery, Joseph Angus, William Steadman, C.H. Spurgeon, J.H. Rushbrooke, M.E. Aubrey and E.A. Payne; minute books of the Particular Baptist Fund (1717-1975); minute books of other Baptist organisations, from 1714; minute books of the Baptist Union of Great Britain and Ireland.

The Congregational Library at Dr Williams's Library, 14 Gordon Square, London, WC1H 0AG holds national Congregational records. Records of the United Reformed Church are not yet available for consultation but the United Reformed Church Scottish Synod Office, PO Box 189, 240 Cathedral Street, Glasgow, G1 2BX can advise on Scottish Congregationalism. Records of the Unitarians can be found at Dr Williams's Library, Harris Manchester College, Mansfield Road, Oxford, OX1 3TD and the John Rylands University Library. Friends House Library (opposite Euston station) houses four broad categories of Quaker materials: the archives of Britain Yearly Meeting and its committees (including Meeting for Sufferings); the archives of London and Middlesex General Meeting and its monthly and local meetings; the archives of some Quaker organisations that are not part of Britain Yearly Meeting, such as Friends Ambulance Unit, and a few non-Quaker organisations, such as the Central Board for Conscientious Objectors; manuscript collections and papers of a wide variety of significant Friends, such as Margaret Fell and Elizabeth Fry. In addition to these national repositories a significant amount of material will be found in local record offices and some specialist archives.

Roman Catholic nonconformists were often known as recusants and there is considerable material at TNA. Fines for recusancy are in E 372, 376-7 and records of seizure of Catholic estates are in E 174 and 368, 379, as well as in the records of the Forfeited Estates Commission in FEC 1-2. Eighteenth-century returns of papists can be found in E 174 and KB 18; the former are returns made by clerks of the peace of the names and estates of Catholics and the latter returns of papists in Lancaster. There are some returns of Catholics taking oaths in PC 1 as well as Dorset recusants in the Shaftesbury Papers in PRO 30/24. The various State Papers Domestic will give references to the activities of Catholic priests in England, the sequestration and sale of recusants' estates and some information on the Gordon Riots.[14]

Between the 16th and 19th centuries various groups of people were required to take oaths of loyalty to the Crown and the Church of England. Oath rolls generally date from after 1673 and can be found at TNA. The 'Solemn Association' oath was for the defence of the king and his succession and was established by Parliament in 1696; all office-holders under the Crown had to take it. The surviving rolls are in C 213-4 and KB 24/1-2. The Corporation Act of 1661 and the Test Act of 1672 restricted the rights of dissenters to hold office; after 1723 Quakers were allowed to take a special affirmation of loyalty and under the Catholic Relief Act 1778 Roman Catholics were allowed to take the oath of allegiance. Relevant records are in PC 1 and C 203. Sacrament Certificates recorded where and when Holy Communion was taken; the names of the clergymen, churchwarden and two witnesses were sometimes submitted to Chancery, King's Bench and Exchequer and are respectively in C 224, KB 22 and E 196. Nearly all them relate to persons living within 30 miles of London and Westminster (Middlesex, Hertfordshire, Surrey and Kent), but there are some records for the Chester Palatinate Court for 1673-1768 in CHES 4. Both oath rolls and sacrament certificates can be found in quarter sessions records at CROs and sometimes in borough records.

Under the 1689 Toleration Act dissenters' meeting houses had to be registered at quarter sessions, with bishops or archdeacons, until the Act was repealed in 1852. Quarter sessions records may also contain oaths of allegiance and registers of estates and wills. Roman Catholic registers and other records may be deposited in a record office but most are still kept in diocesan offices or individual churches. There are fewer Catholic dioceses (22) and some of them have their own archivist. The House of Lords Record Office holds returns of Roman Catholics for 1680, 1706, 1767 and 1781, and further details can be found in its leaflet on sources for family historians; some diocesan (county)

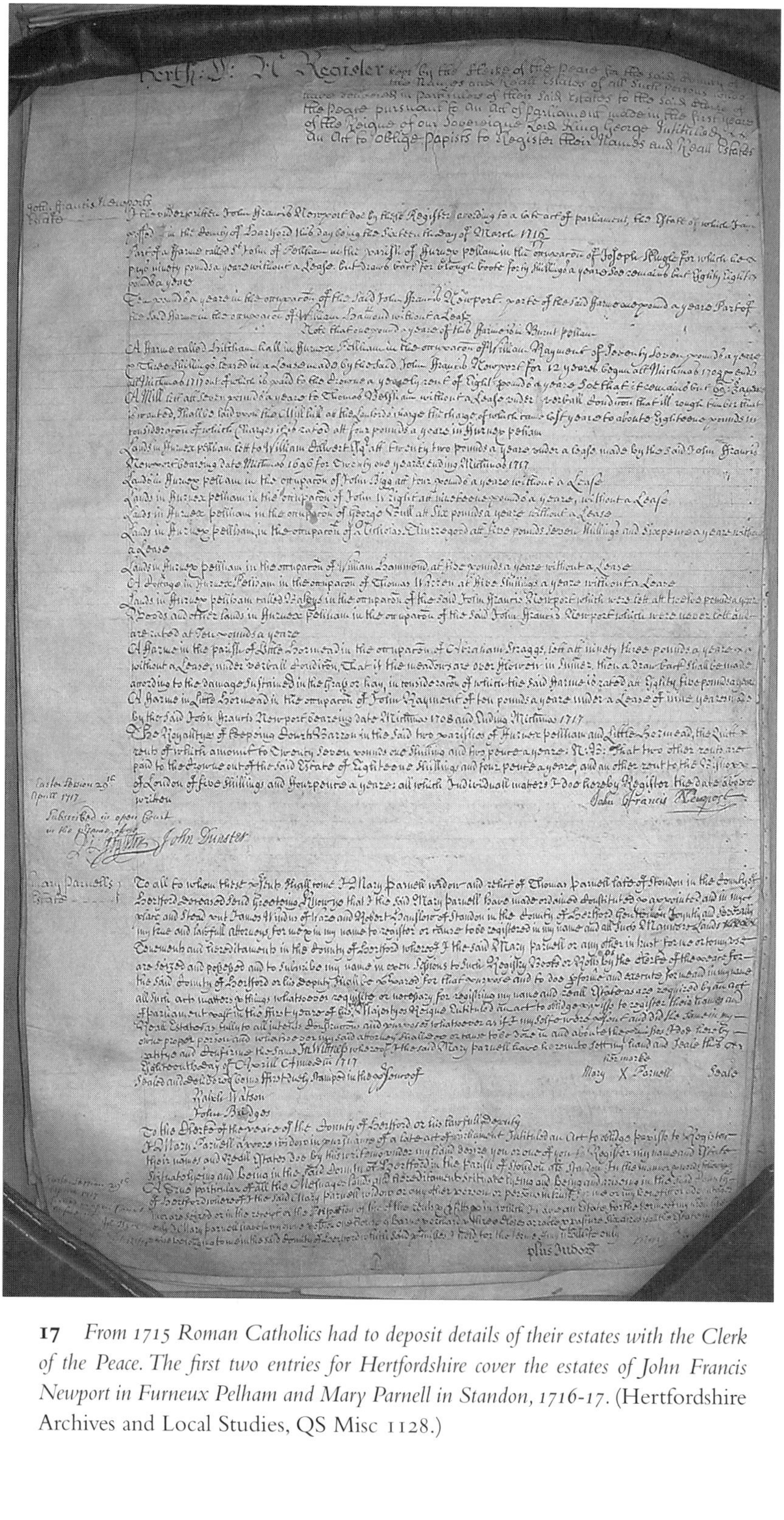

17 *From 1715 Roman Catholics had to deposit details of their estates with the Clerk of the Peace. The first two entries for Hertfordshire cover the estates of John Francis Neuport in Furneux Pelham and Mary Parnell in Standon, 1716-17.* (Hertfordshire Archives and Local Studies, QS Misc 1128.)

record offices have related material and the Catholic Record Society has published two guides to the 1767 returns. Other Roman Catholic records can be found at the Westminster Diocesan Archives, 16a Abingdon Road, Kensington, London, W8 6AF; a prior appointment is necessary. Records of the British Province of the Society of Jesus (Jesuits) are at 114 Mount Street, London, W1Y 6AH and at Stonyhurst College, Clitheroe, BB7 9PZ, where a prior appointment is also required for access.

Jews have been living in Britain since the Norman Conquest but few records appear to have survived before the 19th century. Southampton University has undertaken a survey of Jewish archives, in order to create a computerised database of information about papers relating to individuals, families, organisations, congregations and communities in the UK and Eire, and further details can be found on its web site. Records of the Board of Deputies of British Jews from 1830 are at London Metropolitan Archives and there is further material in other repositories (see the NRA for details).

A census of attendance at religious worship was taken on Sunday, 30 March 1851. It provides detailed information, parish by parish, on the places of worship of each denomination, the number of sittings available, and the numbers attending morning, afternoon and evening services on that day; it also notes the number of children attending Sunday school in the morning or afternoon. These records are now kept at TNA in HO 129; a digest was printed for Parliament[15] but many libraries and record offices have microfilm copies for their area and many returns have been published by record societies.

From 1704 the incomes of poor clergy of the Church of England were supplemented by a fund which drew upon ecclesiastical revenues confiscated by Henry VIII and payments made by clergymen with larger incomes, and known as Queen Anne's Bounty. The Church Commissioners for England, which date from 1948, were formed by joining together Queen Anne's Bounty and the Ecclesiastical Commissioners for England (founded in 1836). In 1856 the Church Building Commissioners, constituted in 1818, had been dissolved and their remaining powers and duties were transferred to the Ecclesiastical Commissioners.

As well as documents in quarter sessions and borough records, others may be found in family and estate records, especially where the family had Catholic sympathies. Dr Williams's Library is the pre-eminent research library of English protestant nonconformity. Among other sources, it holds John Evans's list of meeting houses, 1715, and Josiah Thompson's manuscript providing lists of English and Welsh dissenting congregations, about 1773. An Act of 1736 required the registration of nonconformist trust deeds which are enrolled on the Close Rolls at TNA; the originals should be in the CRO. The House of Lords Record Office holds papists' returns of 1680 and other relevant material, and there are also relevant documents in the British Library Department of Manuscripts.[16] There is a vast collection of printed material for all denominations and researchers are advised to consult the relevant society, Dr Williams's Library or their local record office or library.[17] Most of the major nonconformist denominations have a record society which publishes material of interest, a journal and a history society.

7
Education

During the 16th and 17th centuries England became a semi-literate society, where even some of the humblest members were able to read. A school was available within walking distance for most of the boys and girls whose parents had the means and desire to take advantage of the provision. Schoolmasters' licences, referred to in the previous chapter, show that an expansion of educational provision began in Elizabethan times. The emergence of a sizeable middle class created a demand for superior private schools, especially for girls. Standards were improved by men such as Thomas Arnold of Rugby School but, as Charles Dickens and other writers graphically illustrated, there were still schools where the pupils were badly taught and ill-treated. Information on the nine big public schools can be found in the report of the Clarendon Commission which met from 1861 to 1864 and published its findings as a Parliamentary Paper.[1] Records of private schools are usually still kept by the institution and some of them, such as Eton College, employ a qualified archivist.

A number of present-day schools can trace their history back to the later Middle Ages, but the connection is usually a tenuous one; the character has changed out of all recognition, the original buildings have gone and the site has often been altered. Opportunities for elementary education for the sons of richer and middle classes were widespread and the constitutions, curricula, facilities and aims of the schools were reasonably consistent nationwide. Many of the medieval schools were linked to church chantries and after these were dissolved in the 1540s many parishes were able to use the chantry funds to refound a school. The chantry certificates for the mid-16th century can be found in TNA E319.

Different types of schools emerged as attitudes towards education (primarily of the poor) changed. Concern over the lack of educational provision for poor children led to the formation of charity schools.[2] The Society for the Promotion of Christian Knowledge (SPCK), founded in 1698, was the first national body to build and manage elementary schools for children aged seven to 11 or over. In its first 35 years it helped to form, or reform, over 1,500 schools. It soon became specifically Anglican and its schools provided a basic education for thousands of children, including girls. Its archives are housed in Cambridge University Library and include minutes, reports, account books, correspondence and information on charity schools; the records of the

Scottish Society for the Promotion of Christian Knowledge are at the NAS. Charity schools linked to local churches may be found with other parish records. 'Dame schools' was a rather contemptuous catchall term for many private schools; they were often little more than child-minding establishments, although the more successful ones were listed as private academies in trade directories. They were run by women, often with few or no qualifications, who charged 3d or 4d per pupil a week and taught skills such as reading and writing to a rudimentary level. Dame schools were often held in corners of kitchens or in insanitary cellars while the 'teacher' continued with other household work; it is unlikely that many records survive, but CROs would be the first place to enquire and researchers should try searching the NRA and other network links.[3] Ragged schools, as the name suggests, were charitable foundations which provided a basic education and industrial training for the urban poor. There had been some ragged schools from the 18th century, but they were few and far between. They had been started in areas where someone had been concerned enough to want to help disadvantaged children towards a better life. The schools were given this name because the children who attended had only very ragged clothes to wear and rarely had shoes. During the 19th century many people began to worry about neglected children in London, and more schools were opened. The Ragged School Union (RSU) was formed in 1844, with Lord Shaftesbury as its chairman; initially it provided just 16 schools but by 1861 there were 176 schools in the Union. As well as giving basic lessons many schools provided food and as time went on some also opened refuges where the children could sleep, especially in extremely cold weather. At its peak the RSU represented over 650 schools. Its size allowed new services to be developed: a Fresh Air Fund allowed the Union to take inner-city children into the country for the day, while holiday camps allowed them longer breaks out of the city, or maybe to convalesce. As Ragged Schools were established in Australia, New Zealand and the USA, British schools had the opportunity to offer emigration to their students as a way of making a fresh start. Getting children into employment was a particular focus of the schools; the RSU bought two training ships to prepare boys for a career at sea. As well as teaching vocational skills, they often employed young people in their own small businesses, such as the Wood-Chopping Brigade and the Shoeblack Society. In 1944, the 100th anniversary of the RSU, the organisation changed its name to the Shaftesbury Society to honour the man who had such an influence on its first four decades. The RSU produced a magazine under various different names and published annual reports, and these, together with minutes, are still housed with the Shaftesbury Society;[4] however they relate primarily to London and information on ragged schools in other parts of the country may be harder to find.

Sunday schools were started by Robert Raikes in Gloucester in 1785; the movement spread rapidly among Anglicans and nonconformists and by 1795 Sunday schools were providing a basic education for three-quarters of a million children. By 1851 they had nearly 2.5 million pupils, almost two-thirds of those aged five to 14, and at their peak in 1906 they had over six million, more than 80 per cent of the total in the age range. Few Sunday schools have left adequate records but some may survive in parish and nonconformist collections (see Chapter 6).

In Sunday (and charity) schools the monitorial system was used, whereby senior pupils taught younger ones. The two pioneers of this system were Dr Andrew Bell, an Anglican chaplain to the Indian army, and Joseph Lancaster, a nonconformist who opened a school in London in 1801; Lancaster formed a society in 1808 called the Society for Promoting the Lancasterian System for the Education of the Poor, or the Royal Lancasterian Society, and was supported by a number of prominent evangelical and non-conformist Christians. It was renamed the British and Foreign Schools Society six years later. In 1810 the SPCK established the National Society for the Education of the Poor in the Principles of the Established Church throughout England and Wales, which took over the 230 schools and 40,000 pupils of the SPCK. The National and British Societies competed to build schools, especially in manufacturing towns, and from 1833 they were supported by government grants.[5] The British and Foreign School Society Archive Centre has a fully searchable web site,[6] and is located at the Osterley Campus of Brunel University. Records include: annual reports from 1814, minute books from 1808, correspondence, financial records and information on schools and teachers.[7] (For information on schools connected with other nonconformist denominations see chapter 6.) The records of the National Society are kept in the Church of England Record Centre in South Bermondsey. The archives contain over 15,000 files of correspondence concerning individual schools, many of which are still active today. There are also files on closed schools, and on county schools that were originally founded as church schools; they mostly contain correspondence and papers about applications for grants. The application forms often contain a surprising amount of detail about the building and construction of a school and information on the local population. Trust deeds are a common feature of the files; a condition of any grant was sight of the school's trust deed, so files contain information on these documents, or even a full copy. Trust deeds contain valuable information about a school's foundation date, and the names of the trustees. The archive contains an index of school teachers, compiled from sources within the archives and library, and covering the period 1812-1855; it gives brief educational details of individuals trained by the Society. The history of the Society as a corporate body can be researched in the minute books of its major committees, and in the complete set of its annual reports, both covering the period from 1811 to the present day. Information on church schools can also be found in visitation records and parish records. Parish magazines may have been kept and can contain a surprising amount of information; many of these magazines survive locally in local studies and CRO libraries.

The Catholic Poor School Committee was founded in 1847 under the auspices of the Catholic Bishops of Great Britain to provide primary education for the children of poor Catholics in the United Kingdom. At this time there was an urgent need to address the lack of schools and teachers for Catholic children, who either attended non-Catholic schools or had no formal education at all. The committee was recognised as an intermediary between the Catholic body and the Committee of the Privy Council on Education, with a view to obtaining a share of the Government grant for national education, providing assistance for the building and support of Catholic schools and establishing training colleges for teachers. The Committee purchased a site on which St Mary's College was established in 1850; the records are now held at the present site of the College at Twickenham.[8] The Committee changed its name to the Catholic Schools Committee in 1888 and the Catholic Education Council in 1905. The records include: annual reports, 1848-1981 (incomplete), Annual General Meeting reports of proceedings, 1923-25, including a report on religious inspection of training colleges and files relating to St Mary's College, Strawberry Hill, 1937-1985. The 1849 report included a survey of Roman Catholic voluntary schools returned in 1845.

A great deal of information on schools in every part of the country can be found in various national journals, periodicals, Parliamentary Papers and annual reports. Parliamentary Papers are particularly fruitful and some large towns had their own special enquiries. National reports on grammar schools start with Nicholas Carlisle's *Concise Description of the Endowed Grammar Schools in England and Wales*, published in two volumes in 1818, which includes replies from correspondents to his 18 questions. The first state survey of elementary schools was made in 1816 by a select committee of the House of Commons under the chairmanship of H.P. (later Lord) Brougham; information was supplied by parish clergy. The results were published in the *Digest of Parochial Returns* (HC, 1819 ix); they are arranged by county, provide details of the capacity of endowed, unendowed and Sunday Schools, and distinguish between National, British and dame schools.

From 1833 Parliament allowed an annual sum to assist charities, primarily the National Society and the British and Foreign Schools Society, to build schools; it was originally fixed at £20,000 and increased to £30,000 in 1839. A Committee of Education was created within the Privy Council to supervise the grants. It was from this committee that later departments responsible for education stem: Education Department from 1856, Board of Education from 1899, Ministry of Education from 1944, Department of Education and Science from 1964, Department for Education from 1992 and the Department for Education and Employment from 1995. From 1833 an enormous amount of central government records has been created, relating to the administration, direction and evaluation of education, schools and other related establishments.[9]

The 1851 ecclesiastical census included an investigation into education in England and Wales. This was voluntary and only a few returns survive among Home Office records of the census at TNA in record series HO 129. If there is no individual return for a particular place the *Report of Commissioners for taking a Census of Great Britain on Education* (HC 1852-3 xc) gives details of attendances, pupil ages, capacity of schools, etc. A further key report is that of the Royal Commission appointed in 1858. Chaired by the Duke of Newcastle, the Commission surveyed elementary schools in Britain and abroad and in 1861 published what was probably the most exhaustive 19th-century investigation into education, *Report of the Royal Commission on Education* (HC 1861 xxi).[10] Two reports for Scotland for 1859 and 1866-7 are kept at NAS with references ED 16/13 and 16/14.

The combination of the recommendations of the Newcastle Commission and other pressure from the Education Department, and the Revised Code of 1862, resulted in a system of payment by results; the government grant was dependent on the average attendance and performance levels in examinations. In the words of Robert Lowe, Vice President of the Education Board, 'If it is not cheap, it shall be efficient, if it is not efficient, it shall be cheap'. Despite the work of the voluntary societies, which had expanded rapidly since the 1840s (1.5 million pupils in nearly 7,000 schools by the 1860s), they could not keep up with the increase in population and half the children in Britain did not attend a day-school. It was clear that state intervention was necessary and the Education Act 1870 provided for the election of school boards with power to build and manage schools where the provision by the two voluntary bodies was inadequate. In the biggest cities large Victorian Gothic board schools were built, catering for over 1,000 pupils, and many of them are still in use in some form or other. All schools were subject to government inspection to ensure adequate standards and, once schools were provided, attendance was compulsory. In 1880 all children had to attend up to the age of ten, this was raised by a year in 1893 and to 12 in 1899, except for children employed in agriculture. The school boards paid the fees for poor children from 1876 until all fees were abolished in 1891. Late in the 19th century came the reports of the Taunton Commission (1868-9) and the Bryce Commission (1895), major sources of information on grammar and other secondary schools. A Parliamentary Paper of 1897, *Return of the Pupils in Public and Private Secondary and Other Schools in England*, gives a lot of information about the numbers of schools and pupils, the age of the pupils and the qualification of teachers.[11]

The most significant records in TNA include the following. There are many trust deeds relating to school foundations; from 1735 to 1925 conveyances for land for charitable uses were enrolled in Chancery (see p.99). Further information on trust deeds can be found in TNA in record series T 1 including endowments of Scottish schools. Enrolled deeds for Church of England elementary schools, from 1903 to 1920, under the Mortmain and Charitable Uses Acts 1888-1892, or the Technical and Industrial Institutions Act 1892, can be found in ED 191. There are other trust deeds for 1856 to 1925 in CHAR 12 (indexes in each volume) and CHAR 13, although it seems that some trust deeds were never enrolled. There are Endowment Files, 1853 to 1945, which provide data on private endowments for elementary schools in ED 49, and on those occasions where endowments covered elementary and secondary education the material will be found in ED 27. Applications for government aid for building elementary schools are to the found in ED 103, administered by the Treasury between 1833 and 1839, and then by the Privy Council Committee on Education. These applications are indexed in ED 103/141 and cover England, Scotland and Wales. In addition information regarding grants can sometimes be found in T 1.[12] There are very few plans associated with these applications, but a small number are in ED 228; the appropriate CRO would be the best place to look for early plans. In order to acquire a grant a formal preliminary statement was submitted for consideration, which recorded such details as tenure, any historical establishment details of the school, its financial state and further information regarding the rooms, grounds etc, and staffing. Preliminary statements for elementary schools for the period 1846-1924 are in ED 7 and after 1924 on the school files in ED 21.

Correspondence with school boards of parishes not included in a borough or in the metropolis is contained in the series of Parish Files in ED 2 (confusingly ED 2 relates to parishes with no school or more than one at the time of the 1870 Act). Two other series have parish files. Where there was one school they will be found in the ED 21 file for the parish or in ED 33. Files on schools in receipt of annual grants are in ED 21 where there is information on premises, various statistics, accommodation, inspection, etc. Some papers were either copied or extracted from these files after 1944, and are now found in those records which relate to large numbers of primary schools in ED 161. Central government records for secondary education can be found at TNA in ED 27 (pre 1902) and ED 35 (post 1902) – there is some overlap. Inspection material is in ED 109 with papers relating to the reorganisation of secondary education in ED 152.

The Welsh Department of the Board of Education was established in 1907. Its main papers for general and elementary education are in ED 91 and ED 92. Unfortunately many Welsh schools files were destroyed in the Second World War and later by flooding at the Welsh Department's office in Cardiff in 1960. For more contemporary government data from the 1970s there are datasets on pupil numbers, teaching staff, classes and examination courses. These are accessible via NDAD,[13] as CRDA 13 (ED 267) along with information for 1993.

School inspection was a key part of government intervention when it was made a condition of grant-aid in 1839. Early inspectors' reports were printed in House of Commons Sessional Papers (there are sets from 1839 to 1899 in ED 17) with further reports in ED 2, ED 21, ED 16 or ED 3 (for London). Confidential reports are in ED 9/14. ED 50 also has some reports for 1872 to 1893 on education for the blind in London and on teacher training. There are also a small number of reports on schools for the blind and deaf in the 1890s in ED 17/65-69. Secondary schools pre-1899 inspection reports, made for the Charity Commissioners, are in the endowment files in ED 27 and a few reports on science and art day classes from 1879 to 1905 are in ED 9/13. After 1899 there are abstracts of the reports in the institution files and separately filed full reports on primary schools in ED 156, secondary schools in ED 109, independent schools in ED 172 and special educational schools in ED 195. Some reports on Welsh schools in the early 20th century can be found in ED 91-92 while ED 22 has Welsh inspectorate memoranda for 1907 to 1940. Later reports on Welsh schools are in BD 17 for primary schools, BD 16 for secondary schools, BD 72 for independent schools, BD 71 for special schools, BD 15 for further education establishments, BD 14 for teacher training colleges and collected special reports in BD 19.

The educational system was completely reorganised in 1902 when responsibility for providing elementary, secondary and technical education was given to 330 local education authorities under a central Board of Education; board schools became 'council' schools and there was more emphasis on extending provision for secondary education. From 1906 LEAs could provide school meals and from 1907 a medical service; in 1918 the leaving age was raised to fourteen. The 1944 Education Act replaced the Board of Education with a Ministry and established a tripartite system of secondary education – grammar, technical and secondary modern. The leaving age was raised to 15 in 1947 and to 16 in the early 1970s. In 1965 the comprehensive system, which replaced grammar and secondary modern schools, was adopted as official national policy, although grammar schools have been retained in some parts of the country.

Prior to the 1902 Education Act teacher training was largely carried out under the pupil-teacher system which had been established in 1846. By the end of the 19th century trainee teachers were prepared for the Queen's/King's Scholarship Examination (later the Preliminary Examination for the Certificate) at 18 years of age. After the Elementary Education Act 1870 instruction was no longer to take place at their own schools but at separate establishments; pupil-teacher centres were run by local school boards with teaching practice at their elementary schools. Where these records survive they are in ED 57. Further material on teachers can be found in ED 67, LEA files on the supply of teachers, and other LEA schemes for teacher training in ED 53.

One of the best sources of information for local schools in England is the relevant *Victoria County History* volume. In addition many schools have had their history written and even if this was some time ago, before sources were so easily available, it would still be a good place to start. Many school records will be found in local record offices, both those of school boards and of individual schools. One of the most interesting and numerous are school log books, introduced in 1862 as part of a general move to promote efficiency, economy and accountability in elementary education. Under the Revised Code all elementary schools open to public inspection had to maintain a regular record of activities. Like other sources the survival of school log books is patchy and many will not survive. At first daily entries were required, but this was reduced to weekly ones in 1871. When the inspector paid his annual visit he checked the log book to see that it was being kept properly. Inevitably the bulk of the entries relate to pupils' academic progress, with details of disciplinary problems and teaching methods, including text-books used, songs learnt and poetry recited. As the government grant was partly dependent on attendance levels, there are many references to children's absence because of illness, bad weather or other reasons. In rural areas children were used for seasonal employment and special holidays were granted for haymaking, harvest, fruit and hop picking; sometimes children were absent for less worthy reasons, such as when a circus visited the area. Log books provide valuable information on the wider community: in industrial areas children between the ages of eight and 13 (ten to 13 from the 1870s) were allowed to work on a half-time basis in factories and workshops. Communal events are frequently mentioned, together with national celebrations such as royal jubilees, coronations or war victories. Sometimes log books can yield unexpected results; for example, they have been used by medical researchers to examine the cyclical nature of childhood illnesses. Other school records include punishment books, attendance registers, minutes, accounts, plans and photographs. Records of local education authorities may have been transferred to the local record office or still be held by the relevant authority.

The main role of the universities was to qualify young men for the church but they also attracted the sons of the aristocracy and gentry who did not

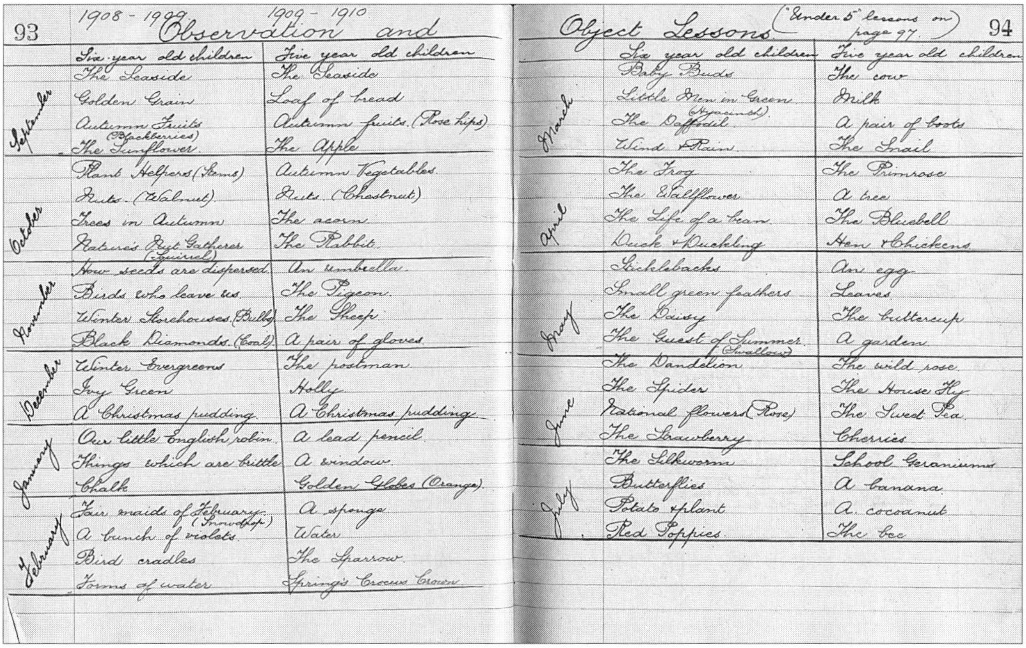

93 1908 - 1909. 1909 - 1910 Observation and Object Lessons ("Under 5" lessons on page 97.) 94

	Six year old children	Five year old children
September	The Seaside	The Seaside
	Golden Grain	Loaf of bread
	Autumn Fruits (Blackberries)	Autumn fruits. (Rose hips)
	The Sunflower.	The Apple
October	Plant Helpers (Stems)	Autumn Vegetables.
	Nuts. (Walnut)	Nuts. (Chestnut)
	Trees in Autumn	The acorn
	Nature's Nut Gatherer (Squirrel)	The Rabbit.
November	How seeds are dispersed	An umbrella.
	Birds who leave us.	The Pigeon.
	Winter Storehouses (Bulbs)	The Sheep.
	Black Diamonds. (Coal)	A pair of gloves.
December	Winter Evergreens	The postman
	Ivy Green	Holly
	A Christmas pudding.	A Christmas pudding.
January	Our little English robin	A lead pencil.
	Things which are brittle	A window.
	Chalk	Golden Globes (Orange).
February	Fair maids of February (Snowdrop)	A sponge
	A bunch of violets.	Water
	Bird cradles	The Sparrow.
	Forms of water	Spring's Crocus Crown

	Six year old children	Five year old children
March	Baby Buds	The cow
	Little Men in Green	Milk
	The Daffodil (Hyacinth)	A pair of boots
	Wind & Rain.	The Snail
April	The Frog	The Primrose
	The Wallflower	A tree
	The Life of a bean	The Bluebell
	Duck & Duckling	Hen & Chickens
May	Sticklebacks	An egg
	Small green feathers	Leaves
	The Daisy	The buttercup
	The Guest of Summer (Swallow)	A garden
June	The Dandelion	The wild rose
	The Spider	The House Fly
	National flowers (Rose)	The Sweet Pea.
	The Strawberry	Cherries
July	The Silkworm	School Geraniums
	Butterflies	A banana
	Potato & plant	A cocoanut
	Red Poppies	The bee

18 *School log books were introduced in 1862 as part of a move to promote efficiency, economy and accountability in elementary education, known as the 'Revised Code'. They provide an unrivalled account of life inside – and often outside – the school. The pages illustrated show the lessons taught in 1908-10.* (Hertfordshire Archives and Local Studies, HEd1/96/4.)

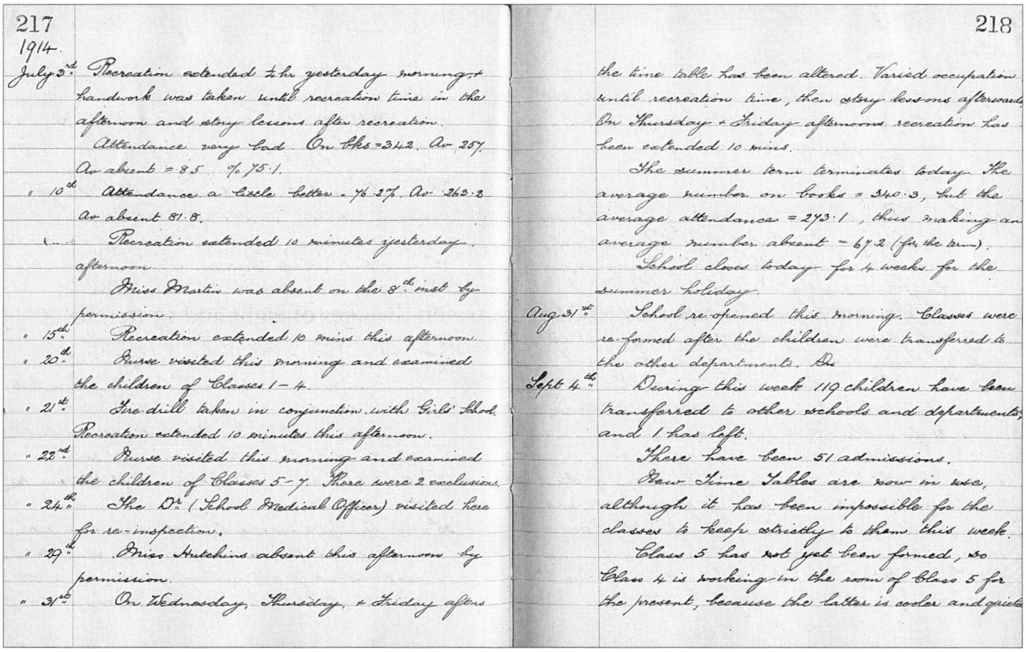

217
1914.

July 3rd. Recreation extended ¼ hr yesterday morning, & handwork was taken until recreation time in the afternoon and story lessons after recreation.
Attendance very bad. On bks = 342. Av. 257. Av absent = 85. % 75·1.

" 10th. Attendance a little better. 76·2%. Av. 263·2 Av absent 81·8.

" Recreation extended 10 minutes yesterday afternoon.
Miss Martin was absent on the 8th inst by permission.

" 15th. Recreation extended 10 mins this afternoon.

" 20th. Nurse visited this morning and examined the children of Classes 1 – 4.

" 21st. Fire-drill taken in conjunction with Girls' School. Recreation extended 10 minutes this afternoon.

" 22nd. Nurse visited this morning and examined the children of Classes 5 – 7. There were 2 exclusions.

" 24th. The Dr. (School Medical Officer) visited here for re-inspection.

" 29th. Miss Hutchins absent this afternoon by permission.

" 31st. On Wednesday, Thursday & Friday afternoons

218

the time table has been altered. Varied occupation until recreation time, then story lessons afterwards. On Thursday & Friday afternoons recreation has been extended 10 mins.
The summer term terminates today. The average number on books = 340·3, but the average attendance = 273·1, thus making an average number absent = 67·2 (for the term).
School closes today for 4 weeks for the summer holiday.

Aug 31st. School re-opened this morning. Classes were re-formed after the children were transferred to the other departments. &c

Sept 4th. During this week 119 children have been transferred to other schools and departments, and 1 has left.
There have been 51 admissions.
New Time Tables are now in use, although it has been impossible for the classes to keep strictly to them this week.
Class 5 has not yet been formed, so Class 4 is working in the room of Class 5 for the present, because the latter is cooler and quieter.

wish to follow that vocation. Oxford was the earliest university in the country, dating from the 12th century, and although Cambridge began in the following century it did not rival Oxford for another 200 years. The next four universities were all in Scotland: St Andrews (1410), Glasgow (1451), Aberdeen (1494) and Edinburgh (1582); Trinity College Dublin dates from 1591. Students attending these universities are listed in the various alumni volumes. There was a considerable gap before any further universities were created, London dating from 1826 and Durham from 1837. During the late 17th and 18th centuries, however, a broader education was available at some of the dissenting academies, especially Northampton and Warrington. Many more universities were created in the 20th century, including the Open University for those studying at home, which awarded its first degrees in 1973. The older universities have a dedicated archive facility for their own records, usually part of the library, and others have specialised in particular subject areas, as indicated elsewhere. Most newer universities retain their own records in the originating departments or in the university library. The 1944 Education Act gave LEAs responsibility for further education; they took over existing provision and built further education colleges specialising in technology, commerce and art; they also assumed responsibility for teacher training colleges. The first polytechnics were created in 1969 and played a significant part in the expansion of higher education. They achieved university status in 1992.

Many union workhouses, established after the 1834 Poor Law Amendment Act, provided a basic education and industrial training for the children in their care. They were required to provide at least three hours a day of schooling for workhouse children, and to appoint a schoolmaster and/or schoolmistress. The children were taught 'reading, writing, arithmetic, and the principles of the Christian Religion, and such other instruction as may fit them for service, and train them to habits of usefulness, industry and virtue'. Most workhouses had their own school rooms or school blocks, some of them quite substantial; Boards of Guardians were, however, sometimes reluctant to spend money on even the most basic equipment such as writing slates. Occasionally, it was even questioned if pauper children needed to be taught basic literacy, but the 1844 Parish Apprentices Act required that 'pauper apprentices be able to read and write their own names unaided'. The quality of the education provided in workhouse classrooms varied considerably, but in some cases was probably better than was available in other types of school. Much material will be found in the poor law union records held at CROs. Records of district schools (mainly London) are in MH 27. Correspondence about workhouse schools run by individual unions will be found in the union and assistant commissioners and inspectors correspondence in MH 12 and MH 32. The later records relating to inspection of the educational and industrial work of these schools are in ED 132 and on local authority education of 'poor law' children from 1929 in ED 95.

Industrial schools had two main objects, to instil in the children the habit of working and to develop the latent potential of the destitute child. One of the earliest attempts to start an Industrial Feeding School, as they were first called, was in Aberdeen in 1846. They were intended to help those children who were destitute but who had not as yet committed any serious crime; the idea was to remove children from bad influences, give them an education and teach them a trade. It was felt that, although the ragged schools were fulfilling a need, what they provided did not go far enough and the children needed to be removed from the environment in which they had been living. Depending on the circumstances, the child either attended the school daily or was able to live in. The timetable was quite a strict one with regimented times for getting up and going to bed. During the day there were set times for schooling, learning trades, housework, religion in the form of family worship, meal times, and there was also a short time for play three times a day. The boys learned trades such as gardening, tailoring and shoemaking; the girls learned knitting, sewing, housework and washing.

At first the industrial schools were run on a voluntary basis. The 1857 Industrial Schools Act gave magistrates the power to sentence children between the ages of seven and 14 years old to a spell in one of these institutions and dealt with those children who were brought before the courts for vagrancy. A further Act in 1861 differentiated between four categories of children. Parents were supposed to contribute to the cost of keeping a child in an industrial school, but this often proved impossible to collect because most of the children were homeless, and the money had to be found from government sources. From 1870 the schools became the responsibility of the Committee on Education. Researchers will find various records at CROs as well as at TNA in MH 102, ED 45 and scattered across several ED series (e.g. ED 30).

In the 19th century the working classes sought self-improvement. The best known organisation was the Mechanics' Institute; the first one was established in Chester in 1810 and by 1826 there were over a hundred others. The movement was particularly important in Lancashire and the West Riding of Yorkshire, which between them contained 27 per cent of all the British institutes. They were the first important national movement in adult education, which in the 19th century included elementary education for those who had had little or no opportunity to study as children. The University extension movement began in 1867 and the Workers' Education Association in 1903; both of these are still in existence although very much changed from their origins. The records of Mechanics' Institutes may include minutes, accounts, reports, etc. and may have been deposited in the local record office; their activities were often reported in local newspapers.

The report from the Select Committee on public libraries was charged with investigating the best means of extending the establishment of free libraries, especially in large towns. It noted the recent and successful policy of allowing public access to institutions such as the British Museum and National Gallery, and included details of the Yorkshire Union of Mechanics' Institutes and other libraries of mechanics' institutes.[14] The Royal Society for the Encouragement of Arts, Manufactures and Commerce was founded in 1754 and its catalogue can be viewed online. There were many other societies involved with technical education and the relevant local library or record office will have more details. The National Association for the Promotion of Technical and Secondary Education's annual reports, from 1888 (with gaps) have been microfilmed and there is further material in the British Library; it had local branches and there may be information in local newspapers.

8

POVERTY

This is one of the subjects that touches on most local historical research and which has generated a lot of interesting records. However, as is often the case, appropriate record survival is uneven. The history of the treatment of poverty in England and Wales can be divided into four periods: before the Old Poor Law (pre 1597-1601); the Old Poor Law (to 1834); the New Poor Law (to 1930); and the modern welfare state. The picture in Scotland is significantly different and complicates any straightforward discussion of the law and records relating to relief. Scotland is therefore dealt with separately below.

In the Middle Ages relief of the poor was legally the responsibility of the manor but was generally accepted by the church; monasteries were especially important as it was seen as part of the religious life to succour the poor and suffering. In addition to the church, gilds and municipal corporations also helped the poor, for example by endowing hospitals. However, because funds were often insufficient many poor people were reduced to begging and the tendency to slip from being a pauper to a vagrant was quite common, so that poverty became inextricably linked with law and order; the government's main concern was to maintain the peace. The term 'social control' beloved of the Victorians has a much older pedigree. An Act of 1399 forbade vagrancy, and up to the reign of Henry VIII the statute book abounded in laws of ever-increasing severity against vagrants.

The earliest law for the relief of the poor was passed in 1531 and distinguished between those found begging and capable of work, and those unable to work who were given licences to beg by magistrates. 1563 saw the compulsory payment of poor rates by householders and an Act of 1572 created the office of overseer of the poor. In the 16th century poverty took new forms and appeared on a much greater scale than before; the problems were exacerbated by the Dissolution of the Monasteries in the 1530s, thus depriving the poor of a traditional source of help. In the last quarter of the century the social condition of the labouring poor changed considerably for the worse; there was dearth and high prices, leading to a starvation crisis in the late 1580s and 1590s which forced the government to take action as once again vagrancy and petty crime increased.

Information for this period will be limited (in comparison with later periods) but there may be evidence in manorial, borough and quarter sessions court records, as well as in early parish vestry accounts, accounts of churches and religious houses and the records of the dissolved monasteries. There will be various references to the poor, instances of poverty and provisions for relief in the records of Star Chamber, Chancery, State Papers Domestic and the special collections (SC) record series at TNA. Finding material will be problematic but as can be seen from the examples below there is much available:

> [1262]: SC 7/33/20: Order to the abbot and convent of the Holy Cross of Waltham to supply the necessaries of life in their house so long as he shall live, to Ambrose de Ponte Tegule, a poor clerk, who on a journey to the apostolic see has been robbed and grievously wounded, provided he reside in person and serve the monastery according to his power;
>
> [1381-1382]: SC 8/19/917: The community of Rye state that their town has been captured several times, and that they have rebuilt their walls on the land side, but that because of their poverty they can do no more, and fear the vulnerability of the town from the sea, especially as last time the town was captured several people were hung and drawn when the invaders returned to France, for not holding it. They request that the excesses and fines levied on victuallers, craftsmen and labourers before the Justices of the Peace in Sussex, except for the justices' wages, might for the next three years be granted for the repair of the walls;
>
> 1432: SC 8/26/1255: Petitioners requesting that the king confirm all and singular the letters, licences, writings, gifts concerning the foundation of a college of five chaplains celebrating divine mass daily for the soul of Whittington and others, and of an alms house next to the church for 13 paupers;
>
> [1548-1553]: Edward VI: STAC 2/18/51: Thomas Key, master of the hospital of Ewelme, defendant, and Robert Noyse, Henry Wale, John Grace, and John Adeane: regarding non-payment of rent due for relief of the poor in the hospital (Oxfordshire);
>
> [1327-1377]: 5 Edward III. C 143/217/8: Henry de Gower, bishop of St David's, to grant a messuage, land, and mills in Gower and the advowson of the church of St Mary, Swansea, to certain chaplains for saying mass and for relief of the poor, retaining messuages and land, two weirs, and a ferry over the water of Tawe. Glamorgan;
>
> 1466-7. E 40/5971: Will of Thomas Gigges of Brunham St Clements ... leaves legacies in money to the church of St Clement where he is to be buried, to the poor house in the parish of St Clement and St Andrew, Brunham ... etc.

A series of Acts of Parliament between 1597 and 1601[1] was a response to the economic and social problems of the late 16th century. They established the parish as the unit of administration and introduced compulsory, rate-financed poor relief. They also provided for the right of the parish vestry (through the office of the overseer of the poor) to raise the rate, decide on any scheme of running the relief system and make various disbursements of money according to its own scheme. The result was a highly discretionary and varied 'national system' of relief. A distinction was made between the deserving and the undeserving poor; the poor law was seen as a safety net to catch those who were not liable to conviction as vagrants but for whom the available charitable resources were inadequate. It would be a mistake to think that the late Elizabethan legislation brought a regular response from the localities. Where there was no recognition of poverty requiring the provisions of the Acts many parishes simply ignored them. It was not until 1660 that a third of the parishes had any regular experience of the Acts' provisions. At the end of the 17th century most English parishes, and the end of the 18th century most Welsh parishes, moved to the more universal position of applying the Old Poor Law.[2]

An assumption that each parish would relieve its own poor was made in the Elizabethan Acts. However, as the Old Poor Law was more regularly adopted in England by the middle of the 17th century, further legislation was needed to make it more explicit; this was the 1662 Act of Settlement.[3] It was enacted under pressure from parishes needing stronger powers to rid themselves of unwanted immigrants who would become a drain on the poor rates. The Act introduced bonds for the security of the parish and temporary settlement certificates for migrant workers. It made life difficult for the working poor as any strangers could be removed forthwith unless they rented a tenement of £10 or found security to discharge the parish of all costs. There were a number of ways of gaining a settlement and individuals could have more than one during their lifetime. The Act was criticised for hindering mobility of labour and preventing the unemployed from finding work, so an Act of 1697 stated that the poor could enter any parish provided they had a settlement certificate; these documents usually constitute the most numerous of all poor law documents and certified that the person, and dependents if appropriate, had a legal settlement in the parish of origin, and that the issuing parish would take them back if necessary and provide poor relief. Alternatively, the issuing parish would undertake to pay for the relief in the 'new' parish, thus relieving the ratepayers there of any improper expenses. Settlement disputes were common as parishes were unwilling to bear the financial weight of dealing with paupers from other parishes. Settlement examinations by magistrates were designed to find the true place of settlement of individuals. Applicants were questioned about their life-histories and the examinations may therefore provide details of where they had lived, the type of work they were employed in, as well as information on their family circumstances. These certificates and examinations, where they survive, can now be found with other vestry records in the appropriate CRO under the relevant parish.[4]

A number of towns gained a local Act, beginning with Bristol in 1696, which gave them greater autonomy in poor law administration and allowed several parishes within the town to join together, pool resources and benefit from any resulting economies of scale. The 1722 Workhouse Act[5] made powers for the establishment of workhouses generally available and Gilbert's Act of 1782[6] enabled parishes to unite for the purpose. *An Account of Several Work-houses for Employing and Maintaining the Poor*, published anonymously by SPCK, can be used as an early directory of parish workhouses in England. Workhouses were

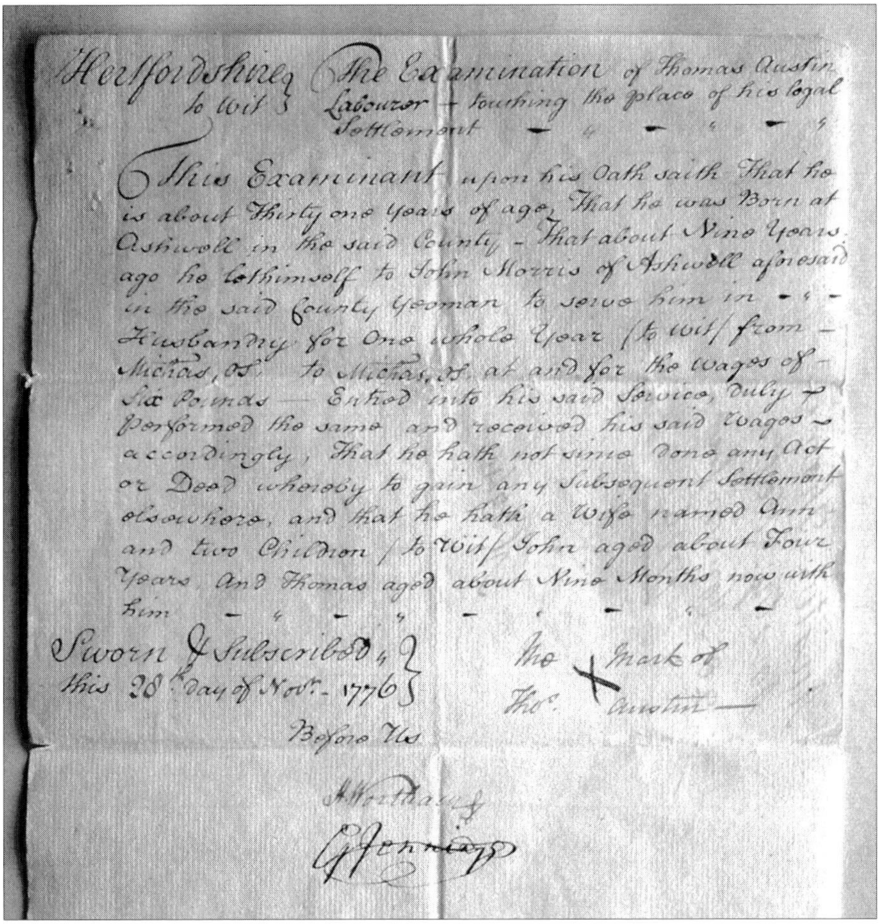

Hertfordshire to Wit } The Examination of Thomas Austin Labourer touching the place of his legal Settlement

This Examinant upon his Oath saith That he is about Thirty one Years of age, That he was Born at Ashwell in the said County – That about Nine Years ago he let himself to John Morris of Ashwell aforesaid in the said County Yeoman to serve him in Husbandry for One whole Year (to wit) from Michas, &c to Michas, &c at and for the Wages of Six Pounds — Entred into his said Service, duly & performed the same and received his said Wages accordingly, That he hath not since done any Act or Deed whereby to gain any Subsequent Settlement elsewhere, and that he hath a Wife named Ann and two Children (to wit) John aged about Four Years and Thomas aged about Nine Months now with him

Sworn & Subscribed this 28th day of Novr. 1776 } the X mark of Thos. Austin

Before Us

[illegible]

G Jennings

19 *The Old Poor Law generated some fascinating documents, none more so than the settlement examination. It was a 'potted biography', drawn up to determine an individual's place of settlement and where he/she was entitled to poor relief. Thomas Austin's examination, taken in 1776, gives brief details of his work and family; what it does not reveal is why the document is found in the Barkway records.* (Hertfordshire Archives and Local Studies D/P 13 13/3.)

supposed to offer economy, efficiency and deterrence but their reputation was poor; they were seen as bleak and austere, and a place of last resort. Joan Kent and Steve King state as much in their work on poor relief in Huntingdonshire and Staffordshire when referring to the Great Staughton workhouse (which was in place by the late 1730s), reflecting 'not only a desire to make the poor more productive, but also to deter them from seeking relief'. Drawing on court records, overseers' accounts and pauper examinations they use several sets of overseers' accounts to establish graphs showing peaks of expenditure, and conclude that the establishment of local workhouses restricted opportunities to procure additional income to care for family members or neighbours.[7] Nationally, in many instances, workhouses achieved significant but short-term economic successes.

From about the middle of the 18th century the poor law was the subject of much discussion and an endless stream of pamphlets on the subject was published. Many people believed that the poor ought to be forced to make provision for themselves but a range of abuses made the system unacceptably harsh in implementation by the middle of the century; in the late 18th and early 19th centuries there was a series of parliamentary investigations on various aspects of poor relief and vagrancy, which brought home the increasing cost of the system.[8] Poor law litigation was especially expensive: between 1776 and 1815 its annual cost rose from £35,000 per year to £287,000, and over half the business at quarter sessions could be taken up with poor law matters, especially illegal removals.[9] A series of statutes in the 1780s and 1790s were designed to make the poor law more humane. The final crisis of the Old Poor Law came in the traditional agricultural sector; a run of poor harvests saw extensive distress and increased published interest in the state of the poor.[10] Schemes such as Speenhamland and the roundsman system dealt with temporary problems but social tension heightened and poor law issues were often the flashpoint.[11] Speenhamland was the fixing of poor relief scales to the price of bread. The roundsman system and labour rate could take differing forms of sending labourers 'round' the employers of the parish: payment of labour by the parish through a contract with the employing farmer for work at an agreed price, payment by both the parish and the farmer via an agreed scale, or an auction of unemployed labour to the highest bidder.

For this period, most of the relevant records will be found with other parish records in CROs and other local record offices, or occasionally libraries. As well as settlement certificates and examinations the available sources can be divided into a number of categories. The key documents are overseers' accounts, which list payments to paupers, income from the poor rates, and so on; payments to the poor were often monetary ones, but sometimes there would be payment in kind, such as rent, medical and nursing expenses, food, clothing, fuel, etc. Other documents relating to settlement include removal orders and documents relating to settlement appeals. Because of its role in putting children out as apprentices, there may be apprenticeship indentures and registers. The problem of illegitimate, orphaned or abandoned children could generate bastardy bonds, filiation orders, and bastardy examinations. Other items which may have been kept include lists of clothing, details of the purchase of a building for a workhouse, workhouse agreements, accounts, menus and inventories, examinations of and warrants to arrest rogues and vagabonds, and various other correspondence. Vestry minutes can be a superb source for references to the poor law, poverty and pauperism, but there is no consistency. Some vestry minutes can go for years simply listing the formal elections or appointments of parish officers with reference to only one or two other events per year while others will give a detailed and fascinating insight into the workings of a parish dominated by poor relief matters.[12]

Because of the role played by the court of quarter sessions, there is much information contained in rolls, minute books and order books. For example, the Cheshire Quarter Sessions records include an especially interesting examination of a vagabond, Joseph Rooke, in 1743:

> This Examinant [Rooke] saith that he was born in the City of New York in America, and when he was about the age of twenty two years he was pressed on board the Britania Man of War and stayed on board about five months ... and stay'd in that ship [the 'Grafton'] until she was taken prisoner by the French, and after he got into England from France ... in which ship this examinant lost his left arm by a cannon ball, after which he was admitted a petitioner from the Chest at Chatham ... [13]

Petitions from paupers appear regularly and the following two examples from the Leicester records illustrate their use for local historians. Elizabeth Newton – whose husband had 'gone for a souldier' – had six small children and the family was in 'Extreame great wants', needing fuel and clothing. She had been refused relief by the overseers and asked for temporary help until her husband returned. John Heptonstall had been imprisoned (presumably for debt) and his family were in an extremely distressed condition; he asked for financial help so 'that I might gaine my Dischairge throwgh the Assistance of allmigtie god I qeston nott butt to Ease the parish boath of the Chairge of my selfe and famly ...'[14] There is also significant correspondence on poverty, poor relief and related matters scattered across the State Papers Domestic and in Home Office correspondence.[15]

The economic distress and increased costs at the end of the French Wars led to several Select Committee reports[16] and the Board of Agriculture's *The Agricultural State of the Kingdom*, 1816,[17] but no real action. The large increases in poor rates in the early 19th century brought much unease and a huge outbreak of suggested changes and pamphleteering; many of these contemporary pamphlets are listed in the bibliography of J.R. Poynter's *Society and Pauperism*.[18] In an attempt to reduce rates many parishes moved to a system of select vestries. In 1818 and 1819 the Act for the Regulation of Parish Vestries and the Act to Amend the Law for the Relief of the Poor (sometimes referred to as the Select Vestries Acts or the Sturges-Bourne Acts) were passed respectively. The former Act established a plural voting system dictated by the rateable value of property; someone owning property worth £50 had one vote and a further vote for every further £25 worth, up to a maximum of six. The latter Act added resident clergymen as ex-officio members of the vestry as well as providing for the employment of salaried overseers, better-kept accounting and either the building or enlargement of workhouses. Further power was given to ratepayers, as under the Act the agreement of two magistrates, rather than one (as previously), was needed to order the vestry to give poor relief. This was to disrupt the perceived problem of the 'generous-minded' magistrate insisting on too-generous assistance. The post-war period also witnessed outbreaks of rioting in 1816 and 1822, and throughout the south and east of the country in 1830 – the 'Captain Swing' riots (see chapter 11);[19] it was these riots that finally precipitated radical change.

In 1832 the government set up a Royal Commission to investigate the poor law system thoroughly.[20] Detailed questionnaires were sent out to a number of parishes, and replies received from just over 10 per cent of the 15,000 parishes in England and Wales, representing about 20 per cent

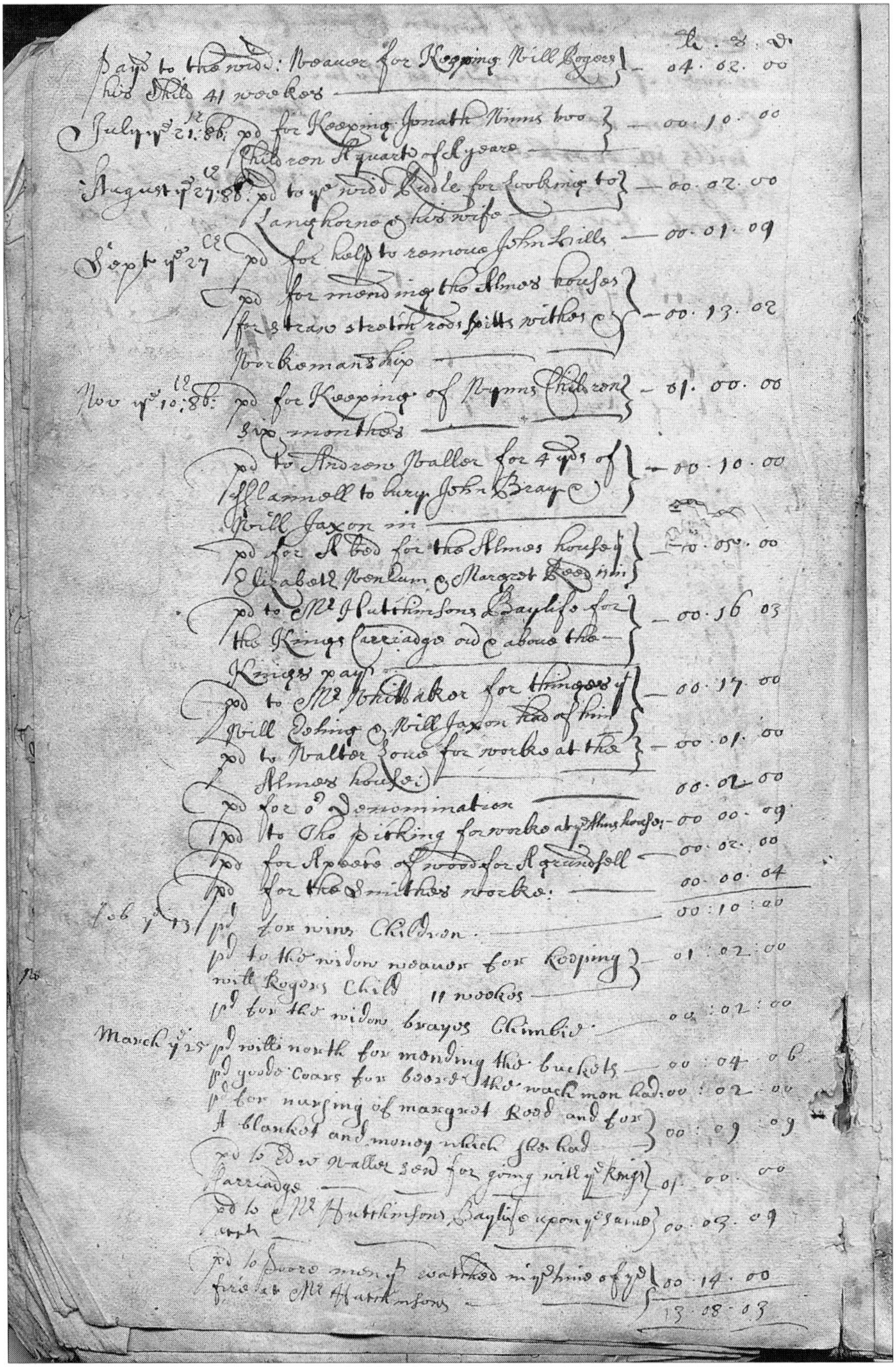

		li. s. d.
	Payd to the widd: Weaver for Keeping Will Rogers his Child 41 weekes	04. 02. 00
July ye 21.86:	pd for Keeping Jonath Nimms two Children A quarter of A yeare	00. 10. 00
August ye 27.86:	pd to ye widd Biddle for looking to Langhorne & his wife	00. 02. 00
Sept ye 27	pd for help to remove John Hills	00. 01. 09
	pd for mending the Almes houses for straw stealth rods spitts withes & workemanship	00. 13. 02
Nov ye 10.86:	pd for Keeping of Nymns Children six monthes	01. 00. 00
	pd to Andrew Waller for 4 yds of fflannell to bury John Bray & Will Jaxon in	00. 10. 00
	pd for A bed for the Almes houses Elizabeth Wonlam & Margret Reed in	00. 05. 00
	pd to Mr Hutchinsons Baylife for the Kings Carriadge over & above the Kings pay	00. 16. 03
	pd to Mr Whittaker for things y Will Eeling & Will Jaxon had of him	00. 17. 00
	pd to Walter Lowe for worke at the Almes house	00. 01. 00
	pd for or Denomination	00. 02. 00
	pd to Tho Pitking for worke at ye Alms house	00. 00. 09
	pd for A peece of wood for A grundsell	00. 02. 00
	pd for the Smithes worke	00. 00. 04
Feb ye 13	pd for nine Children	00 : 10 : 00
	pd to the widow weaver for keeping will Rogers Child 11 weekes	01 : 02 : 00
	pd for the widow brayes Chimbly	00 : 02 : 00
March ye 25	pd will north for mending the buckets	00 : 04 : 06
	pd goode Coars for board the watch man had	00 : 02 : 00
	pd for nursing of margret Reed and for A blanket and money which she had	00 : 09 : 09
	pd to Edw Waller sen for going with ye Kings Carriage	01. 00. 00
	pd to Mr Hutchinsons Baylife upon ye same acct	00. 03. 09
	pd to poore men yt watched ny thing of ye fire at Mr Hutchinsons	00. 14. 00
		13. 08. 03

20 *Overseers of the poor (usually two) were created by an Act of 1572. Their task was a thankless one as the income from the poor rates was often inadequate to help all those in need. The entries for Ashwell in 1686-7 are fairly typical of the cases dealt with by the overseers.* (Hertfordshire Archives and Local Studies D/P7 12/1.)

of the population. In addition assistant commissioners visited parishes to find out the nature and extent of poor law administration. The published report ran to 15 folio volumes and was largely the work of two men, Nassau Senior and Edwin Chadwick; despite reservations about its recommendations, the report is one of the most important social documents of the 19th century.

The 1834 Poor Law Amendment Act[21] marked radical new changes in its unionisation of parishes and particularly its central direction. Three Poor Law Commissioners were appointed and the country was divided into unions of parishes; each parish elected one or more guardians of the poor who met weekly or fortnightly to conduct business. The union boundaries were used later for civil registration and for the decennial census; each union was centred on a market town or some other centre, and many crossed county boundaries. The power of the Commissioners was not so great as it appeared and a determined board could ignore some of their orders and those of the Assistant Commissioners, who acted as the intermediary between the Commissioners and local boards of guardians.[22] The many local studies on the operation of the New Poor Law in various parts of the country have demonstrated that many boards did not adhere to the provisions of the Act; the best example is that outdoor relief to the able-bodied continued in many unions as it was cheaper than indoor relief and preferred by the poor and by many guardians.

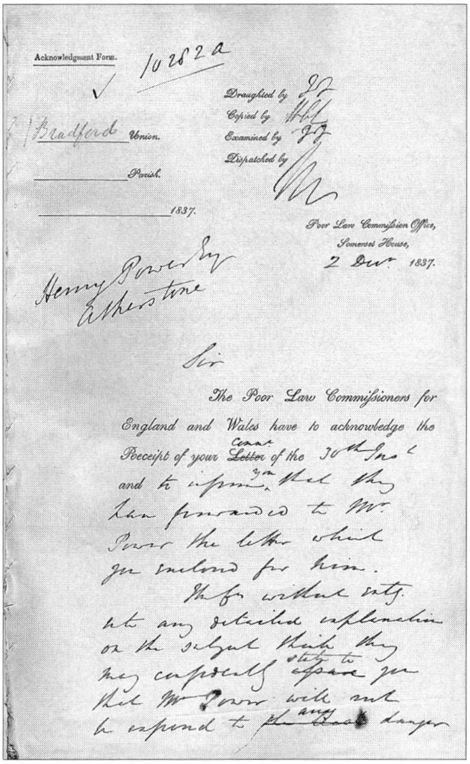
Acknowledgment Form.
10282a
Bradford Union.
Parish.
1837.
Draughted by
Copied by
Examined by
Dispatched by
Poor Law Commission Office,
Somerset House,
2 Dec 1837.
Henry Power Esq
Atherstone
Sir
The Poor Law Commissioners for England and Wales have to acknowledge the Receipt of your Letter of the 30th Inst and to inform you that they have forwarded to Mr Power the letter which you enclosed for him.

21 *Example of the 'Acknowledgement Forms' used by the Poor Law Commission.* (TNA, MH12/14720, Bradford Poor Law Union Correspondence 1834-9, 2 December 1837.)

The twin principles of the New Poor Law were the 'workhouse test' and 'less eligibility'. It was argued that if people were in dire straits they would accept the offer of the workhouse but, if they refused it, this would signify that they did not in fact need relief. The stigma of the workhouse was deliberately fostered as, in physical terms, the workhouse inmate could be better off than the independent worker. Families were separated on entry, made to observe rules and to work for the Union. In times of acute distress, when the workhouse was inadequate for all those needing relief, an outdoor labour test could be established, such as breaking stones for roads. The new legislation had been concerned primarily with reducing pauperism in the rural south and was quite well received there by ratepayers but, as unionisation moved northwards, opposition increased, especially in towns which had run efficient systems under the Old Poor Law. There are examples of Assistant Commissioners and buildings being attacked during the initial implementation of the Act.[23] This opposition was widely reported in the press, not only in local newspapers but in *The Times* and the newly emerging radical press, such as the *Northern Liberator* and the *Northern Star*. Further material on opposition will be found in the early records of the union itself in county and borough record offices. Early correspondence between individual poor law unions and the Poor Law Commission (*c.*1834-1840) will also contain much on opposition, riots and demonstrations against the implementation of the Act where these events occurred. This material is held at TNA in record series MH 12 and can be supplemented by the Assistant Commissioners' correspondence in MH 32. Further material, mainly for the northern counties, is to be found in the general Home Office correspondence for the mid-1830s,[24] as well as in the Assistant Commissioners' papers in HO 73/51-56 and scattered across some of the Constabulary Force papers in HO 73/2-9.

The Poor Law Commission was replaced in 1847 by the Poor Law Board; the Local Government Board took over its responsibilities in 1871 and the Ministry of Health from 1919. Over time poor law unions were given additional duties, such as the vaccination of children against smallpox and became the registration district for births, marriages and deaths. Many features of the Old Poor Law continued under the new, notably the whole system of settlement and removal, apprenticeship and parish rating; it was not until 1865 that 'union chargeability' was introduced and until then many poorer parishes continued to have problems raising their share of the funds required to administer the union and provide for its poor. Studies of the New Poor Law have investigated several areas of its workings and illustrate the wide range of materials historians have been using. Gary Howells introduced new data from the MH 12 correspondence to examine the emigration of over 3,000 Norfolk inhabitants to North America in 1836.[25] Elizabeth Hurren supplemented MH 12 material with guardians' minute books, parochial lists and petty sessions in CROs, British Library Althorp MS, Parliamentary Papers and local newspapers to demonstrate the crusade against continuing out-relief in the 1870s, which angered magistrates, farmers and labourers.[26] Spencer Thomas used the archives of the powerful landowners, the Wyndhams, in his research on paternalism at Petworth.[27]

The New Poor Law continued until 1930, after which there was a curious hybrid period when its responsibilities were transferred to local authorities which set up Public Assistance Committees. The New Poor Law changed considerably from 1834 to the late 1920s, because of particular pressures or changes in public opinion. Unions were often criticised either publicly or privately by central authority as Dick Hunter found in his investigation into the Hackney guardians of the 1890s.[28] The treatment of the elderly, for example, improved as a result of the 1895 *Royal Commission on the Aged Poor* and the *Select Committee on the Aged Deserving Poor* four years later.[29] Similarly attempts were made to give children a better start in life in cottages and scattered homes, which were meant to be more like 'normal' homes than a workhouse. At the end of the 19th century there was again concern in some quarters about the laxness of the poor law and a Royal Commission was set up in 1905, whose remit included Scotland and Ireland. It took over three years to report and its evidence filled 47 folio volumes. When it reported in February 1909 its members were divided and four of them (including Beatrice Webb) produced a minority report.[30] Ironically (and of course tragically) the First World War proved to be an effective cure for pauperism, as unemployment fell and the numbers requiring relief dropped. The figures rose again in the 1920s and the poor law was affected by the General Strike of 1926 and the protracted coal strike which followed (see chapter 11).

Poor law unions employed an army of staff, such as clerks, workhouse masters and matrons, teachers, doctors, nurses, cooks, bakers, relieving officers, and so on; the quality of staff was frequently considered to be low as poor law jobs were not generally well regarded. The clerk was often a local solicitor and his workload grew over time; it has been estimated that he had to keep over one hundred different types of record. A classification drawn up many years ago by the Somerset Record Office identified over two hundred sets of records.

For the researcher the various reports of parliamentary committees are supplemented by the annual reports of the Poor Law Commission (and its successors). Because the system was organised nationally there are extensive and informative records in TNA. The 16,741 volumes of correspondence between the poor law unions and the central authority in London (Poor Law Commission, 1834-1847; Poor Law Board, 1847-1871 and Local Government Board, 1871-1919) must surely be considered one of the jewels of local and social history resources.[31] These records, held in MH 12, are often overlooked by local historians because of the size of the archive and its poor listing (it is organised alphabetically by county and then by union); nevertheless no local study can neglect it.[32] The MH 12 correspondence for Southwell and (the early years for) Manchester is now being drafted for the electronic catalogue; the Southwell material by the Southwell Workhouse Research Group and the Manchester material by TNA staff. In addition the Assistant Commissioners' correspondence in MH 32 provides much local detail usually on a regional basis, as much of the material relates to more than one union. Poor Law Union plans (from 1861) are in MH 14, expenditure summaries in MH 34 and Poor Law Authorities files in MH 68. Staff registers can be found in MH 9 for 1837 to 1921 and these can often be supplemented with references to staff in MH 12, MH 32 and local materials (as described below).

Potentially there is just as much material kept locally but the perennial problem of survival crops up again. Many unions have a full set of minute books, but even these may not have survived, as in Nottingham for example; often unions set up sub-committees, which have their own sets of minutes. Various types of accounts will probably have been retained but their value is limited. Three sets of records that are priceless where they exist are, sadly, all too rare: letter books give an incredible amount of valuable detail unavailable in other series but they were often weeded as modern departmental records in the 20th century; workhouse admission and discharge registers give a lot of personal details on those admitted, but few unions have a complete series

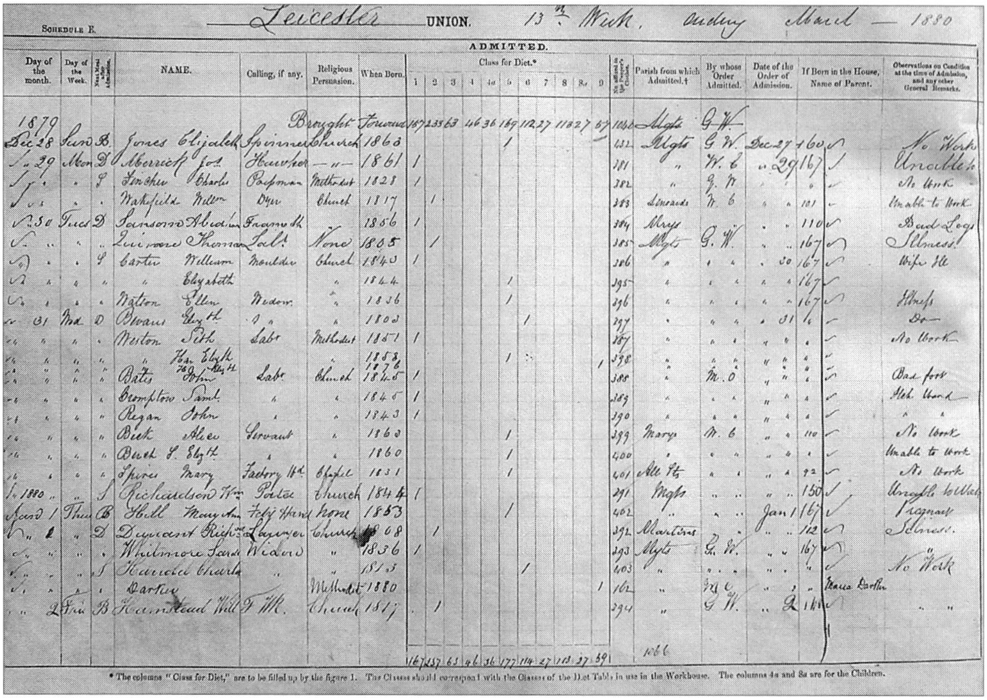

SCHEDULE E. Leicester UNION. 13th Week, ending March — 1880

ADMITTED.

Day of the month	Day of the Week	Meal	NAME	Calling, if any	Religious Persuasion	When Born	No.	Parish from which Admitted	By whose Order Admitted	Date of the Order of Admission	Observations on Condition at the time of Admission, and any other General Remarks
1879					Brought	Forward	1060	Mgts	G. W.		
Dec 28	Sun	B	Jones Elizabeth	Spinner	Church	1863	432	Mgts	G. W.	Dec 27	
29	Mon	D	Merrick Jos.	Hawker	— " —	1861	381	"	W. C.	29	No Work Unable to
		S	Fincher Charles	Packman	Methodist	1828	382	"	G. W.		No Work
			Wakefield William	Dyer	Church	1817	383	Leonards	W. C.		Unable to Work
30	Tues	D	Sansom Abidan	Framesmith		1856	384	Marys			Bad Legs
			Quinmore Thomas	Labt.	None	1805	385	Mgts	G. W.		Illness
		S	Carter William	Moulder	Church	1840	386			30	Wife Ill
			" Elizabeth		"	1844	395				
			Watson Ellen	Widow	"	1836	396				Illness
31	Wed	D	Bevans Elizth		"	1803	397			31	Do
			Weston Seth	Labr	Methodist	1851	387				No Work
			" Han Elizth / Eliz H		"	1858 / 1876	398				
			Bates John	Labr	Church	1845	388		M. O.		Bad foot
			Crompton Saml.	"	"	1845	389				Sick. Hand
			Regan John	"	"	1843	390				
			Beck Alice	Servant	"	1863	399	Marys	W. C.		No Work
			Beck S. Elizth	"	"	1860	400				Unable to Work
			Spires Mary	Factory Hd	Chapel	1831	401	All Sts			No Work
1880		S	Richardson Wm	Potter	Church	1844	291	Mgts			Unable to Walk
Jan 1	Thur	B	Hill Mary Ann	Fcty Hand	None	1853	402			Jan 1	Pregnant
1		D	Durrant Richd	Lawyer	Church	1808	392	Martins			Illness
			Whitmore Sarah	Widow	"	1836	393	Mgts	G. W.		
		S	Harrild Charles		"	1813	403				No Work
			Darker		Methodist	1880	162		M. O.		Maria Darker (parent)
2	Fri	B	Hamstead Will F. M.		Church	1817	294		G. W.	2	
							1066				

* The columns "Class for Diet," are to be filled up by the figure 1. The Classes should correspond with the Classes of the Diet Table in use in the Workhouse. The columns 4a and 8a are for the Children.

22 *Workhouse admission and discharge registers are one of the most important series from the period of the New Poor Law but their survival rate is patchy. These pages from the Leicester union workhouse record the entry of Joseph Merrick, the 'Elephant Man', on 29 December 1879; the reason for his admittance, not surprisingly, was that he was unable to work.* (Record Office of Leicester and Rutland 26D68/987.)

or one that starts at the beginning of the union's life; master's report books are even rarer but are gems if they do exist.[33] Other registers include births and deaths, baths taken and alcohol consumed, to name just a few. Each union was required to send regular (often weekly) returns to the central authority, such as 'Form A' returns which gave details of the numbers in the workhouse, broken down into various categories.[34] Much of the surviving material tends to be for the later period.

A final note on workhouses for both the Old and New Poor Laws. There are some surviving workhouses such as the one just outside Stowmarket in Suffolk and the former Gressenhall House of Industry, dating from 1777, which is owned by Norfolk Museum Service. The National Trust took over the former Thurgarton Incorporation workhouse, built in 1824 at Southwell in Nottinghamshire, which became the workhouse of the Southwell Poor Law Union. It was purchased by the National Trust in 1997 and is now open to the public as a major heritage and educational venue and well worth a visit.[35] Because of the stigma of the New Poor Law many former workhouses have been demolished, but some survive as part of hospitals or used in other ways. The Thackray Medical Museum is housed in a former workhouse building adjacent to St James's hospital in Leeds, and former workhouse buildings in

Ripon house a display relating to the treatment of Yorkshire paupers. Elsewhere, former workhouses and other pauper institutions have been converted into luxury flats, at prices that their former inmates would never have imagined.[36] Union workhouses are instantly recognisable and are a popular subject for study.[37] On a wider scale many workhouses and their infirmaries became sites for National Heath Service hospitals and these modern sites still retain some sections of workhouse buildings even after substantial modernisation.[38]

The dissolution of the boards of guardians in 1930 did not solve the problems in the system and outwardly there was little change; although the workhouse test disappeared it was succeeded by the means test which carried the same emotive connotations. Many policy files relating to Public Assistance Committees can be found at TNA although record series MH 52, MH 57 and MH 61 will be of particular relevance for local historians. The files in MH 52 relate to public health and poor law services taken over by the Ministry of Health from the Local Government Board in 1920. They are particularly important for poor law services after 1929 and specifically in relation to the schemes for administering such services on their transfer from poor law authorities to local authorities. The MH 57 series contains general subject files relating to the administration of public assistance, including poor law relief and related matters, as well as the formulation and operation of the 1948 National Assistance Act. The subject matter is varied and includes correspondence and papers regarding poor law reform and transference of functions from poor law to local authorities. There are also details on the appropriation of poor law infirmaries for public health purposes, vagrancy and casual poor relief, outdoor relief to unemployed persons and strikers' families, as well as wartime distress and air-raid compensation. Files in MH 61 relate to the administration of the Special Areas Acts 1934 to 1937. Subjects include the definition of special areas, various boundary agreements, details of medical services and public health as well as work schemes and housing. Newspaper reports on various aspects of poverty are common; in particular there is a great deal of newspaper and other journalism on unemployment and poverty in the 1930s.[39] Local Public Assistance Committee minutes, relief order books, ledgers and correspondence have now been transferred to county and unitary record offices although there may be examples where they are still kept in former poor law buildings.

For TNA there are three volumes of *Records of Interest to Social Scientists* which provides an overview of the period 1919 to 1939, a detailed look at unemployment insurance records 1911 to 1939, and employment and unemployment between 1919 and 1939.[40] Although TNA may appear to be less useful for the local historian interested in poverty for this period, a brief glance at the *Social Scientists* volumes show this not to be the case; for example there is Home Office correspondence and Ministry of Health material on unemployment riots in Liverpool for 1921, Poplar councillors' imprisonment for 1921-23, circulars on hunger marchers for 1922-23, conditions at Westminster for the able-bodied after a 'strike' by inmates for 1934, administration of outdoor relief in Dorset for 1936-38 and unemployment in South Wales (reports on distress, conferences, examples of relief given and comparison with pre-war pauperism) for 1919-31.[41]

It took another war to change things and a determination to provide a better society. Sir William Beveridge's *Report on Social Insurance and the Allied Services* received an enthusiastic reception in 1942; he saw the state as a maintainer of full employment and provider of a free health service and family allowances. The big difference was that the new welfare state would be available to all, rather than just a service for the poor. The poor law was formally repealed in July 1948 but institutions and records can overlap. For example, the end of the poor law guardians saw the Valley workhouse of the Holyhead Poor Law Union become the Public Assistance Institution (PAI), Valley; in turn the PAI, Valley became the Valley Hospital in 1948 at the creation of the National Health Service. The records relating to the post-Second World War Welfare State are discussed in chapter 9.

It would be wrong to look at poor relief and poverty without providing a short survey on charity sources. Charities have a long history; a fair amount of work has already been done on individual charitable organisations, mainly based on their own accounts, minutes and other records deposited in CROs, in local studies libraries or still with the originating organisation. Some organisations were quite small concerns dealing with a few hundred pounds while others, such as the Peabody Trust in London, accrued gifts and legacies worth around £500,000.[42] Charitable bequests of money, lands or almshouses (or money and land to build them) were often made in wills to the parish officers for the upkeep of the poor, and these records formed part of the overall vestry records.[43] In addition many parishes would initiate subscriptions at times of particular hardship such as the winter of 1800. These types of charitable subscriptions were 'one-offs' and discontinued once the weather, employment and prices improved. Many enclosure Acts refer to leaving land to the poor, but it was usually rented to a local farmer or tradesman and the money used towards poor relief, thus contributing to keeping the rates down rather than providing additional funds towards relief.

Arguably the largest charity devoted to the relief of poverty was the Charity Organisation Society (COS), founded in London in 1869 with the express aim to discriminate between the deserving and undeserving poor, 'to distinguish the proper objects for the exercise of their benevolence'. It was designed to prevent the demoralisation of the poor by the indiscriminate giving of money. It enquired into the circumstances of applicants for charity and gave help, financial or in kind, sufficient to provide assistance without discouraging recipients from using their own efforts to improve their position. By about 1891 about 75 societies had been founded in provincial towns including Leicester, which formed a society in 1876, and which is still in existence. It established a Decisions Committee, comprising five members, which met weekly to consider cases. Householders were given tickets bearing the Society's name which they could give to people seeking help. This was intended to bring the vagrant poor into the COS and its sphere of operations; wherever possible the applicant was to be referred to a local charity. The intention was to restore respectable status to those who had lost it temporarily, generally by re-equipping them with the means of returning to employment. The COS saw itself as 'an ambulance on the fiercely stricken field of modern industrial competition; it picks up the wounded and, if possible, heals them and sets them on their legs again'. From the point of view of those 'wounded' it may appear harsher than this. Its main area of work was in combating unemployment; one of its first projects in Leicester was a small window-cleaning business, and during the Edwardian period it hired mangles and sewing machines as a response to obvious trade fluctuations in the town. This was preferred to financial help that might have disrupted what was perceived to be the legitimate operation of the labour market.

Records of local COSs, which are usually held at the appropriate CROs, will include minutes and case papers; the latter are particularly valuable but may not be open to public inspection because of the sensitive nature of their contents. The Leicester COS was particularly concerned with providing convalescent care in cases of illness in poor families; at first it used private lodgings for this purpose but as private convalescent homes in seaside resorts were established began to take advantage of their facilities. Later on it helped those suffering from consumption and other terminal illnesses. It also became involved with helping people to emigrate, in co-operation with the Board of Guardians and specialist organisations. Janet Martin's research on the Leicester COS[44] concludes that it was not very popular for its first 25 years but in 1903 it appointed a new secretary who transformed the organisation; the number of annual cases rose from 300-400 to over a thousand. The archive also includes records of the Soldiers, Sailors and Airmen's Families Association, the Leicester Children's Aid Association, the Leicester Indigent Old Age Society and other local charities.

Finding evidence of small early charities can be difficult but speculative searches in the TNA catalogue or the NRA, A2A, ANW or SCAN may yield material. There were many instances of misuses of charitable donations and legislation in 1597 and 1691 (the later usually referred to as the Statute of Charitable Uses) was passed to try to regulate trust funds. From 1736 the original aims of the charity was protected further by having the trust deeds enrolled on the close rolls in the Court of Chancery; they provide the names of the original trustees along with some personal information to help identify them. From this period there are good central records for the investigation of local trust deeds.[45]

Central records include, of course, those of the Charity Commission. These are held at their offices in London and Liverpool and can be traced through registers held there. For the early 19th century there are published parliamentary reports of the Charity Commissioners. Records of the Commissioners for Charitable Uses *c.*1558 to *c.*1820 are to be found at TNA in the following series; inquisition and decrees in C 93, depositions in C 91, exceptions (appeals by parties who were aggrieved by the decrees of the Commissioners with other associated paperwork) in C 92, and confirmations and exonerations in C 90. Further records relating to charities and enrolled in the Court of Chancery can be found with regard to land conveyances and trust deeds (land for charitable uses) for the period 1736 to 1925. From 1736 to 1903 conveyances of lands, goods and money in trust for charitable purposes were drawn up and witnessed; they were then enrolled in the Court of Chancery on the Close Rolls in C 54. From 1903 to 1925 they can be found in the Supreme Court Enrolment Books in J 18. There may be earlier deeds as it appears some trustees of existing charities chose to follow the process outlined above. From 1856 documents (wills, deeds, etc.) relating to charities could be voluntarily enrolled in the books of the Charity Commissioners (CHAR 12). From 1888 elementary schoolmasters' houses, public parks and public museums could also be enrolled there instead of at Chancery. In addition gifts of land under the Working Class Dwellings Act 1890 and the Technical and Industrial Institutions Act 1892 could also be enrolled in the books of the Charity Commissioners. From 1926 it was required that all land vested for charitable purposes be recorded in the Charity Commission Enrolment Books (CHAR 13). The trust deeds can be enormously important for local historical research; for example, Hitchin in Hertfordshire has 53 enrolments relating to schools, hospitals, chapels and burial grounds, almshouses, a Mechanics' Institute, and charities to benefit the poor. The 1944 Education Act stated that that all trust deeds for educational purposes had to be recorded with the Ministry of Education, and this was the case until 1960. These trust deeds can be found in ED 21 (some may be earlier than 1944). There are also some deeds relating to elementary schools for the period 1903 to 1920 in ED 191.

Poor relief in Scotland followed a different path. Legislation in 1424 divided the poor into those able to earn to provide for their livelihood and those who could not and were thus obliged to resort to the charity of others. People under 14 and above 70 were not to beg unless they were unable to earn a living; if this was the case they were allocated badges. From 1425 sheriffs were to arrest 'idle' men only to release them for a period of 40 days in order that they might find employment; once the deadline was passed they were to be imprisoned and further punished at the king's will. Further Acts of 1503 and 1535 restricted beggars; the latter established that people were only to beg in their own parish. The 1574 Act for the 'Punishment of Strong and Idle Beggars and Provision for Sustentation of the Poor and Impotent' stated that the poor were only to beg in their own parishes, parish officials were to make and supply badges and parishioners were not to give vagrants money or lodging on pain of a fine. Magistrates in each parish had to draw up lists of the poor and estimate their needs; once this had been done they were to tax the inhabitants (sometimes in kind, such as meat, drink, clothing, etc) to provide for the local poor. A beggar's child (aged five to 14 years) could be taken into the service of a person of good estate and indentured until the age of 18 (for females) or 24 (for males). Those who were entitled to relief through age, illness, etc were to go to the last parish where they had lived for seven years or to the parish of their birth.

By the 17th century the heritors (local landowners) and the Kirk (the lowest ecclesiastical court in the Church of Scotland) jointly managed the parish responsibility to the poor. Records of the heritors and Kirk Sessions records are held at the NAS in record series HR and CH 2. The heritors would often make contributions to a voluntary fund rather than being assessed and taxed; indeed even in the late 18th and early 19th centuries only a minority of parishes was raising a regular assessed rate. The Kirk Sessions themselves would raise income from fines, seat lettings, payments for marriages, baptisms and funerals etc, and this money would also make up the poor's fund. Tracking down distributions to the poor through the heritors and Kirk Sessions records can be difficult as references to poor relief are usually to be found recorded in the other financial business of the parish.[46] In a minority of cases there may be specific accounts or minutes for poor relief.[47] A Royal Commission of Inquiry was appointed, whose recommendations led to reform two years later. R.A. Cage's *The Scottish Poor Law, 1745-1845*, provides a detailed listing of manuscripts, Parliamentary Papers, newspapers, periodicals and contemporary pamphlets.[48]

With the 1845 Poor Law Amendment (Scotland) Act parochial boards took over the responsibility for poor relief apart from the central Board of Supervision in Edinburgh, and after 1894 these were abolished and replaced by parish councils. Parochial boards built poorhouses for those paupers not in receipt of outdoor relief. On most occasions parishes got together to build 'combination poorhouses'.[49] During the second half of the 19th century parochial boards assumed responsibility for the registration of births, deaths and marriages, and for public health. Although abolished in 1894 by parish councils their functions were for the most unchanged. The trade depression following the end of the First World War saw the abandonment of the notion that unemployed men and women were not to have poor relief (Poor Law Emergency Powers (Scotland) Act 1921). After this period parishes tended to keep individual sets of poor law records. Parochial Board records, such as the rolls listing the names, ages, place of birth and family details, are sometime held with the heritor's records, although they are more frequently to be found with the county, district and burgh records. Some Parochial Board records are at the NAS: some parishes in East Lothian, CO 7/7, DC 5/4-5 and DC 7/4; Midlothian, CO 2/77-91 and Wigtownshire, CO 4/30-47. Records which survive for other areas will be found in CROs and other local archives. Appeals could be made to the Sheriff Courts and can be found in the regular business of the court. Some Sheriff Courts had separate records to deal with poor relief affairs and a collection of these are at NAS: Ayr, 1846-1933 in SC 6/82; Banff, 1890-1910, SC 2/7; Elgin, 1846-1851, SC 26/66/1 and Hamilton, 1848-1865 in SC 37/18/8. Like the Parochial Board, the records of the Parish Council are usually held locally.[50]

In 1930 the parish councils were themselves abolished and poor law responsibilities were passed to the county councils, large burghs and cities, acting through Departments of Public Assistance (or Public Welfare). In 1948 the remaining poor law system was finally abolished and replaced by a national system although welfare functions remained with local authorities, including care for the homeless, elderly, mentally and physically handicapped, etc.

It is also advisable to check charitable institutions for their impact on poverty. Some trade and crafts contributed to poor funds. Although many charity records will be held locally and much would be reported in the newspapers for the 19th and 20th centuries, there are collections of large charities at the NAS such as: the King James VI Hospital in Perth (GD 79), the Dean Orphanage in Edinburgh (GD 417), Dr Guthrie's Schools in Edinburgh (GD 425), George Heriot's School in Edinburgh (GD 421) and Trinity House in Leith which was founded for the relief of poor, aged and infirm seafarers (GD 226), including lists of those receiving pensions from the mid-17th century onwards. Parliamentary Papers, as ever, provide much useful information.[51]

9

Sickness and Health

In the distant past the close proximity to illness meant that British people were, as a whole, perhaps more aware of their own mortality than at the beginning of the 21st century. Roy Porter in *Disease, Medicine and Society in England* 1550-1860 states that 'People of all age groups, occupations and social classes … trod the pilgrim's progress of life in the shadow of sickness, disability and death'. He cites as evidence the sermons, works of religious comfort, commonplace books, journals, letters and diaries of the age. He contrasts the popular perception of health in late 20th-century Britain, where health is the normal expectation, interrupted temporarily by illness, with the views of an earlier 17th- and 18th-century age, when illness was an integral part of the life cycle. Explanations of disease (literally dis-ease) ranged from some kind of displacement of equilibrium of the different 'vital forces' for life as well as the correct balance of the humours or key fluids such as blood, to the casting of spells by witches (in decline through the 17th century), and also the fallen condition of man through original sin. Disease and death were brought into paradise by Adam and Eve as a consequence of their disobedience.[1]

Although this may indicate that death and disease were simply regarded as acceptable there were limits; the horror of the Black Death, which killed an estimated 1.5 million people out of a total of four million in England, is a good example. The Black Death was the name given to bubonic plague, a disease which was widespread during the 14th century. Although it occurred in England several times in the century, its impact on England between 1348 and 1350 was appalling. It appears that victims usually died within three days. The kinds of records which historians can turn to are usually ecclesiastical, and many of them give only fragmentary evidence of the plague. The Herefordshire Bishop's Register lists new parish priests, allowing a calculation of the deaths (of priests) in and around 1349, because of the numerous new entries for that year. In a mirror of the labour law of the period (labourers were to work at pre-plague wage rates) the Bishop's Register for June 1349 states that the clergy were not to charge excessive fees.[2] Other surviving records, such as manorial accounts, are scattered across numerous archives and show by the fall in the numbers of tenants how devastating the Black Death was.[3] Speculative searches on the TNA catalogue on 'Black Death' will turn up cases such as 'Edmund de Grey, knight, to retain the manor of Barton in Ryedale, acquired from William, parson of the church of Whitwell, who acquired it from the said Edmund (Nearly all the tenants-at-will of this manor perished in the Black Death.) York'.[4] Other web site searches will turn up early cases relating to health matters, using keywords such as 'surgeon', health', 'disease', etc.[5]

Borough, town and vestry minutes will refer to sanitary regulations, paving and matters relating to the supply of drinking water. Many rural settlements remained dependent on public wells for their water supply well into the 20th century and there are references in manorial court rolls from an early date to the need to keep them free from contamination. The most ambitious scheme to supply water in the early modern period was that of the New River Company, which constructed a pipeline from Hertfordshire to London between 1609 and 1614. Private companies continued to provide water into the Victorian period, but demand increased, both for domestic consumption and for industrial production; by the late 19th century reservoirs were constructed in moorland areas to supply the major centres of population. Most of the records are held locally or with the originating company. Central government papers in Privy Council, State Papers and later Home Office series will refer to plague and outbreaks of other diseases along with ideas on how to combat them (and will include correspondence with localities concerning these matters).[6]

The medical professions, such as the Royal College of Surgeons, created their own records and they will sometimes refer to 'irregular' and non-qualified practitioners. It is difficult to gauge how many medical practitioners there were in Tudor and Stuart times, but there were about 3,000 by the end of the 18th century according to the first 'national register', published between 1779 and 1783. A biographical database of medical practitioners in London has been compiled by Margaret Pelling and Frances White.[7] The various Royal Colleges have web sites which give information on their archives, which can usually be consulted by appointment. The Wellcome Trust is a good starting point for any study of health, hospitals, disease and related topics; its web site should be consulted at an early stage.[8]

During the 17th century the practice grew up in London and the major provincial cities of collating information on burials in parish registers, known as bills of mortality. They were often published in newspapers but should be used with caution. There are some of these records in TNA and they may also be found in local record offices.[9] There was no systematic treatment of disease much before the 19th century. However, there has been some research on disease and mortality, and various aspects of health are popular topics for study. Contemporaries in the medieval and early modern period often did not know the exact nature of an epidemic and used vague descriptions; it is sometimes possible to identify a particular disease from the pattern of recorded burials. The most feared disease was bubonic plague, which was transmitted to humans by fleas carried by rodents (although recent research has questioned whether this is accurate); it struck in the summer months and lay dormant during the winter. As well as the Black Death of the mid-14th century already referred to, it was endemic in Britain and there were further major epidemics in London in 1563, 1603 and 1665, as well as less recorded outbreaks in other parts of the country. Pepys's diary is one of the best known sources of information on the 1665 'Great Plague', which largely disappeared after the 1660s. Rosalin Barker has recently examined the parish register of Great Oakley for 1666 which appears to indicate a disparity between the actual number of plague-related deaths recorded and the huge impact of the epidemic on the communal memory.[10] Most of the other killer diseases remained major health hazards until well into the 20th century. There are significant numbers of archives with reports on 17th-century health matters and these are best picked up through the various archive network links,[11] as well as through records in the Privy Council and State Papers series.

Other potentially fatal diseases included smallpox, diphtheria, dysentery, typhoid, typhus, cholera, tuberculosis, measles and influenza; the term 'ague' described acute fever, with cold, hot and sweating stages, or malaria which was caught in fens and marshes. The 'sweating sickness' of the late 1550s is thought to have been a virulent form of influenza. Smallpox was the major killer of the late 17th and 18th centuries; inoculation against the disease was first reported in England in 1701 and received widespread publicity after Lady Mary Wortley-Montagu inoculated her son in 1716 while in Turkey. Inoculation with a milder form of the disease was the favoured method of protection until Edward Jenner experimented with vaccination using cow-pox in 1796; after initial hostility this method was quickly adopted. Cholera was a water-borne disease endemic in India, which struck Britain in 1831-2, 1848-9, 1853-4 and 1866; the majority of deaths were recorded in the most insanitary parts of industrial towns. 'King' cholera caused fear and alarm and was a catalyst for improved sanitation. Typhoid was an infectious disease and typhus a contagious fever transmitted to humans by body lice or rat fleas; outbreaks of the latter affected the urban poor and armies involved in siege warfare. Dysentery inflames the mucous membrane and glands of the large intestine, causing severe pain and loss of blood; it is transmitted by impure drinking water and malnutrition weakens resistance. Outbreaks were common amongst armies and in sieges, but as late as the 19th century it remained a major concern, especially in industrial towns.

Tuberculosis was a pulmonary disease commonly known as consumption and was often fatal well into the 20th century; isolation hospitals were built from the late 19th century to try to eradicate it. Diphtheria was a winter disease which mainly attacked children under the age of five; in the early modern period it could kill up to 40 per cent of those affected. It remained a major cause of infant mortality until the early 20th century but during the 1950s and 1960s was controlled by vaccination. Other diseases associated with childhood, such as measles, whooping cough, mumps and rubella, are no longer so serious as they once were, due to vaccination, better diet and improved sanitation. In addition to diseases which affected the whole country, there were localised outbreaks of particular diseases in different areas. The most accessible source for information before the 19th century is burial registers, although the information in them cannot be completely trusted. Late 18th- and early 19th-century vestry minutes and overseers' accounts often include references to medical contracts for the poor and to individuals' health problems and payments for treatment. From the late 18th century there is much more

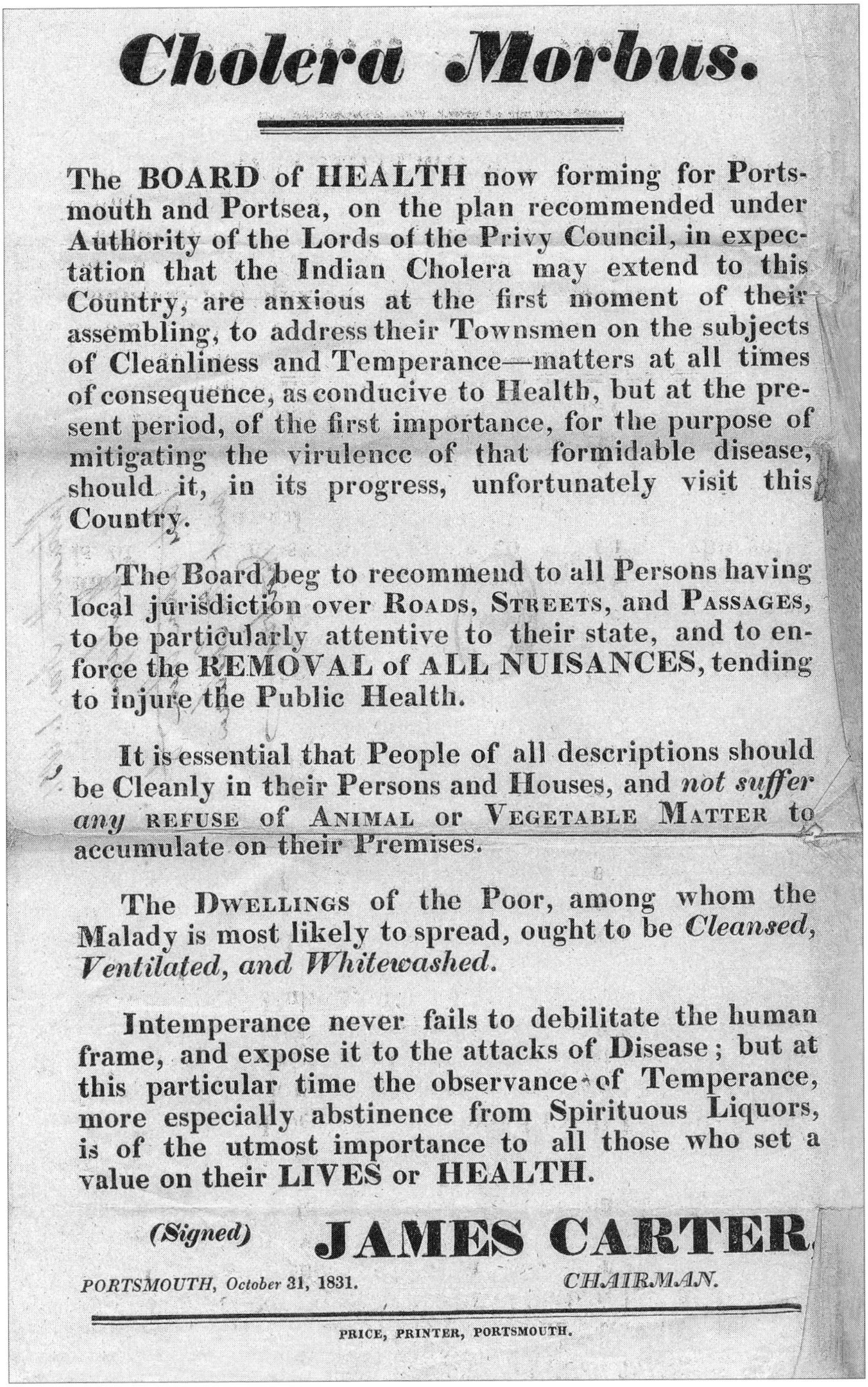

Cholera Morbus.

The **BOARD** of **HEALTH** now forming for Portsmouth and Portsea, on the plan recommended under Authority of the Lords of the Privy Council, in expectation that the Indian Cholera may extend to this Country, are anxious at the first moment of their assembling, to address their Townsmen on the subjects of Cleanliness and Temperance—matters at all times of consequence, as conducive to Health, but at the present period, of the first importance, for the purpose of mitigating the virulence of that formidable disease, should it, in its progress, unfortunately visit this Country.

The Board beg to recommend to all Persons having local jurisdiction over ROADS, STREETS, and PASSAGES, to be particularly attentive to their state, and to enforce the **REMOVAL** of **ALL NUISANCES**, tending to injure the Public Health.

It is essential that People of all descriptions should be Cleanly in their Persons and Houses, and *not suffer any* REFUSE of ANIMAL or VEGETABLE MATTER to accumulate on their Premises.

The DWELLINGS of the Poor, among whom the Malady is most likely to spread, ought to be *Cleansed, Ventilated, and Whitewashed.*

Intemperance never fails to debilitate the human frame, and expose it to the attacks of Disease; but at this particular time the observance of Temperance, more especially abstinence from Spirituous Liquors, is of the utmost importance to all those who set a value on their **LIVES** or **HEALTH**.

(Signed) **JAMES CARTER,**

PORTSMOUTH, October 31, 1831. *CHAIRMAN.*

PRICE, PRINTER, PORTSMOUTH.

23 *Poster/handbill produced for the newly 'forming' Portsmouth and Portsea Board of Health outlining the measures which should be taken in the event of an outbreak of cholera. 31 October 1831.* (TNA, HO 44/24, f. 200.)

reliable information including newspapers, government inquiries and reports of local medical officers. Significant numbers of records regarding health will be found in the records of Poor Law Unions and the Poor Law Commission (and successor bodies), particularly the Poor Law Union correspondence in TNA MH 12 and the Assistant Poor Law Commissioners and Inspectors records in MH 32. Poor health was frequently the cause of poverty (see chapter 8).

As a result of Edwin Chadwick's *Report on the Sanitary Condition of the Labouring Population* in 1842,[12] a Royal Commission on the Health of Towns was appointed the following year. It made a thorough investigation of the sanitary arrangements of 50 English towns and its minute book is at TNA MH 7/1.[13] Local Boards of Health were established as a result of the 1848 Public Health Act, which was designed 'to improve the sanitary conditions of Towns and populous places' and to place the supply of water, sewerage and drainage, and the cleansing, paving and maintenance of urban streets under the same local management and control, subject to the same general supervision.[14] Local boards were responsible to the General Board of Health. They were not universally established or liked and it was often a struggle to have the Act implemented or accepted locally.[15] At Hertford there was no local board because of opposition from the Marquess of Salisbury.[16] Klaus-John Dodds found in his investigation at Reading that even during outbreaks of the disease local politicians opposed sanitary reform, as it would lead to an increase in taxes and disrupt business.[17]

The General Board had powers to enquire into localities petitioning for application of the Act or to initiate inquiries where mortality exceeded 23 in 1,000; if they recommended application of the Act a local board was created. A second Public Health Act in 1858 had additional powers to control building lines when the rebuilding of demolished properties took place, as well as other powers. The General Board of Health was dissolved and its powers split between other government departments. The 1858 Act was widely adopted, especially after the enactment of the 1862 Highways Act. This Act provided that any area subject to the jurisdiction of a local board established under the 1848 or 1858 Acts could not form part of a Highway District. In order to retain control of their own highways and avoid being rated as one constituent part of a larger Highway District, thus subsidising rural roads, many urban areas took an early opportunity to opt for a local board. The 1863 Local Government Act imposed a minimum population limit of 3,000 for local board areas.

The inspectors' reports were of two kinds; the most important and the majority were preliminary inquiries which covered all aspects of the locality's sanitary condition. The others were further inquiries made necessary because the creation of a local board involved the alteration of existing boundaries, or concerned graveyards, drainage schemes and the conduct of existing boards. Besides evidence, correspondence and statistics the reports often specified measures to be taken, offered cost estimates and answered popular misconceptions about the Act, the General Board and powers of local boards. Examples of the sort of information included are: population and mortality figures; meteorological information; privy accommodation in working-class districts; numbers of street lamps and the distances between them; arrestable offences in 1849; the expenses

16

TABLE 1.—Continued

Diseases of the Respiratory Function ...		291
Bronchitis	154	
Inflammation of the Lungs	111	
Asthma	12	
Other Diseases of this Class	14	
Diseases of the Digestive Organs ...		89
Inflammation of Stomach, Bowels, &c.	48	
Obstruction of Bowels	8	
Diseases of Liver	23	
Jaundice	9	
Other Diseases of this Class	1	
Diseases of Urinary Organs		25
Diseases of Children		218
Premature Birth	95	
Teething	31	
Atrophy and Debility	89	
Other Diseases of this Class	3	
Old Age		161
Deaths from Violence		61
Accident or Negligence	49	
Suicide	12	
Other Causes		41
Causes not stated, or ill defined		10

17

TABLE 2.

Shewing the trades or callings of the 51 Male persons registered as dying from Consumption during the year 1866; separating as far as practicable those connected with the staple trades of Leicester, from other trades or callings; omitting all under 15 years of age.

CONNECTED WITH THE STAPLE TRADES.		OTHER TRADES OR CALLINGS.	
Stocking Makers ...	5	Tailors	3
Loom-hands	3	Labourers	2
Warehouseman ...	1	Bricklayers	2
Trimmer	1	Painters	2
Elastic Weavers ...	5	Porters	3
Shoe Makers	5	Commercial Travellers	3
„ Manufacturers ...	2	Gentlemen	2
„ Nailers	3	Clerks	2
„ Finisher ...	1	Collectors	2
„ Clicker ...	1	Gardeners	2
Machinist	1		
Framesmith	1	And one death each from 19 other callings	19
	29		42

24 *Medical Officers of Health were appointed following the 1848 Public Health Act and their reports give an unrivalled description of the sanitary conditions of towns. They usually included tables of deaths from particular diseases and other statistical information, as well as gruesome details of 'nuisances'. These pages are from the Leicester MOH's report for 1866.* (Record Office of Leicestershire, Leicester and Rutland 20D72/1.)

of cultivating a quarter-acre; and dame schools. Most of the reports contain maps showing various relevant features; one for Norwich charts river pollution. In a nutshell, the reports include every topic which, in the inspector's opinion, affected moral and physical welfare, and the government of the locality. London was excepted from the authority of the General Board but the reports cover about 23 per cent of the population outside the capital, although the figures vary considerably from county to county. Thirty-six out of 62 towns with a population of more than 20,000 were visited, as well as many other smaller places. In total 398 reports were published between 1848 and 1857, referring to 296 localities. A complete set is in the library of the Department of Health but this is not normally accessible to the public. Both the British Library and TNA have original or microform copies and there is also a substantial collection in the Wellcome Trust library. There should be a copy in the local reference library for a given locality but some libraries have other reports, some of them quite substantial; apparently Leicester City Library has one report that is not in either the Department of Health or British Library collections. Local newspapers often reproduced the whole report at the time of publication. When a local board was created an inspection of the area's sanitary condition was made but reports often do not survive. Some reports may be found at TNA in PC1 under Public Health and Quarantine.

The general correspondence and draft out-letters of the General Board of Health along with the original petitions for local boards from each locality are in MH 13. This series also includes six boxes of various correspondence and papers on cholera, yellow fever and quarantine for 1848-54. There is further correspondence of the Board in HLG 1 and HLG 46. Board minute books are in MH 5 and MH 6, with other local-related material in HLG 19 and HLG 15-16. In 1858 the General Board of Health published *Papers Relating to the Sanitary State of the People of England* and the Royal Sanitary Commission published three reports between 1868 and 1874, all of which will be useful to the local historian.[18] There may be local evidence of the work of local boards of health, such as the following example from Leicester in 1849: 'I trace their steps in almost every locality, leaving in their course blessings more substantial than the fabled gifts of the deities of olden times. Pigsties, drains, cesspools, and many other similar nuisances have been removed in all these more obvious situations, and, no doubt, time will reveal those that at present lie out of sight'.[19]

The most comprehensive local source is the Medical Officer of Health reports. In 1846 Leicester decided to appoint two medical officers, the first appointed by a local authority in Britain.[20] Their annual reports were printed and also found in the minutes of the Highways and Sewerage Committee. Like similar reports for other towns they include a lot of valuable information and give tables of deaths from various diseases as well as other statistical information. The medical officers reported on anything which they believed affected public health, such as noxious trades, slaughter-houses, water supply and so on. Infant mortality was a particular problem: in 1875 two medical men presented a *Report on the Epidemic Diarrhoea of* 1874 to the borough Sanitary Committee and concluded that the disease was specific to Leicester on account of its low-lying situation and imperfect drainage. They rejected the view of the Medical Officer to the Privy Council that infant mortality was the result of neglect by women who went out to work.[21]

Vaccination against smallpox was not universally accepted and Leicester was a leader in the anti-vaccination movement. Even after the government had passed the legislation in 1867, many parents refused to comply; opposition in Leicester was very strong as shown by a mass anti-vaccination demonstration in 1885. Eventually a local Act made notification of infectious diseases compulsory rather than vaccination itself.[22] The driving force in the campaign against compulsory vaccination was a sanitary and waterworks engineer, J.T. Biggs, who castigated it as 'blood polluting quackery' and organised a highly successful campaign.[23] Even as late as 1934 there were only 98 vaccinations and 3,438 certificates of exemption were recorded. Responsibility for vaccination was given to poor law unions and there is information on the subject with these records (see chapter 8), including details of refusals to vaccinate children and the prosecution of parents.

Following the abolition of the General Board of Health in 1858 staff were transferred to the Local Government Act Office and the Medical Department of the Privy Council. The Sanitary Acts of 1866-70 meant that local authorities were to inspect their districts and deal with nuisances. The resulting reports are in MH 13 and relevant correspondence can be found in HO 45.

The 1872 Public Health Act created urban and rural sanitary authorities and local boards of health became urban sanitary authorities. The Act divided the whole country into sanitary districts, to consist of those parts of each poor law union not within an urban sanitary authority, and in which the boards of guardians were the responsible authority. The 1894 Local Government Act, which established urban and rural district councils, abolished local boards of health and urban and rural sanitary authorities. Local records should include minutes, accounts, correspondence, rate books, maps and plans. The Sanitary Department within the Local Government Board took over responsibility for health from the Local Government Act Office. The Public Health Department dealt with the administrative aspects of public health and vaccination functions transferred from the Privy Council Office and Poor Law Board respectively. The relevant records containing the general correspondence of these two departments, including local authority correspondence, are in MH 25, MH 12, MH 30 and MH 48. The departmental correspondence includes turn-of-the-century material on specific diseases in MH 19. At the end of the 19th century a number of public health surveys were undertaken by the Local Government Board Medical Inspectorate, and the returns of these investigations are to be found in the main Poor Law Union correspondence series in MH 12. The late 19th century saw a huge relative change in terms of health provision, investigation and reports. However, some of the health debates resulted from investigations from outside Parliament such as that undertaken by Charles Booth. His *Inquiry into the Life and Labour of the People in London*,[24] carried out between 1886 and 1903, was one of the most important surveys of working-class life carried out in the 19th century and one for which there is a huge resulting archive. This is held at the British Library of Political and Economic Science (the Library of the London School of Economics and Political Science) and the University of London Library. It is now available online as a searchable resource giving access to archive material from the Booth collections of the British Library of Political and Economic Science and the University of London Library.[25] The research and writing of both Henry Mayhew and Benjamin Seebohm Rowntree are also important for the research of health in 19th-century London and early 20th-century York respectively. Mayhew's *London Labour and the London Poor: A Cyclopaedia of the Condition and Earnings of Those That Will Work, Those That Cannot Work, and Those That Will Not Work* was published in 1861 and his *London Characters: Illustrations of the Humor, Pathos, and Peculiarities of London Life* in 1874. Benjamin Seebohm Rowntree conducted a study of poor families in York in 1899 and drew a poverty line in terms of a minimum weekly sum of money 'necessary to enable families ... to secure the necessaries of a healthy life'. Money was needed for subsistence level covering fuel, light, rent, food, clothing, etc on a scale to accommodate family size. He conducted two further studies of poverty in York in 1936 and 1950. In these later studies he included allowances for things such as newspapers, books, radios, beer, tobacco, etc. He published his results in *Poverty: A Study of Town Life*, 1901; *Progress and Poverty*, 1941 and *Poverty and the Welfare State*, 1951. Some of Rowntree's research papers survive at the Borthwick Institute at York and at Oxford University, Nuffield College; more may be found through the NRA.

Commissioners of sewers dealt primarily with land drainage and their records can go back to medieval times; most records will be found in CROs and other local record offices, although there are records in TNA and a search of the online catalogue will reveal a number of relevant documents. There may also be information in manorial court rolls. The officials were empowered to make regulations for the upkeep and maintenance of banks and ditches but by the early 20th century the system was tangled and confused. Other records include the accounts of the dyke reeve, the officer responsible for a particular length of sea wall, surveys, draft presentments, correspondence and maps. Improvement commissioners were established in many towns between 1748 and 1835; they existed to provide lighting, cleansing and sanitation. They were established by private Act of Parliament, which laid down their powers, and corporations had no control over them. After the Municipal Corporations Act of 1835 boroughs often took over their powers although about 30 continued until 1894 when they were absorbed into urban district councils. Their records include minutes, ledgers, letter books, rate books, maps and plans, and these should be held in borough or CROs.

The 1833 Lighting and Watching Act made provision in individual parishes for inspectors, who were to provide street lighting, paving and a fire brigade; they were also responsible for gas undertakings, for which a special rate was levied. Their records include minutes, ledgers, letter books and rate books. A number of Acts of Parliament between 1852 and 1900 established burial boards which managed non-denominational burial grounds; they were merged with urban district or parish councils in 1894. Many towns have a large cemetery built in the middle of the 19th century and divided into areas for Anglicans and Nonconformists. Their records may still be in the cemetery or transferred to a local record office, and some family history societies have produced name indexes to the burials.

Medieval hospitals were charitable institutions founded by religious bodies, gilds, livery companies and private individuals, and most were dissolved at the Reformation. Some early established hospitals such as St Bartholomew's and St Thomas's in London have records from the 13th and 14th centuries.[26] The numerous almshouses and hospitals of the early modern period were privately founded, often by a bequest in a will. There was a considerable increase in the number of hospitals in the 18th century; most of London's famous institutions date from 1720 to 1745, and by 1800 or soon after most large provincial towns had opened infirmaries and dispensaries as a result of voluntary contributions. They catered for all sections of society but patients had to be nominated by a subscriber and in most cases the local nobility, gentry and clergy head the subscription lists. In towns in the 18th and 19th centuries poor people who were similarly nominated could get free medical treatment at a dispensary.

Specialist hospitals were opened in London, such as the British Lying-in Hospital (1749) and the Lock Hospital for venereal disease (1746). Out-patient treatment began to grow and from 1757 a succession of charities provided home-based maternity care. Thomas Coram's Foundling Hospital, dating from the 1740s, became one of the great sights of London and Handel composed an anthem specially for it. Other early institutions include the Magdalen House for repentant prostitutes and the Female Orphan Asylum at Lambeth (both

1758). Hospital records will be found in local record offices and some may have a published history, which will give more details of the material available.[27] The starting point for these searches is HOSPREC.[28]

In the 19th century hospitals for the poor developed from workhouses, which made provision for the sick; the inability to work due to permanent or temporary illness was a major cause of poverty. The larger institutions had separate wards for particular conditions, such as 'itch', venereal disease and maternity. The records will be found with other poor law material or in the original or a successor building. Both hospitals and former workhouses still stand, although very altered (see chapter 8). A modern problem is the question of clinical records, that is the information on individuals; it would be impossible to keep everything and there is a considerable debate on the issue. Both hospitals and general practitioners have copious personal records, which are increasingly being computerised.

The first asylums for the insane were also private or charitable institutions; the earliest one in England is the Bethlem Royal Hospital, founded as a priory in 1247, which gave its name (corrupted to Bedlam) to other mental hospitals. 'Mad doctoring' became a growing and lucrative profession and mental illness had a special fascination for a literate and propertied public. Private lunatic asylums gave cause for concern and it was often believed that they were prisons by another name. There was legislation in 1774 to regulate them and later in the 18th century a number of provincial asylums were opened. An Act of 1828 empowered JPs to erect and maintain asylums from county rates and a further Act of 1845 compelled them to do so. In 1888 responsibility was transferred to county and county borough councils until the advent of the National Health Service in 1948. Records will therefore be found with quarter sessions, borough and county records; these will usually only comprise administrative material and information on individuals is rare. Again, refer to the HOSPREC database.

Despite opposition from central authority, many workhouses maintained insane wards, which were visited twice a year by the Commissioners in Lunacy. There are records in TNA (MH 19, 51, 83, 85 and 86) and in local poor law records. Researchers should also consult J. Lappin's unpublished 'Central Government and the Supervision of the Treatment of Lunatics, 1800-1913' (1996). As with hospitals, many former asylums still stand, though in another guise: the former Leicester Borough Lunatic Asylum forms the core of Leicester University and the former county asylum is the local headquarters of the Alliance & Leicester Building Society; other institutions have been converted to houses. There were other societies which catered for medical needs, especially for the poor, for which the best source of information is probably local trade directories and newspapers, but there are unlikely to be records.

Knowledge of contraception became much more widespread through the pioneering work of Marie Stopes and the army's distribution of condoms on a massive scale during the First World War in order to limit venereal disease. In the later 20th century new methods of contraception have led to immense social consequences. The wider availability of IVF for infertile couples and 'test tube babies' has also had a considerable impact on family life. The Wellcome Trust is a good starting point for information on these subjects.

TNA holds the records of the Ministry of Health from its creation in 1919. Registers of circulars of the Ministry and its predecessors are in record series MH 10; MH 52 contains Ministry files relating to public health and poor law services, 1916-44. Public assistance administrative papers, including poor law matters, are in MH 57. There are papers relating to various unemployment and hunger marches, strikes, industrial disputes, distressed areas and emigration in these papers and Parliamentary Papers contain reports relevant to health, unemployment and poverty.[29] For papers relating to food, diet and nutrition the records in MH 56 should be consulted and MH 55 contains files, mainly for 1919-36, on mother and child welfare, immunisation and vaccination, hygiene, infectious diseases and nursing. MH 48/61 relates to the 1912-21 tuberculosis scheme. Twentieth-century advances in medicine reduced the levels of disease, which meant that although serious outbreaks involving numbers of deaths were not unusual, epidemics were rare. The commonest diseases remained smallpox, typhoid, diphtheria, tuberculosis and measles. The papers relating to various outbreaks can be found in the local correspondence in MH 52.

During the Second World War William Beveridge published his *Social Insurance and Allied Services Report*,[30] which formed the basis for the legislation of the Labour government in the post-war period. It identified 'idleness, ignorance, disease, squalor and want' as major societal problems and proposed a scheme of social insurance from 'the cradle to the grave'. A national health service, social insurance and assistance, family allowances, and full-employment policies were recommended.

There are some central government records relating to regions, districts and individual hospitals but current listing makes finding material very difficult. MH 96 contains the Welsh Board of Health Registered Files, 1872-1978. The records deal with a variety of subjects including the administration of the poor law, emergency Second World War services, welfare services, maternity and child welfare, hospital services (including the building of hospitals), and the treatment of tuberculosis carried out by the Welsh National Memorial Association, etc. The Ministry of Health and Department of Health and Social Security Registered Files for 1947 to 1991 (File Office E Series in MH 156) contain files covering local authority services, including ambulances, home helps, child welfare, etc. They also refer to confidential enquiries into maternal deaths in England and Wales. MH 160, the Ministry of Health and DHSS Hospitals Registered Files (File Office H Series) for 1948-1994 deal with hospital projects and planning, such as the hospital building programme and grouping, infection control, hospital dental and maternity services, etc.

The HOSPREC database is really the best place to look for records of individual hospitals across the United Kingdom. Where material survives it will include records relating to finance, staff, estate and patient records (although there will be various closure periods for sensitive medical data on patients). In addition to the official documents described above, there will be information and reports on health, accidents and hospitals in local newspapers as well as an increasing number of published works relating to the memoirs, diaries and working papers of members of the medical professions.[31]

10

Housing

Information on this subject is helped by the fact that the buildings themselves may survive, although this overwhelmingly relates to larger and more prestigious houses. Recently the National Trust has extended the range of its responsibilities with such acquisitions as the back-to-backs in Birmingham and the houses in Liverpool where two of the Beatles grew up. Sources for the study of housing can begin from several points and some of the relevant sources are described elsewhere. Estate maps, surveys and rentals can be useful for piecing together patterns of early housing either through a particular map or the description of houses in the surveys and rentals (see chapter 2 for further details). With the advent of parliamentary enclosure local maps became more common (some earlier enclosures also may have maps); from the 1790s maps were a fairly integral part of the award and may indicate any built-up part of the parish or manor.[1] Like the tithe maps from the 1830s-50s the enclosure map needs to be approached with a little caution and housing plots need some form of collaboration before it can be assumed that they give a picture of local housing stock. The larger scale Ordnance Survey maps will of course be useful. The maps produced to assist with rate assessments and the towns mapped under the direction of the Boards of Health (see previous chapter) will also provide relative accuracy. The records of the Valuation Office, from 1910-15, and the National Farm Survey (1941-3) use Ordnance Survey maps as the basis for boundary identification but also provide much detail on specific houses.

A less obvious source for housing is the records of the manor and the vestry.[2] Manor court rolls identify many thousands of cases of cottages being built by squatters on or around areas of waste land or across communal roads or trackways. Often there are complaints about them in the manor court rolls, with a threat of a fine if they are not removed, and the case may be entered in successive rolls over a period of time until the fine is paid. In many instances this was not really a fine *per se* but a mechanism by which the lord of the manor managed potential income from small allotments of the manorial waste. In addition there may be instances of cottages being sub-divided. Several examples can be found in various published transcripts. At Hornsey in Middlesex in 1631 Robert Ruddey was ordered to 'pull downe his hovel standing upon parte of his garden, it being the Lords Waste ... 10s 0d', and in 1633 Mathew Proundley was told he was to 'take downe the cottage which he hath erected in Sawood Lane'.[3] At Acomb in Yorkshire in 1555 the court ordered that 'Every owner in Acome who made 2 dwellings out of 1 cottage ... [was to pay] 10s 0d'. In 1557 'Wm Notyngham [who] had recently built 2 dwellings where there used to be only one ... was to restore the other to a barn as it formerly was ... 40s 0d'.[4] John Middleton, in his report to the Board of Agriculture, objected to the practice of allowing the building of small cottages for the poor, which he claimed was done with the connivance of the parish officers to reduce the poor rates, as it left the commons overstocked and diminished the number of potential dependent agricultural labourers at the disposal of the farming community. In 1798 and again in 1807 he wrote that commons held 'out a lure to the poor man – I mean of materials wherewith to build his cottage, and ground to erect it upon; together with firing, and the run of his poultry and pigs for nothing'. The poor, once gaining such rights, then acquire the 'desire to live, from that time forward, without labour, or at least with as little as possible'.[5] Vestry references to housing may be more varied. It was an important issue in terms of a rising population and rising poor rates. The Hanwell vestry in the late 18th and early 19th centuries had a policy of buying or renting 'parish houses' in which it placed elderly women in need of relief.[6]

Inventories are detailed lists of articles (goods, chattels and sometime land) in the possession of a person at death; they are one of the best sources of information about the contents of houses and, especially when the property to which an inventory relates still stands, can give a graphic picture of the home and working life of people in the past.[7] As well as probate inventories, others will be found among personal papers of well-to-do people; for instance, in the important Panshanger archive at Hertfordshire Archives and Local Studies is an extensive inventory of the contents of the 3rd Earl Cowper's wine cellar and his scientific instruments in his villa in Florence.[8] Inventories also exist for institutions such as workhouses, hospitals and almshouses. They survive from the Middle Ages but an Act of Parliament of Henry VIII (21 Henry VIII, c5) formalised the procedure. It set out that the personal estate (i.e., not including freehold property) of a testator valued at £5 or more should be valued by at least two 'honest and skilful' men within three months of death. The first choice of appraiser was to be someone to whom the deceased was indebted or to whom a legacy was due, and the second choice was the next of kin. Sometimes there was a specialist appraiser in cases where particular trades required a more intimate knowledge of the value of tools or stock, for example, books belonging to the vicar of Stottesdon, Herefordshire in 1687.[9] Some appraisers (nearly all male) became 'semi-professional'; many acted more than once and there are examples of appraisers acting in several cases and sometimes passing on the duty from father to son. At the other end of the scale some appraisers were illiterate – evidenced by the frequency with which they made their mark – but this was not seen as a bar to their doing the work. The inventory protected the executors and relatives and was used as a basis for calculating the court fees.

Thousands of inventories survive, mainly in CROs but also for the Prerogative Courts of Canterbury and York; probate records are at TNA and

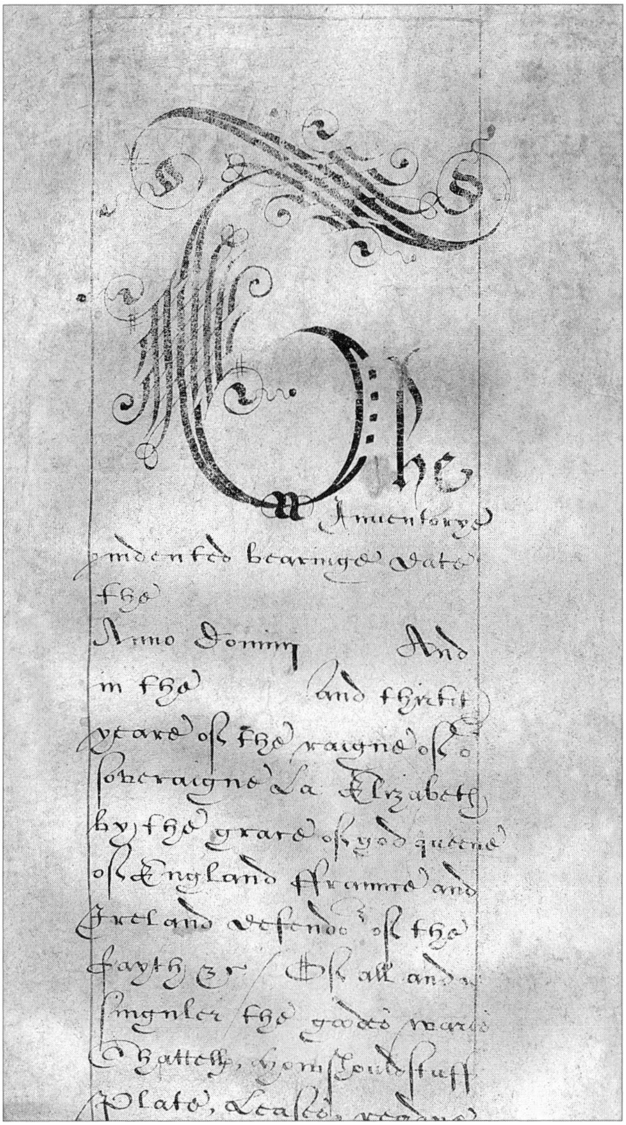
The Inventory
indented bearinge date
the
Anno domini And
in the and thirtie
yeare of the raigne of o[ur]
soveraigne La[dy] Elizabeth
by the grace of god queene
of England ffraunce and
Ireland defender of the
faythe &c / Of all and
singuler the goods wares
Chattells, household stuff
Plate, Leases,

25 *Most inventories will be found with other probate documents but this example comes from the Herrick family papers. It is 53 feet long and records the contents of Nicholas Herrick's goldsmith's shop in London about 1593.* (Record Office of Leicestershire, Leicester and Rutland, DG9/2409.)

the Borthwick Institute respectively. It is difficult to give definitive dates as survival rates will be different for different archives. Inventories were required in ecclesiastical law from the mid-14th century, but the bulk of material survives from 1529 when it was required by statute. Until 1782 it was necessary for an executor or administrator to return an inventory of the deceased's goods, but after that date inventories do not exist in the same quantities. An inventory was only drawn up if required for a case in a church court or for some other interested party; they were often written out by the clerks of the court in an immaculate hand, unlike some earlier documents, and can often be more detailed than ordinary inventories and describe the contents of a house in great detail.

There have been various estimates of the numbers of inventories that survive,[10] and there have been many local studies of the records. M.W. Barley, for example, used them extensively in his book *The English Farmhouse and Cottage* (1961). David Hey has stated that 'No other class of records provides such a rich vein of information on farming systems, old crafts and industries, household arrangements, furniture, utensils and the provision of credit in the form of bills, bonds and mortgages'.[11] Francis Steer, in his leaflet for the Historical Association's *Short Guides to Records* series, asked 'Where else could we get such evidence for the development of, and changes in, household furnishings, the improvement of living conditions, the incidence of particular trades, the names and values of a multitude of objects and goods which reflect the day-to-day needs of all types of society?'.[12] Jon Stobart has recently used inventories and wills to examine rural craftsmen-retailers in Cheshire to highlight their closeness to agricultural pursuits such as ownership of animals and farming equipment.[13]

Inventories listed the furniture and utensils in the house – room by room in larger properties – together with livestock, crops, equipment and tools, and finished goods. It seems obvious but only rooms containing anything that had to be included on the inventory were listed, so that an inventory cannot be seen as a total description of a property. What were known as 'bona paraphernalia' – the widow's clothes and jewels, and some furniture – were also omitted. All tame and confined animals were included but dogs and bees were rarely listed. All crops harvested above ground were included, so long as their cultivation involved manual labour; this could lead to anomalies, as turnips, for example, were sometimes listed although they are a root crop. Although inventories did not include real estate, sometimes leases were noted; debts were invariably given, including 'desperate debts' – i.e., those that had not been collected and probably never would be. They usually begin with 'purse and apparel'; furniture, utensils and linen are invariably listed next, followed by animals, crops and other outdoor items, and finally debts owed to the testator. There is often a phrase 'things forgotten and unseen' to cover all eventualities. The amount of detail varies enormously and appears to have little relevance to the value of the estate.

There are a number of published collections of inventories and some of them are listed by David Hey in *The Oxford Companion to Local and Family History* and by Nancy and Jeff Cox in their four articles in *The Local Historian*;[14] other lists will be found in Mark Overton, *A Bibliography of British Probate Inventories* (1983) and John West, *Village Records* (3rd edition, 1997). West includes detailed information drawn from Worcestershire inventories, including plans of houses reconstructed from five documents. Inventories also lend themselves to statistical analysis and Janet Spavold describes one community project in Derbyshire and Leicestershire using a relational database; over 4,000 entries were input, covering the years 1535 to 1700, and among the more unusual findings were that only two timepieces were mentioned and that chamber pots were very rare.[15]

Local historians have used inventories in helping to recreate the past history of their village or town; members of the local history society in the Leicestershire

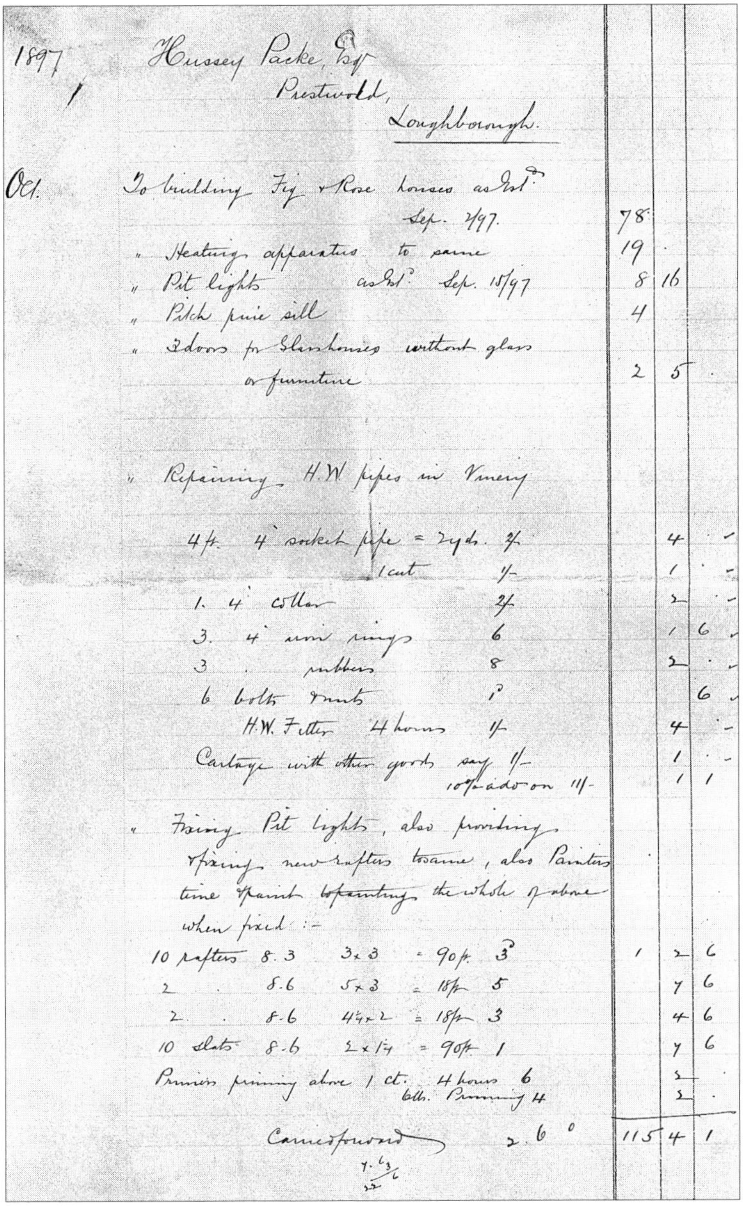

1897 Hussey Packe, Esq
1 Prestwold,
Loughborough.

	£	s	d
Oct. To building Fig & Rose houses as Est^d Sep. 2/97.	78	.	
" Heating apparatus to same	19	.	
" Pit lights as Est^d Sep. 15/97	8	16	
" Pitch pine sill	4		
" 3 doors for Glasshouses without glass or furniture	2	5	.
" Repairing H.W pipes in Vinery			
4ft. 4" socket pipe = 2yds. 2/-		4	-
1 cut 1/-		1	-
1. 4" collar 2/-		2	-
3. 4" iron rings 6		1	6
3 . rubbers 8		2	-
6 bolts & nuts 1d			6
H.W. Fitter 4 hours 1/-		4	-
Cartage with other goods say 1/-		1	-
10% added on 11/-		1	1
" Fixing Pit lights, also providing & fixing new rafters to same, also Painters time & paint to painting the whole of above when fixed :-			
10 rafters 8.3 3x3 = 90ft. 3d	1	2	6
2 . 8.6 5x3 = 18ft 5		7	6
2 . 8.6 4¼x2 = 18ft 3		4	6
10 slats 8.6 2x1¼ = 90ft 1		7	6
Painters priming above 1 ct. 4 hours 6		2	-
6lb. Priming 4		2	.
Carried forward 2.6.0	115	4	1

26 *Messenger & Co of Loughborough built large greenhouses and similar structures in the late 19th and early 20th centuries; some of their products can still be seen, such as the greenhouse at Bodnant Gardens in North Wales. The transfer of the records to the record office demonstrates the problems often facing archivists: the staff were given 24 hours to take what material they could before the rest was destroyed, meaning that no rational selection process was possible. Each file contains drawings, estimates, correspondence, etc and the one illustrated is an estimate for fig and rose houses for Hussey Packe of Prestwold in 1897.* (Record Office of Leicestershire, Leicester and Rutland, DE2121/216/1.)

village of Frisby-on-the-Wreake, for example, undertook a large project a few years ago to 're-furnish' those houses in the village which were 200 or more years old. Inventories are valuable in a study of particular occupations and are an unrivalled source for a study of furnishing styles and demonstrating a rise in standards of domestic comfort. More well-to-do people in the 16th century, for example, had joined chairs and tables whereas poorer folk had to make do with stools, benches and trestles. Certain items, depending on the date of the inventory, can show the relative wealth of an individual – examples include books, window glass and mirrors. Some documents can be very extensive: the will of a goldsmith in London in the Record Office for Leicestershire, Leicester and Rutland, is over fifty feet long and consists of pieces of parchment stitched head to tail.[16]

Inventories at CROs and those at the Borthwick Institute are usually filed with the will or letters of administration. However, they are sometimes kept in a separate series. Those at TNA are in PROB 2 (pre-1660); PROB 3, PROB 4, PROB 5 , PROB 16 and PROB 32 (1660-1782); those for 1722 to 1858 are mainly in PROB 31.[17]

The records of insurance companies are another useful source on all types of buildings, not just houses.[18] Before the 18th century the insurance of property against fire was haphazard and it was not until 1710 that the first fully organised fire insurance concern appeared (in London). The idea spread, principally in London, but by 1790 there were fire offices in Bath, Leeds and Worcester. In return for paying a premium the client received a policy, the details of which were entered into the company's registers; the duplicate registers are therefore an important source. The details include the date and number of the policy, a description of the property, the amount for which the policy was taken out and the rate. The Guildhall Library in London holds the records of over 80 insurance companies and has a leaflet describing the various records. An online index to Sun policy registers Ms 11936/471 – 500, dating from 1816 to 1831, is available on the A2A web site. It is compiled by volunteers from the London Archive Users' Forum and financed by the Heritage Lottery Fund; it includes personal names, occupations and addresses of policyholders, location details of the property insured and the names of any other individuals mentioned. It also gives names of vessels and their masters where these occur. By March 2005 a total of 55 catalogues, containing details of over 95,000 policies, had been input. Local record offices should have information on the location of insurance company records outside London. Specialised plans were produced by insurance companies and examples survive for the Sun and Phoenix companies from the 1780s. The most comprehensive range produced in a standard format was that of Charles E. Goad and his company; he began his work in Canada but returned to the United Kingdom in 1885 and established a British branch of his company, producing his first series of detailed plans for London the following year. Within ten years 53 series of plans had been produced for central districts of major urban areas and commercial and industrial districts. The company is still in business, producing plans for shopping centres.[19]

Other sources of information on houses and buildings generally can be found in deeds, glebe terriers, sale particulars and estate records (see chapter 2),

I *Humphry Repton, the great landscape designer, appears to have also been a clever businessman. He produced a 'red book' (so-called because they were bound in red leather) showing the landscape as it was and how it would look after he had transformed it. This one was drawn up for Earl Cowper of Panshanger in 1799-1800 but the work was never carried out.* (Hertfordshire Archives and Local Studies, DE/P/P21.)

II *The early development of railways in the middle of the 19th century saw the rapid expansion of services across the country, but not everybody was enthusiastic. This anonymous cartoon from 1831 demonstrates the ambivalence felt by many towards this new – and potentially faster and more dangerous – form of transport.* (Hertfordshire Archives and Local Studies, DE/X92/21.)

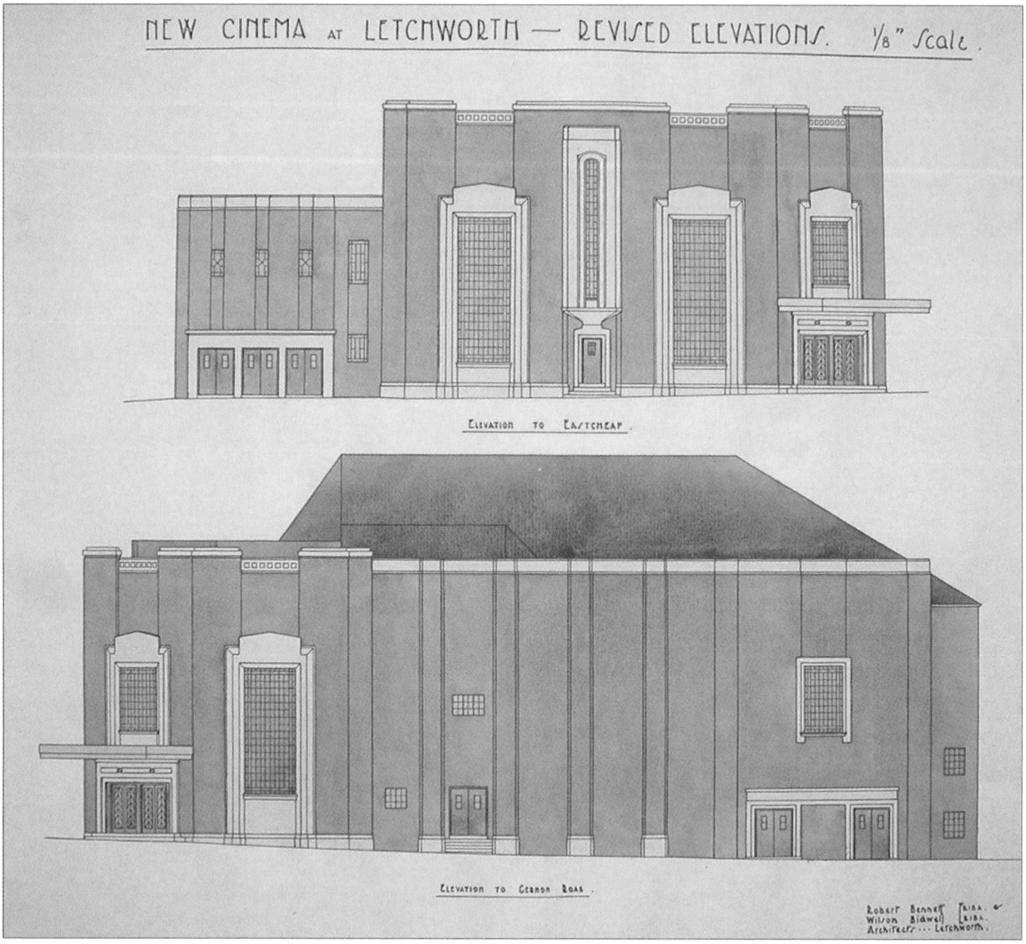

III *Plan of proposed cinema in Letchworth, 1935. The cinema, known as 'The Broadway', is the only one left in the town and is an excellent surviving example of Art Deco. It was reopened in 1996 after a major refurbishment.* (Hertfordshire Archives and Local Studies, OffAcc 189.)

IV *All boroughs were granted a number of charters but this one for Hertford in 1605 is unusually decorative. As well as the hunting scenes shown here, there are paintings of flowers and fruits.* (Hertfordshire Archives and Local Studies, Hertford Borough Records)

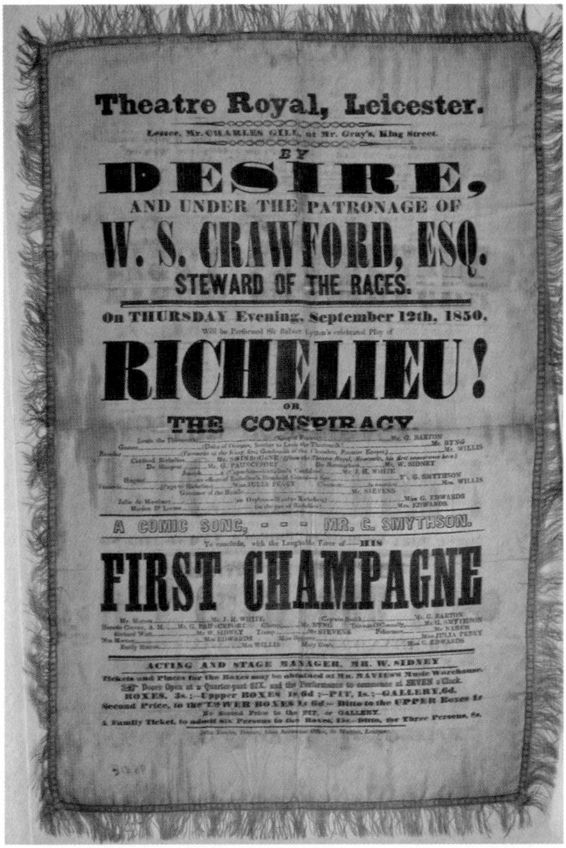
Theatre Royal, Leicester.

BY DESIRE,

AND UNDER THE PATRONAGE OF

W. S. CRAWFORD, ESQ.

STEWARD OF THE RACES.

On THURSDAY Evening, September 12th, 1850.

RICHELIEU!

OR,

THE CONSPIRACY.

A COMIC SONG, - - - MR. G. SMYTHSON.

FIRST CHAMPAGNE

ACTING AND STAGE MANAGER, MR. W. SIDNEY

V *Theatre programmes were usually printed on flimsy paper and few have survived. This example, however, was printed on silk and gives details of the entertainment at the Theatre Royal on 12 September 1850.* (Record Office of Leicestershire, Leicester and Rutland, 31/D/56.)

VI *The Quaker marriage ceremony is simple: the vows are made in a special meeting for worship and at the end everyone present is invited to sign the marriage certificate. This unusual survival, from a private source, records the marriage of Joseph Henry Ellis of Glenfield, Leicestershire, and Sarah Longstreth Thompson of Liverpool, who were married on 9 August 1860; 116 witnesses signed the document.* (Record Office of Leicestershire, Leicester and Rutland, DE 2031.)

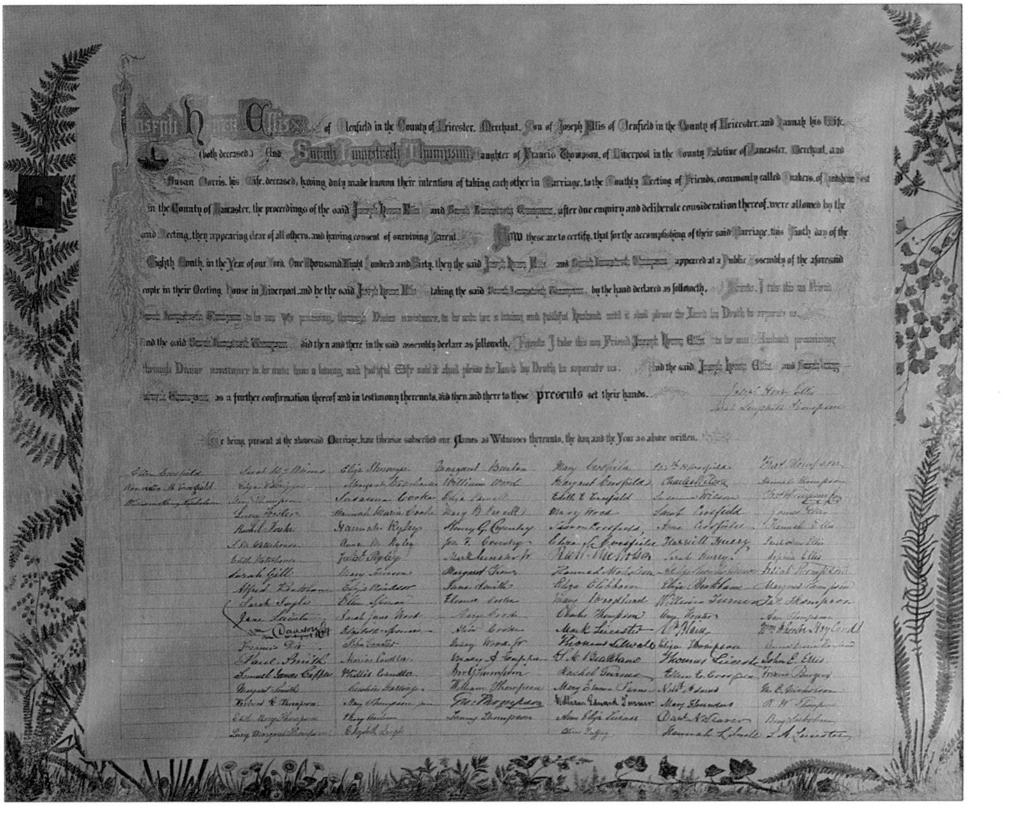

1st Willm 4th 1830 continued

Friday 31st Decr Before Mr Justice Taunton in the Nisi Prius Court contd

Nowch &c. – Puts himself (in Custody) Jury say Guilty – Ho: Corr: at Brixton 6 cal: mos:

32 Richard Stagg 21 – Unlawfully entering with others into certain close with intent to kill game and being found therein at night armed –

2nd Count – Entering certain land with intt to take & destroy Rabbits

2 other Cots Assaulting John Frost a Game Keeper

Puts himself Jury say Guilty To be Hanged &c Judgmt recorded

Repd Trans: Life 33 George Brown 19 – Feloniously Breaking and Entering the Dwelling House of Elizabeth Simpson & Stealing goods v £1. 9. 6

Record made up and with Indt on felony file

Puts himself Jury say Guilty – To be Hanged &c Judgmt record

Repd Trans: 7yrs 34 John Coomber 33 – Stealing a Gelding p £5 of Joseph Lay

2nd Count of Josh Lay and another

Puts himself Jury say Guilty To be Hanged &c Judgmt recorded

Repd Trans: Life 35 William Brain 22 –

Puts himself Like Verdict Like Judgmt recorded

Repd Trans: Life Charles Brain 21 – Feloniously Breaking and Entering the Dwelling House of John Hatton and Stealing goods v £1. 12. 4

Adjourned until Tomorrow at 9 forenoon

Saturday 1st January 1831 – Before Mr Justice Bosanquet in the Crown Court

1 Thomas Atchin
2 Isaac Emanuel Ardley
3 Charles Beville
4 George Bone
5 John Bunce
6 Thomas Barnett

Petit Jury sworn

7 John Child
8 Joseph Dickson
9 James Day
10 Robert Fairbairn
11 David Miller
12 John Whitfield

Confesses himself Guilty To be Hanged &c Judgmt recorded

Repd Ho: Corr: Guildford 1 year 16 James Mills 45

Like confession Like Judgment

Repd Ho: Corr: Brixton 6 cal: mos John Mills 20 – Feloniously Breaking and Entering the Dwelling House of John Best and Stealing his goods v 29/2 and goods v 1/- of Hannah Best

Puts himself Jury say Guilty To be Hanged by the neck until he be Dead

17 James Warner 30 – Maliciously and feloniously setting fire to a Mill of James Franks in his possession with intent to injure him

2nd Count – a Granary

Puts himself Jury say Not Guilty

Daniel Austin 47
George Wilson
William Smith nc

Bill not found Stealing goods v £30. 17 . . of Elizabeth Staley

2nd Count property of James Blaker

VII *Surrey Winter Assizes, 1830. From this particular assizes most of the capital convicts were reprieved. Only James Warner (shown here) is left for execution.* (TNA, ASSI 31/26, p.327.)

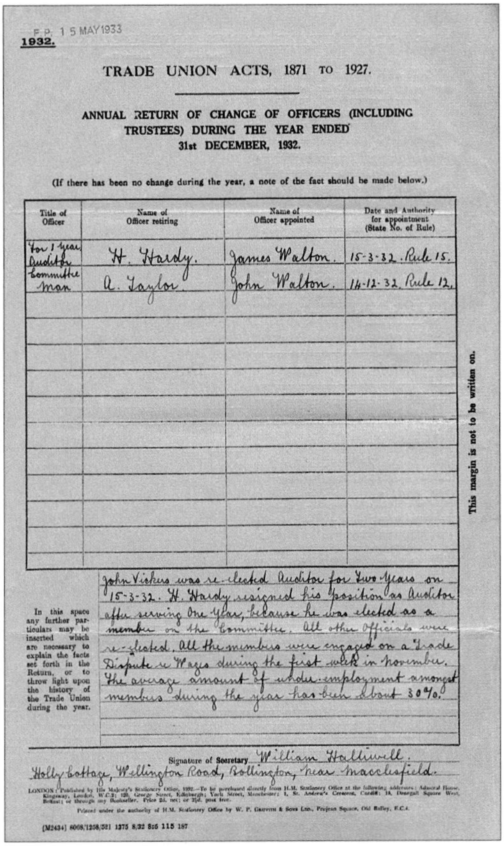

F.P. 15 MAY 1933

1932.

TRADE UNION ACTS, 1871 TO 1927.

ANNUAL RETURN OF CHANGE OF OFFICERS (INCLUDING TRUSTEES) DURING THE YEAR ENDED 31st DECEMBER, 1932.

(If there has been no change during the year, a note of the fact should be made below.)

Title of Officer	Name of Officer retiring	Name of Officer appointed	Date and Authority for appointment (State No. of Rule)
For 1 year Auditor	H. Hardy.	James Walton.	15-3-32. Rule 15.
Committee man	A. Taylor	John Walton.	14-12-32. Rule 12.

This margin is not to be written on.

In this space any further particulars may be inserted which are necessary to explain the facts set forth in the Return, or to throw light upon the history of the Trade Union during the year.

John Vickers was re-elected Auditor for two years on 15-3-32. H. Hardy resigned his position as Auditor after serving one year, because he was elected as a member on the Committee. All other Officials were re-elected. All the members were engaged on a Trade Dispute re Wages during the first week in November. The average amount of under-employment amongst members during the year has been about 30%.

Signature of Secretary William Halliwell.

Holly Cottage, Wellington Road, Bollington, near Macclesfield.

VIII *Final page of the annual return for the Bollington Operative Cotton Spinners Association for 1932.* (TNA, FS 12/347.)

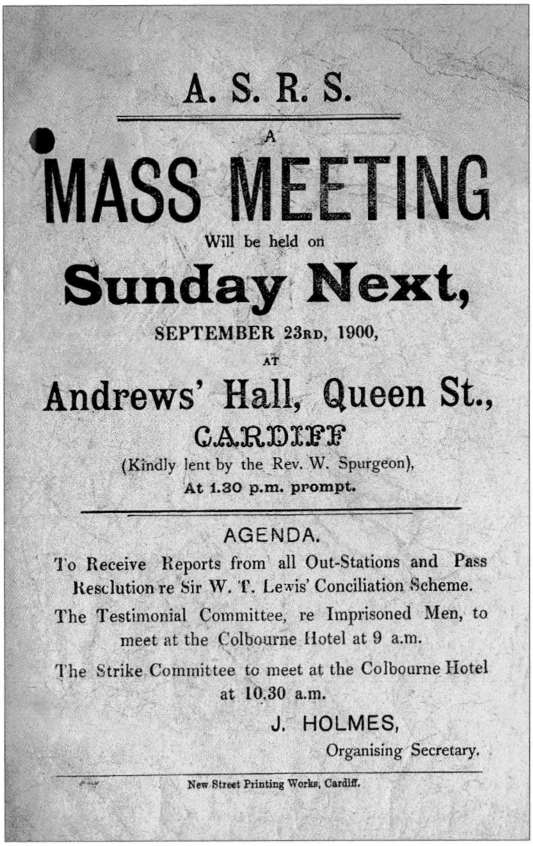

IX *Notice of a mass meeting to be held in Cardiff called by the Amalgamated Society of Railway Servants, 23 September 1900.* (TNA, RAIL 1057/2854.)

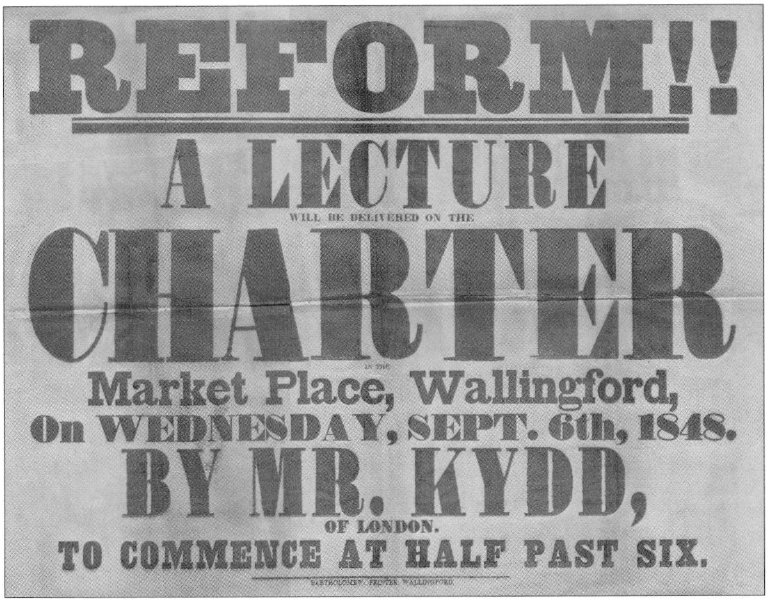

X *Chartist meeting to be held in Wallingford, 6 September 1848.* (TNA, HO 45/2410(3), f. 337.)

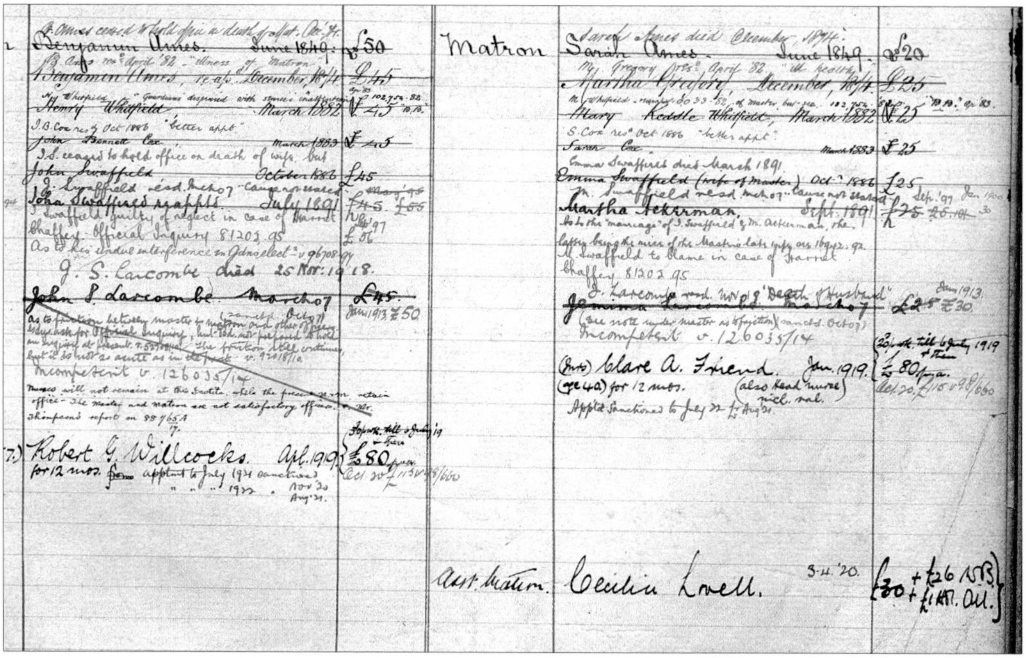

Benjamin Ames. June 1849. £50

Benjamin Ames, re app. December 1874. £45

Henry Whitfield March 1882 £45

John Bennett Cox March 1883 £45

John Swaffield October 1886 £45

John Swaffield reappd. July 1891 £45 £55

J. S. Larcombe died 25 Nov: 1918.

John S. Larcombe March 07 £45. Jan 1913 £50

Incompetent v. 12603S/14

Robert G. Willcocks. Apl. 1919 £80 p.a.

Matron Sarah Ames. June 1849. £20

Martha Gregory December 1874 £25

Mary Keddle Whitfield March 1882 £25

Sarah Cox March 1883 £25

Emma Swaffield (wife of master) Oct. 1886 £25

Martha Ackerman, Sept. 1891 £25 £6.10

Jemima Larcombe March 07 £25 £30.

Incompetent v. 12603S/14

(Mrs) Clare A. Friend. Jan. 1919. £80 p.a.

Asst. Matron. Cecilia Lovell. 3.4.20. £30 + £26 NSB + £1 Lt. All.

XI *Extract from Bridport Union showing the various details for the workhouse matron. Details to the left are for the workhouse master.* (TNA, MH 9/3, p.467.)

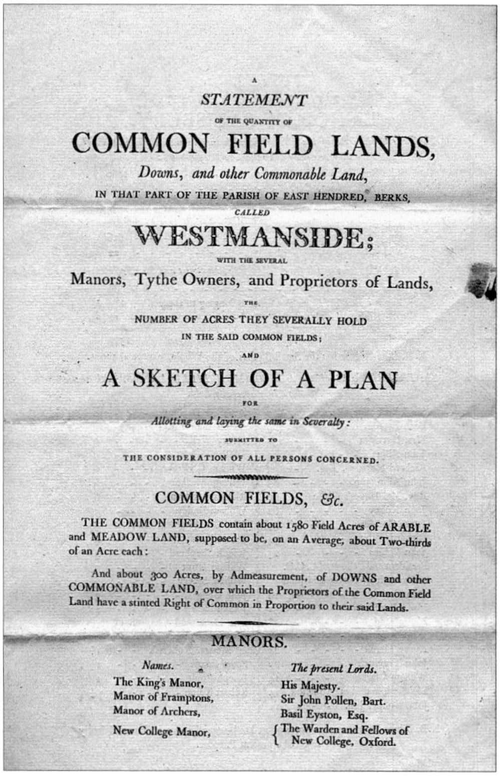

A
STATEMENT
OF THE QUANTITY OF
COMMON FIELD LANDS,
Downs, and other Commonable Land,
IN THAT PART OF THE PARISH OF EAST HENDRED, BERKS,
CALLED
WESTMANSIDE;
WITH THE SEVERAL
Manors, Tythe Owners, and Proprietors of Lands,
THE
NUMBER OF ACRES THEY SEVERALLY HOLD
IN THE SAID COMMON FIELDS;
AND
A SKETCH OF A PLAN
FOR
Allotting and laying the same in Severalty:
SUBMITTED TO
THE CONSIDERATION OF ALL PERSONS CONCERNED.

COMMON FIELDS, &c.

THE COMMON FIELDS contain about 1580 Field Acres of ARABLE and MEADOW LAND, supposed to be, on an Average, about Two-thirds of an Acre each:

And about 300 Acres, by Admeasurement, of DOWNS and other COMMONABLE LAND, over which the Proprietors of the Common Field Land have a stinted Right of Common in Proportion to their said Lands.

MANORS.

Names.	*The present Lords.*
The King's Manor,	His Majesty.
Manor of Framptons,	Sir John Pollen, Bart.
Manor of Archers,	Basil Eyston, Esq.
New College Manor,	The Warden and Fellows of New College, Oxford.

XII *Statement of the common field lands in East Hendred, Berkshire. From the East Hendred enclosure papers, 1800-1805.* (TNA, CRES 2/27.)

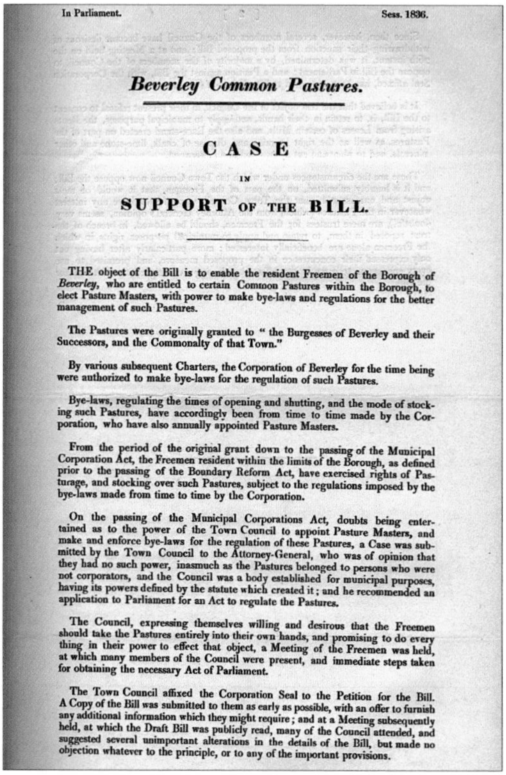

In Parliament. Sess. 1836.

Beverley Common Pastures.

CASE
IN
SUPPORT OF THE BILL.

THE object of the Bill is to enable the resident Freemen of the Borough of *Beverley*, who are entitled to certain Common Pastures within the Borough, to elect Pasture Masters, with power to make bye-laws and regulations for the better management of such Pastures.

The Pastures were originally granted to " the Burgesses of Beverley and their Successors, and the Commonalty of that Town."

By various subsequent Charters, the Corporation of Beverley for the time being were authorized to make bye-laws for the regulation of such Pastures.

Bye-laws, regulating the times of opening and shutting, and the mode of stocking such Pastures, have accordingly been from time to time made by the Corporation, who have also annually appointed Pasture Masters.

From the period of the original grant down to the passing of the Municipal Corporation Act, the Freemen resident within the limits of the Borough, as defined prior to the passing of the Boundary Reform Act, have exercised rights of Pasturage, and stocking over such Pastures, subject to the regulations imposed by the bye-laws made from time to time by the Corporation.

On the passing of the Municipal Corporations Act, doubts being entertained as to the power of the Town Council to appoint Pasture Masters, and make and enforce bye-laws for the regulation of these Pastures, a Case was submitted by the Town Council to the Attorney-General, who was of opinion that they had no such power, inasmuch as the Pastures belonged to persons who were not corporators, and the Council was a body established for municipal purposes, having its powers defined by the statute which created it; and he recommended an application to Parliament for an Act to regulate the Pastures.

The Council, expressing themselves willing and desirous that the Freemen should take the Pastures entirely into their own hands, and promising to do every thing in their power to effect that object, a Meeting of the Freemen was held, at which many members of the Council were present, and immediate steps taken for obtaining the necessary Act of Parliament.

The Town Council affixed the Corporation Seal to the Petition for the Bill. A Copy of the Bill was submitted to them as early as possible, with an offer to furnish any additional information which they might require; and at a Meeting subsequently held, at which the Draft Bill was publicly read, many of the Council attended, and suggested several unimportant alterations in the details of the Bill, but made no objection whatever to the principle, or to any of the important provisions.

XIII *Beverley Common Pastures – Case of promoters in support of saving clause proposed to be struck out on third reading.* (TNA, RAIL 1016/5, pp. 349-52.)

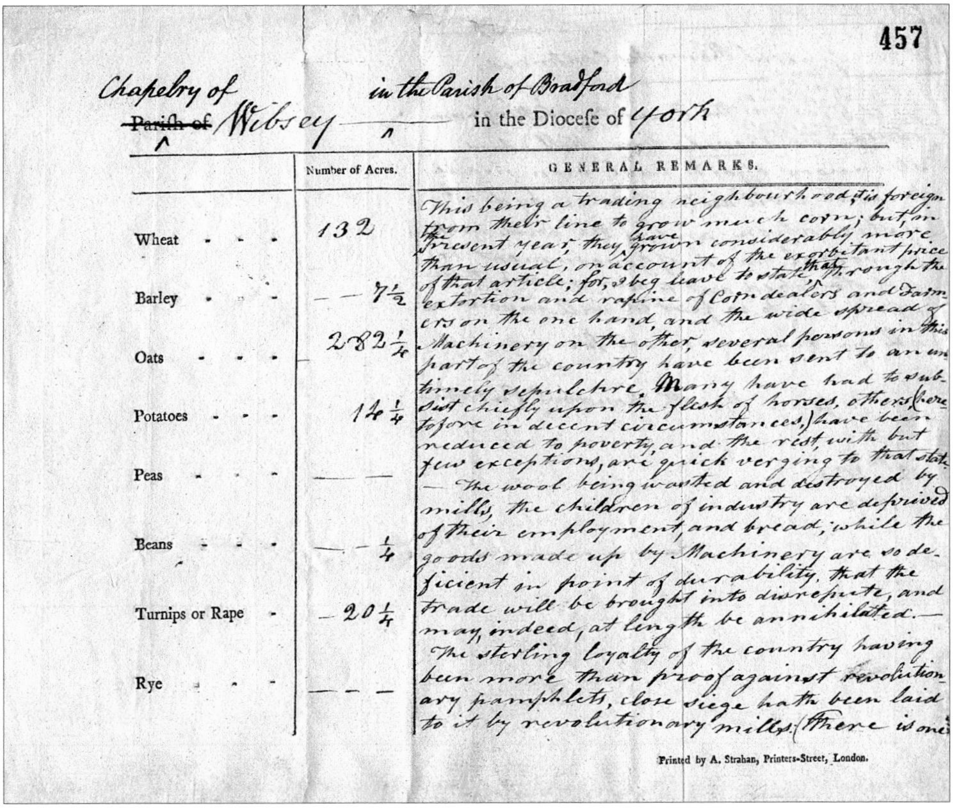

457

Chapelry of ~~Parish of~~ Wibsey in the Parish of Bradford in the Diocese of York

	Number of Acres.
Wheat	132
Barley	— — 7½
Oats	282¼
Potatoes	14¼
Peas	——
Beans	— — ¼
Turnips or Rape	— 20¼
Rye	— — —

GENERAL REMARKS.

This being a trading neighbourhood, it is foreign from their line to grow much corn; but, in the present year, they have grown considerably more than usual, on account of the exorbitant price of that article; for, I beg leave to state, that through the extortion and rapine of Corn dealers and Farmers on the one hand, and the wide spread of Machinery on the other, several persons in this part of the country have been sent to an untimely sepulchre, Many have had to subsist chiefly upon the flesh of horses, others (heretofore in decent circumstances,) have been reduced to poverty, and the rest, with but few exceptions, are quick verging to that state. — The wool being wasted and destroyed by mills, the children of industry are deprived of their employment, and bread; while the goods made up by Machinery are so deficient in point of durability, that the trade will be brought into disrepute, and may, indeed, at length be annihilated. — The sterling loyalty of the country having been more than proof against revolutionary pamphlets, close siege hath been laid to it by revolutionary mills, (There is one

Printed by A. Strahan, Printers-Street, London.

XIV *Return for Wibsey in Bradford, West Riding of Yorkshire. Comments include the increased proportion of corn grown recently due to high prices, local unemployment and poverty, and general political concerns, 1801.* (TNA, HO 67/26/457.)

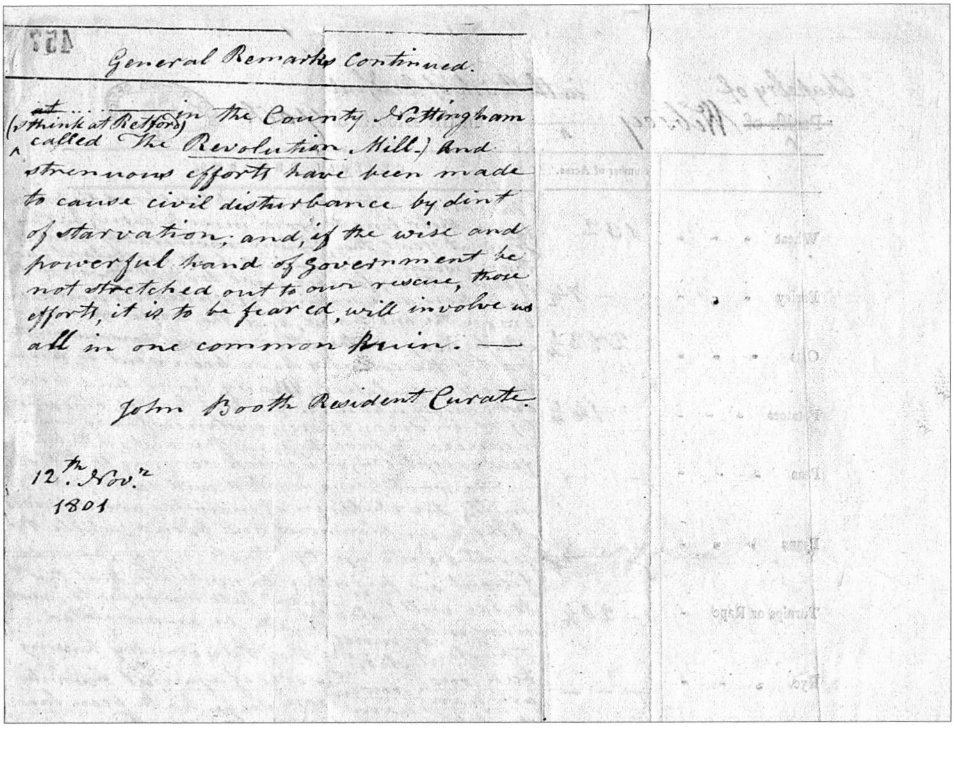

General Remarks Continued.

(I think at Retford) in the County Nottingham called The Revolution Mill.) And strenuous efforts have been made to cause civil disturbance by dint of starvation; and, if the wise and powerful hand of Government be not stretched out to our rescue, those efforts, it is to be feared, will involve us all in one common Ruin. —

John Booth Resident Curate

12th Novr
1801

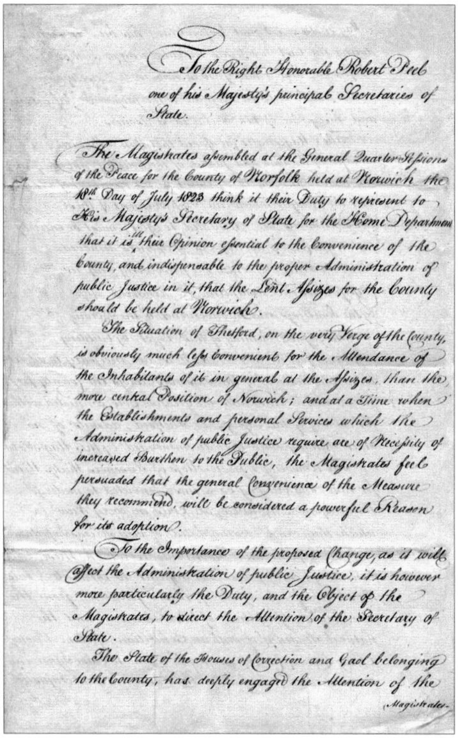

To the Right Honorable Robert Peel one of his Majesty's principal Secretaries of State.

The Magistrates assembled at the General Quarter Sessions of the Peace for the County of Norfolk held at Norwich the 18th Day of July 1823 think it their Duty to represent to His Majesty's Secretary of State for the Home Department that it is in their Opinion essential to the Convenience of the County, and indispensable to the proper Administration of public Justice in it, that the Lent Assizes for the County should be held at Norwich.

The Situation of Thetford, on the very Verge of the County, is obviously much less convenient for the Attendance of the Inhabitants of it in general at the Assizes, than the more central Position of Norwich; and at a Time when the Establishments and personal Services which the Administration of public Justice require are of Necessity of increased Burthen to the Public, the Magistrates feel persuaded that the general Convenience of the Measure they recommend, will be considered a powerful Reason for its adoption.

To the Importance of the proposed Change, as it will affect the Administration of public Justice, it is however more particularly the Duty, and the Object of the Magistrates, to direct the Attention of the Secretary of State.

The State of the Houses of Correction and Gaol belonging to the County, has deeply engaged the Attention of the (Magistrates

XV *Opening page of a letter/petition from the Norfolk magistrates to the Home Secretary stating that the Norfolk Lent Assizes should be held at Norwich rather than at Thetford, Norwich being more central to the county, 5 August 1823.* (TNA, HO 52/3, f. 350.)

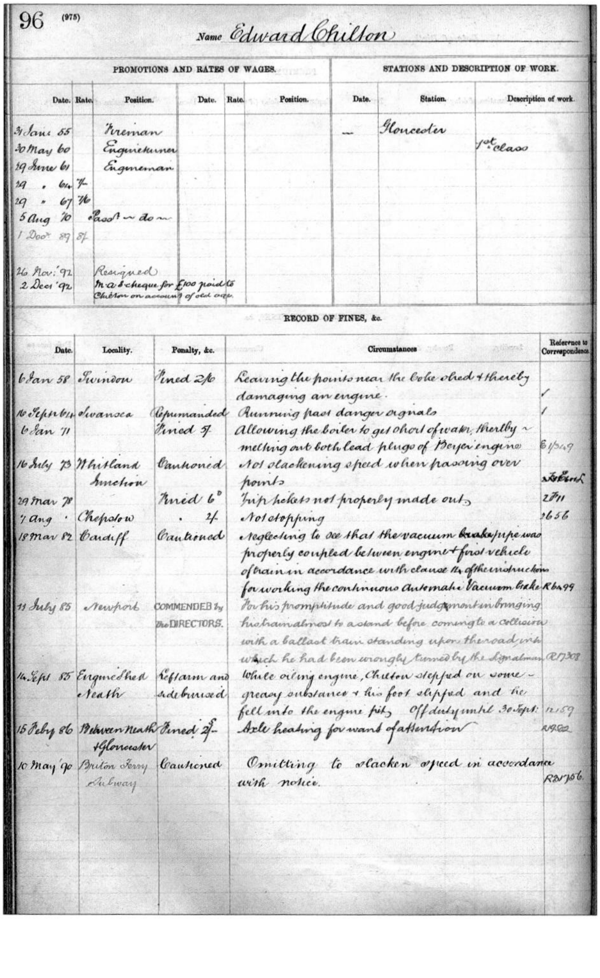

96 (975) Name Edward Chilton

PROMOTIONS AND RATES OF WAGES. / STATIONS AND DESCRIPTION OF WORK.

Date.	Rate.	Position.	Date.	Rate.	Position.	Date.	Station.	Description of work.
31 Jan 55		Fireman				—	Gloucester	1st class
30 May 60		Engineturner						
29 June 61		Engineman						
29 " 64	7/-							
29 " 67	7/6							
5 Aug 70		Pass ~ do ~						
1 Dec 89	8/-							
26 Nov 92		Resigned						
2 Dec 92		M.a & cheque for £100 paid to Chilton on account of old age.						

RECORD OF FINES, &c.

Date.	Locality.	Penalty, &c.	Circumstances	Reference to Correspondence.
6 Jan 58	Swindon	Fined 2/6	Leaving the points near the Coke shed & thereby damaging an engine.	/
16 Sept 64	Swansea	Reprimanded	Running past danger signals	/
6 Jan 71		Fined 5/-	Allowing the boiler to get short of water, thereby melting out both lead plugs of Beyer's engine	61349
16 July 73	Whitland Junction	Cautioned	Not slackening speed when passing over points	[illegible]
29 Mar 78		Fined 6d	Trip tickets not properly made out	2811
7 Aug "	Chepstow	" 2/-	Not stopping	2656
18 Mar 82	Cardiff	Cautioned	Neglecting to see that the vacuum brake pipe was properly coupled between engine & first vehicle of train in accordance with clause 14 of the instructions for working the continuous Automatic Vacuum Brake	Rb 499
11 July 85	Newport	COMMENDED by the DIRECTORS.	For his promptitude and good judgment in bringing his train almost to a stand before coming to a collision with a ballast train standing upon the road, into which he had been wrongly turned by the Signalman	R 17308
14 Sept 85	Engine Shed Neath	Left arm and side bruised	While oiling engine, Chilton slipped on some greasy substance & his foot slipped and he fell into the engine pit. Off duty until 30 Sept.	12159
15 Feby 86	Between Neath & Gloucester	Fined 2/-	Axle heating for want of attention	R 9622
10 May 90	Briton Ferry Railway	Cautioned	Omitting to slacken speed in accordance with notice.	RD 756

XVI *Great Western Railway records. From a register for drivers and firemen, showing date of entering service, promotions, type of work, fines etc. [c.1841-1864: from date joining].* (TNA, RAIL 264/18, p. 96.)

newspapers, journals and other periodicals, photographs and other illustrative material,[20] as well as from the structures themselves where they still stand. Large estates were responsible for building considerable numbers of houses for their workers and these archives will be invaluable in certain areas. Arguably the most important periodical is *The Builder*, which contains numerous articles about public buildings and houses constructed in many parts of Britain during the Victorian era; it is particularly useful for the period 1844-83, when George Goodwin was the editor. It was published from 1842 from 1966 and still continues under the title *Building*.[21] The Royal Institute of British Architects holds an extensive collection of relevant archive material, dating from the 17th century to the present day, including architects' personal papers (correspondence, notebooks and diaries), job files and other records. The records of individual building firms may survive in local record offices.

The Chartists devised a plan to settle many thousands of working people on the land in the 1840s, in 'small farms' of between two and four acres to be cultivated by hand labour; the Chartist Land Plan was essentially the brainchild of Feargus O'Connor. Between 1846 and 1849 five settlements were constructed but only one, Dodford in Worcestershire, was successful; one of the cottages built there has recently been restored under the auspices of the National Trust.[22] Freehold land societies were formed by the lower middle and working classes in the 19th century in order to acquire plots of land on which to build good-quality houses. The combined funds of such enterprises were made available to individual members by ballot and payment was by instalments over many years. Many of the early societies failed but the successful ones were responsible for some interesting mid-Victorian suburbs in many towns. Building societies were smaller, often of 20 to 50 people, and were wound up when all their members had been housed. They began slightly earlier, at the end of the 18th century, especially in northern industrial towns; although most remained local institutions there were a number of mergers and many of the major mortgage lenders today can trace their origins back to these early societies. Records of freehold land societies are rare and may be confined to references in local newspapers, but the records of building societies may have been deposited in a local record office or remain with the present-day organisation.

Planning legislation did not begin until the middle of the 19th century, as part of the provisions of various public health Acts. They were prompted by, and continued under debates reflected in the investigations headed by people such as Edwin Chadwick[23] and Charles Booth.[24] The growth in towns has been well documented and many poorer people lived in slum conditions; graphic details can be found in Medical Officer of Health reports (see previous chapter). Two examples illustrate the type of information given: in Leicester a house in Redcross Street housed a man, his wife and 11 children; they lived in one room measuring 11 ft 6 in by 10 ft 9 in by 6 ft 9 in high. In the graphically-named Porkshop Yard, off Abbey Street, 11 houses were converted pigsties with one room each, containing an average of five persons.[25] There are plenty of similar examples, usually drawn from the local reports to the General Board of Health referred to in the previous chapter. Many towns had back-to-back houses which only had one door onto the street; examples of these survive in places like Bradford, where they have been refurbished and two adjoining houses made into one dwelling.

The 1858 Public Health Act contained adoptive clauses on the control of new buildings and several provincial towns began to regulate particular aspects of building by passing bye-laws under its aegis or by private Acts. Much of the activity was concerned with banning back-to-backs; in 1866 the council in Leeds passed a bye-law which restricted future back-to-back houses to blocks of not more than eight with yard privies between each block. Manchester prohibited cellar dwellings by a local Act in 1853 and in 1867 drew up regulations on room sizes, window areas and the provision of every new house with a small private yard. New bye-laws in Leicester in 1859 stipulated that a minimum space of 150 square feet had to be left at the side or rear of each house, and the depth of this yard was to increase with the addition of a third storey. The minimum height of ceilings was fixed at 8ft 6in for ground floor and basement rooms, and 8ft for others; one room on each floor should have a minimum of 108 sq ft of floor space and one window in each room had to measure at least one-tenth of the floor area. The Sanitary Law Amendment Act of 1874 allowed local authorities to lay down regulations concerning paving and drainage of premises, and the ventilation of rooms, and the Public Health Act of 1875 empowered local authorities to control the sanitary and housing conditions of their districts. Section 157 allowed them to make bye-laws governing the layout, width and construction of new streets, the construction of new buildings, the space around them and the sanitary provisions relating to them.

Lodging houses presented particular problems; the standard of accommodation varied widely and rooms were often shared by people of both sexes and all ages. In Leicester lodging houses were regularly inspected from 1849: the Board of Health recognised minimum standards of cleanliness and specified maximum numbers allowed to share a room. In 1855 there were 38 lodging-houses in the town, accommodating 587 people, a considerable increase from 1845 when the population of lodging-houses was given as 240. A model lodging-house still survives in Leicester and its standards were considerably higher than elsewhere; alcohol was banned, as was smoking upstairs, and lockers were provided.[26]

The 1848 Public Health Act allowed councils to take action on building control, although very few did so. One that did was Leicester and from 1849 there is a marvellous series of plans for every new building and every significant alteration. Other towns which already had private Acts to control development did not start to operate a modern system of building controls until later. The plans vary in a number of ways: their physical condition can range from extremely fragile to fairly robust; they can be works of art or crude drawings. A register was usually drawn up, which listed the plans in order of submission and gave details of the applicant (the owner, developer, architect or owner), location, description, date of application and whether or not the plan was approved. In larger towns contemporary indexes were created, usually by address but sometimes by name of applicant. Most plans have been deposited with local record offices but their sheer bulk means that more ephemeral plans, such as ones for garages and small extensions, may not have been kept. Nevertheless, building plans rank amongst the finest evidence for any study of the physical appearance of Victorian towns and often the buildings themselves have survived as further evidence.[27] The National Monuments Record, part of English Heritage, holds seven million photographs from the 1840s to the present, as well as other material; its public searchroom is in Swindon.

In the 19th century charities made some attempt to alleviate the worst of the inner-city problems. Organisations such as the Metropolitan Association for Improving the Dwellings of the Industrious Classes (founded in 1841) and the Society for Improving the Condition of the Labouring Classes (founded in 1844) were able to make inroads, but it was only a partial solution. The problem of social housing was enormous and required extensive government intervention. London in particular was an example of how big the problem was and this is reflected in the amount of public housing material generated for the capital.[28]

The provision of housing by local authorities was rare before the 20th century; the 1890 Housing of the Working Classes Act authorised the building of houses by public subsidies, but a few authorities, such as Liverpool in 1869, built houses for rent by working-class tenants before then.[29] After the Act 'council houses' began to appear in significant numbers, mainly built by local authorities to clear slums and rehouse families living in insanitary conditions. The 1909 Housing, Town Planning, etc Act gave local authorities planning powers over land for development. By this time working-class housing was rare,[30] but had long been a key political demand,[31] particularly during and after the First World War when 'homes fit for heroes' became a popular phrase. Slum housing remained a real problem throughout the inter-war period particularly (but not exclusively) in the areas designated as Special Areas of Britain.[32] A succession of Acts after the First World War led to the creation of large council estates on the edges of towns and the building of smaller estates alongside villages in many parts of the country. Information on this subject will be found in the records of the housing committee of town councils and individual files may also survive in CROs and local archives; in Leicester, for example, there are detailed specifications for new developments which include details of the houses built, their costs and house plans. Council estates continued until the 1980s when the withdrawal of government subsidies made further building difficult and 'social' housing built since then has been mostly undertaken by housing corporations. Central government policy in the same decade encouraged the 'right to buy' and many former tenants were able to purchase their homes at considerable discounts.

The garden city was the brainchild of Ebenezer Howard, a Hansard writer who sought a way of providing decent housing and other improvements to replace slum conditions in London and other major cities. His ideas were outlined in his book, *Tomorrow: a Peaceful Path to Real Reform*, published in 1898 and republished four years later under the title of *Garden Cities of Tomorrow*. The forerunners of garden cities were model industrial communities, such as Bournville, Port Sunlight and New Lanark. Although Howard was seen as a visionary, he was able to persuade others to help him to put his ideas into practice. With a team of like-minded individuals he established the Garden City Pioneer Company which looked for a suitable estate in which to build the Garden City. Its Articles of Association stated: 'The estate selected [is] to be carefully planned under the best expert advice, so that as the town grows, factories and workshops, the houses of the people, the parks and open spaces, schools, churches and other public buildings, may be placed in the most convenient position'. It was believed that the ideal size for a garden city was between 4,000 and 6,000 acres and a number of possible sites were investigated. The other criteria included that it should be close to a railway line, that a satisfactory water supply was available and that it should be near to London or some other large centre of labour. Howard envisaged a series of garden cities, with 'satellites' surrounding one larger town.

The first garden city (Letchworth) dates from October 1903. The first houses were occupied in July 1904 and the following year a 'Cheap Cottages Exhibition' was held: a £100 prize was offered for the best £150 cottage with living room, scullery and three bedrooms. There were other classes and special prizes were offered for the cheapest cottage, the best wooden cottage and the best concrete cottage. Over 60,000 people visited the exhibition, many of them on cheap day returns from Kings Cross, and most of the houses are still standing.[33] In October 1918 Howard had identified a suitable site for a second garden city (Welwyn).[34] The garden city movement spread throughout the world, with particular interest in Japan, and 21st-century pressure for more housing has demonstrated that the models of Letchworth and Welwyn still have much to commend them; however, there were to be no further garden cities in Britain. Although many of Howard's original ideas were impractical in implementation, his core philosophy of providing better places to live succeeded.[35] The successor to garden cities was the new towns movement, which was first mooted just before the Second World War. In 1944 the Abercrombie Plan suggested the creation of ten new satellite towns to relieve pressure in Greater London. The New Towns Act was passed in 1946 and 14 new towns were designated by 1950, mainly in the south-east; a further eight were named between 1961 and 1967. The first new town was Stevenage, also in Hertfordshire. In many of the new houses the standards of layout and design were high and there were often attempts to build in styles which would harmonise with the local vernacular. Records of the various schemes will be held at local borough or CROs.

Central government records mainly feature from the late 19th century as government became much more of a key player in planning and regulating house building. This followed the various 19th-century debates about poverty and public health and dealt with overcrowding, unemployment, dirt, disease, etc (see chapters 8 and 9). Some of the earliest central records for England and Wales, which refer to housing and in particular overcrowding, are in TNA record series MH and HLG. These records were created or inherited by the Ministry of Housing and Local Government, and of successor and related bodies which included the Local Government Board and Ministry of Health as they related to the administration of local government, housing and town and country planning. With the establishment in 1871 of the Local Government Board a department was created which was able to influence housing initiatives at a local level. As well as holding the administrative records of the Ministry of Housing and Local Government, HLG records also include documents relating to regional offices and committees of the Ministry of Town and Country Planning, housing divisions, rent tribunals, rent assessment panels and rent officers, planning divisions, new towns and development divisions, and the Housing and Planning Inspectorate. Local authority correspondence in MH 48 will give some scattered information on housing, as will MH 13, HLG 1 and HLG 46. HLG 4 holds files concerning general planning schemes of local authorities or joint planning committees and related matters. Where possible the working plans of each scheme have been associated with the appropriate file; extracted maps and plans can be found in HLG 5. Contemporary registers of planning schemes which contain references to HLG 4 files can be found in HLG 95 (1910-1939) with later correspondence in HLG 71 (1932-1980). A key series is HLG 47; these records cover the period 1909 to 1977 and comprise files of correspondence and papers of the Local Government Board, the Ministry of Health and the Ministry of Housing and Local Government on general housing subjects. They are essential when examining local authority schemes for slum clearance and demolition. They also relate to rehousing and problems of overcrowding, unhealthy districts, and redevelopment of land for housing and other purposes. There are also reports of departmental housing inspectors, local authority rehousing schemes and orders for slum clearance etc. Some records regarding permissions for planning schemes to go ahead can be traced through the registers in HLG 66 to records in HLG 26, HLG 23 (1923-1937) and HLG 11. The record series HLG 49 comprises files of the Local Government Board, the Ministry of Health, the Ministry of Housing and Local Government and the Department of the Environment from 1905 to 1971. The records relate to the planned development of housing programmes and schemes. There is material which relates to housing and town development, acquisition of land, district valuers' and surveyors' reports, etc. A useful series for the post-war period is the various maps, plans and associated documents submitted by local authorities to the Ministry of Town and Country Planning in HLG 119, HLG 79 and HLG 71. For information on New Towns see HLG 90, HLG 91, HLG 115 and HLG 116.

There is a considerable amount of information on buildings, other than houses, especially important and substantial structures such as castles and stately homes. This may be difficult to track down, but the major repositories, such as the British Library and Bodleian Library, will hold sources. In the British Library, for example, are 15th-century building accounts for Kirby Muxloe Castle in Leicestershire.[36] The system of listing buildings according to their historical or architectural merit is run by English Heritage. There are three categories, I, II* and II; of the 370,000 buildings currently listed, over 92 per cent are grade II. Buildings in the two higher grades may be eligible for grants towards urgent major repairs and there are restrictions on alterations to any listed building. The National Trust owns hundreds of buildings of all types and states of repair in England, Wales and Northern Ireland and the National Trust for Scotland is the sister body for that country. Apart from the Crown and the Anglican Church, other major landowners include English Heritage and its equivalents in the other home countries. Cadw is the historic environment agency within the Welsh Assembly Government with responsibility for protecting, conserving and promoting an appreciation of the historic environment of Wales, including historic buildings, ancient monuments, historic parks and gardens, landscapes and underwater archaeology. Historic Scotland safeguards the nation's built heritage and promotes its understanding and enjoyment on behalf of Scottish Ministers; there are more than 300 properties in its care and it is responsible for Scotland's listed buildings and scheduled ancient monuments. In Northern Ireland the Environment and Heritage Service has responsibility to protect and conserve Northern Ireland's natural heritage and built environment, to control and regulate pollution and to promote the wider appreciation of the environment and best environmental practices. The various Royal Commissions on Historic Monuments have been subsumed within English Heritage or its equivalent.

Nikolaus Pevsner's *Buildings of England* series comprises detailed volumes on important structures, county by county. They were first published by Penguin Books between 1951 and 1974, and some have been reprinted in recent years; the series is now sold by Yale University Press London and has been extended to Wales, Scotland and Ireland.[37]

The Society for the Protection of Ancient Buildings was founded by William Morris in 1877 to counteract the highly destructive 'restoration' of medieval buildings being practised by many Victorian architects. Today it is the largest, oldest and most technically expert national pressure group fighting to save old buildings from decay, demolition and damage. There are similar societies concerned with particular periods, such as the Georgian Group and the Victorian Society; the latter has some regional groups and both offer lectures and other special events.

11

Radicalism and Unrest

This chapter is aimed at describing material which illustrates local popular politics. This is sometimes a less than precise phrase and there are differing views about whether specific acts are political or not. Were the peasants of the 1381 Peasants' Revolt traitors, were striking miners in 1984–5 really the enemy within and was the breaking of newly erected enclosure fences in 18th-century Essex a piece of wanton vandalism, a pragmatic method of ensuring a particular individual's right to common pasture or a political defence of a communal way of life? Different (but essentially similar) conceptual questions can be asked with regard to poaching, food riots, wage disputes, animal maiming, arson and a host of other subjects. For much of our past politics has been the preserve of the elite – the king, his knights, lords and advisors; it was the sphere of the propertied, and specifically propertied men. In some ways any objection to the power of the lords of manors, employers, vicars, bishops and others by those socially and economically below them may be deemed popular politics.

The fact that much popular politics was considered seditious or purely criminal means that a lot of material will be found in the various criminal records. However, there were undoubtedly many criminal events and cases concerning enclosure, food or wages riots and disturbances which are yet unlisted, difficult to find and underused; therefore speculative searches can be made which yield unexpected results. Until the various criminal records have been fully indexed or calendared, individual researchers will have to rely on their own searches to exhaust these wonderful sources.

Notwithstanding the fact that much work remains to be done in this area, it seems that direct intervention by groups of workers was far more common than may have been thought and this chapter seeks to illustrate the well-known as well as the lesser-known sources regarding popular politics. Sources relating to opposition to unfair taxes, enclosure and new machinery, resistance to wage cuts, refusal to pay tithes, riots over high prices or the removal of local grain stores can be found in many repositories, and the main sources will be described. The chapter ends with a short piece on 'high [parliamentary] politics' and the slow democratisation of the political process.

The Peasants' Revolt of June and July 1381 was a milestone in English politics and its major outlines are clear. The immediate catalyst of the rebellion was the poll tax of 1380–81. The march on London and the confrontation between the king and his men against Wat Tyler and the rebel company are the better known events, but a variety of disturbances leading up to and contemporaneous with those of London occurred in Essex, Kent, Middlesex, Surrey, Suffolk, St Albans, Bury St Edmunds, Norfolk, Cambridgeshire, Ely and York. The records of central government concerning the revolt are mainly found at TNA within tax and criminal records of the Exchequer, records of itinerant justices and the Court of King's Bench. For example:

> E 179: Exchequer: Kings Remembrancer: Particulars of Account and other records relating to Lay and Clerical Taxation, 1190-1690. This series of records include the taxation records of the poll taxes which contributed to the revolt;
>
> JUST 1/103: General Oyer and Terminer Roll, Commissioners of 1381 to deal with the aftermath of the peasants' revolt, roll of indictments, 5 Ric II;
>
> JUST 1/400: General Oyer and Terminer: Inquiry into the Peasants' Revolt, file of indictments. 5 Ric II;
>
> JUST 2/255: Inquisitions held at Colchester by Justices of Oyer and Terminer to inquire into the damage done to the property of Thomas Harding of Manningtree at the time of the Peasants' Revolt (rot 13) 14 Ric II;
>
> KB 9/43: Enquiry Commission, Kent, concerning those who were against the king and his people between Trinity and Corpus Christi (9-13 June 1381) during the Peasants' Revolt, taken at Maidstone, 4-5 July, from West Kent Juries: Indictment file, 1381.

Other TNA series worth consulting are C 54, C 60, C 66, KB 27, SC 8 and CHES 25.[1] Obviously surviving contemporary estate and manorial records may further illuminate the revolt (see chapter 1). A selection of sources (including some mentioned here) has been edited and published in Dobson, *The Peasants' Revolt of 1381* which also includes selections of and references to other contemporary records and chronicles. The bibliography also includes a list of contemporary chronicles some of which can be found on the web.[2]

From the 15th century onwards many of the types of records essential for such research are essentially the same, and it would be pointless continually to reproduce the same list of documents each time. There are a number of overlapping sources which cover: the Pilgrimage of Grace (1536-7), the Western Rebellion (1549), Kett's Rebellion (1559), the Midland Revolt (1607), the series of major protests between 1608 and 1639 against enclosure at Coventry and in North Wales, the increasing demands of landlords (including the Crown) on their tenants in northern England, the opposition of inhabitants of the Fenlands to the Crown's claim of ownership of reclaimed Marshland; and many more.[3] At a local level the existence of substantial private family and estate, manorial and local authority records (vestry, town and borough council, quarter sessions) exist in greater numbers in the early modern period than earlier. Sometimes this will be because of the recent establishment of a particular authority or creation of an estate bureaucracy while in other cases it will be a result of that great historical leveller, document survival.[4] Criminal records and sets of estate papers will also survive in NAS and NLW.

The key central government sources for the subject are the general domestic correspondence and other papers of the Principal Secretaries of State,[5] Privy Council (England and Wales), [6] Treasury Solicitor,[7] as well as specific places that may have come under crown lands, duchy and palatinate of Lancaster and the palatinates of Chester and Durham. Other central repositories such as the British Library and the Bodleian Library will have scattered references to these general features of unrest such as the depositions concerning Kett's rebellion which were taken at Colchester before Benjamin Clere and Robert Flyngant in 1549, the accounts of destruction of enclosures in Fakenham in 1603 and a transcript of Philip Doddridge's letter to those involved in a riot at Brixworth in Northamptonshire in 1736.[8] The House of Lords Journals and House of Commons Journals will also be useful[9] as will legal court records. The latter are perhaps the most daunting for speculative searches. However, there are numerous published calendars for various court proceedings and the researcher should begin by investigating published transcripts and calendars before moving to the archival sources (see also chapter 12).

Direct intervention could occur in economic life: opposition to the introduction of machinery,[10] breaking down enclosure fences,[11] resisting wage cuts, food riots[12] (prompted by local perceptions of unjust high prices) and general murmurings of discontent can be found across various sets of records. For example, the following list is made up from the records of Star Chamber, assizes, Privy Council, Home Office, State Papers and Kings Bench:

> 1526: William Partriche, Herry Savyll, Robert Furneux and others, killing game in Wortley Park;[13]
>
> 22 March 1579: a group of men, mainly local labourers from Cheshunt, broke down the fences of a close at Northaw belonging to the Earl of Warwick. The following week another group of men, this time from North Mimms and Hatfield broke down more [or replacement fences?] in the same place;[14]
>
> September 1603: an unspecified number of men and women armed with shovels, staves and hedge stakes 'broke and digged downe' the ditches of a close called Church or Ox Mead in Kelshall in Hertfordshire;[15]
>
> June 1607: an unspecified number of people broke down the posts and rails of a recent enclosure at Danbury in Essex;[16]
>
> 5 January 1610: John Aylewood, a weaver from Coggeshall, indicted for uttering seditious words in public at Bocking, said 'That the Church of England is nott the true visable Church of Jesus Christ';[17]
>
> 1709: a corn dealer travelling through Suffolk to Norwich related how he was assailed in several places and called 'a Rogue, and Corn Jobber, and some cry'd out Stone him, some Pull him off his horse'. When he asked why they acted in this way towards him they said 'he was a Rogue & was going to carry the corn into France';[18]

> [1740] a North Yorkshire trader in grain was given a ducking in the river and told that by following such a trade he was 'no better than a rebel';[19]
>
> [1795] at Chudleigh in Devon a crowd destroyed the machinery of a local miller in 1795. The miller had recently undertaken to supply the admiralty with ship's biscuits and subsequently had no flour to sell locally. This led 'to an Idea that ive done much infimy to the Community'; hence the destruction of his machinery;[20]
>
> [1800] Emmerson was regarded as the main culprit in ridiculing the Reverend Charles Jeffrys Cottrell. Cottrell was the rector of Hadley, a local JP and the chairman of the local Commissioners of Tax. Emmerson, who along with several other locals, was nursing a grievance against Cottrell in his role regarding taxation, erected a ten-foot high gibbet from which was suspended an effigy in a black coat. Emmerson claimed it was a scarecrow while Cottrell saw it as a personal slight. Cottrell then received through the post a portrait of a parson on a gibbet, exposing his genitals and asking his 'Bretheren [to] behold my exalted station ... O yea I repent from ever been Parson Just Ass and so forth. O what a miserable Shitting Stinking Dogmatick Prig of an April fool I do appear'.[21]

Such events tell us much about what was considered acceptable and what was considered possible. Although such activities were not usually considered to be as dangerous to the state as overt sedition, similar actions in various periods of political peace and political unrest may be viewed differently, treated differently, managed by different government departments and so archived in different record series. The general court records of quarter sessions, assizes and King's Bench as well as the online Old Bailey sessions papers for metropolitan cases will be key records for these types of events.[22] Local archives and CROs may provide local accounts but they may be hard to find and researchers need to know that something happened or be prepared systematically to work their way through the records; central government records of the Treasury Solicitor, State Papers Domestic, Star Chamber and Privy Council should be searched,[23] as well as the later general Home Office correspondence classes.[24] These general sets of records are essential for researchers.

There are some interesting examples from the mid-17th century onwards. In the State Papers Domestic, the English Revolution, the execution of Charles I and Cromwell's introduction of a republic is marked in archival terms with the introduction of Interregnum volumes for the period 1649-60. These records remain as a major series of material sent to central government from local areas and have the additional feature of recording local events and outcomes of the parliamentary or royalist struggle in some detail.[25] The H of LRO British Library is a major national repository for studies of this period, and a key collection of tracts and pamphlets are held there. David Pam's well respected local study of Enfield Chase used several short published accounts now held at the British Library dealing with Enfield inhabitants' clashes with the army over the government's plans to enclose Enfield Chase.[26] Some material has been published; Gerald Aylmer's *The Levellers in the English Revolution* is a good example of this and includes several writings of John Lilburne, William Walwyn and Richard Overton.[27]

Following the Restoration the archival record does not really alter in any significant way but the survival rates undoubtedly change. More survives in the way of private papers, vestry and corporation minutes and papers, and the records of quarter sessions. It is also the case that more material was produced. For example, recorded crime increased from the mid-18th century so the numbers of indictments, depositions and minute or order books which would need to be written up and compiled increased proportionately. For central government records at TNA the triumvirate of State Papers, Privy Council and Treasury records remain the three chief central government departments. The Treasury Solicitor remains key in dealing with the growth in political radicalism from the mid-18th century. In 1782 the record series of State Papers came to an end when the Northern and Southern Departments of the two principal secretaries of state become respectively the Foreign and Home Offices. The nature of the correspondence does not change between the two record series. The list of events for which material survives, which is by no means exhaustive, includes: the Jacobite risings of 1715 and 1745, 18th-century demands for the extension of the political franchise, corresponding societies of the 1790s, trade unionism, Luddism and other machine breaking, 'Peterloo', the 'Swing Riots', reform riots, Chartism, the suffragettes, the rise of the Independent Labour Party, 'the great unrest' (1910-14), the general strike; and many others up to the 20th century. Many local disturbances, if recorded at all, will be found in the generality of records discussed below.

For the Jacobite risings the key central government records at TNA are those of the general Domestic State Papers correspondence in SP 35, SP 45 and SP 44, as well as SP 41, SP 42, SP 45 and SP 55, and to a lesser degree WO 4, WO 5, WO 7, WO 24, ADM 1 and ADM 2. The most useful of the trial records are those of the Court of King's Bench and the Papers of the Treasury Solicitor. The Crown Side *Baga de Secretis* in KB 8 contains material relating to the treason trials which followed both risings. Precedents and Miscellanea in KB 33 contains a diverse collection of criminal material including draft indictments, some trial transcripts and list of prisoners. The Treasury Solicitors Papers in TS 11 and the 1745 Rebellion Papers in TS 20 are rich in material on the judicial and administrative aspects of the proceedings against those captured in 1745 and include trial records, lists of prisoners and material relating both to their backgrounds and their fates.

Although trials of prisoners held outside London were heard by Special Commissioners and the routine business of the assizes courts was suspended after each rising, a few documents and entries relating to the rebels can be found in the assize records for the north-eastern circuit. See ASSI 41-47 and those for Chester in CHES 21 and CHES 24, Durham in DURH 17 and DURH 19 and Lancashire in PL 25-28. The estates of many rebels were forfeit to the Crown. After the 1715 rising a Forfeited Estates Commission was established; the papers are in FEC 1 and books in FEC 2 of the Commissioners for England and Wales.[28] The records of Greenwich Hospital in ADM 74-80 contain many estates and some family records of the Earl of Derwentwater whose lands, after forfeiture, passed to the hospital. A smaller collection of records, relating to forfeiture after the 1745 rising, is in T 64. There are some High Court of Justiciary records relating to the post-1745 rising at the NAS in JC 7. There are also a number of certificates for the transportation of Jacobite prisoners to America in 1770 in JC 41 and papers relating to the settlement of forfeited estate on soldiers following the 1745 rebellion in E 700-788. There are also several useful publications listing prisoners and giving accounts of the trials.[29]

Jonathan Oates discusses material for Jacobite studies in his *Sources for the Study of the Jacobite Rebellions* ... and identifies later publications (including transcripts and lists of original documents), contemporary publications (including newspapers), records held locally and these at national repositories; the last includes the British Library (particularly the Newcastle MSS and the Hardwicke MSS for the '45), National Army Museum, National Library of Scotland, Nottingham University Library (correspondence between Henry Pelham and the military), as well as NAS and TNA.[30]

The early 1790s witnessed an upsurge in political interest, the concerns of ordinary people with regard to their social and economic condition and their aspiration to take part in politics to change that condition. Corresponding societies began during the 1790s in towns and cities such as Derby, Edinburgh, Dundee, Glasgow, London,[31] Leeds, Norwich, Nottingham, Perth and Sheffield. They were inspired, at least in part, by the publications of the radical writer Thomas Paine and the ideas of the French Revolutionaries. The societies met to discuss the cost of provisions, levels of wages and (most important) political change. Even more radical for this period, they began to discuss (through correspondence with similar groups around the country) ways in which political change could be secured, as well as organising lecture tours to promote their ideas.[32] Worried by the popularity of these societies, the government decided to repress the movement and embarked on a course of collecting material which would both inform them of planned activities and act as evidence against the leadership in any court action. As they were local societies there may be material in CROs, but there is also much material in several national specialist repositories such as the Modern Records Centre, Working Class Movement Library, National Maritime Museum and the British Library. Because of the government's obvious role in home defence TNA is one of the best places to look for this type of material; in the various Home Office,[33] and Privy Council correspondence and entry books for the period, papers in TS 11 and TS 24 as well as King's Bench and other criminal courts, there are documents relating to sedition and related matters. These include: handbills and posters advertising the general ideas and planned meetings of the societies; details of petitions; letters between various societies; and names of members. Trials of prominent leaders took place and resulting records can be found in both TNA and the NAS. The government developed an internal spy system. Much of the accounts, correspondence and miscellaneous papers relating to Home Office secret service expenditure are in TNA HO 387 but are difficult to interpret (see also published trial material).[34]

Part of the government's fears regarding this new political interest was the real or perceived connection to the military. Naval mutinies at Spithead and the Nore in 1797 appeared to many in authority to be especially dangerous when looking across the channel to revolutionary France. TNA ADM series and Home Office Criminal Entry Books in HO 13 give useful accounts of the mutineers. The National Maritime Museum also contains much useful material on the mutinies.[35]

The period of the corresponding societies overlapped with generalised legislation against trade unionism (see also chapter 5). During the 18th century legislation was usually introduced against specific groups of workers. In general confederacies, combinations and conspiracies by groups of workers to raise their wages were criminal at common law.[36] There were 18th-century statutes against tailors, weavers, hatters, etc until the legislation was generalised in 1799 and 1800 with the Combination Acts, essentially outlawing any combination of workers acting to raise wages; such combinations remained illegal until the Acts were repealed in 1824.

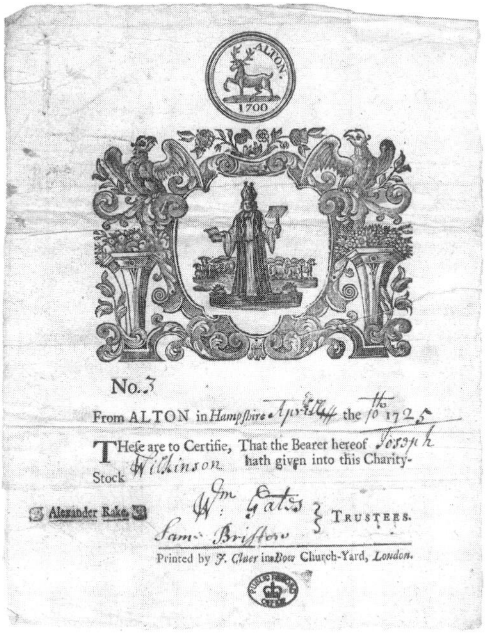
ALTON
1700
No.3
From ALTON in Hampshire the 1725
THese are to Certifie, That the Bearer hereof Joseph Wilkinson hath given into this Charity-Stock
Alexander Rake
Wm Gates
Sam Bristow
TRUSTEES.
Printed by J. Cluer in Bow Church-Yard, London.

27 *Trade Union or 'charity' ticket taken as evidence in the prosecution of workers at Alton, Hampshire.* (TNA, KB 1/3.)

Documentary evidence of early trade unions (before the middle of the18th century) or combinations are rare; they had no permanent structure, and references to their activities may be found in private papers and also in newspapers.[37] There may be some material in local and CROs,[38] as well as central collections such as the Modern Records Centre, British Library, Working Class Movement Library and TNA. A key set of records is the general court records of quarter sessions, assizes and perhaps to a lesser degree King's Bench (see also chapter 12). Information on strikes and combinations to increase wages (or resist wage cuts) is common in the criminal records, as the following examples illustrate. In 1725 Edward Palmer and Richard Palmer prosecuted woolcombers at the small Hampshire town of Alton. A strike involving seven of the men had been called to enforce a closed shop and regulations concerning apprenticeship. The case was heard in the Court of King's Bench. The Crown's affidavits give a mass of local detail and included is a union card of one of the woolcombers, Joseph Wilkinson. The card itself, complete with an image of Bishop Blaize (the patron of the woolcombers), indicates that the Alton branch of the union (or charity) was in existence by 1700. At times when economic dislocations were followed by widespread disturbances, defiance by a local workforce and the establishment (and activity) of trade unions, many local employers and local authorities would inform the Privy Council, Principal Secretaries of

State and (after 1782) the Home Office. From the middle of the 18th and into the early 19th centuries central government departmental involvement in the monitoring and prosecution of trade unions and their members means that State Papers Domestic, Privy Council and the Treasury Solicitor may be useful as well as the early Home Office correspondence classes.[39]

The Luddite disturbances took place in Nottinghamshire, Lancashire, Cheshire, Derbyshire, Leicestershire and Yorkshire during the period 1811-1816 (sometimes historians restrict it to 1811-13). Led by a fictional leader called 'Ned Ludd', the Luddites attacked new machinery and mills in an attempt to maintain the 'price' paid to them as textile workers and control over their work practices. The most violent incident took place in the West Riding of Yorkshire in 1812 when a mill-owner called William Horsfall was murdered. Disconcerted by the machine breakers' actions, the government responded by despatching large numbers of troops to the disaffected areas. CROs and TNA hold a fascinating and varied collection of material on the disturbances. Although mainly remembered for machine-breaking, the Luddites had initially suggested a new taxing scheme for the new machinery to raise revenue to train displaced workers in new skills. They also selected the newer (bigger) machines for destruction, usually leaving the traditional technology alone, demonstrating they had no aversion to machinery *per se*.

Concerned by the violent outbreaks of machine-breaking many people wrote to the Home Office to keep the government informed and ask for assistance in quelling the disturbances. This correspondence is ideal for local historians interested in studying Luddism. Not only do the correspondents provide accounts of Luddite activity but also in many instances provide a detailed background to the attacks, mentioning local conditions of living, the state of trade, etc. There is valuable material in HO 40, HO 41, HO 42, HO 43, HO 44 and HO 50. In fact with the outbreak of Luddite activities the Home Office began to compile a specific and separate set of related correspondence – 'disturbances' correspondence – and a complementary set of entry books (HO 40 and HO 41). Notwithstanding the relative difficulties of using Home Office records, there is a great deal of material for local historians interested in Luddism and other related trade union activity, and seditious political organisation in the localities. The particular problems concerning HO 42 can be partially overcome by published selected transcriptions of the material. Both A. Aspinall's *The Early English Trade Unions: Documents from the Home Office Papers in the Public Record Office* and M.I. Thomis's *Luddism in Nottinghamshire* provide full or partial transcriptions from Home Office papers.[40] These books are useful not only for the actual transcripts included in the volumes themselves but for providing general examples of HO 42 material for other studies.

Perhaps not surprisingly the government took a harsh line against the threat posed by the Luddites. Not only were an estimated 12,000 troops sent to the northern counties to deal with the disturbances but frame- or machine-breaking was made a capital offence. Every attempt to secure successful prosecutions of persons suspected of being Luddites was made, and many of the trial (as well as pre- and post-trial) records can be found at TNA. Many of these trials would have taken place at assize and quarter sessions level. The local historian would also be well advised to make an initial search of TS 11.[41] Since this class is not arranged in chronological order, a search for useful information should be made by relevant keywords on the online catalogue. The material contained in TS 11 will provide various details of the charge or indictments and names of people being prosecuted, witness statements and other details of Luddite activity. The government was concerned with the spread of Luddism and there is still some work to be done in uncovering to what degree they were in contact with the rest of the country.[42]

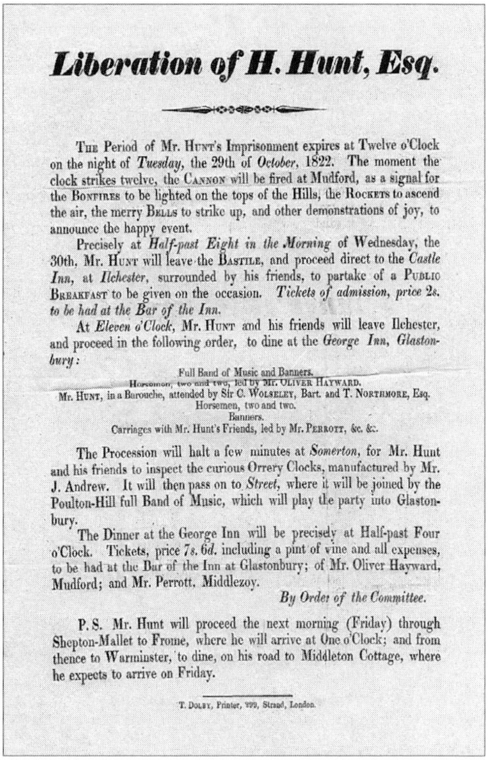

Liberation of H. Hunt, Esq.

The Period of Mr. Hunt's Imprisonment expires at Twelve o'Clock on the night of *Tuesday*, the 29th of *October*, 1822. The moment the clock strikes twelve, the Cannon will be fired at Mudford, as a signal for the Bonfires to be lighted on the tops of the Hills, the Rockets to ascend the air, the merry Bells to strike up, and other demonstrations of joy, to announce the happy event.

Precisely at *Half-past Eight in the Morning* of Wednesday, the 30th, Mr. Hunt will leave the Bastile, and proceed direct to the *Castle Inn*, at *Ilchester*, surrounded by his friends, to partake of a Public Breakfast to be given on the occasion. *Tickets of admission, price 2s. to be had at the Bar of the Inn.*

At *Eleven o'Clock*, Mr. Hunt and his friends will leave Ilchester, and proceed in the following order, to dine at the *George Inn, Glastonbury:*

Full Band of Music and Banners.
Horsemen, two and two, led by Mr. Oliver Hayward.
Mr. Hunt, in a Barouche, attended by Sir C. Wolseley, Bart. and T. Northmore, Esq.
Horsemen, two and two.
Banners.
Carriages with Mr. Hunt's Friends, led by Mr. Perrott, &c. &c.

The Procession will halt a few minutes at *Somerton*, for Mr. Hunt and his friends to inspect the curious Orrery Clocks, manufactured by Mr. J. Andrew. It will then pass on to *Street*, where it will be joined by the Poulton-Hill full Band of Music, which will play the party into Glastonbury.

The Dinner at the George Inn will be precisely at Half-past Four o'Clock. Tickets, price *7s. 6d.* including a pint of wine and all expenses, to be had at the Bar of the Inn at Glastonbury; of Mr. Oliver Hayward, Mudford; and Mr. Perrott, Middlezoy.

By Order of the Committee.

P. S. Mr. Hunt will proceed the next morning (Friday) through Shepton-Mallet to Frome, where he will arrive at One o'Clock; and from thence to Warminster, to dine, on his road to Middleton Cottage, where he expects to arrive on Friday.

T. Dolby, Printer, 299, Strand, London.

28 *Notice of a procession to celebrate the release of Henry Hunt following his arrest, conviction and imprisonment for the 'Peterloo' meeting in 1819.* (TNA, HO 52/1, f 236.)

From the end of the French Wars the British government was faced with a series of events, movements and political demands from below. These are briefly summarised: a series of provincial Hampden Clubs arguing for reform of the political system following the establishment of the London Hampden Club in 1812; riots in the agricultural districts in Essex, Suffolk and Norfolk and at Spa Fields in London in 1816; march of the Blanketeers and the Pentrich rising in 1817; the 'Peterloo Massacre' in 1819; the Cato Street Conspiracy; 'Radical War in Scotland'; the Queen Caroline affair in 1820; and further riots in East Anglia in 1822. This non-exhaustive list marks out the disturbed social history of Britain in the second half of the 1810s and early 1820s. After 1815 radical journalists began to publish cheap periodicals such as *The Cap of Liberty* and *The Black Dwarf*. In 1816 William Cobbett amended the style of his *Weekly Political Register* (originally started in 1802) and reduced the price to 2d; it soon reached a circulation of more than 40,000.[43] Although not easy (or quick) to work through, these periodicals can be excellent for local historians.

During the second half of 1830 and the first few weeks of 1831 over 1,000 separate incidences of machine-breaking, arson attacks, threatening letters and other disturbances took place, mainly in counties across the south and east of England.[44] Prompted by a long decline in the prices of agricultural produce and wages, the introduction of threshing machines and an influx of lowly paid Irish labour, the agricultural labourers were desperate to improve their standards of living. Although initially slow to react, the government eventually sent troops to quell the disturbances and undertook to prosecute all those involved in the riots. Over 2,000 people were arrested, of whom 19 were executed and over 500 transported. Most rural communities in south-eastern England were affected by the 'Swing' disturbances and CROs and TNA hold many letters and other material connected with the subject. A search for relevant information should start in the CRO for quarter sessions, estate papers and newspaper reports (including the national press). Various Parliamentary Papers, including those on agriculture, policing and crime, and the poor laws, should be consulted, as should the assize records and Home Office material at TNA; good sources are the Criminal (Rewards and Pardons) correspondence and Secret Service reports for 1820-1840 in HO 64, as well as the general Home Office correspondence.[45]

The records described above will provide accounts of the disturbances, local reaction in the form of posters and handbills advertising rewards for the capture of offenders, examples of threats made to farmers and landowners, requests for military assistance in quelling the disturbances, names of persons suspected of involvement, names of landowners and farmers targeted by the rioters, and the response of the military. The less well used (and poorly listed) policing returns in HO 73 also refer to agricultural disturbances in the early and mid-1830s (see also chapter 12).

The government took strong action. Troops were despatched to the disturbed areas and financial rewards were offered for information leading to the capture of Swing rioters; these tactics were by no means ineffective. For the local historian, the prosecution of the rioters has left a wealth of information which can be used to further local study. Of particular importance are the ongoing publications of Jill Chambers whose compilations of 'Swing' source material, on a county-by-county basis, has so far covered Berkshire, Buckinghamshire, Dorset, Essex, Gloucestershire, Hampshire and Wiltshire; further volumes will follow.[46] Most of the material surviving at TNA relating to the trials is in the various assize and Home Office classes but some has ended up amongst the records of the Treasury Solicitor in TS 11. Local historians interested in the following counties should check to see if there are records of interest: Berkshire, TS 11/849; Buckinghamshire, TS 11/865; Kent, TS 11/943; Oxfordshire, TS 11/1031; and Sussex, TS 11/1007.

The early part of the 1830s was dominated by parliamentary, factory and poor law reforms. These agitations were greatly inter-mixed and the repositories and even the archives within them will span several areas of interest. Factory reformers who sought to limit the ages of the workforce, hours worked and working conditions were often involved in opposing the New Poor Law; parliamentary reformers seeking to extend the franchise would often support factory reform; factory reformers would also be involved in other issues of the day, such as support for the Tolpuddle Martyrs (the six Dorset agricultural trade unionists), the Merthyr Rising, the attempt to create large general unions, the reduction or abolition of 'stamped' or taxed newspapers and the rise of co-operative ideals. For an example of a family history which grew into a substantial local and then regional, national and international history through newspapers, local, county, specialist and national archives, see Ross Johnson's *Sentenced to Cross the Raging Sea*; his ancestor was transported to Australia for taking part in the Bankside Riots in Oldham in 1834.[47]

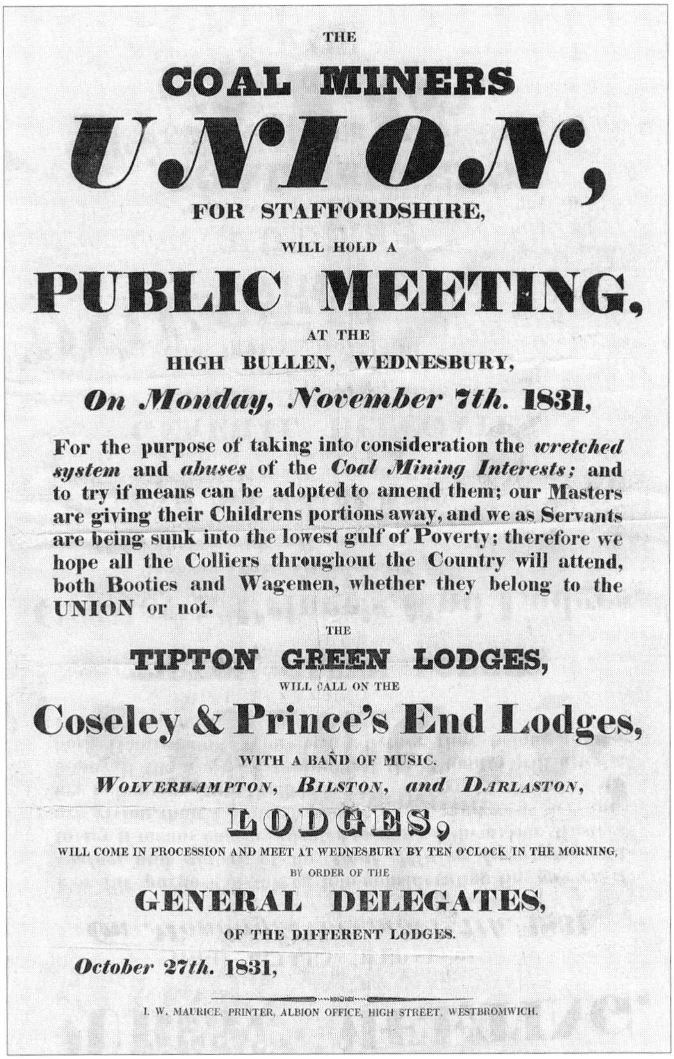
THE

COAL MINERS

UNION,

FOR STAFFORDSHIRE,

WILL HOLD A

PUBLIC MEETING,

AT THE

HIGH BULLEN, WEDNESBURY,

On Monday, November 7th. 1831,

For the purpose of taking into consideration the *wretched system* and *abuses* of the *Coal Mining Interests;* and to try if means can be adopted to amend them; our Masters are giving their Childrens portions away, and we as Servants are being sunk into the lowest gulf of Poverty; therefore we hope all the Colliers throughout the Country will attend, both Booties and Wagemen, whether they belong to the UNION or not.

THE

TIPTON GREEN LODGES,

WILL CALL ON THE

Coseley & Prince's End Lodges,

WITH A BAND OF MUSIC.

Wolverhampton, Bilston, and Darlaston,

LODGES,

WILL COME IN PROCESSION AND MEET AT WEDNESBURY BY TEN O'CLOCK IN THE MORNING,

BY ORDER OF THE

GENERAL DELEGATES,

OF THE DIFFERENT LODGES.

October 27th. 1831,

I. W. MAURICE, PRINTER, ALBION OFFICE, HIGH STREET, WESTBROMWICH.

29 *Poster/handbill advertising a public meeting at Wednesbury called by the Staffordshire Coal Miners Union during the reform agitation of the early 1830s, 1831.* (TNA, HO 44/24, f. 203.)

As well as CROs, other useful places to search for this period are the Home Office, Treasury Solicitor and Privy Council records at TNA and other central archives, such as the House of Lords Record Office, British Library, NAS and NLW. In addition smaller archives such as the Modern Records Centre and the Working Class Movement Library will have useful material. Newspapers will be particularly important. As well the national and local press there was a substantial radical output, such as William Carpenter's *Political Letters and Pamphlets*, *Poor Man's Advocate*, *The Voice of the West Riding*, Henry Hetherington's *Poor Man's Guardian* and James Watson's *Working Man's Friend*. It is believed that more than 550 illegal journals were published between 1830 and 1836. The reform of the poor law in England and Wales means that information can be found on its opposition,[48] in administration records at CROs and local archives as well as the correspondence material in MH 12 and MH 32 held at TNA (see

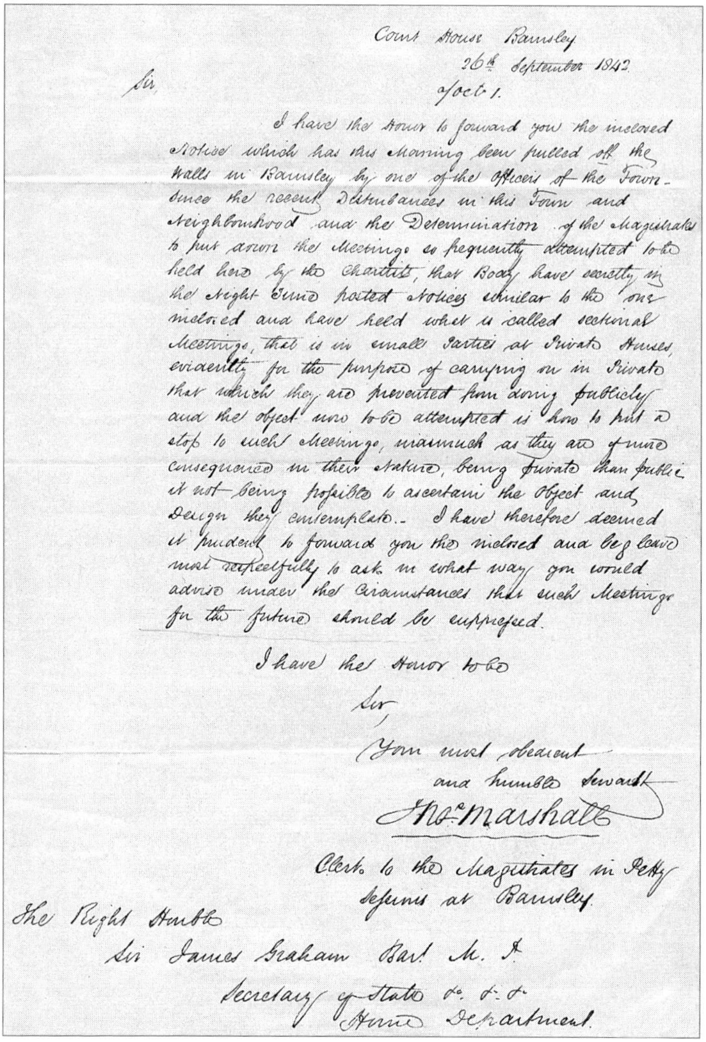

Court House Barnsley
26th September 1842.
Sir, 2 Oct 1.

I have the Honor to forward you the inclosed Notice which has this Morning been pulled off the Walls in Barnsley by one of the Officers of the Town - Since the recent Disturbances in this Town and Neighbourhood and the Determination of the Magistrates to put down the Meetings so frequently attempted to be held here by the Chartists, that Body have secretly in the Night Time posted Notices similar to the one inclosed and have held what is called sectional Meetings, that is in small Parties at Private Houses, evidently for the purpose of carrying on in Private that which they are prevented from doing publicly and the object now to be attempted is how to put a stop to such Meetings, inasmuch as they are of more consequence in their Nature, being Private than public it not being possible to ascertain the Object and Design they contemplate.- I have therefore deemed it prudent to forward you the inclosed and beg leave most respectfully to ask in what way you would advise under the Circumstances that such Meetings for the future should be suppressed.

I have the Honor to be
Sir,
Your most obedient
and humble Servant
Thos Marshall

Clerk to the Magistrates in Petty Sessions at Barnsley.

The Right Honble
Sir James Graham Bart. M. P.
Secretary of State &c. &c. &c.
Home Department.

30 *Letter from the magistrates in Barnsley, West Riding of Yorkshire, to the Home Office, reporting on Chartist meetings (in private houses) in the town and asking for advice on how to deal with them, 26 September 1842.* (TNA, HO 45/264B.)

chapter 8).[49] Published material flourished for this period through government Parliamentary Papers as well as the manuscript and published accounts of both sides in the various struggles.[50]

The Chartist movement, which dominated the political scene in the late 1830s and throughout the 1840s, was the first mass working-class political movement. It can trace its roots back to demands for parliamentary reform which had led to the 1832 Great Reform Act, factory reform, the anti-poor law movement and the demand for an unstamped press. Unlike earlier radical agitations, Chartism drew support from much of the country and could claim to be a national organisation. The Chartists' primary objective was to achieve universal manhood suffrage but they strongly believed that once the working class had the vote they would be able to introduce further legislation to improve their working and living conditions. This belief undoubtedly broadened their appeal. Perhaps not surprisingly, the government and local authorities were very concerned about the rise of Chartism, and local and central government were flooded with reports from many parts of the country expressing their concerns; this will greatly assist the researcher to build up a picture of any local Chartist activity.

The popularity of the movement saw thousands of people become actively involved at a local level, and worried local authorities kept the Home Office very well informed of activity in their area, often accompanying their missives with examples of Chartist propaganda, posters, handbills and publications. Much of this material has survived amongst the correspondence records of the Home Office as well as in War Office miscellaneous papers in WO 30. There may also be material in the poor law administration papers at a national or local level. For example, Charles Mott, Assistant Poor Law Commissioner, included information in his reports on several public meetings, including those concerning Chartism, at Leeds in 1842,[51] and in Colonel A. C. a'Court's correspondence he includes reports of disturbances related to Chartism in 1846.[52]

The government was concerned by the activities of the Chartist movement and attempts to crack down on it and bring rioters to trial were made whenever appropriate; this has left the local historian with a wealth of information. Of some interest are the records relating to the interview of over 70 Chartist prisoners in 1840 in HO 20/10; for each of the prisoners interviewed there is a form listing personal details, information regarding their offence and subsequent punishment, their diet, treatment and health; and an account of their conduct in prison.[53] There is also material in TS 11, containing information relating to a number of trials of Chartists, amongst which can be found: accounts of Chartist activity in various regions, 1838-1840; details of the Bull Ring Riot in Birmingham, 1839; an account of the Newport Uprising of 1839 (including a calendar of prisoners, map of the site of the riot and a local newspaper account); trials of Chartists for events taking place in Lancashire, Yorkshire, Cheshire and Staffordshire in 1842; trials of Chartists for events taking place in Birmingham, London, Bingley, Manchester, Chester and Liverpool in 1848.[54]

The scale and influence of the Chartist Movement means that several of the national repositories will have extensive material. The papers of Sir C.J. Napier at the British Library contain some of the correspondence of Colonel Thomas James Wemyss, the Assistant Adjutant-General for the Northern District, consisting mainly of letters and various enclosures, to Napier, dated 1839-1848. The papers concern control of civil unrest and the deployment of the military in the northern counties of England.[55] The following, quite exceptional, document gives us some idea of the alien nature felt towards working people by those in a position of social and economic power at a local level. It is a letter from the Reverend Forrest Frew to his daughter, Catherine, in 1841; in it he refers to several issues, including the dissolution of parliament, the corn laws and sugar and timber duties, Chartist opposition to them and the Chartists' desire for universal suffrage. He goes on to say that:

> The views of the Chartists are Utopian, and quite ridiculous. None can manage the government of this country but Whigs or Tories. I wish poor working people would mind their work and let politics alone. It is an engine

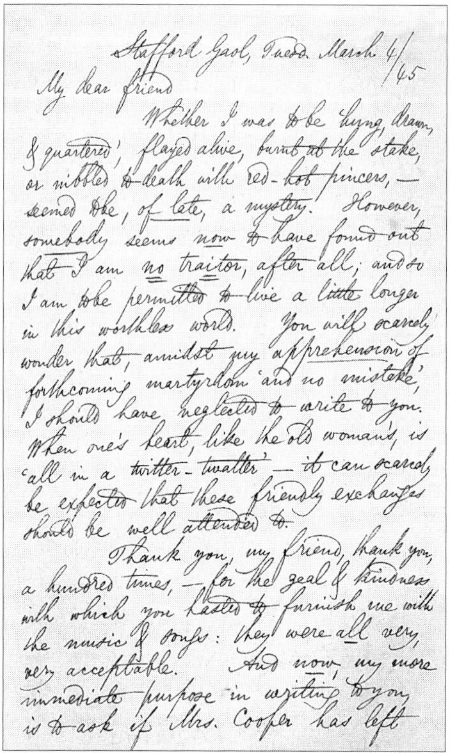
Stafford Gaol, Tuesd. March 4/45

My dear friend

Whether I was to be hung, drawn, & quartered, flayed alive, burnt at the stake, or nibbled to death with red-hot pincers, — seemed to be, of late, a mystery. However, somebody seems now to have found out that I am no traitor, after all; and so I am to be permitted to live a little longer in this worthless world. You will scarcely wonder that, amidst my apprehension of forthcoming martyrdom 'and no mistake', I should have neglected to write to you. When one's heart, like the old woman's, is 'all in a twitter-twatter' — it can scarcely be expected that these friendly exchanges should be well attended to.

Thank you, my friend, thank you, a hundred times, — for the zeal & kindness with which you hasted to furnish me with the music & songs: they were all very, very acceptable. And now, my more immediate purpose in writing to you is to ask if Mrs. Cooper has left

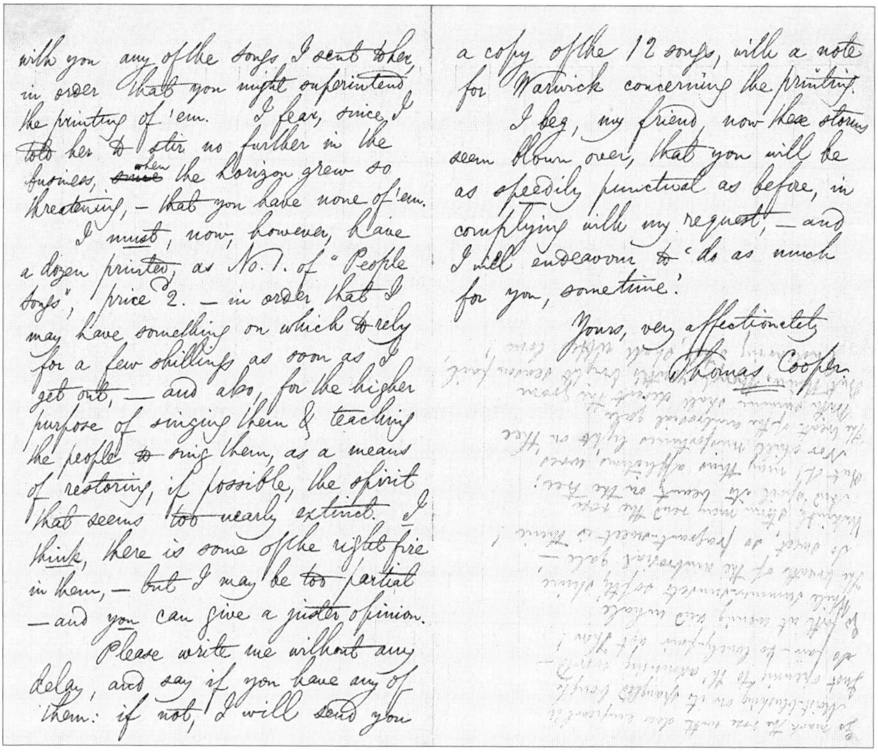
with you any of the songs I sent to her, in order that you might superintend the printing of 'em. I fear, since I told her to stir no further in the business, when the horizon grew so threatening, — that you have none of 'em.

I must, now, however, have a dozen printed, as No. 1. of "People Songs", price 2. — in order that I may have something on which to rely for a few shillings as soon as I get out, — and also, for the higher purpose of singing them & teaching the people to sing them, as a means of restoring, if possible, the spirit that seems too nearly extinct. I think, there is some of the right fire in them, — but I may be too partial — and you can give a juster opinion.

Please write me without any delay, and say if you have any of them: if not, I will send you a copy of the 12 songs, with a note for Warwick concerning the printing.

I beg, my friend, now these storms seem blown over, that you will be as speedily punctual as before, in complying with my request, — and I will endeavour to 'do as much for you, sometime.'

Yours, very affectionately,

Thomas Cooper

31 *Thomas Cooper was a Chartist from Leicester and a great self-publicist; in 1872 he published* The life of Thomas Cooper written by himself. *This letter, written from Stafford Gaol on 4 March 1845, two months before his release, concerns the publication of some of his songs; the recipient is unknown.* (Record Office of Leicestershire, Leicester and Rutland, DE 2964/17.)

> of Satan to ruin immortal souls, when common people spend so much time in worldly politics.[56]

There is much published material on local Chartist activity, in particular bibliographies of modern publications (although the *Bibliography of the Chartist Movement* is now a little out of date)[57] and the multi-volume *Dictionary of Labour Biography*. David Jones' account of the Newport insurrection in 1839, as well as being extremely well footnoted, includes a brief but very useful list of the main sources.[58] Web sites[59] and Parliamentary Papers relating to civil unrest for this period will be useful but will not necessarily have the word 'Chartism' in them; for example, the 1844 Report of the Commissioners of Inquiry for South Wales reads

> ... for the purpose of making a full and diligent inquiry into the present state of the laws, as administered in South Wales, which regulate the maintenance and repair of turnpike roads, highways and bridges; and also into the circumstances which have led to recent acts of violence and outrage in certain districts of that country.[60]

Locally, there is a lot of information in newspaper reports of Chartist meetings, including of course the pro-Chartist newspapers such as the *Poor Man's Guardian*, *Northern Star* and the *Red Republican*. There are autobiographical publications of Chartists, such as Thomas Cooper's *The Life of Thomas Cooper*, first published in 1872 and republished by Leicester University Press in 1971.

By the second half of the 19th century trade unions were an established part of British life. In the 1860s and 1870s they strove for respectability but there were also some outbreaks of violence at this period, such as 'outrages' – whereby 'scab' or under-price labour was attacked.[61] The rise of 'New Unionism' (unions for the unskilled) and the Independent Labour Party saw a return to independent workers' voices in the very late 1880s and 1890s. The suffragettes, who adopted militant methods to campaign for the parliamentary vote for women, and the strike wave known as the 'Great Unrest' give the early 20th century a particular radical edge. Labour unrest through this period, up to the First World War, can be found across CROs and local archives,[62] specialist archives such as the Modern Records Centre, Bishopsgate Institute, South Wales Miners' Library, labour collections in university archives such as the Universities of Huddersfield and of Hull,[63] as well as national repositories such as the NAS,[64] NLW and TNA. There may be surviving minute and meeting books, accounts, correspondence at branch and national level and papers of individual trade unionists.[65] For those interested in the late 19th century TNA still has some reports of unrest and trade union disputes, but the creation and spread of county and borough policing make the Home Office a less likely place for general searches; although even for this period the general correspondence is useful for particular subject areas such as suffragettes and trade union disputes. The John Rylands Library and the Women's Library (previously the Fawcett Library) in particular have important collections of material concerned with the suffragettes and the 'Genesis' web site database holds descriptions of women's history collections from libraries, archives

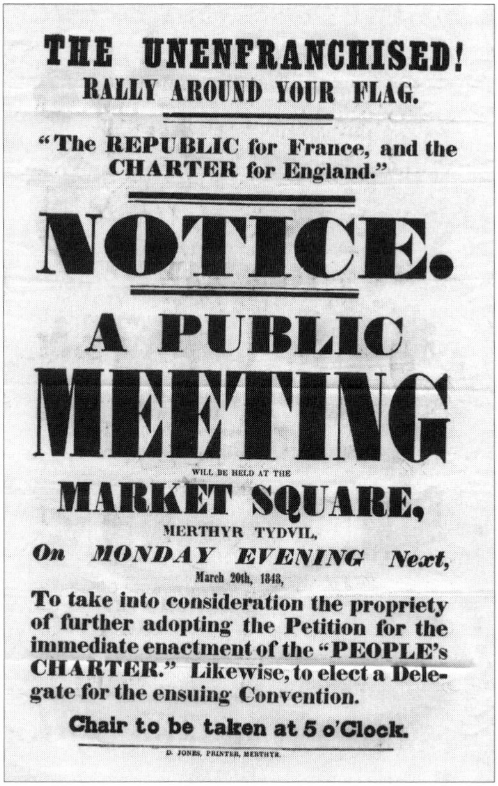

32 *Chartist poster advertising a meeting at Merthyr Tydfil, Glamorgan, 20 March 1848.* (TNA, HO 45/2410(5), f. 1001.)

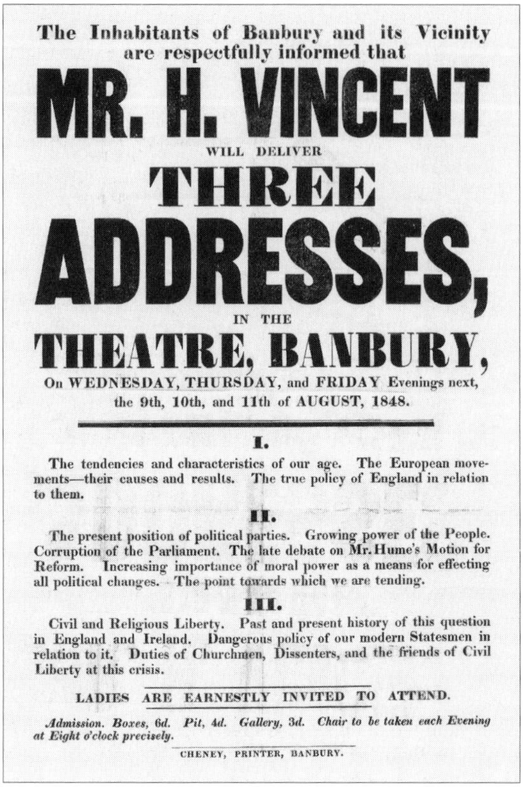

33 *Chartist/reform poster advertising a meeting at Banbury, Oxfordshire, 9-11 August 1848.* (TNA, HO 45/2410(3), f. 1265.)

and museums from around the British Isles (including that of the Women's Library).[66] Most local political party records are held at CROs and other local archives, while the British Library, NAS and NLW will have records relating to them. The records of the Communist Party, Labour Party and Independent Labour Party at national level are held at the Labour History Archive and Study Centre in Manchester, and at the London School of Economics and Political Science.[67] TNA holds the James Ramsay MacDonald papers in record series PRO 30/69, which include much material regarding the British left-wing from the late 19th century through to the 1930s.

The General Strike took place between 3 and 12 May 1926 and was called by the Trades Union Congress (TUC) to defend 'miners' wages and hours'.[68] It had been planned that initially only workers in front-line industries, such as the dockers, printers, railway and transport workers, and builders would come out on strike but many second-line workers, those employed in the textile industries for example, also stopped work. In total, it has been estimated that between two and three million workers came out in support of one million miners. Although the miners were adamant that they would remain on strike until their demands were met, the TUC entered into negotiations to end the strike; the miners, however, remained on strike until October when poverty and hardship forced them to return to work.

There will be much material at CROs, the Modern Records Centre and published in local and national newspapers. The effects of the General Strike were felt in most areas of the country so TNA, NAS and the NLW also have material. A good place to start at TNA are the records of the Cabinet Office, of which the most appropriate classes are CAB 21, CAB 23, CAB 24 and CAB 27. Amongst these records local historians could expect to find: daily bulletins regarding the progress of the strike; letters between the government and various trade union officials; copies of wage agreements and Acts relative to the dispute; reports on the situation in certain districts (these tend to be coal-mining districts in South Wales and the North-East); details of working conditions and terms of employment in various areas; and a diary of negotiations taking place before, during and after the General Strike.

LAB 27 is a class of documents relating to the Coal Dispute and General Strike of 1926. Again, most of the material is national in nature but it is possible to find material relating to certain localities. Another useful source are the records of the Home Office, in HO 45 and HO 144. Using these records it is possible to find details such as incidents occurring during the strike, police behaviour and the response to it, as well as situation reports. Material relating to the General Strike can also be found amongst the records of the Ministry of Health. Many of the people involved in the strike and the coal-mining dispute were forced to fall back on the poor relief system and the impact that this had on local authorities is reflected in the records. The most useful classes are MH 57 and MH 68. Both make reference to place-names in their piece descriptions which makes identifying the relevant file relatively easy. Amongst the material contained in these classes, local historians could expect to find details of wages in certain areas, how the local authority felt about the dispute, local reaction to the strike and working and living conditions in certain localities. A further, and perhaps unexpected, source of information is the records created by various railway companies. The railway industry was heavily affected by the General Strike and many files on the subject have survived. In order to use this material, it is necessary to know which railway company passed through a particular locality, since this is how the RAIL classes are arranged. It is possible to find material relating to the number of trains that could be run (including information on food supply to different areas), the number of people on strike in different localities, situation reports in various places along the railway line and the number of persons belonging to a union or trade federation.

The county franchise had long been restricted to the 40-shilling freeholder but prior to the 1832 Reform Act there was no fixed qualification for the borough franchise. Eligibility for the vote depended on local tradition and criteria varied, such as paying certain rates, being an apprentice or freeman, etc. The 1832 Reform Act gave the franchise to middle-class householders, copyholders and others. In 1867 it was extended to householders with 12 months' residence and lodgers paying at least £10 per annum (in boroughs) and to all house occupiers rated to at least £12 (in counties), and all householders with property of at least £4 annual value (the urban working-class vote).

In 1884 the county franchise was equalised with that of the borough (rural working-class vote). In 1918 the property and residence qualification was abolished (to ensure the vote was awarded to those who served abroad in 1914–18) and all men over 21 and women aged 30 (or who were graduates), had the vote. In 1928 voting rights were equalised between men and women and in 1948 plural voting was abolished. The private papers of MPs and peers are widely distributed and searches should be made at the British Library and on the NRA, A2A, ANW and SCAN.

There is currently a project to bring together a huge amount of research into the lives and activities of individual MPs and peers – the History of Parliament project. It was initially conceived by Josiah Wedgwood, MP for Newcastle-Under-Lyme from 1906; he was a minister in the Labour government of 1924 and a keen local historian. A number of people from his own family had previously served as MPs and as a result of his historical interests he sought to persuade the government to fund a national parliamentary biography. This was to be a large undertaking which would eventually record and identify all the 75,000 MPs up to 1918. Some unfunded work took place during the 1930s but it was not until 1940 that the History of Parliament Trust was founded and only in 1951 did the Treasury finally agree to fund it. By early 2005 there are 28 published volumes, covering eight periods: 1386–1421, 1509–1558, 1558–1603, 1660–1690, 1690–1715, 1715–1754, 1754–1790 and 1790–1820 (the texts of 23 volumes were reissued in 1998 as a CD-ROM). In April 1999 a new section was launched to give a comprehensive account of the House of Lords in the governance of Great Britain and the United Kingdom from 1660 to 1832.[69]

Part of the local aspect of parliamentary elections can be traced through the poll books and electoral registers. Poll books were first authorised by an Act of Parliament of 1696 and were published until 1871; they were issued after contested elections. They were not issued as a matter of course but only if there was local demand for them. Information in the poll book varies; the person's name and details of who they voted for will be given, but sometimes addresses and occupations are included. With the advent of secret voting in 1872 poll books were discontinued. From 1832 electoral registers were drawn up listing every person qualified to vote. They provide addresses, and prior to 1918 details of the property which entitled a person to vote. Both poll books and electoral registers are usually held at the CRO or other local archives,[70] but see the caveat on page 30. For election results on a constituency-by-constituency basis, providing all the candidates, votes and results, see F.W.S. Craig's series of *British Parliamentary Election Results*.[71]

12

Law and Order

The records that will help to illuminate aspects of law and order within particular localities can be widely distributed. They are also voluminous, many written in Latin (until 1733) and composed in a jargon sometimes difficult to understand.[1] That should not deter the local historian, as (problems notwithstanding) they can be excellent records for local research. This chapter will deal with the following records: courts; hulks and prisons; transportation; the principal secretaries and Home Office; and the police.

The easiest way to understand the various levels of criminal courts is to look at the severity of criminal acts which they dealt with. For England and Wales (see below for Scotland) the main courts were the assizes, quarter sessions and petty sessions. There were other courts, such as manor courts leet (see also chapter 2), King's Bench and Court of Star Chamber. King's Bench records, which are included in the general discussion below, are organised in such a way as to make searches by location extremely problematic; Star Chamber records are found in class TNA STAC 1 to 9 but the court was only in existence from 1487 to 1641.

Until the 17th century manor courts leet retained a working and significant criminal jurisdiction. For example, whereas only 23 cases of assault in the manor of Prescott in Lancashire were accounted for in the Lancaster Quarter Sessions there were 1,252 recorded at the manor leet,[2] so that prior to the 18th century these courts record significant numbers of criminal matters. There are many thousands of criminal cases in manorial records such as those of Elizabeth Petty who 'made affray and drew blood from Margaret Rider', John Linley and John Marsden who 'hunted and killed hares in the snow against the statute', and Richard and Mary Lawson who 'made affray and drew blood of Jane Harrison'.[3] From this time onwards these types of cases were heard either by magistrates acting alone, or in twos or more at petty sessions or at quarter sessions.

From the 13th century until 1971 the assizes were held in each county; the counties were grouped into a number of circuits. During the early years of the system judges, and sometimes senior lawyers, were commissioned to hold the king's courts across the country, and two judges would cover a circuit. (Some places were not included in the system proper and are dealt with separately below.) Initially they only tried property disputes, but their remit was extended to criminal cases and their records are in TNA JUST 1- 4.[4] From 1482 to 1559 there is a break in the surviving records. Some information can be gleaned by using the King's Bench indictments in KB 9 which had been returned from lower courts, sometimes via the assizes, into King's Bench. In addition there are surviving letters from the judges, who reported to central government on the political condition of the country in SP 1 (and continually through State Papers Domestic).

From the late 1550s, the period at which records of the Home Circuit start to survive in large numbers, the assizes were dealing with more serious criminal offences, such as homicide, infanticide and thefts of large amounts (in money or value). However, relatively less serious crimes could also be dealt with by assizes and there is no way of determining which court would deal with a particular offence; the main difference was that usually only the assizes, by the late 16th century, was inflicting capital punishment locally.[5]

Prior to 1733 most assize records are in Latin. After this date there are a small number of Latin phrases which are often used and these are given with their translation in the table:

Latin Abbreviation	Full Latin Version	English Translation
ca null	*catalla nulla*	no goods/chattels to forfeit
cog ind	*cognovit indictamentum*	confessed to the indictment
cul	*culpabilis*	guilty
ign	*ignoramus*	we do not know i.e. no case to answer
non cul nec re	*non culpabilis nec retraxit*	not guilty and did not flee
po se	*ponit se super patriam*	puts himself on the country, i.e. opts for jury trial and pleads not guilty
sus	*suspendatur*	let him be hanged

There are other issues which local historians should consider; for example, criminal aliases were common, and occupations and place-names may be suspect.[6]

The main records for assize cases are the indictments[7] (formal statements of the charge against the defendant), depositions (written evidences) and gaol/minute books (these list the accused and summarise cases heard including those found not guilty) often noting the plea, verdict and sentence. The records are held at TNA and the key at appendix 4 gives the relevant ASSI series.

There are several omissions and anomalies from this list. The equivalent Old Bailey Sessions for London and Middlesex up to 1834 were held in London. The Old Bailey Sessions Papers, which contain 100,621 trials from April 1674 to October 1834, are now available online.[8] The online site also has some of the Ordinary's Accounts which are essentially short biographies of convicts compiled just before they were executed.[9] Original papers with other records of the court relating to the City are in the Corporation of London Records Office and those for the rest of London and Middlesex in the London Metropolitan Archives. After 1834, the Central Criminal Court acted as the assize court for London, Middlesex and extended into parts of Essex,

Kent and Surrey as London effectively grew into these counties. There are some printed proceedings for London and Middlesex cases from 1801 to 1834 in TNA PCOM 1. From 1834 to 1912 the Central Criminal Court Sessions Papers are in CRIM 10; some shorthand notes in cases which interested the Director of Public Prosecutions or Treasury Solicitor are in DPP 4 (after 1846) and TS 36 (unlisted); cases referred to the Court of Criminal Appeal are in J 82 (after 1945).

Bristol Sessions records prior to 1832 are held by Bristol Record Office; Ely assize records for the 17th and 18th centuries are at Cambridge University Library, while the Court of Great Sessions for Wales, 1543-1830, are held by the National Library of Wales.[10] From 1830, the Welsh records are held at TNA and are included in the appendix. Chester, Durham and Lancaster were palatinates with their own assize jurisdiction until 1830 for Chester and 1876 for Durham and Lancaster. The relevant record series have also been included in the appendix.

Transcripts of proceedings or shorthand notes of what was actually said in court do not normally survive (and were rarely created). The best place to find such material is in contemporary newspapers or pamphlets. Where no assize records have survived for a particular county for the period *c.*1714-1832, the incomplete sheriffs' assize vouchers in TNA E 389 may prove useful. Copies of indictments removed to the Court of King's Bench by writs of *certiorari* and returns in KB 9 of those granted benefit of clergy (prior to 1660) may also be useful where assize records do not survive.

The tier below the assizes was the court of quarter sessions.[11] The office of Justice of the Peace or magistrate goes back to the Statute of Winchester in 1285; the system of quarterly meetings of the magistrates for each county and county borough began in 1361. Quarter Sessions became more important under the Tudors, and the gentry saw the Commission of the Peace (which appointed magistrates) as the true source of local power. Magistrates tried non-capital crimes and had a number of non-criminal responsibilities which are dealt with elsewhere. Quarter Sessions in the 17th and 18th centuries had more and more administrative duties laid on them, because they were the only truly active local body. The County Rates Act 1739 allowed a general rate to be levied; a Treasurer had to be appointed by the magistrates, proper books were to be kept and they were to submit quarterly accounts. The County Surveyor, a new official, was responsible for bridges and county buildings, especially the county hall and gaol.

The most important documents in relation to the business of quarter sessions are the sessions rolls, one for each session; they contain: lists of officers, writs, presentments, indictments, and other documents. The writ was issued to the sheriff, to summon juries, officers, defendants and others. The presentment was a detail of offences, mainly of the 'nuisance' type; they were informal and sometimes in English. The indictment was a formal accusation sometimes based on the presentment; common offences were larceny, assault, unlicensed or disorderly alehouses, poaching, false weights and measures. The deposition was an examination of the defendant and witnesses. The recognizance was a bond, mostly to secure the appearance of the defendant, prosecutor or witnesses, to

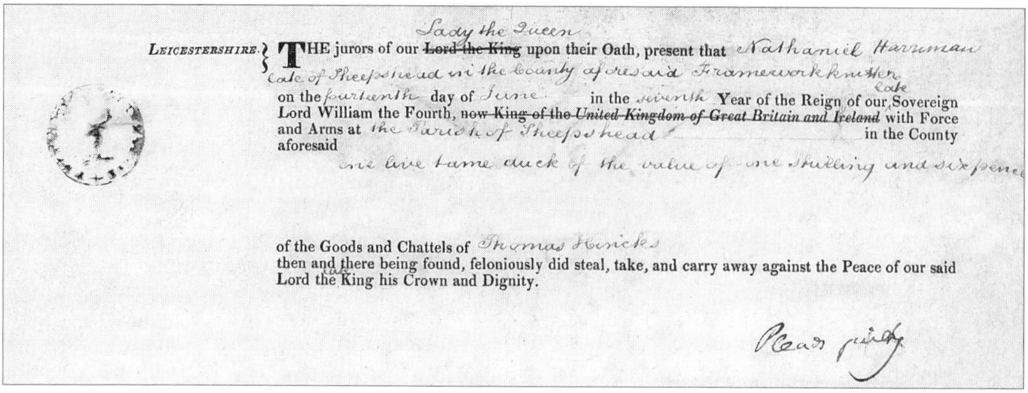

LEICESTERSHIRE. } THE jurors of our ~~Lord the King~~ Lady the Queen upon their Oath, present that Nathaniel Harriman late of Shepshead in the County aforesaid Framework knitter on the fourteenth day of June in the seventh Year of the Reign of our late Sovereign Lord William the Fourth, ~~now King of the United Kingdom of Great Britain and Ireland~~ with Force and Arms at the Parish of Shepshead in the County aforesaid one live tame duck of the value of one shilling and sixpence

of the Goods and Chattels of Thomas Hicks then and there being found, feloniously did steal, take, and carry away against the Peace of our said late Lord the King his Crown and Dignity.

Pleads guilty

34 *The Court of Quarter Sessions dealt with particular offences and the sessions rolls contain much valuable material. The presentment shown here deals with the case of a framework knitter, Nathaniel Harriman of Shepshed, accused of stealing a duck in 1837. Framework knitting was a very unpredictable trade and the 1830s was a period of severe depression; Harriman almost certainly stole the duck to feed his family.* (Record Office of Leicestershire, Leicester and Rutland, QS3/518.)

be of good behaviour or to keep the peace. Other documents which may be found are jury lists, calendars of prisoners, petitions, complaints, certificates and testimonials by individuals or a number of local inhabitants. Summary convictions were held by one or two magistrates, out of sessions, for minor offences including profane swearing.

Sessions books are rough minutes, kept in the court by the Clerk of the Peace, and containing notes of verdicts, orders, recognizances, justices present, persons taking oaths, persons fined and calendars of prisoners; they are likely to be hastily written and difficult to read. Process or indictment books were memoranda recording indictments; they contain very brief particulars, but may give the name, address and occupation of the defendant, with details of the offence, plea, verdict and sentence. Order books were the formal records of the proceedings of the court and often have contemporary indexes. The records of the court of quarter sessions form the bedrock of many CROs and a number have been published by county record societies.[12] Both assizes and quarter sessions were important local political events where judges and magistrates delivered their 'charges' to the grand juries reminding them of their importance in the delivery of justice and the dangers inherent in crimes, disobedience and idleness going unpunished. A collection of mainly 18th-century charges has been published.[13]

Petty sessions were courts of summary jurisdiction (no juries) held by two or more magistrates for trying lesser offences or to enquire into indictable offences. The modern equivalent is the Magistrates' Court. They effectively replaced hundred and manorial courts and their development was rather slow and haphazard, and varied from county to county. The divisions within which the magistrates acted corresponded to the hundreds. In the 18th century they began to deal with minor business which was not sufficiently important to go to quarter sessions, such as appointing overseers of the poor and surveyors,

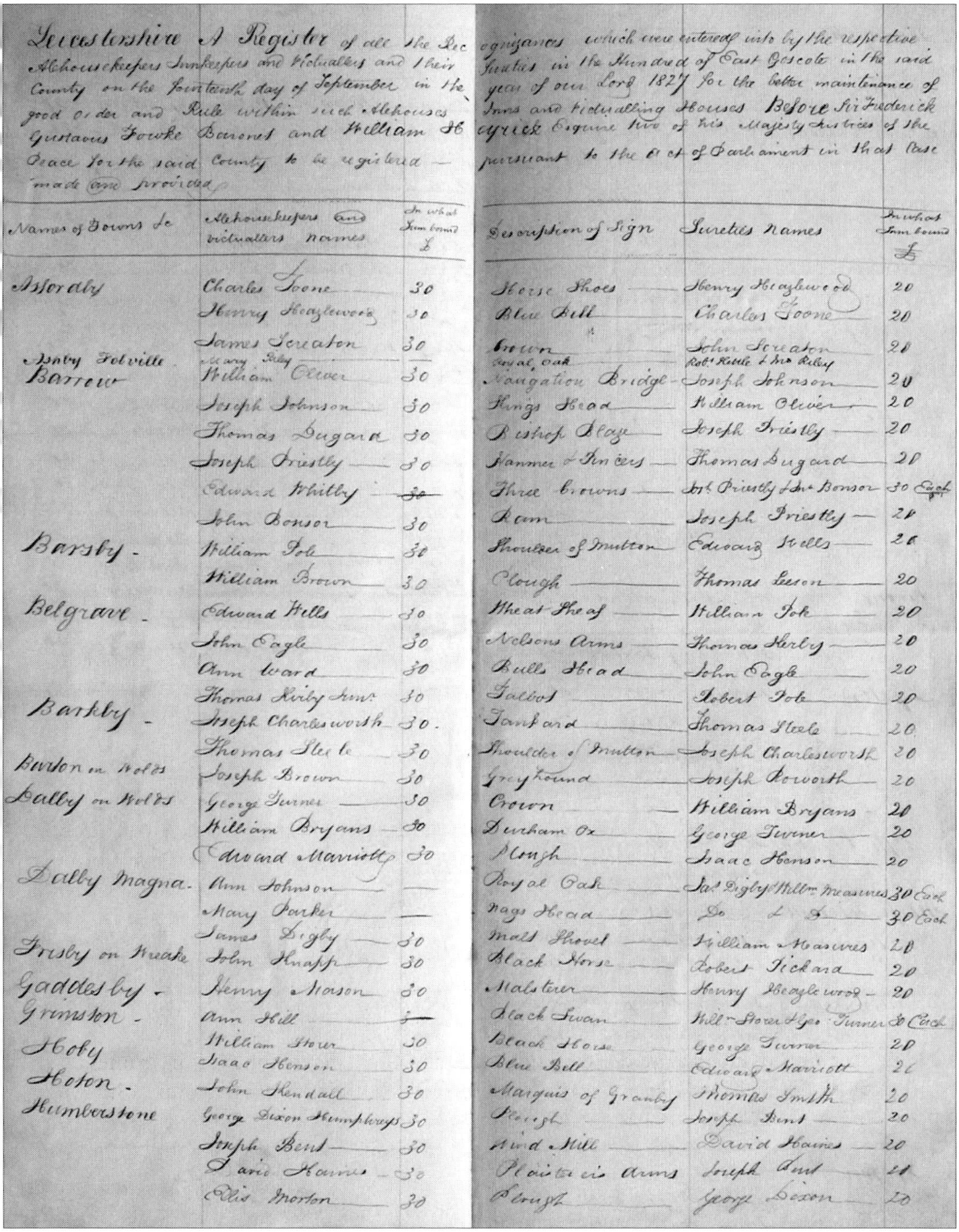

Leicestershire A Register of all the Recognizances which were entered into by the respective Alehousekeepers Innkeepers and Victuallers and their Sureties in the Hundred of East Goscote in the said County on the fourteenth day of September in the year of our Lord 1827 for the better maintenance of good order and Rule within such Alehouses Inns and Victualling Houses Before Sir Frederick Gustavus Fowke Baronet and William Herrick Esquire two of his Majesty's Justices of the Peace for the said County to be registered pursuant to the Act of Parliament in that Case made and provided

Names of Towns &c	Alehousekeepers and victuallers names	In what Sum bound £	Description of Sign	Sureties names	In what Sum bound £
Asfordby	Charles Toone	30	Horse Shoes	Henry Heazlewood	20
	Henry Heazlewood	30	Blue Bell	Charles Toone	20
	James Screaton	30	Crown	John Screaton	20
Ashby Folville	Mary Riley		Royal Oak	Robt. Kettle & Jno. Riley	
Barrow	William Oliver	30	Navigation Bridge	Joseph Johnson	20
	Joseph Johnson	30	Kings Head	William Oliver	20
	Thomas Dugard	30	Bishop Blaze	Joseph Priestly	20
	Joseph Priestly	30	Hammer & Pincers	Thomas Dugard	20
	Edward Whitby	~~30~~	Three Crowns	Jos. Priestly & Jno. Bonsor	30 Each
	John Bonsor	30	Ram	Joseph Priestly	20
Barsby	William Pole	30	Shoulder of Mutton	Edward Wells	20
	William Brown	30	Plough	Thomas Leeson	20
Belgrave	Edward Wells	30	Wheat Sheaf	William Pole	20
	John Eagle	30	Nelsons Arms	Thomas Kirby	20
	Ann Ward	30	Bulls Head	John Eagle	20
	Thomas Kirby Junr.	30	Talbot	Robert Pole	20
Barkby	Joseph Charlesworth	30	Tankard	Thomas Steele	20
	Thomas Steele	30	Shoulder of Mutton	Joseph Charlesworth	20
Burton on Wolds	Joseph Brown	30	Greyhound	Joseph Rowarth	20
Dalby on Wolds	George Turner	30	Crown	William Bryans	20
	William Bryans	30	Durham Ox	George Turner	20
	Edward Marriott	30	Plough	Isaac Henson	20
Dalby Magna	Ann Johnson	—	Royal Oak	Jas. Digby & Willm. Measures	30 Each
	Mary Parker	—	Nags Head	Do & Do	30 Each
	James Digby	30	Malt Shovel	William Measures	20
Frisby on Wreake	John Knapp	30	Black Horse	Robert Pickard	20
Gaddesby	Henry Mason	30	Malsters	Henry Heazlewood	20
Grimston	Ann Hill	—	Black Swan	Willm. Storer & Geo. Turner	30 Each
Hoby	William Storer	30	Black Horse	George Turner	20
	Isaac Henson	30	Blue Bell	Edward Marriott	20
Hoton	John Kendall	30	Marquis of Granby	Thomas Smith	20
Humberstone	George Dixon Humphreys	30	Plough	Joseph Bent	20
	Joseph Bent	30	Wind Mill	David Haines	20
	David Haines	30	Plaisterers Arms	Joseph Bent	20
	Ellis Morton	30	Plough	George Dixon	20

35 *Under an Act of 1552 people who ran licensed premises had to be licensed at the Court of Quarter Sessions; after 1753 these 'recognizances' were to be entered into annual registers. Later on the name of the public house was given, as shown here for 1827.* (Record Office of Leicestershire, Leicester and Rutland, QS 36/2/10.)

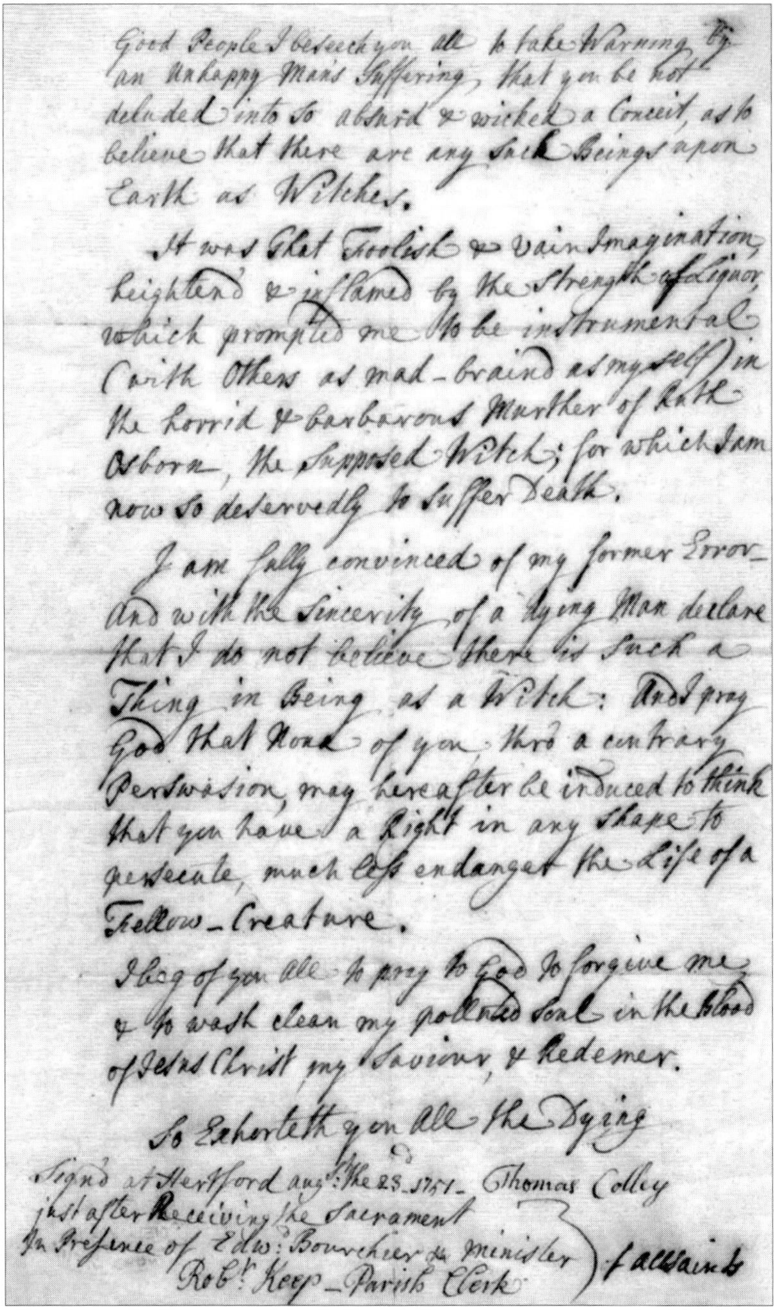

Good People I beseech you all to take Warning by an Unhappy Man's Suffering, that you be not deluded into so absurd & wicked a Conceit, as to believe that there are any such Beings upon Earth as Witches.

It was that Foolish & vain Imagination, heighten'd & inflamed by the Strength of Liquor, which prompted me to be instrumental (with Others as mad-brain'd as myself) in the horrid & barbarous Murther of Ruth Osborn, the supposed Witch; for which I am now so deservedly to suffer Death.

I am fully convinced of my former Error— And with the Sincerity of a dying Man declare that I do not believe there is such a Thing in Being as a Witch: And I pray God that None of you, thro' a contrary Perswasion, may hereafter be induced to think that you have a Right in any shape to persecute, much less endanger the Life of a Fellow-Creature.

I beg of you all to pray to God to forgive me & to wash clean my polluted Soul in the Blood of Jesus Christ my Saviour, & Redeemer.

So Exhorteth you all the Dying

Sign'd at Hertford Augt: the 25 1751 Thomas Colley
just after Receiving the Sacrament
In Presence of Edw: Bourchier de minister of All Saints
Robt: Keep Parish Clerk

36 *The main local sources for law and order in local archives are the records of the Court of Quarter Sessions but material will be found elsewhere. Thomas Colley was one of the people responsible for the death of Ruth Osborn, a reputed witch, who was drowned in Tring in 1751. This document is in a collection relating to family properties in Wheathampstead and there is further material about Ruth Osborn in the Panshanger archives.* (Hertfordshire Archives and Local Studies, DE/LW/Z22/13.)

signing settlement certificates and fixing local rates. Their proceedings became more formal and in 1828 quarter sessions were empowered to divide up the county into petty sessional divisions. There are few records of petty sessions (and magistrates acting alone) although some have now been transcribed and published;[14] they may include registers of licences, minutes, settlement examinations and correspondence. Both quarter and petty sessions records, as well as magistrates notebooks where they survive, are held at CROs.

Towns and boroughs had civil courts, as well as quarter and petty sessions. These could include the mayor's court, manorial court and piepowder court (the last settled disputes, regulated measures and maintained order in markets). The records should be found with other borough records.

The Court of King's Bench had jurisdiction over both civil and criminal cases, but only the 'Crown Side' or criminal cases are dealt with here. It had an original jurisdiction regarding all criminal and public matters as the *custos morum* of all the subjects of the realm; it also had supervisory powers over inferior courts and a local jurisdiction whereby the rights of other courts (across the country) were extinguished if King's Bench entered the county in which the inferior court was sitting (although the court was fixed at Westminster by the 15th century). Although it was the highest criminal law court it was able to hear an extensive range of cases; the records are in Latin until 1733 and are written in distinctive legal scripts. The records are held at TNA; they are complex and their current arrangement makes their use by local historians almost impossible unless there is other evidence that a case was taken to King's Bench. Depositions for the period 1682-1985 are in record series KB 1; only a few of them date from before 1714 but from the 1730s they are mainly complete. Various items of interest can be found in the depositions, such as printed ephemera and early newspapers. There are supplementary affidavits for 1689-1737 in KB 2.

There are some indexes for different periods. London and Middlesex defendants for 1673 to 1843 are indexed in IND 1/6669-6677 while provincial defendants for 1638 to 1704 and from 1765-1843 are IND 1/6680-6684. A further set of London and Middlesex defendants (as well as some defendants in northern counties for 1682 to 1699) are in IND 1/6678-6679. London and Middlesex indictments files from 1675 to 1844 are in KB 10 while the provincial files for the same years can be found in KB 11. For the very short period, 1844 to 1859, there is a card index to the plea rolls (KB 28), giving the names of prosecutors and defendants. These records give the outcome of cases in which judgement was entered. Many cases did not reach this stage and so are not recorded in this set of records. The controlment rolls in KB 29 (1329-1843) list all the prosecutions with a numerical reference to the indictment or information in KB 10, for London and Middlesex until 1844, KB 11 for the provincial or counties until 1844, or KB 12 for all counties after 1845. The indictments are formal documents which give the basic allegation against the defendant in a sometimes quite obscure manner, but which is often summarised by an annotation such as riot, assault, nuisance, etc. Criminal libel comes to dominate ordinary criminal informations but cases of forgery, perjury and riot are also common. For sedition or treason cases the list for Baga de Secretis in

KB 8 should be consulted; this refers to material for trials of concern to the state. Some coroners' inquisitions survive with the out-county indictments in KB 11, with further records in KB 13 and KB 140. Inquisitions on prisoners who died in the King's Bench prison are in KB 14.

The principal court records for Scotland are the records of the High Court of Justiciary (HCJ), the highest criminal court in Scotland, with jurisdiction over serious crimes such as murder, treason, heresy and counterfeiting. It also acted as a court of appeal from cases heard in the Sheriff courts.[15] The records are held at the NAS. There are typescript indexes for the period 1611 to 1631 and 1699 to 1720. Records include both cases heard at the HCJ in Edinburgh and on local circuits from 1537. Books of Adjournal record the proceedings at Edinburgh from 1576. The Minute Books of the court proceedings with verdict and sentence are in record series JC 2-9. The North, South and West Circuit Courts minute books from 1655 are in JC 10-14. Processes, which are also known as 'small papers', include various papers including confessions and depositions in JC 26.[16] Precognitions, the written reports of the evidence given by witnesses to crimes, are in record series AD 14-15. These are excellent records and may give much background information on the economic conditions and attitudes toward particular crimes, but the survival rate is poor before 1812. Many criminal cases were heard by the Privy Council (prior to its abolition in 1708). Many of these were people of above average social standing or concerned accusations of witchcraft and sedition. The 35 volumes of the Registers of the Privy Council are fully indexed.

Sheriff Courts usually heard cases of a less serious nature, such as common assault and petty theft. These records are also held at NAS and sometimes include locally taken precognitions. Franchise Courts were local courts for which a local landowner held a franchise to hear civil and criminal cases. Regality Courts had the jurisdiction as the high court in criminal cases and were abolished in 1747. Barony Courts heard cases of minor crime. The records of these courts are in RH 11 but some (being local courts under the direction of individual landowners) can be found in private papers. Crimes on the high seas or in harbours were heard in the Admiralty Court. The records run from 1557 to 1830 when the court was abolished. Early cases from the Admiralty Court have been published.[17] A selection of records to illustrate Scottish criminal history has been listed and published.[18]

The microfilm collection of *British Trials 1660-1900* republishes an organised, indexed and accessible collection of published material which was produced for sale to the public; most are verbatim transcripts. From 1750 these were compiled from shorthand experts while 17th-century reports tended to be brief summaries. Cases from across England, Scotland and Wales (as well as from Ireland) referring to murder, cruelty, duelling, highwaymen, forgers, burglars, political radicals, Chartists and trades unions, treason, sedition and riot were printed. There is a set of multi-indexes allowing, for example, searches by defendants, plaintiffs and locations of the trials.

Before the middle of the 19th century many prisons were privately owned lockups and gaols; perhaps a couple of hundred in the 16th to 18th centuries, with the county gaol under the direction of the sheriff. Such prisons were places in which people were kept until their sentences (death or transportation) were carried out. In the modern period magistrates established houses of correction for those found guilty of less serious crime. Bridewells were houses of correction for prisoners, originally vagabonds and vagrants, and took their names from the Bridewell in London, established in 1552. By the 1630s every county in England and Wales had similar institutions for petty offenders.

Special debtors' prisons, notably the Fleet in London, were supervised by sheriffs. The post of gaoler was usually sold to the highest bidder, who recouped his costs from the prisoners. Prisoners convicted of a felony (i.e., a serious crime) were entitled to an allowance, known as the 'county bread'. A study of prisons provides information on social as well as criminal topics.[19] The vast majority of prisons were administered locally and were not the responsibility or property of central government,[20] so that most early records of prisons are held in CROs. The exceptions to this were the crown prisons attached to the central courts such as King's Bench, Marshalsea and Fleet prisons (debtors' prisons) and Newgate Gaol, for which there are substantial records at TNA.[21] The various King's Bench, Marshalsea and Fleet registers are in record series PRIS 1-10 for the late 17th through to the mid-19th centuries. Newgate registers and those from other prisons can be found in PCOM 2, HO 24 and HO 23. Some of these are mid-19th-century registers for local prisons where central government were renting the cells for convicted felons. For a useful summary of the whereabouts of prison registers see the appendices in David Hawkings, *Criminal Ancestors*.[22]

It could be argued that the first move towards a central system of prisons was the establishment of prison hulks moored at Chatham, Plymouth, Portsmouth, Sheerness and Woolwich. Between 1776 and 1787 a temporary expedient (which lasted much longer than initially envisaged) was introduced, in which disused warships were used to house convicts. Shortly before the end of transportation to Australia convicts were transported to Bermuda and Gibraltar, where they were also held on prison hulks. Before being transported the convicts on the hulks were used to build various shore establishments. One hulk, the *Dunkirk* moored at Plymouth, held female convicts. The hulks were maintained by private contractors who were also responsible for the maintenance and care of the convicts held on board; the costs incurred were met by the Treasury. In order to claim payment the overseers of the hulks had to send in quarterly returns listing all convicts on board, giving such details as age, place of conviction and date when transferred to another hulk or sent on board a transportation ship. The various registers and other records for the hulks can be found at TNA in HO 7-10, ADM 6 and PCOM 2.

There is much Home Office correspondence relating to prison building in the late 18th and early 19th centuries. The first of the new prisons, Millbank, was completed in 1816, and was followed by others, such as Pentonville, Winchester, and Dartmoor. It was not until the Prisons Act 1877 that all prisons were placed under the administration of a new central Prison Commission. Subsequently, with the increased role of central government, there are various records of these prisons (registers, finance matters, plans, etc) spread between TNA and the appropriate CROs (as well as those held by the Prison Commission and the prisons themselves).[23] Most of the surviving prison records date from the first half of the 19th century but 24 gaols have records before 1800; the Fleet, Northampton and Norwich have records for the 17th century. The late 19th-century registers may include photographs. The information recorded varies from county to county and can be very detailed; a precise description may have been kept in order to identify an absconding prisoner. Some prisons have registers of personal effects, which list the clothing the prisoner was wearing on admittance, together with all his other possessions. Other records which may survive are prison journals kept by governors, medical officers and chaplains, calendars of prisoners and records of prisoners' educational achievements.

The fact that the 19th century was one of centralisation should not obscure the fact that an estimated 317 local prisons were in existence in 1812, and even at the time of the Prisons Act 1877 there were 166 prisons. From 1791 to 1849 there are criminal registers for prisoners committed for trial in London and Middlesex; they are in HO 26 and end in 1849. From 1805 to 1892 similar registers can be found for England and Wales in HO 27 (London and Middlesex cases are included from 1850). From 1868 to 1909 there are calendars of prisoners tried at assizes and quarter sessions in record series HO 140. Other large repositories have prison material. For example, the British Library has 'reports' on 'The State of His Majesty's Gaol of Newgate'. This document covers the period 29 April 1816 to 27 February 1819 and was compiled by the keepers John Newman and William Brown. The reports give the number, sex and category of the prisoners was well as the number receiving medical treatment. There are also occasional reports on their health, the state of the prison and 'Particular Occurrences during the week'. It covers the period of the Spa Fields riots, 2 December 1816, and some of the entries refer to the authorities' reactions in regard to the disturbances.[24]

Prisons featured in the local press and were also the subject of several published investigations such as William Smith's *State of the Gaols in London, Westminster and Borough of Southwark*, John Howard's *State of the Prisons* and James Neild's *State of the Prisons in England, Scotland, and Wales … with documents … and remarks, adapted to … improve the condition of prisoners in general.*[25] The disgraceful state of prisons in the 18th century led John Howard to campaign for improvement; he had been appointed sheriff of Bedfordshire in 1773 and was responsible for the county gaol and, when he looked into conditions there, was appalled by what he found. He recommended that the gaoler be paid a salary and this led to his published survey in which he gave details of the inmates. Howard's work led to the Prisons Act of 1778 but abuses continued and new regulations were often ignored. Under the Act gaols and inmates were to be cleaned and there was to be provision of sick rooms and medical help. Uniform standards were not imposed until 1856, when the number of prisoners was increasing after the abolition of transportation and the creation of county police forces. In 1877 responsibility for prisons was transferred to the Home Secretary. There are several key Parliamentary Papers regarding prisons,[26] including: *Royal Commission … to Inquire into the Condition and Treatment of the Prisoners Confined to Birmingham Borough Prison and the Report*

... *on the Present State of Discipline in Gaols and House of Correction*.[27] There are also numerous 'prison biographies'; some of these have been brought together to reflect prisoner's attitudes towards issues such as incarceration, hard labour, prison diets, discipline and prison staff. A bibliography of this material can be found in P. Priestley's *Victorian Prison Lives*.[28]

In Scotland prisons were mainly the responsibility of burghs prior to 1839, and from that date were usually the responsibility of central government; prison material for specific prisons may therefore be found in burgh records (local or CROs) and central government records (NAS). For Scotland a number of prison registers are held at NAS in the papers of the Home and Health Department in record series HH 21. These include registers for Edinburgh (Carlton) Prison and Bridewell, 1798 to 1874; Glasgow Duke Street and Barlinnie, 1841 to 1966; Aberdeen, 1809 to 1960 and Perth, 1867 to 1961, as well as some registers for smaller prisons.[29] There are some prison administration papers in HH 13. There are some further prison registers in Sheriff Court records: Angus, 1805-27 at SC 47/55/2; Ayr, 1860-3, SC 6/57/1; Fort William, 1893-1936, SC 28/32/1; Jedburgh, 1839-93, SC 62/72/1; Kirkcudbright, 1791-1811, SC 16/28/2; Selkirk, 1828-40, SC 36/63/3 and Stirling, 1822-9, SC 67/47/5-6.

Records relating to transportation are numerous and will be found in CROs and TNA. The Western assizes compiled a specific set of transportation order books from 1629 to 1819. The TNA Treasury records in T 1 contain lists of prisoners on board ships awaiting transportation to America and similar lists can be found in record series T 53.[30] With the loss of the American colonies Britain turned to Australia to continue its policy of transportation. HO 11 is lists of convicts for transportation to Australia for 1787 to 1867. Contracts for transportation for the 1840s-60s are in TS 18 with Privy Council correspondence in PC 1 and the registers in PC 2 (listing the convicts to be transported). Orders in Council, providing lists of those to be transported during the 1780s and '90s, are in HO 31. There may also be records in quarter sessions, such as the payment of £59 4s. 0d. to Cornelius Wilson, the Hertfordshire county gaoler, 'for conveying 37 Convicts on Board a Hulk at Woolwich'.[31]

Further records concerning prisoners and the administration of the criminal justice system will be found in State Papers Domestic and (after 1782) the Home Office at TNA. For State Papers there is a set of Criminal Entry Books in SP 44.[32] After 1782 there are several sets of Home Office records, such as Judges Reports in HO 47 for 1783-1830,[33] Recorders and Judges Returns in HO 6 for 1806-40, Criminal Petitions for mercy in HO 17 and HO 18,[34] for *c*.1819-54 (with registers in HO 19). These records are concerned with the pardoning process which was a major part of the criminal justice system at this time.[35] The Criminal Entry Books from 1782 onwards in record series HO 13 are well indexed and contain a huge amount of information on individual cases and criminal administration. Other important Home Office records are the Criminal Papers (Old Series) for 1849-71 in HO 12 (with a subject index in HO 15); and prison correspondence and in-letters for 1820-43 in HO 20 (complemented by the Prisons Entry Books in HO 21 and HO 22). General Home Office correspondence will also contain much information on crime, criminals, prisons and punishments.[36] Convicts' licences, which allowed convicts

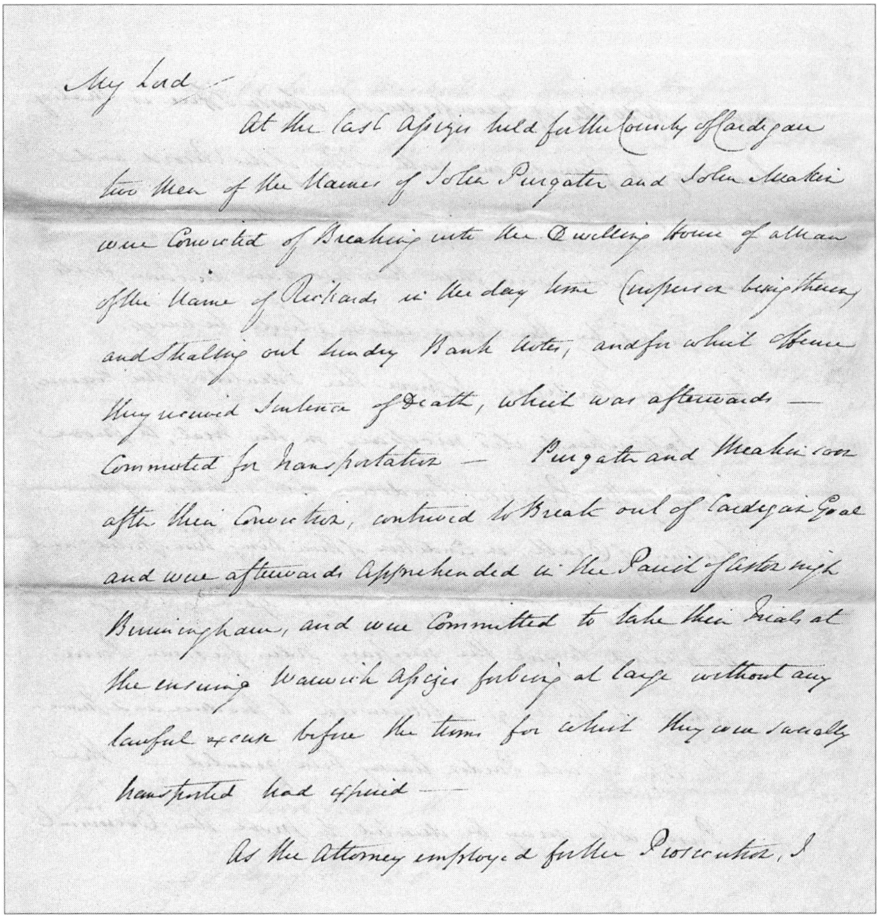

My Lord:–

At the last Assizes held for the County of Cardigan two Men of the Names of John Purgater and John Meakin were Convicted of Breaking into the Dwelling House of a Man of the Name of Richards in the day time (no person being therein) and Stealing out sundry Bank Notes, and for which Offence they received Sentence of Death, which was afterwards — Commuted for Transportation — Purgater and Meakin soon after their Conviction, contrived to Break out of Cardigan Goal and were afterwards Apprehended in the Parish of Aston nigh Birmingham, and were Committed to take their Trials at the ensuing Warwick Assizes for being at large without any lawful excuse before the term for which they were severally transported had expired —

As the Attorney employed for the Prosecution, I

37 *In-letters relating to convicts and prisons. Letter from Richard Bird to Lord Sidmouth regarding prisoners who escaped from Cardigan Gaol but were taken up at Birmingham and will be tried at Warwick Assizes for being at large, 20 March 1819.* (TNA, PC 1/67.)

to live at large, are in PCOM 3 and PCOM 4 for the period 1853-87 with the registers in PCOM 6. Captions or orders of court for the imprisonment or transportation of convicts are in PCOM 5 for 1847-65 with transfer papers for 1856-65 in PCOM 5.[37]

Medieval policing was very different from what is now understood by the term. The modern police service is very much a late 18th- or even 19th-century creation. Initially policing was governance through self-regulation, based upon local community units of the tything where members had a responsibility for maintaining the law. If the law was being broken people were expected to make a 'hue and cry'; with other members of the community they would seek to capture the felons and take them to the hundred court. Lists of tythings can be found in manor court records where the View of Frankpledge was claimed (see Chapter 2 for locating this type of material). Borough archives may have surviving 'watch and ward' records as watches developed under the

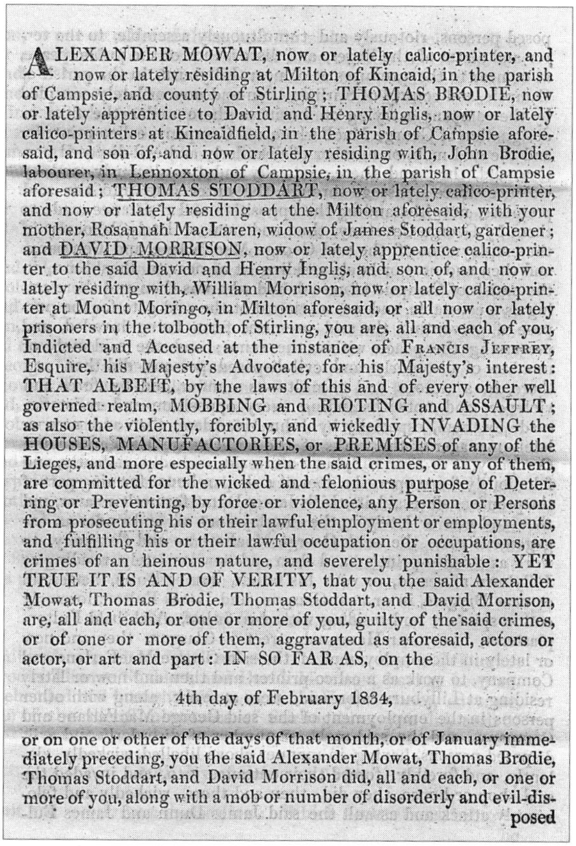
ALEXANDER MOWAT, now or lately calico-printer, and now or lately residing at Milton of Kincaid, in the parish of Campsie, and county of Stirling; THOMAS BRODIE, now or lately apprentice to David and Henry Inglis, now or lately calico-printers at Kincaidfield, in the parish of Campsie aforesaid, and son of, and now or lately residing with, John Brodie, labourer, in Lennoxton of Campsie, in the parish of Campsie aforesaid; THOMAS STODDART, now or lately calico-printer, and now or lately residing at the Milton aforesaid, with your mother, Rosannah MacLaren, widow of James Stoddart, gardener; and DAVID MORRISON, now or lately apprentice calico-printer to the said David and Henry Inglis, and son of, and now or lately residing with, William Morrison, now or lately calico-printer at Mount Moringo, in Milton aforesaid, or all now or lately prisoners in the tolbooth of Stirling, you are, all and each of you, Indicted and Accused at the instance of FRANCIS JEFFREY, Esquire, his Majesty's Advocate, for his Majesty's interest: THAT ALBEIT, by the laws of this and of every other well governed realm, MOBBING and RIOTING and ASSAULT; as also the violently, forcibly, and wickedly INVADING the HOUSES, MANUFACTORIES, or PREMISES of any of the Lieges, and more especially when the said crimes, or any of them, are committed for the wicked and felonious purpose of Deterring or Preventing, by force or violence, any Person or Persons from prosecuting his or their lawful employment or employments, and fulfilling his or their lawful occupation or occupations, are crimes of an heinous nature, and severely punishable: YET TRUE IT IS AND OF VERITY, that you the said Alexander Mowat, Thomas Brodie, Thomas Stoddart, and David Morrison, are, all and each, or one or more of you, guilty of the said crimes, or of one or more of them, aggravated as aforesaid, actors or actor, or art and part: IN SO FAR AS, on the

4th day of February 1834,

or on one or other of the days of that month, or of January immediately preceding, you the said Alexander Mowat, Thomas Brodie, Thomas Stoddart, and David Morrison did, all and each, or one or more of you, along with a mob or number of disorderly and evil-disposed

38 *From a collection of petitions, indictments and other associated paperwork concerning a number of calico printers for 'mobbing, rioting and assault' at the Lillyburn premises of Macfarlane and Co. Campsie, Stirling, 1834.* (TNA, HO 17/22 (BH 5).)

1285 Statute of Winchester. As the tything man became the more familiar constable, appointed to maintain the king's peace and enforce the king's law, his work was the taking of those apprehended before a local court and receiving the fees and payments for doing so, as this remained an unpaid community function.

The office of the petty constable is the oldest of the parish offices and survived until the advent of paid police officers. It was manorial in origin, being the link between the lord and his tenants, and has been recorded as early as the 13th century; this is sometimes reflected in the alternative titles which are found such as headborough, thirdborough, verderer, borsholder, tithingman or chief pledge. When manors became less important the constable was appointed by the parish vestry, although in some parts of the country his appointment had to be confirmed by the court leet until the 19th century. Women were rarely appointed although there are isolated examples, such as Jane Kitchen, a widow, who served as constable for Upton (Nottinghamshire) in 1644.[38]

Early references to the work of constables in the early modern and modern period can also be found in manor and vestry records. The accounts may only indicate money claimed next to brief entries of duties undertaken, but they are important for showing how minor crimes were dealt with at the local level.

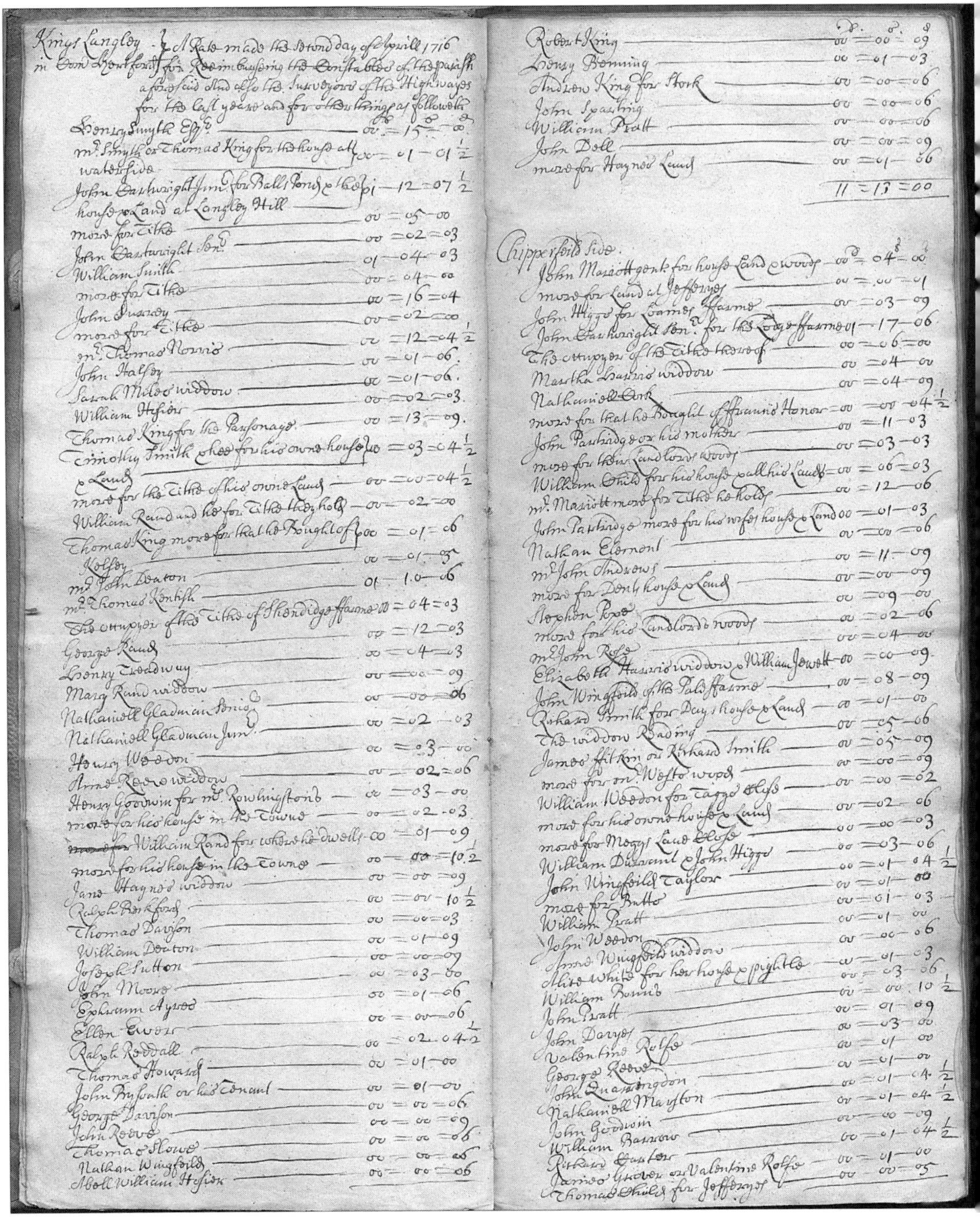
Kings Langley } A Rate made the second day of Aprill 1716 in Com Hertford for Reimbursing the Constables of the parish aforesaid And also the Surveyors of the Highways for the last yeare and for other things as followeth

Henry Smyth Esq.	00 = 15 = 00
Mr Smyth or Thomas King for the house at waterside	00 = 01 — 01 ½
John Cartwright Jun. for Balls Pond & the Hospi[tal]	01 — 12 — 07 ½
house & Land at Langley Hill	00 = 05 — 00
more for Tithe	00 = 02 = 03
John Cartwright Sen.	01 — 04 — 03
William Smith	00 = 04 — 00
more for Tithe	00 = 16 = 04
John Hardy	00 = 02 — 00
more for Tithe	00 = 12 = 04 ½
Mr Thomas Norris	00 = 01 — 06
John Halsey	00 = 01 — 06
Sarah Miles widdow	00 = 02 = 03
William Hester	00 = 13 = 09
Thomas King for the Parsonage	00 = 03 = 04 ½
Timothy Smith Clerk for his owne house & Land	00 = 00 = 04 ½
more for the tithe of his owne Land	00 = 02 = 00
William Rand and he for tithe he holds	00 = 01 = 06
Thomas King more for that he bought of Kolsey	00 = 01 = 05
Mr John Eaton	01 — 1 — 06
Mr Thomas Kentish	00 = 04 = 03
The occupyer of the tithe of Shendish Farme	00 = 12 = 03
George Rand	00 = 04 = 03
Henry Treadway	00 = 00 = 09
Mary Rand widdow	00 = 00 = 06
Nathaniell Gladman Senior	00 = 02 = 03
Nathaniell Gladman Jun.	00 = 03 = 00
Henry Wooden	00 = 02 = 06
Anne Rees widdow	00 = 03 — 00
Henry Goodwin for Mr Rowlingstons	00 = 02 — 03
more for his house in the Towne	00 = 01 — 09
William Rand for where he dwells	00 = 00 = 10 ½
more for his house in the Towne	00 = 00 = 09
Jane Haynes widdow	00 = 00 — 10 ½
Ralph Berkford	00 = 00 = 03
Thomas Davison	00 = 01 — 09
William Dorton	00 = 00 = 09
Joseph Sutton	00 = 03 — 00
John Moore	00 = 01 — 06
Ephraim Aywood	00 = 00 — 06
Ellen Ewer	00 = 02 . 04 ½
Ralph Reddall	00 = 01 — 00
Thomas Howard	00 = 01 — 00
John Bysouth or his tenant	00 = 00 — 06
George Davison	00 = 00 = 09
John Reeve	00 = 00 = 06
Thomas Slowe	00 = 00 = 06
Nathan Wingfeild	00 = 00 = 06
Abell William Hester	

Robert King	00 = 00 = 09
Henry Benning	00 = 01 — 03
Andrew King for Stork	00 = 00 = 06
John Spalding	00 = 00 = 06
William Pratt	00 = 00 = 06
John Doll	00 = 00 = 09
more for Haynes Land	00 = 01 — 06
	11 = 13 = 00

Chipperfeild side.

John Mariott gent for house Land & woods	00 = 04 = 00
more for Land at Jefferys	00 = 00 = 01
John Higgs for Barnes Farme	00 = 03 — 09
John Cartwright Sen. for the Lodge Farme	01 — 17 — 06
The occupyer of the tithe thereof	00 = 06 = 00
Martha Harris widdow	00 = 04 — 00
Nathaniell Clark	00 = 04 — 09
more for that he bought of Francis Honor	00 = 00 — 04 ½
John Partridge or his mother	00 = 11 — 03
more for their Landlords woods	00 = 03 — 03
William Child for his house & all his Lands	00 = 06 — 03
Mr Mariott more for tithe he holds	00 = 12 — 06
John Partridge more for his wifes house & Land	00 = 01 — 03
Nathan Eleanor?	00 = 00 — 06
Mr John Andrews	00 = 11 — 09
more for Dorts house & Land	00 = 00 — 09
Stephen Rose	00 = 09 — 00
more for his Landlords woods	00 = 02 — 06
Mr John Rose	00 = 04 — 00
Elizabeth Harris widdow & William Jowett	00 = 00 — 09
John Wingfeild of the Pale Farme	00 = 08 — 09
Richard Smith for Days house & Land	00 = 01 — 00
The widdow Rading	00 = 05 — 06
James Aitkin or Richard Smith	00 = 05 — 09
more for on Westewood	00 = 00 — 09
William Wooden for Tayes Close	00 = 00 = 02
more for his owne house & Land	00 = 02 — 06
more for Moggs Land Close	00 = 00 = 03
William Durrant & John Higgs	00 = 03 — 06
John Wingfeild Taylor	00 = 01 — 04 ½
more for Butts	00 = 01 — 00
William Pratt	00 = 01 — 03
John Wooden	00 = 01 — 00
Anne Wingfeild widdow	00 = 00 — 06
Alice White for her house & pightle	00 = 01 — 03
William Burnb	00 = 03 — 06
John Pratt	00 = 00 — 10 ½
John Dayes	00 = 01 — 09
Valentine Rolfe	00 = 03 — 00
George Reeve	00 = 01 — 00
John Quarrington	00 = 01 — 00
Nathaniell Marston	00 = 01 — 04 ½
John Goodwin	00 = 01 — 04 ½
William Barrow	00 = 00 — 09
Richard Gaster	00 = 01 — 04 ½
James Grover or Valentine Rolfe	00 = 01 — 00
Thomas Child for Jefferys	00 = 00 — 05

39 *The petty constable was the oldest of the parish officers and has been recorded as early as the 13th century. He had extensive duties, not all of them concerned with the maintenance of law and order. The pages illustrated give details of the money raised in Kings Langley in 1716; other entries will provide information on how this was spent. Only a few constables' accounts appear to have survived.* (Hertfordshire Archives and Local Studies, D/P 64 9/1.)

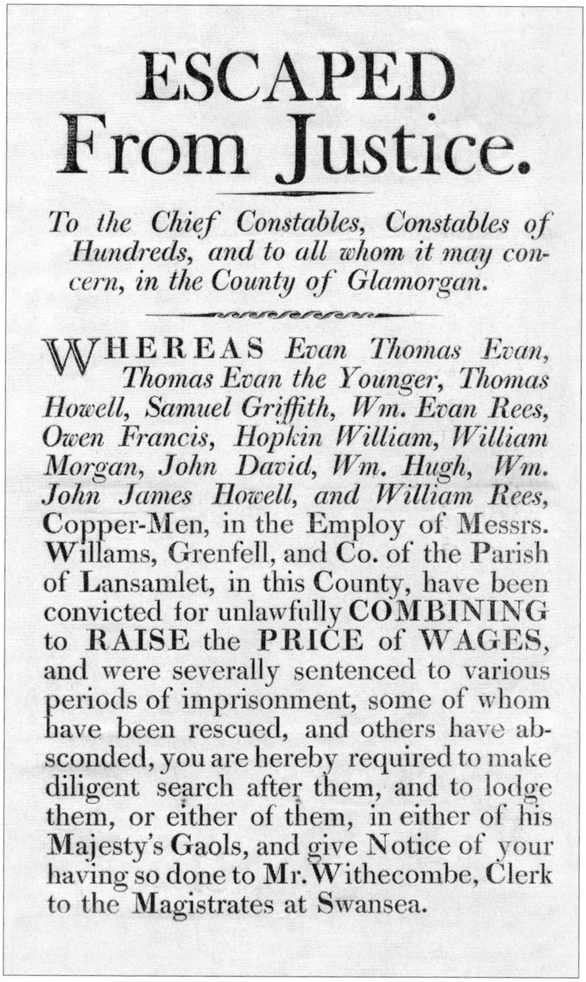

ESCAPED From Justice.

To the Chief Constables, Constables of Hundreds, and to all whom it may concern, in the County of Glamorgan.

WHEREAS *Evan Thomas Evan, Thomas Evan the Younger, Thomas Howell, Samuel Griffith, Wm. Evan Rees, Owen Francis, Hopkin William, William Morgan, John David, Wm. Hugh, Wm. John James Howell, and William Rees,* Copper-Men, in the Employ of Messrs. Willams, Grenfell, and Co. of the Parish of Lansamlet, in this County, have been convicted for unlawfully COMBINING to RAISE the PRICE of WAGES, and were severally sentenced to various periods of imprisonment, some of whom have been rescued, and others have absconded, you are hereby required to make diligent search after them, and to lodge them, or either of them, in either of his Majesty's Gaols, and give Notice of your having so done to Mr. Withecombe, Clerk to the Magistrates at Swansea.

40 *'Escape from Justice'. Notice to the local authorities in Glamorgan that some of the 12 men lately convicted for a trade union 'combination' have been rescued and are to be found, 1820.*(TNA, HO 52/1, f. 439.)

With the paucity of petty sessions and magistrates notebooks these are key records for unrecorded crime; for example 'William Rangham taken up and whipped according to law and sent away by pass. Issac Billington and Thomas Bray Constables'.[39] Constables' accounts can reveal interesting information on individuals, who are often named in the accounts – as constables or other officers, as poor persons or vagrants, or malefactors. As well as their link with the churchwardens, the constables also worked closely with the overseers of the poor; they escorted vagrants and others who had no right of settlement in the parish, to the boundary, so that they were taken 'from constable to constable' until they reached their ultimate destination. In a footnote to his book on churchwardens' accounts, Tony Palmer says that at the end of his term the constable passed on the parish armour to his successor and a receipt was issued which normally listed the armour in detail; he concludes that one parish in Hertfordshire had been selling surplus items to neighbouring parishes and that the constable had transferred the proceeds to the churchwardens.[40] Accounts can sometimes be found in a Town Book with the accounts of

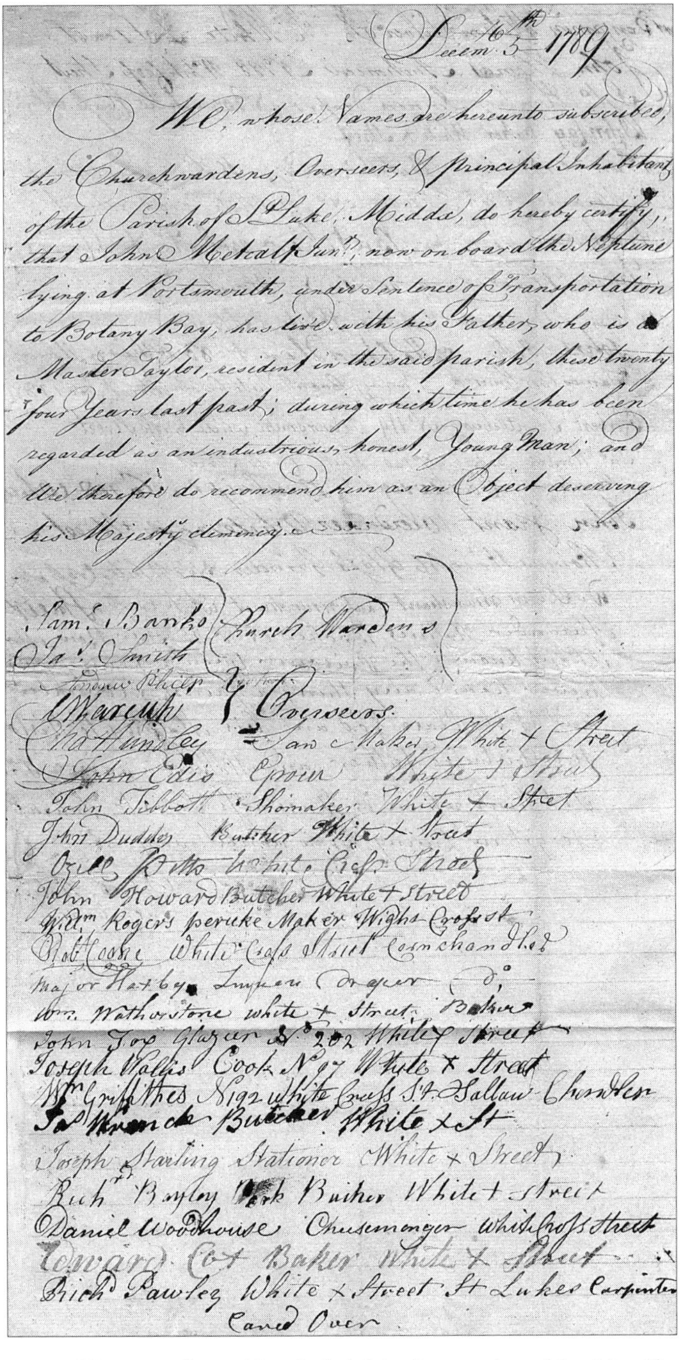

Decem 16th 1789

We, whose Names are hereunto subscribed, the Churchwardens, Overseers, & principal Inhabitants of the Parish of St Luke, Middx, do hereby certify, that John Metcalf Junr, now on board the Neptune lying at Portsmouth, under Sentence of Transportation to Botany Bay, has lived with his Father, who is a Master Taylor, resident in the said parish, these twenty four Years last past; during which time he has been regarded as an industrious, honest, Young Man; and We therefore do recommend him as an Object deserving his Majesty's clemency.

Saml Banks
Jas Smith } Church Wardens
Thomas Phelps
J Wareup } Overseers
Thos Hunsley Saw Maker White + Street
John Edis Grocer White + Street
John Tibbott Shoemaker White + Street
John Dudley Butcher White + Street
Ozell Potts White Cross Street
John Howard Butcher White + Street
Willm Rogers perucke Maker Whight Cross st
Robt Moore White Cross Street Cornchandler
Major Hatbyn Linen Draper do
Wm Wathorstone White + Street Baker
John Joo Glazier No 202 White + Street
Joseph Wallis Cook No 97 White + Street
Wm Griffithes No 192 White Cross St Tallow Chandler
Jas Wrench Butcher White + St
Joseph Starling Stationer White + Street
Richd Bayley Pork Butcher White + Street
Daniel Woodhouse Cheesemonger White Cross Street
Edward Cox Baker White + Street
Richd Pawley White + Street St Lukes Carpenter
Carried Over

41 *First part of a petition (included in the report) on John Metcalf convicted at the Reading Borough Sessions in April 1789, for theft. Forty-one people have signed the petition, from St Luke's in Middlesex, including churchwardens and overseers of the poor (many occupations are given).* (TNA, HO 47/10, f. 168.)

the other parish officers. The 'golden age' of accounts appears to have been the 17th and 18th centuries when a greater number seem to have survived; they will usually be found with other non-ecclesiastical parish records, although they do turn up in unexpected places.[41] Even at this period the constable was not a modern police officer and little proactive investigation would be expected. Two general introductions to the subject of this difference are Joan Kent's *The English Village Constable,* 1580-1642 and Keith Wrightson's chapter on 'Two Concepts of Order: Justices, Constables and Jurymen in 17th Century England'.[42]

In the 18th century property owners got together to form associations for preventing crime and to bring offenders to book; the most common name was 'Association for the Prosecution of Felons'. If records survive they are usually to be found in CROs and may include minute books and handbills offering rewards; some may be found with vestry records.[43] References to these associations may also be found in newspapers.

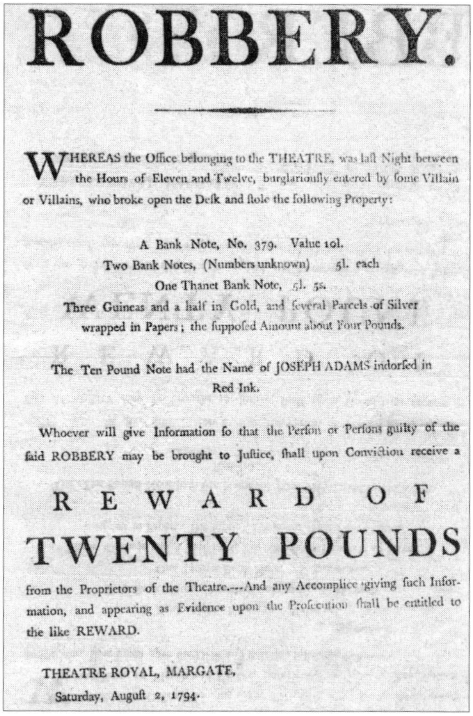
ROBBERY.

WHEREAS the Office belonging to the THEATRE, was laſt Night between the Hours of Eleven and Twelve, burglariouſly entered by ſome Villain or Villains, who broke open the Deſk and ſtole the following Property:

A Bank Note, No. 379. Value 10l.
Two Bank Notes, (Numbers unknown) 5l. each
One Thanet Bank Note, 5l. 5s.
Three Guineas and a half in Gold, and ſeveral Parcels of Silver wrapped in Papers; the ſuppoſed Amount about Four Pounds.

The Ten Pound Note had the Name of JOSEPH ADAMS indorſed in Red Ink.

Whoever will give Information ſo that the Perſon or Perſons guilty of the ſaid ROBBERY may be brought to Juſtice, ſhall upon Conviction receive a

REWARD OF
TWENTY POUNDS

from the Proprietors of the Theatre.---And any Accomplice giving ſuch Information, and appearing as Evidence upon the Proſecution ſhall be entitled to the like REWARD.

THEATRE ROYAL, MARGATE,
Saturday, Auguſt 2, 1794.

42 *Reward notice concerning a robbery at the Theatre Royal, Margate, Kent, 2 August 1794.* (TNA, HO 42/33, f. 23.)

The idea of a modern police force grew with the anxieties which arose from industrialisation and urbanisation in the late 18th century. Writers and criminal administrators all commented on perceptions of rising crime at this time.[44] The first police force was established at Bow Street in the mid-18th century under magisterial control. By the end of the century the old watches were organised into a small regular patrol for the City of London and this continued into the 19th century. The 1829 Metropolitan Police Act gave responsibility for policing to a new disciplined and professional force. The original Metropolitan Police District was a seven-mile radius from Charing Cross; this was extended in 1839 to include Middlesex and those parishes in the counties of Surrey, Hertfordshire, Essex and Kent not more than 15 miles from Charing Cross (in both instances the City of London was excluded). The extensive records of the Metropolitan Police are held at TNA. The main collection of correspondence and papers is in MEPO 2 and a supplementary series in MEPO 3. These files relate to the general organisation of the force, financial matters (including pay and allowances, expenses and economy measures), meetings and demonstrations, stations and other buildings, special constables, recruitment of women, as well as files on particular crimes. Letter books (entry books) are in MEPO 1 while registers of

43 *Leytonstone Police Station, 1908.* (TNA, MEPO 13/36.)

habitual criminals are in MEPO 6. There is a series of registers regarding murders and deaths by violence from 1891 in MEPO 20.

There was some consultation on policing in the 1830s which has resulted in detailed local material at TNA in HO 73/2-9 and 16, dated 1835-8.[45] By the middle of the 1850s legislation decreed that county and borough police forces were to cover the country; records of individual police forces are not held centrally but the appropriate CRO should have details. Ian Bridgeman and Clive Emsley's *A Guide to the Archives of the Police Forces of England and Wales* gives further details of what may be found in other police archives.[46] For more general information the Police History Society publishes a regular journal and also has links on its web site to the various regional, county and local police force history societies.[47] The European Centre for the Study of Policing is based at the Open University in Milton Keynes and promotes research into the history of modern policing (from *c.*1750); it advertises seminars, conferences and publications and welcomes researchers.[48]

There are numerous Parliamentary Papers of interest to the local historian with regard to policing, such as the *Returns of Police Forces, 1840-56* in 1856, and the *Report of the Committee on the Police Service* in 1919; there are many others and researchers should search BOPCRIS for further information.[49]

13

National and Local Administration

The United Kingdom Parliament is one of the oldest representative assemblies in the world today and can trace its origins back to the middle of the 13th century; the upper and lower chamber system started in the 14th century in England. How the two Houses work is governed by an amalgam of convention and parliamentary Act. Wales was represented from 1523 and Scottish MPs sat in Westminster from 1707. The most important of the parliamentary functions are 'to make all UK law, to provide, by voting for taxation, the means of carrying on the work of government, to protect the public and safeguard the rights of individuals, to scrutinise government policy and administration, including proposals for expenditure, to examine European proposals before they become law, to hear appeals in the House of Lords, the highest Court of Appeal in Britain, and to debate the major issues of the day'.[1]

This is not the place to sketch out a history of parliament as there are many secondary sources.[2] However, it is fair to say that for much of its history it has been involved in firstly an assertive campaign to curtail the arbitrary powers of the crown, and then a more defensive campaign to defend its own undemocratic powers with regard to people at large. The records of parliament and government are highly dispersed for several reasons and are set out in brief here.[3] The Parliamentary Archives[4] hold the records of both houses of Parliament, including Acts,[5] deposited plans, journals and appeal cases.[6] Many of the Acts which will help local historians (enclosure, canal, turnpike road building,[7] etc) will be found in the collections built up by CROs, and the printed parliamentary journals can be found at other large archives (such as TNA), university libraries and elsewhere; it may not always be necessary to go to the House of Lords Record Office to see them. There is also a collection of private papers of almost 200 people, bodies and other groups, mainly of members of the Commons or Lords such as Lord Beaverbrook, Bonar Law, Lloyd George and Herbert Samuel, or bodies and groups such as the Britain into Europe Campaign,[8] and the Forests and Commons Preservation Society (these latter papers date back to the late 19th century).[9] The records of the departmental activities of government are held at TNA (and have been described in earlier chapters).

Records of debates in the Houses of Parliament began in the 17th century. T.C. Hansard took over responsibility in 1743 and from 1803 a verbatim account was kept, which is still known as *Hansard*.[10] Reports of debates were published in newspapers and journals, such as the *Historical Register* and *Gentleman's Magazine*. Contemporary political broadsheets may be found in local libraries and record offices. The History of Parliament Trust is a major academic project to create a scholarly reference work describing the members, constituencies and activities of the Parliament of England and the United Kingdom.[11]

Statute rolls, which contain all Acts of Parliament since 1500, are kept in the House of Lords Record Office; this includes Acts which have not been printed. Public Acts from 1485 to 1702 have been printed as *Statutes of the Realm* and from 1702 as *Statutes at Large*. Local, personal and private Acts from 1797 are kept among the Parliament Rolls at TNA in records series C 65. Printed sets of local and personal Acts are available at the British Library, and most reference libraries and record offices will have sets relating to their area.

The borough was an enclave separate from the county and granted certain privileges. Its characteristics included the following rights: to perpetual succession, to sue and be sued as a legal entity, to hold property corporately, to use a common seal, to make bye-laws,[12] and to elect members to Parliament. Its origins lie in the Anglo-Saxon 'burh', a fortified place. Trade was particularly important and the key to prosperity, so trading rights were jealously guarded. Some boroughs were seigneurial, that is, they did not have a mayor and corporation but did have a measure of independence from the local lord of the manor; the lord often retained the right to the market tolls and exercised authority through the manorial court. Many towns were seigneurial boroughs and the leading townsmen, called burgesses, administered their affairs through an institution, often a gild. Leicester is a good example of a seigneurial borough and acquired privileges from both royal and seigneurial sources; when the Duchy of Lancaster was united with the Crown in 1399 grants were made by the monarch, sometimes as king and sometimes as Duke of Lancaster. Cities were large towns that were episcopal or ancient royal boroughs, or granted city status, mostly in the 19th and 20th centuries.

Borough officers included a mayor (the chief magistrate), aldermen, town clerk, recorder, chamberlains (financial officers) and coroner. The Corporation Act of 1661 excluded non-Anglicans from standing for office. Until the 18th century most British towns were small by continental standards and local migration from the country to the town was often the only way of sustaining their size, let alone allow them to grow. In the 18th century the weaknesses in administration became apparent, showing that corporations were not equipped to deal with new kinds of problems such as lighting and sanitation. There were no major changes in government until the 19th century but some small improvements, such as private Acts establishing improvement commissioners, and standards of paving, lighting and street-widening improved.

The Municipal Corporations Act of 1835 swept away inadequate and corrupt boroughs and put in their place elected bodies with greater accountability more suited to the needs of an increasing population.[13] Many towns grew by more than 100 per cent between 1801 and 1831; the period was one of technological improvement, an expanding economy and opportunities for men of ability and ambition to prosper. Many became substantial citizens

To the Honorable House of Commons, in Parliament assembled.

THE

PETITION

Of the Inhabitant Householders of the Ancient Town and Borough of Southwark, in Town-Hall assembled, on Wednesday, Nov. 22nd, 1820.

Humbly Sheweth,

THAT your Petitioners beg leave to represent to your Honorable House, that it appears to them His Majesty's Ministers have for a great length of time, most grossly misconducted the Government of the Country.

THAT in the measures His Majesty's Ministers have pursued, they have exhibited a total disregard of the Economy which circumstances have rendered so imperiously needful; that, by their profusion and waste, they have added enormously to the Taxation and Burthens, by which the Agricultural, the Manufacturing, and the Commercial Orders of the Community, are already so severely oppressed, and have augmented the Distresses, under which the Labouring Ranks of the People have been suffering, to a degree that has become scarcely supportable.

THAT the Motives by which these Ministers have been actuated, appear to your Petitioners to have been the preserving, at all hazards, the Possession of their Places and Emoluments, and to sacrifice all considerations of public Good to the perpetuation of their Power, and the gratification of a pernicious and unprincipled Ambition.

THAT in the pursuit of their destructive Purpose, it appears to your Petitioners that His Majesty's Ministers have attempted the most daring Encroachments on the ancient and constitutional Privileges of the Subject; and by means of Influence, Patronage, and Corruption, and in defiance of all expostulation and reason, have, in several instances, succeeded in abridging, to a most alarming extent, the Liberties and Birth-rights of the British Nation.

THAT with the same desperate determination to retain Office at the expence of all moral or prudential feeling, their Councils have latterly led to proceedings by which the personal character of the Monarchy has been injured and degraded, and the affections and loyalty of the People towards their Sovereign in a very extensive degree estranged.

THAT the true and simple remedy for these manifold Grievances would be such a Reform in your Honorable House, as should insure a more adequate Representation of the People; and a due regard to the Expenditure, the Complaints, and the Discontents which are now so universally expressed.

THAT sooner or later such Reform is inevitable, but whether such Reform be immediately effected or not, it is indispensable to the welfare, the security, and the honor of the Country, that the Government should be no longer entrusted to the management of Individuals so unworthy the confidence of the People, and of your Honorable House.

THAT *on these several grounds, your Petitioners most humbly pray that your Honorable House would be pleased to withdraw your Support from His Majesty's present Ministers, who have so shamefully betrayed the best Interests of the Country; that you would proceed to amend the defective Representation of the People, and effect, under the immediate controul of your Honorable House, a general and an efficient Reform of Abuses, and a diminution of Expenditure.*

AND your Petitioners, as in duty bound, will ever pray, &c.

The above PETITION lies for SIGNATURES at the

BAILIFF'S OFFICE, TOWN-HALL.

☞ *The Petition to His Majesty will be presented when a Levee takes place.*

44 *Petition from Southwark against the management of the government and in favour of political reform, 22 November 1820.* (TNA, HO 52/1, f. 568.)

with considerable economic power and wealth but with little or no say in the running of the country, so that those who wished to exercise political power had to look to their own localities for opportunities to do so. Leicester has been cited as the classic example of the success of the Act in practice, as the corrupt Tory corporation was replaced by an enlightened Liberal one, although this rather simplifies the situation.[14] The mayor of a corporation was normally the *ex officio* magistrate for the borough; the mayor and corporation were sometimes lords of the manor and usually had jurisdiction over markets and fairs.

There was a series of Acts from the second half of the 19th century: the 1846 Baths and Wash-houses Act empowered corporations to provide public baths and wash-houses; the 1850 Public Libraries Act made the borough a library authority; the 1856 Police Act made local forces compulsory. (Further information on sanitation, education and public transport will be found in the relevant chapters.) It should always be taken into account that, in addition to records in CROs and other local archives, there will be policy material and correspondence with central government in various TNA series, especially the Home Office and Local Government Board. There was a further Municipal Corporations Act in 1882 which disenfranchised a number of small boroughs. There were four statutory borough officers – town clerk, medical officer, surveyor and treasurer; others were appointed as new legislation was introduced.

Many sets of borough records have been published, some up to 1835 only; the original documents will usually be found in the local record office. They normally include a number of common series, but inevitably each borough will be slightly different. Charters granted various rights, including freedom from certain tolls, trade privileges, pardons and exemption from particular legislation;[15] Leicester's earliest surviving charter dates from 1103–18 and frustratingly grants to the merchants their customs and gild held in the time of William I, with no further details. Unusual rights include the expulsion of all Jews forever and permission to change the law of inheritance from ultimogeniture to primogeniture. There are relevant records at TNA, particularly the Patent Rolls in C 66 and Charter Rolls in C 53. There is also a collection of charters of incorporation of boroughs, colleges, hospitals, etc. in C 248. Custumals were handbooks for the guidance of officials. Minute books may be called by different names; Leicester's, for example, were called Hall Books and date from 1467, in Exeter they were known as city act books and in Southampton assembly books. They give information on many aspects of life in the town, such as public health, charities, poor relief, education, law and order and markets. Loose papers may also survive, which have sometimes been bound into volumes to preserve them better. Records of freemen and apprentices were important, as only freemen had the right to trade. Letters, if they survive, give valuable details about the life of a town. Information about the town's officers could include orders, details of wages and applications for jobs. The assize of bread and ale dealt with the price of these staple commodities. An important section dealt with town property from which it usually derived its income and power. Most towns had a number of charities and there will be information about them, including lists of recipients, accounts and letters. Fee farm was an annual rent paid to the Crown and there may be locally held documents relating to its administration; there are several sets of records at TNA including those of the Exchequer in E 351, E 134, E 367, E 304, E 307, E 315, E 317 and E 320 (catalogue searches will find less important series concerning fee farms).

Boroughs had to provide men for military service and muster rolls may have been kept, as well as those in quarter sessions records. There are also sets of musters books and pay lists at TNA; there are several series but the main collections are in WO 13/4160-4621 for the period 1797 to 1814 with further material for the Middlesex and County of London regiments in WO 70. Financial records will feature prominently and there may be more than one series of accounts; Leicester has mayors' accounts from 1300 and chamberlains' accounts from 1376. Judicial records will include sessions rolls and other documents relating to the administration of justice. Electoral records will include poll books and lists of voters. Gild rolls are important because of their link to the town's trade, and may include more than one series; Leicester has a set of merchant gild rolls from 1196 (one of the earliest in the country) and Corpus Christi gild records from 1458. There will be other interesting material for any particular town and just one example will demonstrate this: there was a royal progress by James I to Leicester in 1614 and a small group of documents relates to it; it includes a copy of a letter from the mayor certifying that the town was free of disease, an itinerary of places at which the king intended to stay and a report of his arrival.[16]

Post-1835 records are potentially less interesting and will be more familiar to researchers. They will include minute books, accounts, correspondence, title deeds, records of public utilities and departmental working records. Although the earlier records should have been deposited in a record office, they may often still be found in the council offices. Urban history is now a discipline in its own right and there are many useful secondary sources for anyone interested in the subject. London is a special case and there are records which are not found elsewhere, such as bills of mortality; London became a county council in 1888 and the 1963 London Government Act created the Greater London Council, which absorbed the whole of Middlesex and parts of neighbouring counties. It was abolished in 1986 along with the short-lived metropolitan county councils created in 1974.

Outside towns the only form of 'big local government' before the end of the 19th century was the court of quarter sessions (see below). Elected county councils were created by the 1888 Local Government Act which also created county borough councils for towns with a population of more than 50,000. They were abolished in 1974 and there is no longer a uniform pattern; some county councils remain in existence in much the same way as they have for the last 100 years and others have lost some or all of their powers to other authorities. One of the responsibilities of county councils is for the archive service.

At first the powers of county councils were limited although they acquired housing and planning powers in 1890. In 1902 they took over responsibility

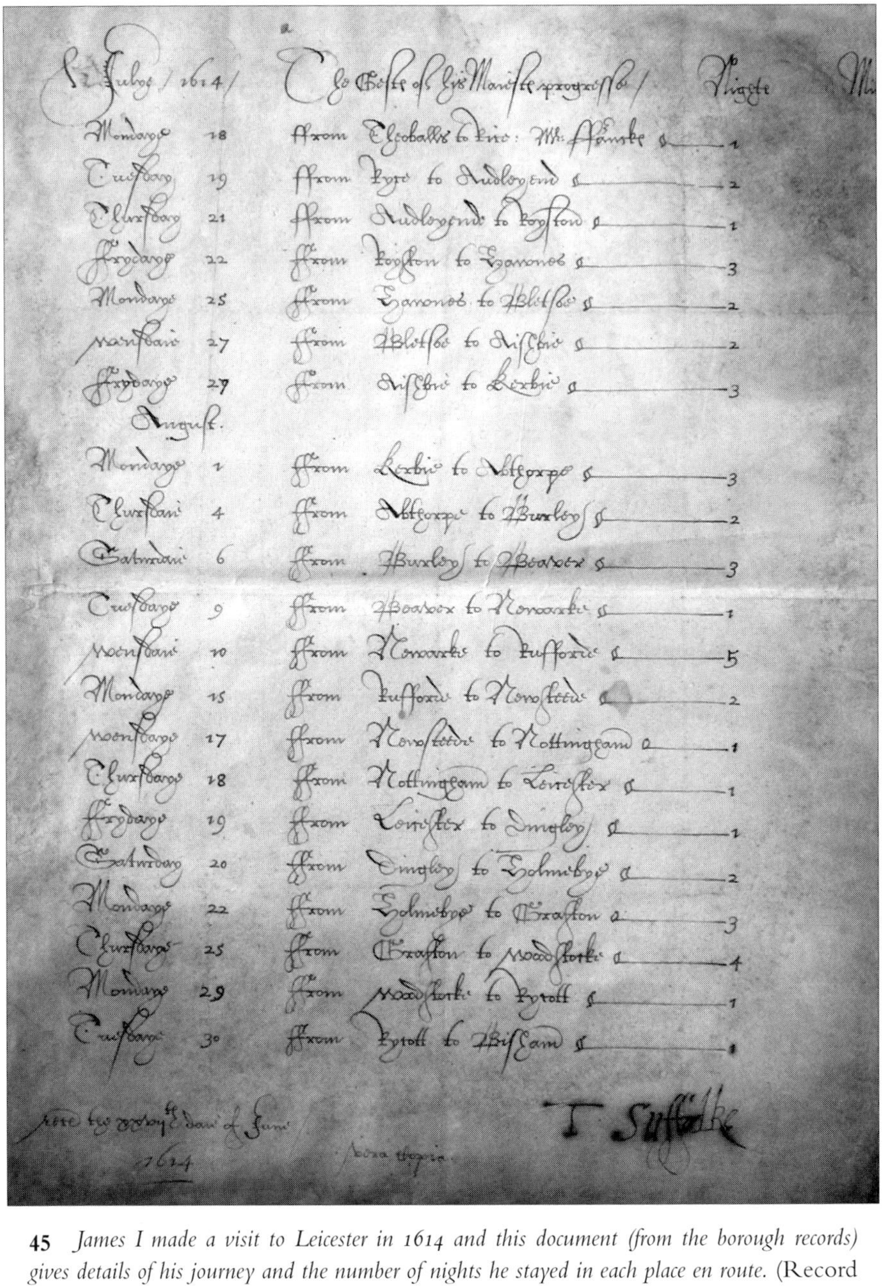

12 Julye / 1614 / The Geste of his Maiesties progresse / Nights

Monday	18	From Theobalds to Ware: Mr Fanshawe	1
Tuesday	19	From Ware to Audleyend	2
Thursday	21	From Audleyend to Royston	1
Friday	22	From Royston to [illegible]	3
Monday	25	From [illegible] to Bletsoe	2
Wednesday	27	From Bletsoe to [illegible]	2
Friday	27	From [illegible] to Kerbie	3
August			
Monday	1	From Kerbie to Althorpe	3
Thursday	4	From Althorpe to Burley	2
Saturday	6	From Burley to Bever	3
Tuesday	9	From Bever to Newarke	1
Wednesday	10	From Newarke to Rufforde	5
Monday	15	From Rufforde to Newsteede	2
Wednesday	17	From Newsteede to Nottingham	1
Thursday	18	From Nottingham to Leicester	1
Friday	19	From Leicester to Dingley	1
Saturday	20	From Dingley to Holmbye	2
Monday	22	From Holmbye to Grafton	3
Thursday	25	From Grafton to Woodstocke	4
Monday	29	From Woodstocke to Rycott	1
Tuesday	30	From Rycott to Bisham	1

T Suffolke

45 *James I made a visit to Leicester in 1614 and this document (from the borough records) gives details of his journey and the number of nights he stayed in each place en route.* (Record Office of Leicestershire, Leicester and Rutland, BRII/17/3.)

for the education service and this now accounts for the largest percentage of expenditure. The Clerk of the Peace for the quarter sessions became the clerk of the county council and other posts included a medical officer of health and inspectors of weights and measures; as new powers were added there were new appointments, such as a director of education and a county land agent. In 1947 county councils took over responsibility for the fire service and became the planning authority. Under the National Health Service Act 1946 and Children's Act 1948 they became responsible for health and welfare services; some of these were lost later and the remaining services subsumed in social services departments.

It is impossible to detail all the changes over time but the local library or record office will be able to provide relevant information. County council records will include: council and committee minutes and related papers, financial records, correspondence, title deeds, contracts and agreements, departmental working papers and so on. There should be a records management system in operation, whereby records are selected for permanent preservation dependent on their historical importance. (More information on particular subjects will be found in other chapters; for details on education records, for example, see chapter 7.)

In 1894 Urban and Rural District Councils were created, with responsibility primarily for public health matters (see chapter 9 for further information). In 1974 the structure of local government was completely reworked and in most parts of the country a system of two-tier authorities was introduced; the county council had responsibility for the major services, such as education, social services and libraries, while the new district councils dealt with smaller services including refuse collection and leisure provision. In some areas, especially large conurbations, a system of unitary authorities was later introduced, which have responsibility for all the services in their area. The records of these authorities are naturally much less extensive than those of county councils but will include similar material; some material has been deposited in record offices but there is still a considerable quantity kept in the council offices.

Parishes are both civil and ecclesiastical and the boundaries of the two may not be the same. A civil parish was defined in 1866 as a place for which a separate poor rate was levied; some large parishes, more so in the north, were divided into townships. The Tudors began to use the parish as the local administrative unit instead of the township or manor; the township was the smallest unit of local government, largely synonymous with a vill. The Local Government Act 1894, which created UDCs and RDCs, divided England and Wales into 14,000 parishes with boundaries roughly the same as the old civil parishes, and with responsibility for non-ecclesiastical matters at the local level. They are still in existence but have very limited powers. Their records are very similar to those for other councils and will include minutes, financial records and correspondence. Details of pre-1894 records, such as the accounts of various parish officers, will be found in chapters 4, 8 and 12.

There are a number of printed sources for local administration, such as the *Municipal Year Book* and *County Councils Gazette*, and local reference libraries will be able to provide further information on current and non-current titles. Modern local authorities publish a large amount of literature, much of which is of historic interest. In the 19th century special statutory bodies were created to deal with a number of issues which were not catered for adequately elsewhere. Most of these were concerned with public health and are dealt with in chapter 9; poor law unions are covered in chapter 8 and highway boards in chapter 4.

The Court of Quarter Sessions, as its name indicates, met quarterly in each county in England and Wales, usually in the county town. The Tudor monarchs used the magistrates as a means of administering the country, although the office dated from much earlier. They were given more and more administrative responsibilities in the 17th and 18th centuries, because they were the only effective local body, and the sessions became longer and busier. By the 19th century new bodies were created and powers were taken away from quarter sessions, and many of their non-judicial responsibilities were gradually transferred to county councils; the court was finally abolished in 1971. Petty Sessions was the lowest tier of the judicial system and there are very few non-judicial records. (See chapter 12 for details of legal records.)

Quarter Sessions records form the bedrock of all English and Welsh county record offices; they can be a very rich source and provide information rarely found elsewhere. Many of the records have been published by county councils, record offices or record societies, and indexes to the more important records have been compiled; the earliest volume to be published was in 1886 by the Middlesex County Record Society.[17] The date from which the records have survived will vary from county to county, but several have material from the 16th century; one of the strengths of quarter session records is that they often form an unbroken series from the date of the earliest documents to the abolition of the court or the transfer of responsibilities.

The non-judicial records are usually divided into administrative records and those which were enrolled, registered or deposited under various pieces of legislation. The first category includes records relating to bridges, buildings, highways, police and prisons. Under an Act of Parliament of 1552, licensed victuallers had to take out a recognizance to ensure good behaviour in their premises. From 1563 to 1772 badgers, higglers and other dealers had to be licensed. From 1815 parish overseers (and later, clerks to poor law unions) had to send an annual return of pauper lunatics.

The Clerk of the Peace was the recipient of a number of documents which had been ordered to be deposited, enrolled or registered with him. Records which may well be of interest include: details of barges, wherries, etc on navigable rivers and canals (see chapter 4); lists of freemasons (under the Unlawful Societies Act of 1799 which exempted existing lodges provided that each lodge supplied a list each year); registers of friendly societies from 1793, loan societies from 1836 and literary societies from 1844; gamekeepers' deputations (an Act of 1710 allowed the lord of a manor to appoint one gamekeeper with power to kill game whose name had to be registered with the Clerk of the Peace); rules of savings banks from 1817; jury lists from 1696 (apparently few survive but they crop up regularly in the St Albans records); names and addresses of owners of printing presses from 1799 to 1869; various religious oaths and declarations, such as sacrament certificates, association rolls and papists' oaths of allegiance, which all contain names; game duty registers for 1784-1807; and records of vagrancy, such as examinations and removal orders. One very large set of records relates to the payment of Land Tax which was connected with the right to vote in the counties.[18] Before the first Reform

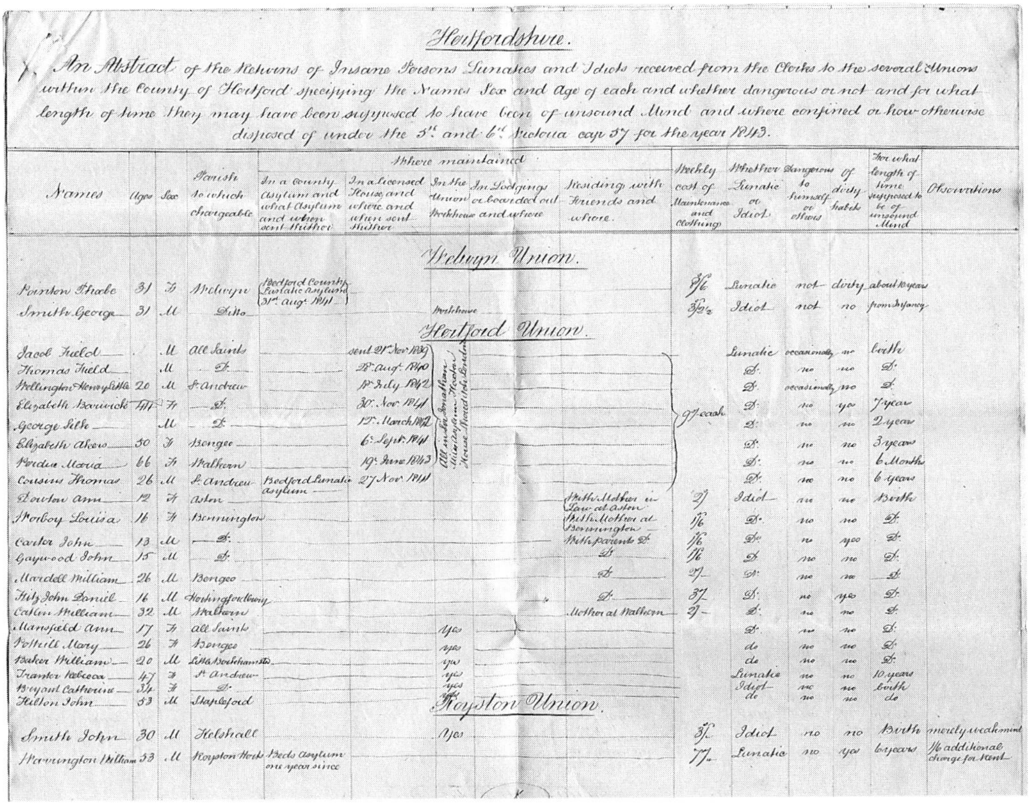
Hertfordshire.

An Abstract of the Returns of Insane Persons Lunatics and Idiots received from the Clerks to the several Unions within the County of Hertford specifying the Names Sex and Age of each and whether dangerous or not and for what length of time they may have been supposed to have been of unsound Mind and where confined or how otherwise disposed of under the 5th and 6th Victoria cap 57 for the year 1843.

Names	Ages	Sex	Parish to which chargeable	Where maintained: In a County Asylum and what Asylum and when sent thither	In a licensed House and where and when sent thither	In the Union Workhouse	In Lodgings or boarded out and where	Residing with Friends and where	Weekly cost of Maintenance and Clothing	Whether Lunatic or Idiot	Dangerous to himself or others	Of dirty habits	For what length of time supposed to be of unsound Mind	Observations
Welwyn Union.														
Pointon Phoebe	31	F	Welwyn	Bedford County Lunatic Asylum 31st Aug. 1841					8/6	Lunatic	not	dirty	about 10 years	
Smith George	31	M	Ditto			Workhouse			3/2½	Idiot	not	no	from Infancy	
Hertford Union.														
Jacob Field		M	All Saints		sent 21st Nov. 1839	All in Sir Jonathan Miles Asylum Hoxton House Hoxton London				Lunatic	occasionally	no	birth	
Thomas Field		M	D.		28th Aug. 1840					D.	no	no	D.	
Wellington Henry Little	20	M	St. Andrew		1st July 1842					D.	occasionally	no	D.	
Elizabeth Barwick	44	F	D.		30th Nov. 1841					D.	no	yes	7 year	
George Lilly		M	D.		1st March 1842				9/- each	D.	no	no	2 year	
Elizabeth Akers	30	F	Bengeo		6th Sept. 1841					D.	no	no	3 years	
Perdue Maria	66	F	Walkern		19th June 1843					D.	no	no	6 Months	
Cousins Thomas	26	M	St. Andrew	Bedford Lunatic Asylum	27 Nov. 1841					D.	no	no	6 years	
Dowton Ann	12	F	Aston					With Mother in Law at Aston	2/	Idiot	no	no	Birth	
Worboy Louisa	16	F	Bennington					With Mother at Bennington	1/6	D.	no	no	D.	
Carter John	13	M	D.					With parents D.	1/6	Do.	no	yes	D.	
Gaywood John	15	M	D.					D.	1/6	D.	no	no	D.	
Mardell William	26	M	Bengeo					D.	2/-	D.	no	no	D.	
Fitz John Daniel	16	M	Hertingfordbury					D.	3/-	D.	no	yes	D.	
Catlin William	32	M	Walkern					Mother at Walkern	2/-	D.	no	no	D.	
Mansfield Ann	17	F	All Saints			yes				D.	no	no	D.	
Pottill Mary	26	F	Bengeo			yes				do	no	no	D.	
Baker William	20	M	Little Berkhamsted			yes				do	no	no	D.	
Tranter Rebecca	47	F	St. Andrew			yes				Lunatic	no	no	10 years	
Bryant Catherine	34	F	D.			yes				Idiot	no	no	birth	
Hillon John	53	M	Stapleford			yes				do	no	no	do	
Royston Union.														
Smith John	30	M	Kelshall			yes			3/-	Idiot	no	no	Birth	merely weak in mind
Warrington William	53	M	Royston Herts	Beds Asylum one year since					7/-	Lunatic	no	yes	6 years	1/6 additional charge for Rent

46 *Parish overseers and (from 1834) clerks to poor law Guardians had to submit annual returns of pauper lunatics, with brief details. This extract shows the entries for three Hertfordshire unions in 1843.* (Hertfordshire Archives and Local Studies, QS Misc B3.)

Act of 1832 only those who held freehold property worth at least 40s a year could vote in such elections in 1745.

Two of the more unusual sets of documents which may be found are Hair Powder Duty certificates and 'Tyburn Tickets'. Items which have attracted taxation over the years are many and varied, such as dogs, carriages and servants, but one of the most unusual was the requirement that those who used hair powder had to buy an annual certificate costing a guinea. The clergy, unless wealthy, were exempt and those whose names appear in the registers are mostly the gentry and their servants. The Act soon became irrelevant once the fashion for powdering hair stopped. Under an Act of 1699, not repealed until 1827, any person who successfully apprehended and prosecuted a felon to capital conviction was entitled to a certificate exempting him from serving any offices in the parish where the crime was committed. These certificates were nicknamed 'Tyburn Tickets' and could be transferred; they became marketable commodities which could attract quite large sums of money, and copies were enrolled with the Clerk of the Peace.

The sessions rolls, which are dealt with more fully in chapter 12, can also contain non-judicial documents, especially poor law material. Most counties

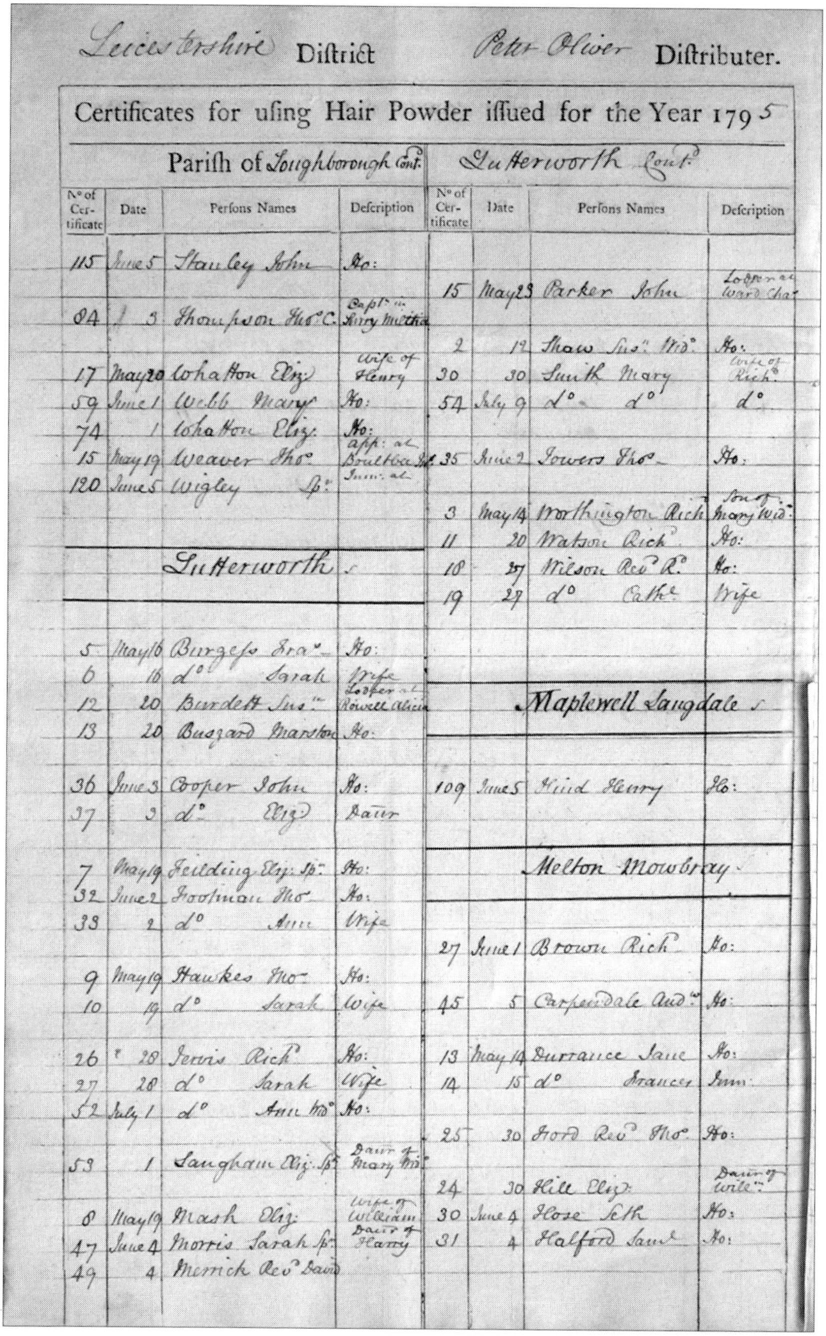

Leicestershire District Peter Oliver Distributer.

Certificates for using Hair Powder issued for the Year 1795

Parish of Loughborough Cont.

Nº of Certificate	Date	Persons Names	Description
115	June 5	Stanley John	Ho:
84	3	Thompson Thos C.	Capt. in Army Militia
17	May 20	Whatton Eliz:	Wife of Henry
59	June 1	Webb Mary	Ho:
74	1	Whatton Eliz.	Ho:
15	May 19	Weaver Thos	app: at Boulton [illegible]
120	June 5	Wigley Sp:	Journ: at

Lutterworth

Nº of Certificate	Date	Persons Names	Description
5	May 16	Burgess Fra.	Ho:
6	16	do Sarah	Wife
12	20	Burdett Jno.	Lodger at Powell Alice
13	20	Buszard Marston	Ho:
36	June 3	Cooper John	Ho:
37	3	do Eliz	Daur
7	May 19	Feilding Eliz: Sp.	Ho:
32	June 2	Footman Thos	Ho:
33	2	do Ann	Wife
9	May 19	Hawkes Thos	Ho:
10	19	do Sarah	Wife
26	28	Jervis Rich.	Ho:
27	28	do Sarah	Wife
52	July 1	do Ann Wid.	Ho:
53	1	Langham Eliz: Sp.	Daur of Mary Wid.
8	May 19	Marsh Eliz:	Wife of William
47	June 4	Morris Sarah Sp.	Daur of Harry
49	4	Merrick Revd David	

Lutterworth Cont.

Nº of Certificate	Date	Persons Names	Description
15	May 23	Parker John	Lodger at Ward Cha.
2	12	Shaw Jno. Wid.	Ho:
30	30	Smith Mary	Wife of Rich.
54	July 9	do do	do
35	June 2	Towers Thos	Ho:
3	May 14	Worthington Rich	Son of Mary Wid.
11	20	Watson Rich.	Ho:
18	27	Wilson Revd R.	Ho:
19	27	do Cathe	Wife

Maplewell Langdale

Nº of Certificate	Date	Persons Names	Description
109	June 5	Hind Henry	Ho:

Melton Mowbray

Nº of Certificate	Date	Persons Names	Description
27	June 1	Brown Rich	Ho:
45	5	Carpendale Andw	Ho:
13	May 14	Durrance Jane	Ho:
14	15	do Frances	Inm:
25	30	Ford Revd Thos	Ho:
24	30	Hill Eliz:	Daur of Wille
30	June 4	Hose Seth	Ho:
31	4	Halford Saml	Ho:

47 *One of the more bizarre ways of raising taxation was Hair Powder Duty. By an Act of 1795, those who used hair powder had to take out an annual certificate bearing stamp duty of a guinea. The document illustrated shows entries for the larger towns of Loughborough, Lutterworth and Melton Mowbray in 1795.* (Record Office of Leicestershire, Leicester and Rutland, QS570.)

will have good sets of quarter session records but there will be gaps; for example, Hertfordshire has a marvellous set of militia lists, compiled during the Napoleonic Wars (and indexed by the county family history society) but Leicestershire has none. Some of the records are indexed by name, place and subject and these are likely to grow as more local projects come on stream; some of them are also beginning to appear on web sites.

The 'golden age' of the sheriff was 1066 to about 1300; in the 11th and 12th centuries he was the only source of 'local government'. He was a royal viceroy and was in close touch with the Curia Regis and Exchequer. His responsibilities included: collecting royal revenues in his county; holding the county court and tourn; the local military forces; police and gaols; juries; execution of royal writs; the county castle; and the impounding of stray animals. He was appointed by the king and became hereditary in some areas. Some counties, such as Essex and Hertfordshire, shared a sheriff. By the beginning of the 14th century many of the sheriff's powers had disappeared and by the middle of the 15th century he had lost practically all of them. In 1551 king's lieutenants were put in charge of the county militias, with responsibility for musters and beacons, and became known as lords lieutenant. They became a valuable means of passing on local news to central government, and the Militia Act of 1662 made the office permanent, giving the lieutenant complete control over the county militia; deputy lieutenants were also appointed. The system was reorganised under the 1757 Militia Act and there were further alterations in 1786 and 1802, but in 1871 the lieutenant lost all militia duties as a result of Cardwell's army reforms; county regiments began in the same year.

The offices of high sheriff and lord lieutenant still exist but only as local representatives on ceremonial occasions. Until 1971 the sheriff was responsible for organising the assizes but became redundant in 1972, although he is still 'chosen' by the Queen. There are few records of either the sheriff or lord lieutenant held locally but what there is will usually be found with quarter sessions records and dating from the 18th century; most county record offices have at least one example of a quietus, the annual receipt-roll of the Exchequer for the royal dues and fines accounted for by him. Other records which may survive are minutes of general meetings, correspondence, clerks' papers and papers relating to the militia; in maritime counties there may be vice-admiralty papers as the lieutenant was the local representative of the court of admiralty. Detailed returns in 1797 and 1803 were called for from every county, listing the names of men fit to act as guides or pioneers, the influence they could muster and the number of carts available; millers had to give details of the amount of flour they could provide and bakers the number of loafs they could make. There may be papers in family collections relating to the office, which was often held by a major landowner. From 1757 minute books of the Clerk to the Lieutenancy may survive as well as records relating to the muster, but these are not very extensive.

Every county was divided into a number of hundreds (known as wapentakes in the Danelaw) from the 10th century onwards. They had military, judicial and administrative functions, some of which continued into the modern period;

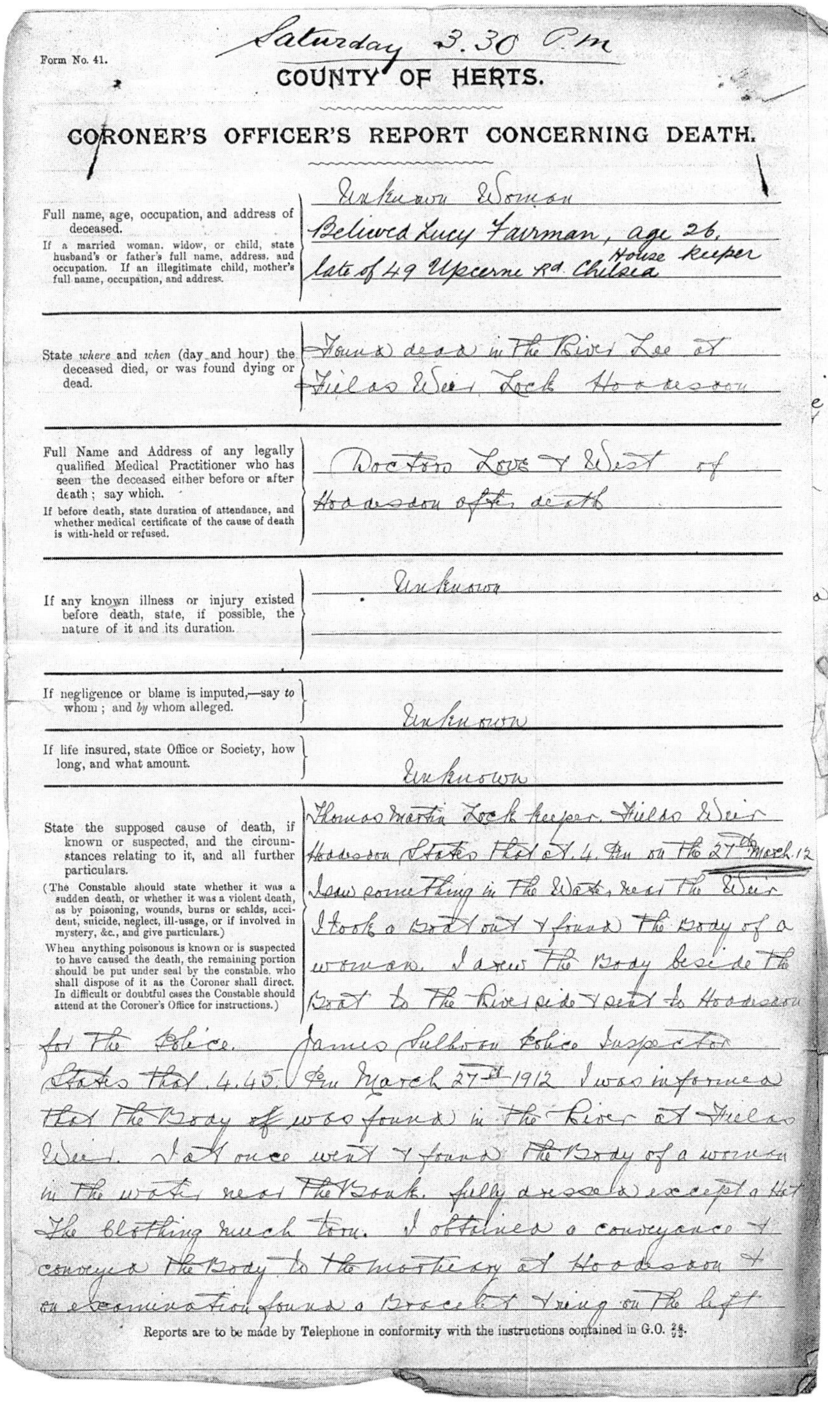

Saturday 3.30 P.m

Form No. 41.

COUNTY OF HERTS.

CORONER'S OFFICER'S REPORT CONCERNING DEATH.

Full name, age, occupation, and address of deceased. If a married woman, widow, or child, state husband's or father's full name, address, and occupation. If an illegitimate child, mother's full name, occupation, and address.	Unknown Woman Believed Lucy Fairman, age 26. late of 49 Upcerne Rd Chelsea House keeper
State *where* and *when* (day and hour) the deceased died, or was found dying or dead.	Found dead in The River Lee at Fields Weir, Lock Hoddesdon
Full Name and Address of any legally qualified Medical Practitioner who has seen the deceased either before or after death; say which. If before death, state duration of attendance, and whether medical certificate of the cause of death is with-held or refused.	Doctors Love & West of Hoddesdon after death
If any known illness or injury existed before death, state, if possible, the nature of it and its duration.	Unknown
If negligence or blame is imputed,—say *to* whom; and *by* whom alleged.	Unknown
If life insured, state Office or Society, how long, and what amount.	Unknown
State the supposed cause of death, if known or suspected, and the circumstances relating to it, and all further particulars. (The Constable should state whether it was a sudden death, or whether it was a violent death, as by poisoning, wounds, burns or scalds, accident, suicide, neglect, ill-usage, or if involved in mystery, &c., and give particulars.) When anything poisonous is known or is suspected to have caused the death, the remaining portion should be put under seal by the constable, who shall dispose of it as the Coroner shall direct. In difficult or doubtful cases the Constable should attend at the Coroner's Office for instructions.)	Thomas Martin Lock keeper, Fields Weir Hoddesdon States That at 4. P.m on The 27th March 12 I saw something in The Water near The Weir I took a boat out & found The Body of a woman. I drew The Body beside The Boat to The Riverside & sent to Hoddesdon

for The Police. James Sulhorn Police Inspector States That 4.45 P.m March 27th 1912 I was informed That The Body of was found in The River at Fields Weir. I at once went & found The Body of a woman in The water near The Bank. fully dressed except a Hat The clothing much torn. I obtained a conveyance & conveyed The Body to The mortuary at Hoddesdon & on examination found a Bracelet & ring on The left

Reports are to be made by Telephone in conformity with the instructions contained in G.O. 28/13.

48 *Statement relating to the death by drowning of an unknown woman, thought to be Lucy Fairman, aged 26, in 1912. This document is one of a series of items from the Hertford coroner's records.* (Hertfordshire Archives and Local Studies, off Acc 1376.)

for example hearth tax and militia records were organised by hundred. The hundred court died out in the Middle Ages and was superseded by manorial courts. The territorial organisation of the Anglican church follows hundred boundaries and rural deaneries usually correspond to them. The great hundred court (sheriff's tourn) was held at Easter and Michaelmas and was not officially abolished until 1887. There are some records for this court at TNA in SC 2 (Special Collections, Court Rolls). This set of records comprises court rolls and books of manors, honors, hundreds and other local jurisdictions, including those of the Marcher lordships of the Duchy of York. The majority of these jurisdictions belonged to the Crown or came to it with forfeited lay and ecclesiastical estates. It also includes the court rolls of the Marcher Lordship of Ruthin or Dyffryn Clwyd from 1294 to 1654.

The genesis of the office of coroner was in 1194, when two persons were to be elected in each county to enquire into cases of sudden and unexplained death; in 1274 their duties were well defined and they acted in the absence of the sheriff. They were elected in the county court and were unpaid until the reign of Henry VIII; ultimately there were four for each county, until the 19th century. They acquired other responsibilities, such as hearing the confessions of felons in sanctuary, confiscating property from outlaws and keeping a record of crimes in the county. Two acts of 1887 and 1926 created the modern office.[19]

Inquest records are held in CROs but are closed for 75 years after their creation. Cases of sudden death will almost always be reported in local newspapers. References to inquests sometimes appear in quarter sessions records, such as in St Albans in 1792 when information was taken from several witnesses concerning the death of Thomas Humbley. He had been driving a wagon when the horses were frightened by a recruiting party beating drums and waving a flag, and he was crushed by the wagon.[20] Records of inquests where cases were subsequently heard at assizes are usually held with the court papers; records of inquests for the northern and north-eastern circuits for some of the 17th- and 18th-century cases are in the depositions and case papers in TNA ASSI 45. The North and South Wales Circuit, Chester and North Wales Division, coroners' inquisitions from 1798 to 1799 and 1817 to 1891 are in ASSI 66. This set of records are coroners' inquisitions mainly for Cheshire but some from Anglesey, Denbighshire, Flintshire and Merionethshire (it seems there are no inquisitions from Welsh counties after 1877). Other assize material may hold or refer to inquests in unlisted ASSI series (for example there are a few 19th-century coroners inquests in ASSI 47: Assizes: Northern and North-Eastern Circuit: Miscellanea, 1605–1950).

The vestry is the room in a church used for the keeping of vestments and was originally where parish meetings were held, so that the word has come to mean the local body. Membership of the vestry comprised the minister, churchwardens and leading parishioners who were either co-opted (close or select vestry) or elected (open vestry). In the 16th and 17th centuries the vestry assumed many of the old functions of the manorial court, such as appointing the constables, as well as taking on new responsibilities for the poor and highways. It lost these roles during the 19th century, and after 1834 was only important in London as the major rate raising and spending function (poor relief) passed to

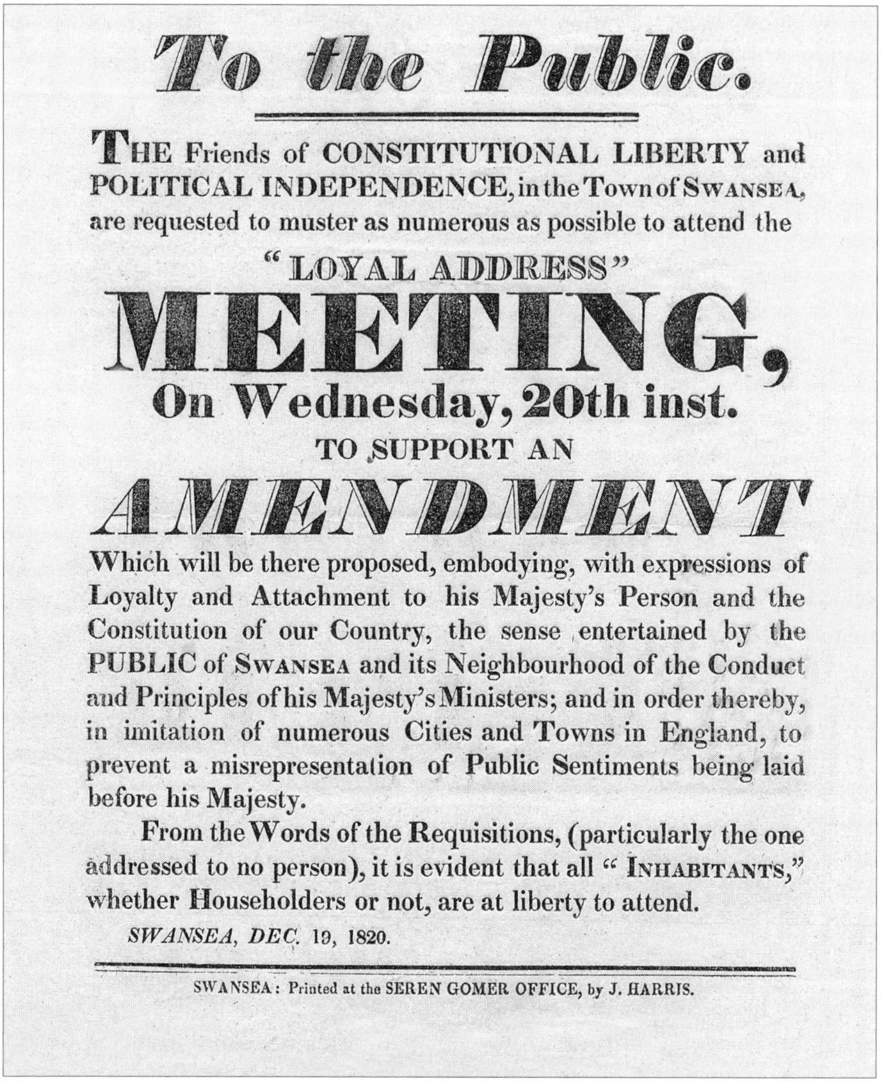

To the Public.

THE Friends of CONSTITUTIONAL LIBERTY and POLITICAL INDEPENDENCE, in the Town of SWANSEA, are requested to muster as numerous as possible to attend the

"LOYAL ADDRESS"

MEETING,

On Wednesday, 20th inst.

TO SUPPORT AN

AMENDMENT

Which will be there proposed, embodying, with expressions of Loyalty and Attachment to his Majesty's Person and the Constitution of our Country, the sense entertained by the PUBLIC of SWANSEA and its Neighbourhood of the Conduct and Principles of his Majesty's Ministers; and in order thereby, in imitation of numerous Cities and Towns in England, to prevent a misrepresentation of Public Sentiments being laid before his Majesty.

From the Words of the Requisitions, (particularly the one addressed to no person), it is evident that all "INHABITANTS," whether Householders or not, are at liberty to attend.

SWANSEA, DEC. 19, 1820.

SWANSEA: Printed at the SEREN GOMER OFFICE, by J. HARRIS.

49 *'Loyalist' meeting to be held in Swansea to affirm attachment to the Crown and constitution, 19 December 1820.* (TNA, HO 52/1, f. 613.)

the new Poor Law Unions. Other functions were transferred to parish councils and parish meetings in 1894. Vestries became very corrupt but there were some efficient ones, such as Liverpool which had salaried officials, an annual audit and standing committees. The 1831 Hobhouse Act introduced manhood suffrage and annual elections to vestries, but was only adoptive and not very effective. The main records of vestries are minutes, some of which have been printed; there may also be accounts, lighting and watching records and papers relating to the registration of electors. All of these records should now be available in CROs or local borough libraries, although in some instances they may still be held at the church.

14

FAMILY AND SOCIAL LIFE

Family and social structure have become popular topics for historians and there have been a number of studies looking at the subject from various viewpoints.[1] Lawrence Stone's 1977 book, *The Family, Sex and Marriage in England, 1500-1800*, was the first attempt to describe changes over a long period of time. Despite some criticism it remains popular, although it has been partly superseded by more recent books.[2] The nuclear family was founded on marriage although many were cut short through premature death. In England marriage usually took place several years after puberty and required parental consent after 1754. The average age at which people married fell slightly in the 18th century, from about 25-27 at the beginning; among the aristocracy and upper gentry age at marriage was slightly later. The mean age at which women married fell from about 26 to 23 by the early 1800s, which in part led to an increase in population.[3] In the early modern period up to a quarter of the population never married and it was particularly difficult for younger children of the gentry; the figures fluctuated over time.[4] The peak period when people married coincided with the ending of annual service contracts, i.e., springtime in pastoral farming districts and late autumn in arable areas; marriages were prohibited in Lent. Some clergy performed clandestine marriage ceremonies; prison chapels were often used and there were 217 marriages at the Fleet prison on the day before Hardwicke's Act came into operation. Parson Gaynam of the Fleet chapel had personally presided over 36,000 persons when he married his servant-maid in 1737. Tampering with parish registers was a capital offence from 1754. TNA has about 300 registers of clandestine marriages (see chapter 6). There was no legal divorce for most people but they found other ways of solving the 'problem', such as wife-selling.[5]

Women had few rights after they married. Judicial separation was the only way out but from the late 17th century it was possible to divorce by private Act; there were only 200 divorces by this route up to 1857, of which six were at the suit of women. Desertion was more common and there are examples of men abandoning their families in the poor law records. Common-law marriages took place and by the early 18th century the church was losing a quarter to a third of all marriages to 'irregular unions of one kind or another'. In one in three of all marriages the wife died young. Remarriage was common, especially for widowers with children. In 1765 Thomas Turner, a Sussex shopkeeper, and widowed since 1761, confided his motives for remarriage to his diary. Despite his own stormy relationship with his wife, it was, he wrote, 'a state agreeable to nature, reason and religion and in some manner the indispensable duty of Christians'.[6] From February 1858 the Court for Divorce and Matrimonial Causes made such separations easier; the records are at TNA with the case files in J 77 and the indexes in J 78. From 1938 most have been destroyed.

Marital disputes and cases of adultery that threatened the peace were dealt with in church and manorial courts (see chapters 2 and 6). Rough music was the use of a rude cacophony of sound and simple dramatic performance to ridicule or express hostility towards those who had offended against communal values and moral standards. Regional variations for the practice include 'skimmington', 'riding the stang' and continental historians use the term 'charivari'. (There is a good example in Thomas Hardy's *Mayor of Casterbridge*.) The victim was often portrayed by an effigy supported on a pole or donkey, and the performance sometimes included mime and dance, lewd representations and reciting of verses. The victim might be an adulterer, wife-beater, cuckold or simply a masterful woman, virago or scold, and sometimes might be driven away by the hostility he or she had aroused.[7] Marriage was under attack in certain quarters: in the 1750s Ann Lee and her 'shaking Quakers' at Bolton reanimated medieval heresies by advocating complete celibacy, and after her departure to America in the 1770s a similar view was taken by followers of Joanna Southcott.

The size of families varied over time and infant mortality was relatively high until the 20th century; for the 19th century the census provides invaluable data (see chapter 3). In pre-industrial England 34.4 per cent of deaths were of children under ten.[8] Childbirth continued to be dangerous to women well into the 19th century (and beyond) and was a major cause of second marriages. Historians are divided about how children were treated: some said they were not looked after and there was no perception of childhood, but there are examples of children who died being mourned, and evidence of baptism being a cause for celebration. Although parents wanted to provide for their children's future, it was not cheap to apprentice children to a prosperous trade; marriage portions were given to girls.[9]

Two of the prime sources for the study of families are parish registers (see chapter 6) and wills; only a small percentage of people made a will and, even if a person had property to leave, may have made provision before death. After 1858 the proving of wills was a civil matter and the wills are held by the Court of Probate; they can be accessed at the Probate Search Room, First Avenue House, 42-49 High Holborn, London, WC1V 6NP. There is a detailed index to wills, the *National Probate Calendar*, which is more widely available (at least up to 1943); it gives the date of death and usually additional information. It can be seen on microfiche or microfilm, at TNA, FRC, the Society of Genealogists and the Guildhall Library (all in London) and in some local libraries and record offices. At TNA there is a seven per cent sample of papers relating to cases of disputed probate; they are listed by the full name of the testator whose will was being disputed, and the name of the suit. The series is in J 121 and is easy to search online. Other records relating to disputed wills are in Chancery Proceedings. Many people left estates which were liable for death duties and

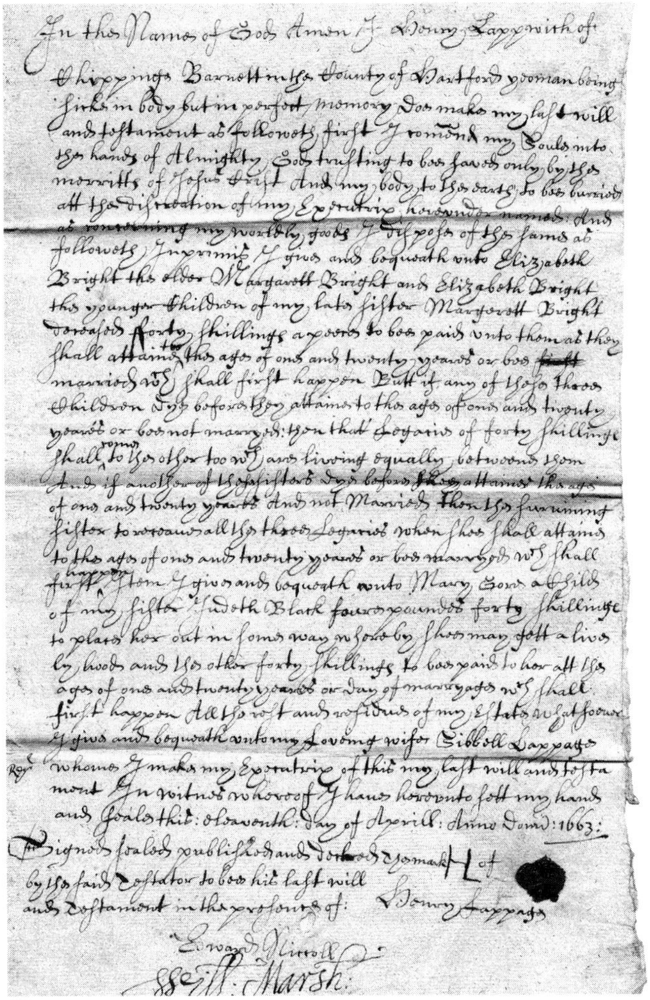

In the Name of God Amen I Henry Lappwith of
Chippinge Barnett in the County of Hartford yeoman being
sicke in body but in perfect memory doe make my last will
and testament as followeth first I commend my Soule into
the hands of Almighty God trusting to bee saved only by the
meritts of Jesus Christ And my body to the earth to bee burried
att the discretion of my Executrix hereunder named And
as concerning my worldly goods I dispose of the same as
followeth Inprimis I give and bequeath unto Elizabeth
Bright the elder Margarett Bright and Elizabeth Bright
the younger children of my late sister Margarett Bright
deceased forty shillings a peece to bee paid unto them as they
shall attaine to the age of one and twenty yeares or bee ~~first~~
married wch shall first happen Butt if any of those three
Children dye before they attaine to the age of one and twenty
yeares or bee not marryed: then that Legacie of forty shillinge
shall come to the other too wch are living equally betweene them
And if another of those sisters dye before they attaine the age
of one and twenty yeares And not Married then the surviving
sister to receave all the three Legacies when shee shall attaine
to the age of one and twenty yeares or bee marryed wch shall
first happen Item I give and bequeath unto Mary Gore a Child
of my sister Judeth Black foure pounds forty shillinge
to place her out in some way whereby shee may gett a live
lyhood and the other forty shillings to bee paid to her att the
age of one and twenty yeares or day of marriage wch shall
first happen All the rest and residue of my Estate whatsoever
I give and bequeath unto my Loving wife Sibbell Lappath
whome I make my Executrix of this my last will and testa
ment In witnes whereof I have hereunto sett my hand
and seale this: eleaventh: day of Aprill: Anno Domi: 1663:

Signed sealed published and declared the mark H L of
by the said Testator to bee his last will
and Testament in the presence of: Henry Lappath

Edward [illegible]
Will: Marsh:

50 *Most wills are found in the records of probate courts and can go back to the late 14th century; they will also be found with property deeds. Only a small percentage of testators left a will but this does not detract from their historical value. Henry Lappwich of Chipping Barnet left bequests to four nieces as well as to his wife, in 1663.* (Hertfordshire Archives and Local Studies, 100AW16.)

the death duty registers run from 1796 to 1903. From 1858 there should be a death duty record for all estates worth more than £20. However, unless the assets were valued at £1,500 or more, the taxes were often not collected, and so the register entry was not filled in with all the details. Tax was payable on bequests to anyone other than a husband or wife. The information in the death duty registers is not the same as that given in wills or grants of administration. In particular, they show what *actually* happened to a person's estate after death (rather than what they hoped would happen), and what it was *actually* worth, excluding debts and expenses. They can also give the date of death, and information about the people who received bequests, or who were the next-of-kin, such as their exact relationship to the deceased. Because the registers could be annotated for up to fifty years after the first entry, they can include a wealth of additional information such as dates of death of spouse; dates of death or marriage of beneficiaries; births of posthumous children; change of address; references to law suits in Chancery delaying the settling of the estate, etc. Many of the registers for the 1890s were destroyed by fire. The records are at TNA in IR26 with the registers in IR27.[10]

Inventories are discussed in chapter 10; there is other probate material, such as letters of administration (where no will was made), probate accounts, and so on. By Acts of 1666 and 1678 no corpse was to be buried in any garment other than one made of wool, and burial in woollen certificates may be found with other parish records. The civil registration of births, marriages and deaths began in July 1837 and the indexes only are kept at the FRC, which also contains information on related matters such as adoption. The FRC is jointly run by the General Register Office and TNA. Births, marriages and deaths indexes on fiche are held at TNA.

The first documentary evidence of heraldry is found in 1127 and the rules and terminology were laid down in the 13th century; by the early 15th century the Crown was attempting to control the use of armorial bearings that did not date from time immemorial (fixed as before the accession of Richard I in 1189). The Heralds were part of the royal household and incorporated as a College of Arms by Richard III in 1484. In 1530 they began a programme of county surveys, known as visitations, which continued until 1688; major surveys were made in about 1580, 1620 and 1666. The records are held at the College of Arms in London. Many of these records have been published by the Harleian Society and county record societies, and they are a useful source for pedigrees of families claiming the right to bear arms; the Harleian Society was founded in 1869 and has published over 200 volumes. Heraldry is a complex subject but a certain amount of knowledge is useful when studying funerary monuments, stained glass and the like.

The practice of fixed, hereditary surnames spread slowly down the social scale and was adopted widely throughout western Europe in the Middle Ages. Norman barons took the name of their estate as a surname, giving a useful link with property. By the 15th century most English people had acquired surnames but Welsh names did not take an English form until the following century. The study of the etymology of surnames has been led by British scholars (see bibliography) and they have divided them into four main types: locative, patronyms, occupational and nicknames. The English Surnames Survey began in 1965 and is housed at the Centre for Local History, Leicester University, and has a searchable database.

Social surveys are essentially a resource of the 20th century, of which the best known is probably Mass-Observation, a pioneering social research organisation which is concerned with ordinary people's lives and experiences and has, over the years, solicited opinion on topics from wartime rationing to the death of Diana, Princess of Wales. The accumulated archive, kept at the University of Sussex, offers researchers material in such volumes, and on such a broad range of themes, that it is possible to measure social change and gauge popular opinion through the study of highly subjective responses. Mass-Observation has traditionally made no distinction between the personal and the political, and values topics traditionally thought of as too 'trivial' for academic study as highly as the more usual subjects which concern sociologists.

The Cambridge Group for the Study of Population and Social Structure (CAMPOP) has systematically applied the technique of family reconstitution

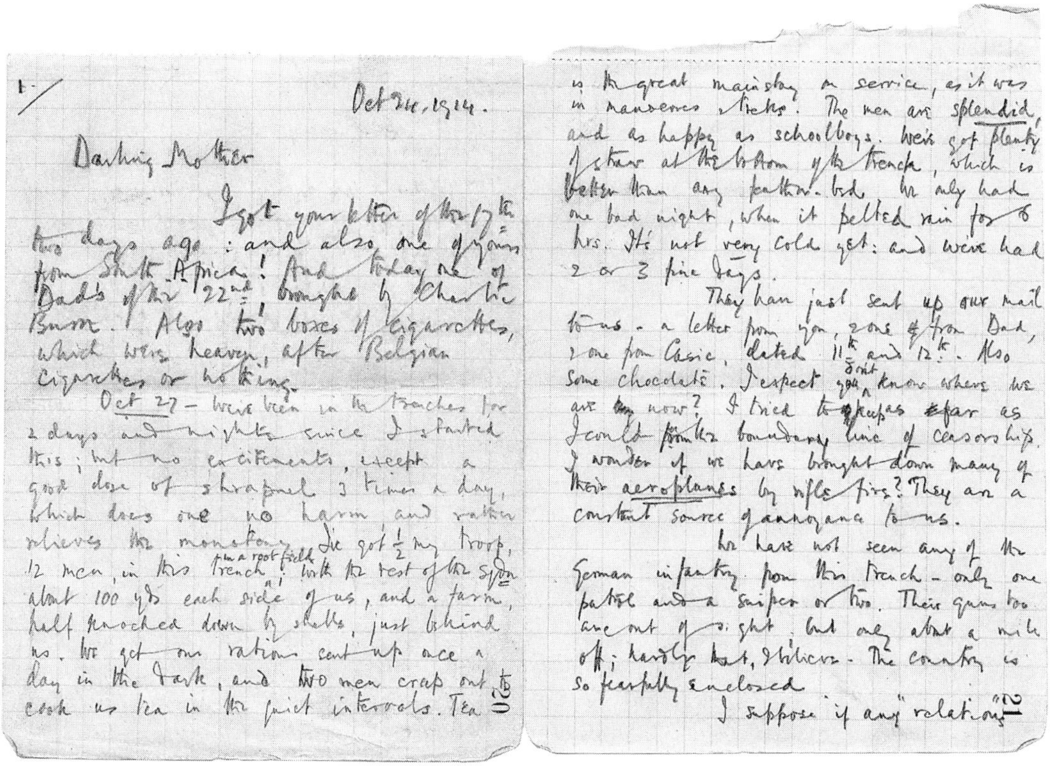
1 -/ Oct 24, 1914.

Darling Mother

I got your letter of the 17th two days ago: and also one of yours from South Africa! And today one of Dad's of the 22nd, brought by Charlie Burn. Also two boxes of cigarettes, which were heaven, after Belgian cigarettes or nothing.

Oct 27 – We've been in the trenches for 2 days and nights since I started this; but no excitements, except a good dose of shrapnel 3 times a day, which does one no harm and rather relieves the monotony. I've got ½ my troop, 12 men, in this trench in a root field with the rest of the Sqdn about 100 yds each side of us, and a farm, half knocked down by shells, just behind us. We get our rations sent up once a day in the dark, and two men creep out to cook us tea in the quiet intervals. Tea 2

is the great mainstay on service, as it was in manoeuvre treks. The men are splendid, and as happy as schoolboys. We've got plenty of straw at the bottom of the trench, which is better than any feather-bed. We only had one bad night, when it pelted rain for 8 hrs. It's not very cold yet: and we've had 2 or 3 fine days.

They have just sent up our mail to us – a letter from you, 2 one from Dad, 2 one from Casie, dated 11th and 12th. Also some chocolate. I expect you don't know where we are now? I tried to express as far as I could from the boundary line of censorship. I wonder if we have brought down many of their aeroplanes by rifle fire? They are a constant source of annoyance to us.

We have not seen any of the German infantry from this trench – only one patrol and a sniper or two. Their guns too are out of sight, but only about a mile off; hardly that, I believe. The country is so fearfully enclosed.

I suppose if any "relations" 3

51 *Julian Grenfell was the eldest son of Lord and Lady Desborough of Taplow Court, Buckinghamshire and was killed in May 1915 on the Western Front. His letters, mostly to his mother, cover his school and university education and military service in India and South Africa, as well as in the First World War; they will shortly be published by the Hertfordshire Record Society. In 1916 Lady Desborough privately published Julian's letters, along with those of his brother Billy who was also killed in the war, but sometimes changed the text – a warning to local historians not to trust secondary sources!* (Hertfordshire Archives and Local Studies, DE/Rv/C1135/684.)

to the study of parish registers in order to investigate such matters as the age at marriage, completed family size and child and infant mortality. There have also been a number of studies based on the census returns, often the 1851 census which was the first one to record details such as family relationships and occupations.[11]

Friendly societies began in the early 18th century but their heyday was during the Victorian and Edwardian period. Their main purpose was to act as a benefit club in times of sickness and death, but the larger ones provided other services, such as public halls with social and educational facilities, and some lent money for mortgages. They often had strange names – the Independent Order of Oddfellows, the Loyal Order of Ancient Shepherds, the Royal Antediluvian Order of Buffaloes – to name but a few. Many societies still flourish and further details can be found on the Association of Friendly Societies' web site at www.afs.org.uk. Records may be with the society, where it still exists, or in a local record office; friendly societies had to register with the Clerk of the Peace from 1793 so there will be some information in Quarter Sessions records (see also chapter 5).

The concept of leisure was unknown for many people before the 20th century, although there were a number of games in which people could take part before the age of mass spectator sports. The rise of professional sport in the second half of the 19th century has become a popular topic of research; the Sir Norman Chester Centre for Football Research is part of the Sociology Department of Leicester University. In the Middle Ages people generally worked six days a week but this was offset by frequent 'holy-days', the enforcement of periods of idleness by gilds and the casual nature of much employment. Many religious festivals were abolished in the 16th century and others suppressed by the puritans during the Commonwealth. Sunday was never a working day and church attendance was almost universal. With the coming of factories and the need for more regular working hours trade unionists began to agitate for a half day on Saturday, which was first achieved in the textile industries in 1850 and other trades soon after.[12]

The coming of the railways brought a new dimension to leisure time; families could now travel cheaply to the coast or country for a day or longer. Thomas Cook pioneered the railway excursion (although his first venture was to a temperance rally in 1841) and his first overseas trip was to the Paris International Exhibition in 1855. Factories found it more efficient to close down completely for a week or fortnight in the summer and in some parts of the country this still happens, though it is less and less common. Bank holidays began for bank clerks in 1871 but the days when banks were closed soon became public holidays. Paid holidays did not become generally available until the 20th century; the 1938 Holidays with Pay Act covered about half the manual workers in the country.

Football was an ancient pastime but had few rules before the Victorian period. Surviving historic games suggest that there were large numbers of participants and matches lasted for several hours. The Sheffield Football Club, founded in 1857, is recognised as the oldest in the world. The National Football Association was founded in 1863 as a result of public school interest; the FA Cup was first contested in 1871 and the first real international match, between England and Scotland, took place in 1872. The Football League, established in 1888, reflected working-class interest in the game and the desire of supporters for regular entertainment. By 1885 the employment of paid players was officially recognised by the Football Association. An indication of the popularity of football is demonstrated by the attendance of 65,000 at the Cup Final of 1897. The National Football Museum is located in Preston, Lancashire.

Rugby is named after the public school where it apparently originated; it was popular among the middle classes and also among working-class communities in south Wales. There are two codes, with different rules; Rugby League is traditionally played in Lancashire and Yorkshire and Rugby Union in other areas. The Rugby Union was founded in 1871. The origins of cricket can be traced back to the 18th century in Hampshire and Kent. The professional game began with teams playing for wagers and with challenge matches such as those featuring a top-hatted All England XI which toured the country and played up to 40 matches a season, often against twice as many opponents. The players remained a curious mixture of well-to-do amateurs and paid professionals – known at the time as Gentlemen and Players. W.G. Grace popularised the sport in the 1870s and 1880s, and the first Test Match was played against a visiting Australian team in 1878. Other early games include boxing, wrestling and running, and new middle-class games achieved prominence towards the end of the 19th century, such as golf and lawn tennis.

Cycling became very popular in the last quarter of the 19th century, especially among the working classes. Bicycles were relatively cheap and purchasers came from all levels of society. Although the penny-farthing had been invented a decade or so earlier, the first modern-pattern cycle was the Rover Safety Cycle of 1885; Hans Renold's bush roller chain (1880) and J.B. Dunlop's development of the pneumatic tyre by 1888 led the way to mass production of cycles. The cycle provided a new form of transport, in the first place for the middle-class young gentleman who could not afford a horse, and then for the working man; it was a new and cheap way of getting to work, and into the countryside. A Bicycle Touring Club was founded in 1878 and over 2,000 other clubs followed; by 1900 the Cyclists' Touring Club had around 60,000 members. Modern cycles could be ridden by women and played their part in their emancipation.

Cock-fighting was originally an outdoor activity, held in circular pits dug into the ground, and the preserve of the gentry; throwing stones at cocks was a traditional pastime of apprentices on Shrove Tuesday. During the 17th and 18th centuries smaller cockpits were constructed indoors; one is marked on Speed's 1610 map of Leicester. A wide section of society was attracted by the violence and by gambling on the winner. Cock fights were frequently depicted in satirical cartoons, and newspapers often carried advertisements for them. Bear-baiting and bull-baiting were commonly practised in market towns and at country feasts. Bulls were tied to a post and attacked by a group of bulldogs (bigger and fiercer than the modern breed); part of the attraction was gambling on which dog was judged the bravest. As bears were in shorter supply they were baited less often than bulls; bears which were trained to dance to music were made to perform in streets well into the 20th century. All these 'sports' were suppressed in the first half of the 19th century.

Country pursuits – hunting, shooting, fishing, etc – were traditionally upper- and middle-class sports. The early Stuart kings made Newmarket famous by their patronage and it became the seat of racing's ruling body, the Jockey Club. Despite its royal connections, horse racing was enjoyed by all classes of society. New courses were laid out in the 18th century for a variety of reasons. The major classic race, the Derby, was first run in 1780; the first Grand National was held in 1839. Gambling was always part of the appeal of horse-racing. Greyhound racing attracted less people and is seen as more of a working-class sport. The first man in England to have a pack of foxhounds was said to have been Thomas Boothby of Desford, Leicestershire; by the end of the 18th century Leicestershire was the most famous fox-hunting county in the country, with Melton Mowbray being the centre of the sport and of the glittering social life which followed it; in other parts of the country stag-hunting still takes place. All forms of hunting may soon join cock-fighting, bear- and bull-baiting in being outlawed. A rather unusual sport was quoits, which could be played almost anywhere; the game was well established in 1467 when Leicester Corporation prescribed imprisonment for anyone playing for silver at 'dyce, cardyng, haserding, tenes, bowlys, pykking [pitching] with arrows, coytyng with horsshon, penypryk [penny-prick – either throwing oblong pieces of metal at a mark or throwing to dislodge coins from sticks], foteball ne cheker in the myre'[13] [perhaps an alternative name for nine men's morris]. Archery began as a method of warfare; in late medieval England practice with the longbow was a statutory requirement and fear of a French invasion led to the statute's revival in 1543. Men in every town and village had to practise at the butts after church on Sundays and holidays, but the legislation lapsed during the 17th century.

Records of sports clubs and activities may be difficult to track down. Larger clubs may have deposited their records in the local record office but others, especially professional football clubs, prefer to retain them; many of them have established club museums. Local and national newspapers will carry reports of matches, and ephemera, such as programmes, may be found in local libraries or museums. There is very little material in TNA but there are references in legal records to social activities causing problems:

> SC 8/98/4858. The Prioress of Clerkenwell petitioned the King requesting a remedy for the fact that the people of London trample down and destroy her corn and her meadows with their miracle-plays and their wrestling-matches and so prevent her from profiting from her lands, and states she can have no remedy against them at law. [*c.*1275-*c.*1300];
>
> C 1/47/276. William Smyth, alias Saunder, against the Sheriffs of London: Selection by John Fynour of the parish of St Sepulchre's, London, as the venue in an action of trespass against complainant for the loss of a purse, although both parties at the time of the alleged loss were admittedly playing tennis at East Barnet, 1386-1486;
>
> C 1/146/48. William Lucasse and Richard Tailler, the churchwardens of the church of St James, Pulloxhill, Bedfordshire against John Russell, of Pulloxhill for the detention of the profits of a play promised to the use of the church, 1486-1529;
>
> STAC 2/16 Lewis Gryffyth v Richard Godfrey, John Whelpley, and others for assault arising out of dispute as to betting on an archery match at Salisbury, Wiltshire (1509-1547).

Similarly, a search in the Old Bailey Sessions Papers reveals the following two later cases:

> 18 April 1683. Henry Conway, was Tryed for Killing John Griffeth, on the 3d. of March last, the which upon Evidence appeared that the Prisoner and the deceased being together all night and playing at Dice, the deceased lost, and not having mony to answer his loosing the Prisoner called him Cheat,

at which the deceased being offended told him he should answer it another time, and so breaking up, they went into Lambs-Conduict Field, and there fought, when after several passes Griffith fell down dead being run into the Body 6, Inches, the Prisoner being likewise run through the Body, and wounded in several other places but no prepence Malice appearing he was found Guilty of Manslaughter;

27 May 1691. Edward Griffeth, Esq; was Indicted for Killing Thomas Thomson, Gent. on the 4th of this Instant May. They were both playing at Bowls together at Mary-Bone; and some difference happened to arise about the Game concerning Betting, Mr Griffeth said, That he would give 10 l. to see Mr Thomson lose; and Mr Thomson reply'd, That he would give 20 l. to see his Throat cut: After which Mr Thomson drew his Sword, and made several Passes at the Prisoner; upon which the Prisoner drew, and gave him a Wound, near the Navel, of the depth of six Inches, of which he dyed on the next day; but there was no precedent Malice betwixt them. The Prisoner did not deny the Matter of Fact, so he was found Guilty of Manslaughter.

Examples such as these indicate the socio-historical value of criminal/legal records without which much leisure history would be lost. Parish feasts or wakes were important in local communities. 'Church ales', events at which ale and food was provided by churchwardens to raise money for the church, were popular events and information may be found in churchwardens' accounts and related records. Church courts may give information on cases of bull-baiting, over-indulging in drink, wrestling or boxing, etc, and bishops' registers may give instructions on dealing with boisterous revelry at church services. Games, plays and sporting activities may be recorded in estate records, commonplace books and diaries, but should be used with caution as they will only give one view of events. In the 18th century the authorities renewed their attentions against pleasure and hiring fairs as these were large gatherings where people would gather, gossip, drink and take part in other dubious activities. Newspapers, handbills and posters may all advertise specific public events and antiquarian collectors of customs and folklore were busy in the late 18th and 19th centuries noting remnants of past customs.[14] A related aspect of such material can be found in collected songs of the past, such as those contained in Roy Palmer's *The Sound of History*.[15]

Drama was an integral part of the civic ritual of the Middle Ages, but performances were not held in permanent theatres. Churches were often used for plays as they had few or no pews, and some forms of theatre such as mystery plays had a religious theme. Churchwardens' accounts may include references to plays, such as an entry for Bishops Stortford in 1524-5: 'Item received of the profites of the pley'.[16] Travelling bands of actors are recorded in provincial towns and cities from the 1530s. The 1572 Vagabonds Act required companies of travelling players to seek royal or aristocratic patronage and therefore forced them to be based in London. They played in some of the first theatres to be built in Britain, such as the Swan, Rose, and Globe – the last now reconstructed. The London companies toured the provinces in summer and records of performances indicate the use of great houses, college halls, inn yards and the like. Theatres were banned by the puritans during the Commonwealth, but were re-established in London after the Restoration; Pepys' diary is a major source for the 1660s. In the 18th century provincial urban drama flourished as never before; by mid-century every self-respecting town had to have a playhouse, some of which survive (such as the one in Richmond, Yorkshire). Records of theatres tend to be ephemeral, such as posters and programmes. Some of this material will be found in CROs and further information will be found in local newspapers.

The first public film show in Britain was in 1895 and the heyday of the cinema was before and after the Second World War. The buildings were often decorative but few of them survive in their original form, despite a minor revival at the end of the 20th century. Similar records to those for theatres may survive, but personal testimony and the evidence from the buildings themselves are perhaps more valuable. A number of cinema histories have been written.[17]

In towns throughout Britain the middle classes formed musical, scientific, philosophical and literary societies, and circulating libraries and book clubs. Music was traditionally played or sung in churches and chapels but the 19th century saw the foundation of numerous brass bands, choirs, glee clubs and amateur operatic societies. Literary and philosophical societies date from the second quarter of the 18th century and were set up to discuss the intellectual issues of the day and to sponsor cultural activities. The records of these organisations may be in the local record office.[18]

The history of seaside resorts has become popular, with John K. Walton one of the foremost authors on the subject. The fashion for sea-bathing started with the aristocracy and gentry in the mid-18th century and soon spread to the middle classes. Resorts grew to meet the need for accommodation; Scarborough, Margate and Brighton were the first to be developed in the 1730s and attracted the same type of clientele as spas. Sea-bathing was thought to be beneficial as well as enjoyable. The conversion of George III's court to sea-bathing at Weymouth between 1789 and 1805 established the town's reputation, and the Prince of Wales made Brighton fashionable. The golden years of the British seaside resort were in the late Victorian and Edwardian era. Guidebooks to the various resort are a major source for the subject. The fashion for visiting spas for the supposed healing properties of the waters was imported from the continent in the 16th and 17th centuries, but didn't become fashionable until the 18th century. Spas such as Bath, Wells and Epsom offered social activities out of the London season in addition to their medical provision. Many spa towns retain the buildings erected in their heyday. The Grand Tour became fashionable for the upper and middle classes and diaries and letters of those who spent some time in countries such as Italy may be found in estate and family collections.[19] Middle-class interest in arts such as painting and sculpture may generate records in family and estate collections.

The British tradition of collecting began in the 16th century and the British Museum was founded in 1753. Others in London and the provinces followed from the early 19th century and grew considerably in the 20th, so that now many towns and villages have their local museum. As many of these institutions pre-date record offices they often contain considerable archive material, as well as photographic and ephemeral collections of interest. Some of the archives held by museums are extensive but are becoming better known by initiatives such as A2A.[20]

Christmas replaced an older mid-winter festival in which excessive eating and drinking was an essential feature. In the Middle Ages and early modern period it was followed by 12 days of celebration, during which activities which would have been banned at other times were tolerated. It was suppressed by the puritans, but the law was repealed with the restoration of the monarchy; from that time to the 19th century it was on the wane, until there was a self-conscious attempt to maintain its traditions. The Victorians are credited with 'inventing' the modern festival, with the tree introduced by Prince Albert, the sending of cards and the use of holly for decoration. Similarly church carol services date only from the Victorian period.

From the late 12th century onwards the right to hold a fair was granted by a royal charter; the greatest period of creation was between the Norman Conquest and the Black Death. Before the 19th century many fairs were held all over the country; some lasted several days and many were held on the eve, day and morrow of the patron saint of the parish church, whereas others were one-day events devoted to a particular commodity. In 1889 the government published a report on market tolls and rights, which included a list of markets and fair charters up to 1483.[21] The staple commodity of most fairs was cattle, followed by sheep and horses; the most famous in Britain was held at Stourbridge, on the outskirts of Cambridge, which Defoe described as the greatest in the world. Place-names are a good indicator of where fairs were once held, even in large urban centres. Martinmas hiring fairs were known as 'statute' fairs because annual contracts between farmers and labourers expired on Old Martinmas Day (23 November), the end of the farming year. The practice of holding such fairs survived in market towns until Edwardian times and all the farmers and workers came together to negotiate new contracts. Reference to fairs is a staple part of VCH volumes. The associated funfairs were greatly enjoyed by young people at a dreary time of year; most had a reputation for rowdiness. By the 1820s and 1830s Easter and Whitsun funfairs were being held in, or close to, major centres of population. Others were new ones created simply for recreation. By the last quarter of the 19th century steam roundabouts and organs were an essential part of the attraction.[22] Most British towns have a long history as market centres but there were many more in the Middle Ages than today. The right to hold a market also required a royal charter. By the 18th century market activity in the larger towns had increased to the extent that new locations had to be found. Because of the link between fairs and markets, and towns, records of their activities will be found with other borough records.

Appendix 1

Record Offices, Libraries, etc

Only the principal national repositories are listed below; details of all other offices open to the public, including private archives which allow access, can be found on The National Archives web site (under 'Search other archives' and going to the Archon directory) or in the latest (2002) edition of *British Archives*, edited by Janet Foster and Julia Sheppard.

The National Archives
Ruskin Avenue
Kew
Richmond
Surrey
TW9 4DU
Tel: 0208 876 3444
Web site: www.nationalarchives.gov.uk

British Library
96 Euston Road
London
NW1 2DB
Tel: 0207 412 7513
Web site: www.bl.uk

National Archives of Scotland
HM General Register House
Edinburgh
EH1 3YY
Tel: 0131 535 1314
Web site: www.nas.gov.uk

National Library of Scotland
George IV Bridge
Edinburgh
EH1 1EW
Tel: 0131 4662812
Web site: www.nls.uk

National Library of Wales
Aberystwyth
SY23 3BU
Tel: 01970 632800
Web site: www.llgc.org.uk

Public Record Office of Northern Ireland
66 Balmoral Avenue
Belfast
BT9 6NY
Tel: 028 90 255905
Web site: www.proni.gov.uk

National Archives of Ireland
Bishop Street
Dublin 8
Tel: 00353 1407 2300
Web site: www.nationalarchives.ie

Jersey Heritage Trust
Clarence Road
St Helier
Jersey
JE2 4JY
Tel: 01534 833333
Web site: www.jerseyheritagetrust.org

Isle of Man Public Record Office
Unit 40a Spring Valley Industrial Estate, Braddan
Douglas
Isle of Man
IM2 2QS
Tel: 01624 693569
Web site: www.gov.im/deptindex/reginfo.html

Bodleian Library
Broad Street
Oxford
OX1 3BG
Tel: 01865 277158
Web site: www.bodley.ox.ac.uk/dept/scwmss

Appendix 2

Useful Web Sites

www.ordnancesurvey.co.uk	Ordnance Survey
www.notttingham.ac.uk/english/research/EPNS	English Place Name Society
www.nrm.org.uk	National Railway Museum
www.consignia.co.uk/heritage	Post Office Archives
www.btplc.com/Thegroup/Btshistory/BTgrouparchives	BT Archives
www.bahs.org.uk	British Agricultural History Society
www.lse.ac.uk/library/archive	London School of Economics
www.dwlib.co.uk	Dr Williams's Library
www.catholic-history.org.uk	Catholic Archives Society/Catholic Record Society
www.english-heritage.org.uk	English Heritage
www.thewaterwaystrust.org.uk	Waterways Trust
www.visionofbritain.org.uk	Vision of Britain
www.rgs.org	Royal Geographical Society
www.hitchinbritishschools.org.uk	Hitchin British Schools
www.spck.org.uk/about_spck/archives.php	Society for Promoting Christian Knowledge
www.natsoc.org.uk/society/archives.php	National Society
www.raggedschoolmuseum.org.uk	Ragged School Museum
www.nationalfootballmuseum.com	National Football Museum
www.workhouses.org.uk	A very useful site all about workhouses and associated subjects
www.wellcome.ac.uk	Wellcome Trust
www.bethlemheritage.org.uk	The Bethlem Hospital
www.policehistorysociety.co.uk	Police History Society
www.harleian.co.uk	Harleian Society
www.massobs.org.uk	Mass Observation Society
www.national-army-museum.ac.uk	National Army Museum
www.nmm.ac.uk	National Maritime Museum
www.rafmuseum.org.uk	RAF Museum
www.iwm.org.uk	Imperial War Museum
www.oralhistory.org.uk	Oral History Society
www.bfi.org.uk/collections/preservation/index.html	British Film Institute
www.bl.uk/collections/sound-archive/listen.html	British Library Sound Archive
www.ihgs.ac.uk	Institute of Heraldic and Genealogical Studies
www.lambethpalacelibrary.org	Lambeth Palace Library
www.bopcris.ac.uk	British Official Publications Collaborative Reader Information Service
http://serials.abc-clio.com	Historical Abstracts
www.englandpast.net	Victoria County History
www.history-journals.de	Worldwide web site for history periodicals
www.british-history.ac.uk	British history online

www.scan.org.uk	Scottish Archive Network
www.charity-commission.gov.uk	Charity Commission
www.afs.org.uk	Association of friendly societies
www.businessarchivescouncil.org.uk	Business Archives Council
www.archive.co-op.ac.uk	Co-operative Society archives
www.ice.org.uk/knowledge/library_heritage.asp	Institution of Civil Engineers
www.landregistry.gov.uk	Land Registry
www.rsa.org.uk/library/index.asp	Royal Society
www.pevsner.co.uk	Site related to Nikolaus Pevsner
www.spab.org.uk	Society for the Protection of Ancient Buildings
www.victorian-society.org.uk	The Victorian Society
www.georgian-group.org.uk	The Georgian Group
www.architecture.com	Royal Institute of British Architects
www.riba.org.uk	
www.nationalarchives.a2a.gov.uk	Access to archives project
www.aim25.ac.uk	AIM25 archives project
www.archiveshub.ac.uk	Archives Hub project

Appendix 3
Short Subject/Source Guides

3.1 Parliamentary Papers

Parliamentary Papers (PPs) are a fantastic source for local historians, particularly for the early 19th century onwards. The various reports, covering a multitude of subject areas (workhouses, poverty, crime, churches, taxes/rates, trade unions, agriculture and industry, communications, education etc) may be short and statistical or long and accompanied by detailed minutes of evidence.

Complete sets can be found at the British Library and the House of Lords Record Office. Incomplete sets may be found at the Institute of Historical Research, most university libraries and good reference libraries. Many archives, reference and university libraries have PPs on microfiche from 1801. There are published paper indexes for PPs as well as a CD ROM index (for 1801 onwards) which is searchable by keyword. Many good reference libraries have copies.

A useful guide to the records (in subject order) was produced as part of the 'Helps for Students of History' series; W.R. Powell, *Local History From Blue Books: A Select List of Sessional Papers from the House of Commons,* 1962.

BOPCRIS provides a Web-based bibliographic database which enables researchers to search and browse for relevant government publications, read abstracts and view detailed consistent subject indexing in order to decide if they would be useful for research; http://www.bopcris.ac.uk

3.2 National Register of Archives and Archives Network Links

Much more searching for documents, their location, their references (and less common the images of the materials themselves) is now done online. It is the way of historical research and for the uninitiated the time spent coming to grips with the web will repay the researcher many times over. The difficulty for many, and this includes those who have taken the time to get to know and love their computers, is the number and variety of places to search online. The following note is to help you get the best out of this book – but is by no means a comprehensive view on the subject. It relates not to the individual catalogues of specific archives but to those sites which bring together lists of different archives or other institutions with significant archival holdings.

The National Register of Archives (NRA) is perhaps the best place to start to collect information about the nature and location of manuscripts relating to British history. It currently consists of over 44,000 unpublished lists and catalogues that describe archival holdings in the United Kingdom and overseas. These can be consulted at TNA in the main Research Enquiries Room. The lists and catalogues have been indexed according to corporate bodies, persons and families and the indexes are available online. The lists can be searched at www.nra.nationalarchives.gov.uk/nra.

Other sites are:

Archives Network Links. ANLs are sites containing descriptions, references and locations of archival holdings. They are essential for research. Get to love and to cherish them ...

A2A Describes archives held throughout England from the 900s to the present. The catalogues are fully searchable and (like those below) regularly updated. www.nationalarchives.gov.uk/a2a.

AIM25 Archives of higher education institutions and learned societies in London and the M25 area. www.aim25.ac.uk

Archives Hub Access to the archives of UK universities and colleges. www.archiveshub.ac.uk

ANW Archives Network Wales allows easy searching and gives descriptions of collections of documents held by record offices, universities, museums and libraries in Wales. www.archivesnetworkwales.info

GASHE Gateway to Archives of Scottish Higher Education provides access to descriptions of the archives produced by 10 higher education institutions (and their predecessors) in Scotland. The material dates from 1215 to the present. www.gashe.archives.gla.ac.uk

JANUS Describes archive and manuscript collections held throughout the University of Cambridge. janus.lib.cam.ac.uk/

SCAN the Scottish Archive Network. www.scan.org.uk

3.3 Equity Courts (Chancery and Exchequer)

Both the Chancery and Exchequer courts dealt with cases between parties and the rather brief description here will outline the major proceeding of the two courts as well as giving some detail on where the records will be found and a description of the major set of records the researcher could expect to find. The records are held at TNA. Equity disputes in Chancery and Exchequer are varied: inheritance and wills, debts, marriage settlements, apprenticeships, manorial rights, tithes, titles of land, common rights; the list is endless. Until the records are listed in detail their potential for local and social historians is seriously undermined; work is being undertaken on Chancery at the time of writing but it will be some time before comprehensive, consistent and useful lists will be produced – the records of equity are huge and run to many hundreds of thousands of documents. However, there are several ways in which you may be able to approach these records and they are explained, along with the records themselves, below. A general word of warning; just because a case begins in either of these courts it should not be expected that the courts always record the final resolution. Informal agreements made outside the courts would not be noted and the case would simply fall out of the record.

Chancery	
C 1 bundles	*Date range*
1–82	1386–1486

83-235	1486-1529
236-377	1500-1515
378-457	1515-1518
458-600	1518-1529
601-694	1529-1532
695-934	1532-1538
935-1094	1538-1544
1095-1285	1544-1551
1286-1324	1551-1553
1325-1397	1553-1555
1398-1488	1556-1558
1489-1519	[1386-1558]

Table 1: Early Chancery Pleadings.

Chancery: someone wishing to begin a case (suit) against another person would need to have a bill of complaint drawn up setting out the grievance. The person submitting the bill (the plaintiff) is essentially asking the Lord Chancellor to deliver an equitable solution in their favour against the offences committed by the defendant/s. The defendant was then asked to submit an answer to the initial bill. This could be followed by the plaintiff's replication and a subsequent rejoinder by the defendant. This could continue with both sides effectively answering back (together these documents are referred to as pleadings) until they have got to the point where there are agreed differences between the parties. These documents were then used for the next stage of the process; the gathering of evidence.

Date Range	*Catalogue reference*
1558-*c.*1649	C 2
1558-*c.*1660	C 3
1570-1714	C 8
1613-1714	C 5
1620-1714	C 7
1625-1714	C 6
1640-1714	C 10
1649-1714	C 9
1715-1758	C 11
1758-1800	C 12
1800-1842	C 13
1842-1852	C 14
1844-1864	C 18
1853-1860	C 15
1861-1875	C 16
1876 onwards	J 54

Table 2: Chancery Pleadings from 1558.

The court commissioned men to examine those considered by the parties as competent to give evidence regarding the suit and an agreed set of people (deponents) would be established. Set questions were compiled (interrogatories) and the deponent would supply their answers (depositions). There are also voluntary affidavits taken during the period of a suit.

The suit could be referred by the judge to a Master in Chancery to investigate. The Master's report to the court (based on the pleadings and depositions) would form the basis of the final decree (the outcome of the suit). The records of specific suits can therefore be spread across pleadings, depositions, orders, Masters' reports and decrees.

The early Chancery pleadings, up to 1558, are in record series C 1 and are set out in Table 1 above. From 1558 to 1714 the pleadings are in several record series and these are set out in Table 2.

Depositions for the early pleadings can be found with the pleadings in C 1 with some in C 4 (although none survive until the mid-15th century). Town depositions (London) survive from 1534 until 1853 in C 24 from which period they can be found with the pleadings themselves (and from 1880 with the country depositions). Country depositions survive from 1558 in C 21 and C 22 until 1714 from which time they are filed with the pleadings. From 1880 the town and country depositions are both together in J 17. Affidavits for 1611 to 1875 are in C 31 and C 41.

Record Series	*Master's Name*	*Date Range*
C 103	Master Blunt	*c.*1200-1859
C 104	Master Tinney	13th century-1856
C 105	Master Lynch	1481-1829
C 106	Master Richards	13th century-1853
C 107	Master Senior	*c.*1250-1851
C 108	Master Farrar	*c.*1220-1847
C 109	Master Humphrey	*c.*1180-1857
C 110	Master Horne	1306-1853
C 111	Master Brougham	13th century-1857
C 112	Master Rose	1270-1857
C 113	Master Kindersley	1235-1837
C 114	Unknown Masters	1566-1841
C 115	Duchess of Norfolk Deeds	1085-1842
C 116	Court Rolls (extracted from the other series)	1295-1808
C 171	Six Clerks' Office	*c.*1350-c1850

Table 3: Chancery Masters' Exhibits.

Any order made during the course of the suit and the final decree may be found in early suits (before 1544) on the back of the bills. After this time you would need to consult the Entry Book of Decrees and Orders in C 33 (although there are a few in C 38). From 1876 the Entry Books are in J 15. From 1955 to 1966 the records were destroyed with only samples surviving from 1966. Enrolled Decrees are in C 78 and C 79 and cover the period 1538 to 1903. Masters' Reports survive from 1544 in C 38 and J 57.

During the course of a suit both parties may produce 'exhibits' into the court as evidence to support their side of the case. Upon completion the exhibits would be claimed by the parties. However, unclaimed exhibits were retained by the court and make up a private collection of material in several series of Masters' Exhibits. The listing of this material is fair and the local historian may decide to begin searches here and work back into the pleadings.

There are other sets of records which may prove useful to the local historian and which add information to the main series explained above.[1]

Exchequer

The process of the Exchequer Equity Court has (of course) similarities to that of equity in Chancery and some of the process will be similar. Exchequer equity records run from 1559 to 1841 when the Exchequer lost its equity jurisdiction and remaining business was removed into Chancery.

Record Series	*Documents*	*Years covered*
E 111	Bills and answers	Hen VII–Eliz I
E 112	Bills and answers	Eliz I–Victoria
E 193	Replications and rejoinders. Apparently strays from E 112.	Eliz I-Victoria
E 133	Depositions before the Barons. These are cases concerning actions relating to places within a radius of 10 miles around London. This is extended to a 15-mile radius in the 19th century.	1559-1841
E 134	County depositions (outside the London radius).	1559-1841
E 178	Special Commissions of Enquiry	Eliz I-Victoria
E 207	Affidavits	Eliz I-1774
E 103	Affidavits	1774-1842
E 218	Affidavits	1695-1822
E 140	Exhibits: C 106, C 121, E 101, E 219, E 163, E 167)	1319-1842
J 90	Documents exhibited or deposited in court (mainly Chancery exhibits but some from Exchequer)	*c.*1700-1918.
E 161	Minute Books	1616-1841
E 128	Decrees and Orders	Eliz I –1663
E 131	Orders Files	1660-1842
E 130	Decree Files	1660-1841
E 123-125, 127	Entry Books of Decrees and Orders	Eliz I-Victoria

Table 4: Main series of Exchequer Equity Records

The plaintiff would submit a written 'bill of complaint' to the court detailing the wrongs committed against him/her by the named defendant(s). The defendant would then respond by producing a written document known as an 'answer', refuting all or part of the issues raised in the complaint. The plaintiff could then respond to the defendant's answer by issuing a 'replication' and the defendant respond again with a 'rejoinder'. This series of claim and counter-claim are known as 'proceedings' or 'pleadings' and are found in E 111 and E 112. The Records in E 111 are not really Exchequer documents but are strays drawn from the Court of Requests and other courts. The records in E 112 are chronologically arranged by reign and (importantly for the local historian) by county. Once the pleadings have established the main points at issue the court could draw up a series of written questions. These are known as 'interrogatories', which were then put to witnesses. The answers, or 'depositions' in E 133 and E 134 were then considered by the court as evidence. Other evidences include 'affidavits' and 'exhibits'. Affidavits are sworn voluntary informations and are in E 207, E 103 and E 218, while exhibits, items that were brought into the court as evidence and subsequently left unclaimed, are in E 140, E 219, C 106 and C 212 (the latter two being mainly Chancery exhibits but including material from Exchequer). The 'decrees and orders' of the court relating to suits were written up in the Entry Books in E 123-125 and E 127 as a record of the court's decisions during, and at the end of, the suit. Decrees and Orders are also to be found in E 128, E 130 and E 131.[2]

3.4 State Papers Domestic: Henry VIII-1782

The various State Papers Domestic series held at TNA contain much of interest for the local historian; finance and trade affairs, enclosure, law and order, religious policy (such as the Dissolution of the Monasteries), sedition,

Jacobite risings, general domestic security and intelligence and issues relating to Crown Estates. The types of material will vary but will include (mainly in-coming) private and official letters, petitions, returns, memoranda, orders in council, council minutes, warrants, newsletters, reports, memoranda, and draft parliamentary bills. The distinction between private and public papers was loose with the result that Secretaries of State would often take papers with them when they retired. This means that 'state' papers can be found in private collections held elsewhere, most notably the Lansdowne, Harleian and Cottonian papers held at the British Library and papers at Hatfield House. The records are arranged in rough chronological order with regard to the reign of individual monarchs apart from the obvious exception of the period of the English republic in the mid-17th century.

Some of the early material is in Latin or written in secretary or italic hands. These can be difficult (but not impossible after a little practice) to read. From the late 17th and early 18th centuries the material is much easier to read.

The list given below provides the main sequence of State Papers from the Letters and Papers of Henry VIII (which are a mixed collection of domestic and foreign material) to the State Papers Domestic for George III. In 1782 the Foreign Office and Home Office were created and so the records of State Papers Domestic now move to the TNA Home Office series.

Immediately following each series of state papers listed are the (mainly published) calendars. These are indexed and provide the local historian with the main means of reference. Many reference and university libraries have copies of the published calendars. At TNA you will find the required 'keys' to convert the *Calendar* entries to TNA references:

State Papers (incoming)

- Henry VIII: SP 1 and SP 2: Brewer, J.S., Gairdner, J. and Brodie, R.H. (eds.), *Letters and Papers, Foreign and Domestic, of the Reign of Henry VIII* (1862-1932). See also SP 5, Miscellanea relating to the Dissolution of the Monasteries and to the General Surveyors, Henry VIII, 1517-1560.
- Edward VI, SP 10 (1547-1553), SP 15 (1547-1625): Knighton, C.S. (ed), *Calendar of State Papers, Domestic Series, of the Reign of Edward VI*, 1547-1553, (1992) and Green, M.A.E. (ed.), *Calendar of State Papers, Domestic: Elizabeth*, 1601-1603*; with Addenda*, 1547-1565 (1870).
- Mary, SP 11 (1553-1558), SP 15 (1547-1625): Knighton, C.S. (ed.), *Calendar of State Papers, Domestic, Mary I*, 1553-1558 (1998) and Green, M.A.E., (ed.), *Calendar of State Papers, Domestic: Elizabeth*, 1601-1603*; with Addenda*, 1547-1565 (1870).
- Elizabeth I, SP 12 (1557-1660), SP 13 (1158-1603), SP 15 (1547-1625): Lemon, R. and Green, M.A.E. (eds.), *Calendar of State Papers, Domestic: Edward VI, Mary, and Elizabeth* (1856-1870).
- James I, SP 14 (1603-1640), SP 15 (1547-1625): Green, M.A.E. (ed.), *Calendar of State Papers (Domestic Series) of the reign of James I* (4 vols; 1857-1859) and *Calendar of State Papers Domestic, Addenda, Elizabeth-James I*, 1558-1623.
- Charles I, SP 16 (1625-1665), SP 17 (1625-1651): Bruce, J., Hamilton, W.D. and Lomas, S.C., (eds.), *Calendar of State Papers Domestic, Charles I* (23 volumes, 1858-1893).
- Council of State SP 18 (1649-1660): Green, M.A.E., (ed.), *Calendar of State Papers, Domestic Series (of the Commonwealth)*, (13 vols; 1875-1886).
- Committee for the Advance of Money: Books and Papers, SP 19 (1642-1656): Green, M.A.E., (ed.), *Calendar of the Proceedings of the Committee for Advance of Money*, 1642-1656, (1888).
- Sequestration Committee: Books and Papers, SP 20 (1643-1653). Supplementary information on cases in this series may be found in Green, M.A.E. (ed.), *Calendar of the Proceedings of the Committee for Compounding, etc* 1643-1660, (5 vols; 1889-1892).
- Committee for Compounding with Delinquents, SP 23 (1643-1664): Green, M.A.E. (ed.), *Calendar of the Proceedings of the Committee for Compounding, etc* 1643-1660 (5 parts; 1889-1892). Selections are printed in vols 21 and 22 of Bruce, J., Hamilton, W.D. and Crawford, S. (eds.), *Calendar of State Papers, Domestic Series of the Reign of Charles I* (23 vols; 1858-1897).

- Trustees for Crown Lands and Fee Farm Rents: Books, SP 26 (1650-1660).
- State Paper Office: Deeds and Other Miscellaneous Documents SP 27 (1650-1659): Most of these records are calendared in Green, M.A.E. (ed.), *Calendar of State Papers, Domestic Series (of the Commonwealth)*, (13 vols; 1875-1886).
- Charles II, SP 16 (1629-1685), SP 30 (1660-1688): Green, M.A.E., Daniell, F.H.B. and Bickley, F. (eds.), *Calendar of State Papers Domestic, Charles II* (28 vols; 1860-1947).
- James II, SP 31 (1685-1688): Timings, E.K., *Calendar of State Papers Domestic, James II* (3 vols; 1960-1972).
- William and Mary, SP 32, SP 33 (1689-1702): Hardy, W.J. and Bateson, E. (eds.), *Calendar of State Papers, Domestic Series, of the Reign of William and Mary* (1895-1937).
- Anne, SP 34 (1702-1714): Mahaffy, R.P. (ed.), *Calendar of State Papers Domestic, Anne* (2 vols; 1916-1924); only to 1704.
- George I, SP 35 (1714-1727): SP 35/1-76 are calendared in *State Papers Domestic George I* (List and Index Society, vols. 136, 144, 155 and 165, 1977-1980) with indexes in *State Papers Domestic George I* (List and Index Society, 173, 1981).
- George II, SP 36 (1727-1760): The records are calendared in typescript to 1745 (Oct), with an index to 1744. A manuscript descriptive list covers the remainder of the series, supplying foliation, date, nature and provenance only, and is un-indexed. The calendar and manuscript descriptive list are available at TNA.
- George III, SP 37 (1760-1783, after this period see Home Office classes): For 1760 to 1775 (SP 37/1-17 and 22) see the mis-named Redington, J. and Roberts, R.A., *Calendar of Home Office Papers of the Reign of George III* (4 vols; 1878-1899).

Entry Books
- SP 44 State Papers Domestic Entry Books, 1661-1828. Miscellaneous books with copies of out-letters from the King, the secretaries, as well as warrants, reports, licences, passes. The subject base in enormous covering the whole range of governance.

Various/Miscellaneous
- SP 45 State Papers Domestic Various, State Papers Office and other Bodies: Various Administrative Records, Precedents and Proclamations Edward VI to 1862.
- SP 46 State Papers Domestic Supplementary, 1361-1829.
- PRO 30/32 Leeds Papers, Mainly official records of the administration, as Lord High Treasurer (1673 to 1679), of Sir Thomas Osborne, later Viscount Latimer and Earl of Danby, and first Marquis of Carmarthen and first Duke of Leeds, 1661-1717.
- PRO 30/70 Hoare (Pitt), some correspondence of the elder and younger Pitts, Sir Edward Hoare's papers include some of John, 2nd Earl of Chatham, and also correspondence and other material of the Taylor family. There are official, semi-official, estate, personal and family correspondence and much of the Chatham/Pitt correspondence is made up of solicitations for appointments, promotions and preferments, 1667-1946.

3.5 Home Office Correspondence and Entry Books: 1782-1959

The Home Office records continue from where the State Papers series end (this is a general point as there is some overlap). As with State Papers the records cover a wide range of subjects, many of which relate to life in England, Wales and Scotland such as law and order, riots and public order, sedition, political movements, trade unions, regulation of aliens and naturalisation, control of explosives, charities, electoral administration, and civil defence to name but a few. The records here are essential for the study of late 18th- to 20th-century domestic history. From the mid-19th century the Home Office established a central registry system to deal with the variety and sheer weight of incoming correspondence. For local historians the main (incoming) correspondence records are listed in the first section below:

Home Office: General Correspondence

HO 42, 1782-1820	Home Office: Domestic Correspondence, George III
HO 40, 1812-1855	Home Office: Disturbances Correspondence
HO 52, 1820-1850	Home Office: Counties Correspondence
HO 45, 1841-1945	Home Office: Registered Papers
HO 144, 1879-1959	Home Office: Registered Papers, Supplementary

Home Office Registers
HO 46: Daily Registers, 1841-1957 (the papers were mainly placed in HO 45 and HO 144 where they survive).

Specific Correspondence
HO 12, (OC-Old Criminal Papers), 1849-1871.
HO 317, Private Office, 1840-1987.
HO 326, Long Papers (literally papers too bulky for filing), 1897-1963.

Entry Books
General Entry Books, HO 43, 1782-1898.
Disturbances Entry Books, HO 41, 1815 to 1916.

Scotland
Some material relating to Scotland will be found in the series listed above. However, the following should also to be used in Scottish historical studies.

HO 102: Home Office Scotland: correspondence and papers, 1782-1853; Home Office letters and papers relating to Scotland; includes petitions, circuit letters (and other criminal matters), treasonable practices material etc.

HO 103: Home Office: Scotland: Domestic Entry Books, 1763-1894; entries of general Home Office out-letters relating to Scotland. Includes letters to the Lord Advocate, prisons in Scotland and the Board of Supervision of Poor Relief in Scotland.

HO 104: Home Office: Scotland: Criminal Entry Books, 1762-1849. Entries of Home Office out-letters relating to criminal cases and matters in Scotland.

3.6 Records of the Privy Council

The Privy Council dealt with a wide variety of local, national and international issues such as commercial and maritime law, law and order, trade and industry and naval and military policy. Its jurisdiction also covered offences against the king's person or property and appeals from petitioners. Some of the records of the Privy Council have been lost due to fire in 1698 and through some dispersal into state papers and private collections. This latter point was because some of the material was seen as private papers by the clerks of the Council (hence papers originally part of the Council may survive amongst private collections).

The main incoming correspondence is in TNA record series PC 1 where there are petitions, letters, reports, appeals, proclamations, orders and minutes. Amongst the subjects of interest to the local historian are charters of incorporation, poor law, crime and legal appeals in general, defence and law and order, ecclesiastical policy (including reports of recusancy and returns of papists), public health, regulation of smuggling, riots, inventions, food supplies (most particularly between the early 1790s and the end of the war with France in 1815).

Original correspondence from 1860 is in PC 8. This can include material on boundaries, charters of incorporation, education, local government and public health. Further material from 1898 is in PC 12. Out-letters relating to a variety of Council-related work can be found in PC 7 for the period 1825 to 1952 with miscellaneous registers of correspondence for 1660 to 1900 in PC 6. Transcripts of correspondence to and from the Council may be recorded in the Privy Council registers from 1540 in PC 2 (transcripts were not included as a matter of course). The 44 published volumes that make up *The Acts of the*

Privy Council of England provide transcriptions between 1542 and 1631 of the daily register of the council proceedings.

The records of the Scottish Privy Council are held at NAS. The Council was sometimes more important than the Scottish parliament in dealing with domestic affairs. The Privy Council registers (which are published from 1545-1691) include political, administrative, economic and social affairs of Scotland. The council oversaw the administration of the law, trade and shipping, granted licences, administered oaths, banished beggars and gypsies etc. The Scottish Privy Council was abolished in 1708.

3.7 Treasury Board Letters and Papers, 1557-1920

As one of the major decision-making bodies of state the Treasury considered applications for (payment) expenditure with regard to services to and by the state. The records of the Treasury also contain a wide variety of types of material including policy papers, reports, draft board minutes, schemes, estimates, accounts and expenses, and proposals of various kinds. The subject matters of the Treasury are so vast (and the records seemingly complex) that many researchers are put off from using these records. This is a mistake as local historians interested in transportation, poverty, (various) political matters, canals, roads and railways, tithe commission issues, Crown Estate correspondence, additional police recruited to catch 'Jack the Ripper' in the Whitechapel area of London in 1888 – and pretty much everything else – will find things of interest. The decisions taken by the Treasury Board can be found in the Fair Minutes until 1849. From this period 'important' decisions were recorded and these are to be found in T 29.

The surviving letters and papers are held in T 1 (with additional and supplementary material in T 98 and PRO 30/32) for the period 1557 to 1920. Many of the earliest papers were lost as they were used as firepaper by Treasury staff to keep warm. The early period is characterised by a patchy survival pattern. The first paper is dated January 1556/7, then it moves to November 1596-July 1597, to January 1615/6, May 1627, 1636, 1641. From the mid- to late 1640s the survival rates increases significantly.

1557-1719	Calendar of Treasury Papers
1660-1718	Calendar of Treasury Books
1729-1745	Calendar of Treasury Books and Papers

Table 5: Treasury Papers.

Access to records is by the series list, by three sets of published calendars (describing the records in chronological order) and by three sets of contemporary registers. This is complicated by the fact that not all of the Treasury papers were registered (see additional material in the boxes of unregistered papers). Details of unregistered papers are in the T 1 lists. For the periods 1557 to 1719 and 1729 to 1745 you will need to consult the published *Calendars of Treasury Books*, *Calendars of Treasury Papers* and/or the *Calendar of Treasury Books and Papers*. There are copies at TNA but the researcher may initially be able to find copies in local reference libraries to determine if there is appropriate material prior to visiting TNA. Not only are the records for this period well indexed via the *Calendars* but the numbers in the volume can be converted to modern TNA references. Simply convert the Roman number followed by an Arabic number, for example CCCXVII no. 8 next to an entry becomes T 1/317. Within this document turn to the eighth item.[3]

For the period 1719-1729 there is only a brief entry in the T 1 list. However, from 1746, there are 'expanded' lists that, while providing much less detailed information than the calendars, are enough at least to indicate the subject matter. They are well indexed for 1746-1758 (and for 1764 and 1799). Each entry for the other years is arranged under subject headings so you will need to know roughly the subject and context. The Treasury Board Papers for most of the 19th century are unlisted. After 1782 you will need to use the Name Registers in T 2, 1777 to 1920 (personal and public office names) or the Subject Registers in T 108, 1852 to 1920. The Skeleton Registers in T 3 should be consulted before moving to the T 1 list. If an entry has a black tick through it, it means the paper/s survives; a red tick means it has been destroyed. The T 1 series comes to a close in May 1920 and the surviving records can then be found in series T 160 to T 164.

There are some additional papers, the Leeds Papers, from February 1668/9 until Michaelmas 1689, relating to Treasury matters, mainly journals and minute books, in record series PRO 30/32. The remainder of the Leeds Papers are at the British Library under references Add MSS 28074-28077.

3.8 Records of the Treasury Solicitor

In 1661 the duties of the Treasury Solicitor, or the Solicitor of the Exchequer as the position was termed, were defined. From 1806 the post-holder could be a barrister but he would not be allowed to work in private practice. It was a post which attracted additional duties over time:

- 1685: agent of the Crown in political prosecutions.
- 1842: acting as solicitor to other government departments (eg. Home Office, Foreign Office, Colonial Office and Privy Council Office)
- 1876: administration of certain intestate estates and the post of Procurator General (this included responsibility for admiralty prize cases, certain matrimonial cases and some international court cases).

As part of the huge reforms in criminal administration in the second half of the 19th century the post of the Director of Public Prosecutions (DPP) merged with that of the Treasury Solicitor between 1884 and 1908. In all, the importance of the role increased and becomes an important source with regard to local criminal and political cases.

The main record series of papers are TS 11 (1584 to 1880), TS 18 (1517 to 1953) and TS 27 (from 1843 onwards). The Treasury Solicitor acts as prosecutor on behalf of the Crown in political cases. These records will include state trials, trade unionists, Chartists and rioters, suffragettes; in fact, any group that was linked to threats to the state/state prosecutions will have come to the Treasury Solicitor's attention. Some of the TS 11 material relating to the Jacobite risings are cross-referenced to TS 20 Jacobite Rebellion Prosecution Papers. In addition to these papers there are various other series that contain material on political repression in TS 24. These relate to prosecutions for seditious libel against the state and monarchy and cover the period 1732 to 1901. Also included here are some copies of alleged seditious publications such as Thomas Paine's *Rights of Man*. The Treasury Solicitor administered *bona vacantia* estates (estates that fell to the Crown as the owner died intestate with no private claim on the lands). The records are scattered across TS 17, TS 30 and TS 33. Royal Wills are found in TS 18. Copies of local statutory rules and rules and instruments are in TS 37 while manorial documents of some of the land purchased by the Crown can be found in TS 19. On occasions divorce proceedings required a decision by the Treasury Solicitor and these records are in TS 29.

3.9 'General Views' County Reports of the Board of Agriculture

The prevailing ideas on agricultural improvement during the 1790s to the 1810s saw the newly established Board of Agriculture arrange for the publication of general surveys of agriculture for each county (although some counties had more than one general survey published). The volumes vary in the quality and quantity of matters they refer to. Some are confined to the purely agricultural: types of crops grown, livestock, condition and types of soil etc., while other volumes are more extensive, giving details on the state of roads, labourers' wages, price and mode of land occupation, size of farms, poor rates, common rights and tithes, and touching on crime, public houses and manufacture.

The books were designed to promote features of what we would now refer to as 'agrarian capitalism' and so need to be seen as a source created for that purpose. They are nevertheless very good for local historians interested in rural matters (and often beyond) for the late 18th and early 19th centuries.

Appendix 4

Key for Criminal Trials at Assize, 1559-1971 (England and Wales)

English Counties	*Crown and Minute Books*		*Indictments*		*Depositions*	
Beds	1863-76	ASSI 32	1658-98	ASSI 16	1832-76	ASSI 36
	1734-1863	ASSI 33	1693-1850	ASSI 94	1876-1971	ASSI 13
	1876-1945	ASSI 11	1851-1971	ASSI 95		
Berks	1657-1971	ASSI 2	1650-1971	ASSI 5	1719-1971	ASSI 6
	1847-1951	ASSI 3				
Bucks	1863-76	ASSI 32	1642-99	ASSI 16	1832-76	ASSI 36
	1734-1863	ASSI 33	1695-1850	ASSI 94	1876-1971	ASSI 13
	1876-1945	ASSI 11	1851-1971	ASSI 95		
Cambs	1902-1943	ASSI 31	1642-99	ASSI 16	1834-1971	ASSI 36
	1863-1971	ASSI 32	1692-1850	ASSI 94		
	1734-1863	ASSI 33	1851-1971	ASSI 95		
Cheshire	1532-1831	CHES 21	1831-1945	ASSI 64	1831-1944	ASSI 65
	1341-1659	CHES 24	1945-1971	ASSI 83	1945-1971	ASSI 84
	1831-1938	ASSI 61				
	1835-83	ASSI 62				
	1945-51	ASSI 79				
Cornwall	1730-1971	ASSI 21	1801-1971	ASSI 25	1861-1971	ASSI 26
	1670-1824	ASSI 23			1951-3	ASSI 82
Cumb	1714-1873	ASSI 41	1607-1876	ASSI 44	1613-1876	ASSI 45
	1665-1810	ASSI 42	1877-1971	ASSI 51	1877-1971	ASSI 52
Derbs	1818-1945	ASSI 11	1868-1971	ASSI 12	1862-1971	ASSI 13
			1662, 67, 87	ASSI 80		
Devon	1746-1971	ASSI 21	1801-1971	ASSI 25	1861-1971	ASSI 26
	1670-1824	ASSI 23			1951-3	ASSI 82
Dorset	1746-1971	ASSI 21	1801-1971	ASSI 25	1861-1971	ASSI 26
	1670-1824	ASSI 23			1951-3	ASSI 82
Durham	1770-1876	DURH 15	1582-1877	DURH 17	1843-1876	DURH 18
	1753-1858	DURH 16	1876-1971	ASSI 44	1877-1971	ASSI 45
	1858-1944	ASSI 41				
Essex	1734-1943	ASSI 31	1559-1688	ASSI 35	1825-1971	ASSI 36
	1826-1971	ASSI 32	1689-1850	ASSI 94		
			1851-1971	ASSI 95		
Glos	1657-1971	ASSI 2 , ASSI 3	1662-1971	ASSI 5	1719-1971	ASSI 6
	1847-1951					
Hants	1746-1971	ASSI 21	1801-1971	ASSI 25	1861-1971	ASSI 26
	1670-1824	ASSI 23			1951-3	ASSI 82
Heref	1657-1971	ASSI 2	1627-1971	ASSI 5	1719-1971	ASSI 6
	1847-1951	ASSI 3				
Herts	1734-1943	ASSI 31	1573-1688	ASSI 35	1829-1971	ASSI 36
	1826-1971	ASSI 32	1689-1850	ASSI 94		
			1851-1971	ASSI 95		

Hunts	1902-1943 1863-1971 1734-1863	ASSI 31 ASSI 32 ASSI 33	1643-98 1693-1850 1851-1971	ASSI 16 ASSI 94 ASSI 95	1851-1971	ASSI 36
Kent	1734-1943 1826-1971	ASSI 31 ASSI 32	1559-1688 1689-1850 1851-1971	ASSI 35 ASSI 94 ASSI 95	1812-1971	ASSI 36
Lancs	1524-1843 1686-1877	PL 25 PL 28	1660-1867 1877-1971	PL 26 ASSI 51	1663-1867 1877-1971	PL 27 ASSI 52
Leics	1818-1864 1864-75 1876-1945	ASSI 11 ASSI 32 ASSI 11	1653, 6 1864-75 1876-1971	ASSI 80 ASSI 35 ASSI 12	1862 1863-75 1876-1971	ASSI 13 ASSI 36 ASSI 13
Lincs	1818-1945	ASSI 11	1868-1971 1652-79	ASSI 12 ASSI 80	1862-1971	ASSI 13
London and Middlesex	1834-1949	CRIM 6	1834-1957 1833-1971	CRIM 4 CRIM 5	1839-1992 1923-1966	CRIM 1 CRIM 2
Monm	1657-1971 1847-1951	ASSI 2 , ASSI 3	1666-1971	ASSI 5	1719-1971	ASSI 6
Norfolk	1902-1943 1863-1971 1734-1863	ASSI 31 ASSI 32 ASSI 33	1606-99 1692-1850 1851-1971	ASSI 16 ASSI 94 ASSI 95	1817-1971	ASSI 36
Northants	1818-1864 1864-76 1876-1945	ASSI 11 ASSI 32 ASSI 11	1659-60 1864-75 1876-1971	ASSI 80 ASSI 95 ASSI 12	1862-1971 1864-75	ASSI 13 ASSI 36
Northumberland	1714-1944 1665-1810	ASSI 41 ASSI 42	1607-1971	ASSI 44	1613-1971	ASSI 45
Notts	1818-1945	ASSI 11	1868-1971 1663-4, 82	ASSI 12 ASSI 80	1862-1971	ASSI 13
Oxford	1657-1971 1847-1951	ASSI 2 , ASSI 3	1661-1971 1688	ASSI 5 PRO 30/80	1719-1971	ASSI 6
Rutland	1818-1864 1864-76 1876-1945	ASSI 11 ASSI 3276 ASSI 11	1667, 85 1864-75 1876-1971	ASSI 80 ASSI 95 ASSI 12	1862-1971 1864-73 1876-1971	ASSI 13 ASSI 36 ASSI 13
Shrops (Salop)	1657-1971 1847-1951	ASSI 2 , ASSI 3	1654-1971	ASSI 5	1719-1971	ASSI 6
Somerset	1730-1971 1670-1824	ASSI 21 ASSI 23	1801-1971	ASSI 25	1861-1971 1951-3	ASSI 26 ASSI 82
Staffs	1657-1971 1847-1951	ASSI 2 , ASSI 3	1662-1971 1662	ASSI 5 ASSI 80	1719-1971	ASSI 6
Suffolk	1902-1943 1863-1971 1734-1863	ASSI 31 ASSI 32 ASSI 33	1653-98 1689-1850 1851-1971	ASSI 16 ASSI 94 ASSI 95	1832-1971	ASSI 36
Surrey	1734-1943 1826-1971	ASSI 31 ASSI 32	1559-1688 1689-1850 1851-1971	ASSI 35 ASSI 94 ASSI 95	1820-1971	ASSI 36
Sussex	1734-1943 1826-1971	ASSI 31 ASSI 32	1559-1688 1689-1850 1851-1971	ASSI 35 ASSI 94 ASSI 95	1812-1971	ASSI 36
Warw	1818-1945	ASSI 11	1868-1971 1652, 88	ASSI 12 ASSI 80	1862-1971	ASSI 13
Westmor	1714-1873 1718-1810	ASSI 41 ASSI 42	1607-1876 1877-1971	ASSI 44 ASSI 51	1613-1876 1877-1971	ASSI 45 ASSI 52
Wilts	1746-1971 1670-1824	ASSI 21 ASSI 23	1729, 1801-1971	ASSI 25	1861-1971 1951-3	ASSI 26 ASSI 82
Worcs	1657-1971 1847-1951	ASSI 2 ASSI 3	1662-1971	ASSI 5	1719-1971	ASSI 6
Yorks	1718-1863 1658-1811 1864-1876	ASSI 41 ASSI 42 ASSI 11	1607-1863 1864-76 1877-1971	ASSI 44 ASSI 12 ASSI 51	1613-1863 1868-76 1877-1971	ASSI 45 ASSI 13 ASSI 52

Welsh Counties	*Crown and Minute Books*		*Indictments*		*Depositions*	
Angle	1831-1938	ASSI 61	1831-1945	ASSI 64	1831-1944	ASSI 65
	1835-83	ASSI 62	1945-1971	ASSI 83	1945-1971	ASSI 84
	1945-51	ASSI 79				
Brecon	1841-2	ASSI 74	1834-1945	ASSI 71	1837-1944	ASSI 72
	1844-1946	ASSI 76	1945-1971	ASSI 83	1945-1971	ASSI 84
	1945-51	ASSI 79				
Caernarvonshire	1831-1938	ASSI 61	1831-1945	ASSI 64	1831-1944	ASSI 65
	1835-83	ASSI 62	1945-1971	ASSI 83	1945-1971	ASSI 84
	1945-51	ASSI 79				
Cardigan	1841-2	ASSI 74	1834-1945	ASSI 71	1837-1944	ASSI 72
	1844-1946	ASSI 76	1945-1971	ASSI 83	1945-1971	ASSI 84
	1945-51	ASSI 79				
Carmarthenshire	1841-2	ASSI 74	1834-1945	ASSI 71	1837-1944	ASSI 72
	1844-1946	ASSI 76	1945-1971	ASSI 83	1945-1971	ASSI 84
	1945-51	ASSI 79				
Denbigh	1831-1938	ASSI 61	1831-1945	ASSI 64	1831-1944	ASSI 65
	1835-83	ASSI 62	1945-1971	ASSI 83	1945-1971	ASSI 84
	1945-51	ASSI 79				
Flint	1831-1938	ASSI 61	1831-1945	ASSI 64	1831-1944	ASSI 65
	1835-83	ASSI 62	1945-1971	ASSI 83	1945-1971	ASSI 84
	1945-51	ASSI 79				
Glam	1841-2	ASSI 74	1834-1945	ASSI 71	1837-1944	ASSI 72
	1844-1946	ASSI 76	1945-1971	ASSI 83	1945-1971	ASSI 84
	1945-51	ASSI 79				
Merion	1831-1938	ASSI 61	1831-1945	ASSI 64	1831-1944	ASSI 65
	1835-83	ASSI 62	1945-1971	ASSI 83	1945-1971	ASSI 84
	1945-51	ASSI 79				
Mont	1831-1938	ASSI 61	1831-1945	ASSI 64	1831-1944	ASSI 65
	1835-83	ASSI 62	1945-1971	ASSI 83	1945-1971	ASSI 84
	1945-51	ASSI 79				
Pemb	1841-2	ASSI 74	1834-1945	ASSI 71	1837-1944	ASSI 72
	1844-1946	ASSI 76	1945-1971	ASSI 83	1945-1971	ASSI 84
	1945-51	ASSI 79				
Radnor	1841-2	ASSI 74	1834-1945	ASSI 71	1837-1944	ASSI 72
	1844-1946	ASSI 76	1945-1971	ASSI 83	1945-1971	ASSI 84
	1945-51	ASSI 79				

Notes

Preface, pp.vii–ix

1. Further information can be found under The Community Access to Archives Project (CAAP) team on TNA's website; there are a number of other project partners including the national repositories and Hackney Archives Department.
2. See bibliography for relevant titles; David Hey's *The Oxford Companion to Local and Family History*, for example, includes references to Wales, Scotland and Ireland as well as England.
3. J. Foster and J. Sheppard, *British Archives: A Guide to Archive Resources in the United Kingdom*, 4th edn (2002).

Chapter 1: Introduction to Sources, pp.1–10

1. This will be true of whatever competing notion of local the researcher may decide on; see A.J.L. Winchester, 'Parish, Township and Tithing: Landscapes of Local Administration in England Before the 19th Century', *The Local Historian*, 27 (1) 1997, pp.3–17 and J.D. Marshall, 'Communities, Regions and Local History: Perceptions of Locality in High and Low Furness', *The Local Historian*, 26 (1) 1996, pp.36–47.
2. A number of regional MLAs have undertaken surveys of archives held by museums.
3. For the use of some of the TNA Ministry of Health files in examining emigration, see G. Howells, 'Emigration and the New Poor Law: The Norfolk Emigration Fever of 1836', *Rural History*, 11, 2 (2000), pp.145–64.
4. www.archiveshub.ac.uk
5. A starting place for England is *A Guide to English County Histories*, edited by C.R.J. Currie and C.P. Lewis (1994); it was produced as a tribute to Christopher Elrington, when he retired as general editor of the *VCH*.
6. VCH website www.englandpast.net/about.html. Volumes can also be found on www.british-history.ac.uk
7. Finding that someone has been engaged in researching 'your' particular subject matter in 'your' particular place should not discourage your own research. Historical study generates debate, disagreement and (mostly!) reasoned argument. Finding previous published work should not prevent you from continuing. It should encourage you to engage in what has gone before. You may wish to agree, disagree, prove wrong (by introducing new evidence) or set new questions for the earlier evidence which was brought to light.
8. http://historyonline.chadwyck.co.uk/info/annreg.htm. Check if your library subscribes to the site.
9. www.bodley.ox.ac.uk/ilej
10. We use the phrase 'non-academic local historians' here in the sense of someone not deriving an income from teaching, researching and/or writing history.
11. B. Berryman (ed.), *Mitcham Settlement Examinations*, 1784-1814 (1973).

Chapter 2: The Land, pp.11–28

1. For parts of Northumberland and Durham, there is the so-called 'Domesday Book of the North': this is the Boldon Book, a survey taken in 1183, of the estates of the Bishop of Durham in those counties. This was published as part of the Phillimore edition of Domesday Book in 1982.
2. Published by Phillimore; this is also available on CD-Rom.
3. J. Kissock, 'Medieval Feet of Fines: A Study of Their Uses With a Catalogue of Published Sources', *The Local Historian*, 24, 2 (1994), pp.66–82; M. David and J. Kissock, 'The Dangers of Shortcuts: the Feet of Fine and Lansdowne Manuscripts 306, 307 and 308', *The Local Historian*, 31, 2 (2001), pp.107–9.
4. N.W. Alcock, *Old Title Deeds* (1986).
5. For an extremely readable recent description of the changes of land tenure from 1550-1850 see M. Overton, *Agricultural Revolution in England: Transformation of the Agrarian Economy* 1500-1850 (1996).

6. W.B. and F. Marcham, *Court Rolls of the Bishop of London's Manor of Hornsey* 1603-1701 (1929), p.xxvii.
7. 'Rentals and Surveys' is used here for a large variety of manorial documents: custumals, extents, rentals, surveys, terriers and valors.
8. P.D.A. Harvey, *Manorial Records of Cuxham, Oxfordshire, c.*1200-1359 (1976).
9. For a detailed discussion on manorial records and their use see M. Ellis, *Using Manorial Records*, PRO Readers' Guide no. 6, PRO Publications/Royal Commission on Historical Manuscripts, 2nd edn (1997); for Welsh manors see H. Watt, *Welsh Manors and Their Records* (2000).
10. See Appendix 3/2. National Register of Archives and Archives Network Links.
11. *Returns from the Commissioners of ... Crown Lands and Royal Forests*, xiii.3 (128), 1831. A copy is on open access in the Map and Large Document Room at TNA.
12. See S. Hollowell, *Enclosure Records for Historians*, 2000; an essential guide to the multitude of records the enclosure process could produce.
13. B. English, *Yorkshire Enclosure Awards*, 1985; J. Chapman and S. Seeliger, *A Guide to Enclosure in Hampshire*, 1700-1900, 1997.
14. See Appendix 3/3, Equity Courts.
15. Work undertaken to calendar the rolls in this series is described in M.W. Beresford, 'The Decree Rolls of Chancery as a Source for Economic History, 1547-*c.*1700', *Economic History Review*, 2nd series, 32 (1979), pp.1-10. As a result of this work a small sample has been calendared and is available in the paper lists at TNA.
16. See L. Wilkinson, 'Completing the Calendar of Patent Rolls, Elizabeth I', *The Local Historian*, 35, 1 (2005), pp.30-43.
17. See Appendix 3/4, State Papers Domestic.
18. W.E. Tate, *A Domesday of English Parliamentary Enclosure Acts and Awards* (1978).
19. J.E. Chapman, *A Guide to Parliamentary Enclosures in Wales* (1992).
20. M. Turner and T. Wray, 'A survey of sources for parliamentary enclosure: the House of Commons' Journal and Commissioners' working papers', *Archives*, XIX, 85 (1991), pp.257-88.
21. The nature of the records collected and included in these enclosure papers means that many records were created after the award was enrolled. In such cases they can contain valuable information on the enclosures themselves as well as the subsequent history of particular pieces of land. For example CRES 35/1537, Hampton and Teddington manors crown allotments under enclosure covers the period from 1799 to 1930.
22. Maps and plans have often been extracted from the various rolls, bundles, volumes etc. and provided with a separate reference.
23. TNA CRES 2/27.
24. TNA CRES 2/2.
25. TNA CRES 2/27.
26. TNA CRES 2/43.
27. TNA CRES 2/609.
28. TNA CRES 2/127.
29. TNA CRES 2/152.
30. TNA CRES 35/337.
31. TNA C 107/179.
32. TNA C 104/189.
33. TNA ADM 76/95.
34. TNA RAIL 1016/5.
35. TNA HO 42/36.
36. TNA HO 67/26/457.
37. TNA HO 67/15/129.
38. TNA HO 67/15/446.
39. TNA HO 67/15/10.
40. TNA HO 67/10/40.
41. D. Williams, 'The Acreage Returns of 1801 for Wales', *Bulletin of the Board of Celtic Studies*, 14 (1950-52), pp.54-68 and 139-54; D. Thomas, 'The Acreage Returns of 1801 for Wales: An Addendum', *Bulletin of the Board of Celtic Studies*, 18 (1958-60), pp.379-83; M. Turner, *Home Office Acreage Returns (HO 67) List and Analysis Part I Bedfordshire-Isle of Wight* 1801, List & Index Society (1982); M. Turner, *Home Office Acreage Returns (HO 67) List and Analysis Part II Jersey-Somerset* 1801, List & Index Society (1982); M. Turner, *Home Office Acreage Returns (HO 67) List and Analysis Part III Staffordshire-Yorkshire* 1801, List & Index Society (1983); M. Turner, *Home Office Acreage Returns (HO 67) Index* 1801, List & Index Society (1983).
42. E.J. Evans, *Tithes: Maps and Apportionments and the* 1836 *Act*, 2nd edn (1993), pp.27-8.
43. R.J.P. Kain and R.R. Oliver, *Tithe Maps and Apportionments of England and Wales* (1995).
44. R.J.P. Kain and H.C. Prince, *Tithe Surveys for Historians* (2000).
45. E.A. Cox and B.R. Dimmer, 'The Tithe Files of the Mid-19th Century', *Agricultural History Review*, 13 (1965) pp.1-16.
46. R.J.P. Kain, *An Atlas and Index of the Tithe Files of Mid-Nineteenth-Century England and Wales* (1986).

47. The national (but not local) statistics for 1866 to 1966 have been published in *A Century of Agricultural Statistics,* 1866-1966 (1968).
48. See the UK National Digital Data Archives of Datasets (UKNDAD) at www.ndad.nationalarchives.gov.uk.
49. P. Anderton, 'Milking the Sources: Cheshire Dairy Farming and the Field Notebooks of the 1910 "Domesday" Survey', *The Local Historian*, 34, 1 (2004), pp.2-16.
50. G. Beech and R. Mitchell, *Maps for Family and Local History* (2004), p.57. If you are thinking of doing any research requiring you to track down and investigate tithes, valuation office or national farm survey records you must consult this book.
51. G. Neville, 'Eviction and Reclamation in World War II: The Case of a Worcester Farm', *The Local Historian*, 29, 2 (1999) pp.76-90.
52. J. Godfrey and B. Short, 'The Ownership, Occupation and use of Land on the South Downs, 1840-1940: A Methodological Analysis of Record Linkage Over Time', *Agricultural History Review*, 49, I (2001), pp.56-78.
53. *Maps and Plans of the British Isles* (1967).
54. P. Hindle, *Maps for Historians* (1998).
55. R. Gard, *The Observant Traveller: Diaries of Travel in England, Wales and Scotland in the County Record Offices of England and Wales* (1989).

Chapter 3: The People, pp.29-37

1. W.B. Stephens, *Sources for English Local History* (1994), chapter 2.
2. *Local Population Studies* and the Cambridge Group for the History of Population and Social Structure, popularly known as Campop.
3. See Anne Whiteman, 'The Compton census of 1676' and Tom Arkell, 'A method for estimating population totals from the Compton census returns' in Kevin Schurer and Tom Arkell (eds.), *Surveying the People* (1992). See also A. Whiteman, *The Crompton Census of 1676: A Critical Edition* (1986).
4. See C. Chapman, *Pre-1841 Censuses & Population Listings in the British Isles* (1996); J. Gibson and M. Medlycott, *Local Census Listings,* 1522-1930*: Holdings in the British Isles*, 2nd edn (1994).
5. W. Spencer, *Records of the Militia and Volunteer Forces* 1757-1945 (1997).
6. It is now possible to choose not to be included on the electoral register which will create problems for researchers in the future.
7. www.york.ac.uk/res/dlb.
8. M. Jurkowski, C. Smith and D. Crook, *Lay Taxes in England and Wales,* 1188-1688 (1998).
9. In 1332, a fractional tax was levied at the rate of a fifteenth and tenth (a tenth in the cities, boroughs and royal ancient demesne lands, a fifteenth elsewhere). In 1334, another tax was levied at the same rate, and instead of making new assessments of individuals, the collectors were simply to demand from each taxation unit (village, town, etc) a sum equal to or greater than that collected in 1332. The amounts collected in 1334 became the basis of all such taxes for the next three centuries, and a system of fixed quotas on individual townships was introduced, the same amount being due every time a tax was granted. Some of these quotas were reduced by statute in 1433 and 1446, and some were altered depending on local circumstances (natural disasters, population changes, etc.), but the system remained in place for all grants of fifteenths and tenths until the last such grant in 1624.
10. W. Illingworth and J. Caley, *Rotuli Hundredorum* (1812-18).
11. See, for example, A.J. Camp, *Wills and their whereabouts*, 4th edn (1974); J.S.W. Gibson, *Wills and where to find them* (1974); more recently see the excellent K. Grannum and N. Taylor, *Wills and Other Probate Records: A Practical Guide to Researching Your Ancestors' Last Documents* (2004).
12. For further details see J.G. Gibson and A. Dell, *The Protestation Returns* 1641-42 (1995).
13. The enumerator was the individual responsible for the distribution of a schedule to each household within the area to which he (women were only able to act as enumerators from 1891) had been assigned prior to census night. He would then later collect the completed schedules and copy them in the Census Enumerators Books. It is these books which make up the enumerators returns.
14. The exception to this is the preservation of the returns in TNA HO 71. These are returns by parish clergy across England and Wales, the Channel Islands and the Isle of Man. They give numbers of baptisms, burials and marriages in each parish for each year between 1821 and 1830. There is some further statistical information and numbers regarding illegitimate children born in 1830.
15. Microfilms of the census books for 1841-91 are held at the Family Records Centre, 1 Myddelton Street, London, EC1R 1UW; The vast majority of local studies libraries and CROs have fiche or film copies of these records. The 1901 census is available online at www.1901census.nationalarchives.gov.uk where relevant pages can be downloaded for a fee. The 1861 to 1891 censuses are also available at www.ancestry.co.uk (there are plans to add 1851 and 1841 at a later date)
16. Hertfordshire Archives and Local Studies, County Hall, Hertford, SG13 8EJ, ref 67578.
17. Michael Barke, 'An 1811 Census Manuscript from North Shields', *The Local Historian*, 34, 1 (2004), p.30.
18. Edward Higgs, *Making Sense of the Census* (1989), p.15.
19. *Ibid.*, p.12.
20. See, for example: R.L. Greenall, *The Population of a Northamptonshire Village in* 1851*: A Census Study of Long Buckby* (1971); Kathryn M. Thompson (ed.), *Rothley in* 1851 (1994).

Chapter 4: Transport, Communications and Trade, pp.38-47

1. Flintshire Record Office, Dee and Clwyd River Authority Records, 1542-1978, DC series.
2. East Sussex Record Office, Archive of Rye Corporation [RYE/45–RYE/51]: RYE/47/81/3, 11 July 1612.
3. For an example of the information to be found in some of the formal records of canal companies see C. Richardson, *Minutes of the Chesterfield Canal Company* 1771-80 (1996).
4. TNA SC 8/99/4939.
5. Leicestershire RO, 3D42/M37/6/1-18.
6. Accessed via http://viewfinder.english-heritage.org.uk.
7. For a discussion on road and trackways and their implication see P. Hindle, *Roads and Tracks*, 2001.
8. Descriptions of the poor state of local roads can be found in many of the *General Views* reports. See appendix 3.9. 'General Views' County Report of the Board of Agriculture.
9. C. Vancouver, *General View of the Agriculture of the County of Devon* (1808, rep. 1969), p.368.
10. *Local History News*, no 74, spring 2005, p.7 and front cover.
11. C. Vancouver, *General View of the Agriculture of the County of Devon* (1808, rep. 1969) pp.368-9.
12. TNA MPF 1/2, MPF 1/247, MPH 1/14/4 (the latter a much later copy of a 1750 survey of Perthshire and Aberdeenshire). There is relevant material in T 1, Long Bundles; T 1/3962, 4170-4172 and 4205 may contain hitherto unrecorded maps.
13. www.nls.uk/digitallibrary/map/military/index.html.
14. *British Railways pre-grouping atlas and gazetteer* (1976 *et seq*).
15. C. Edwards, *Railway Records: A Guide to Sources* (2001).
16. *Exp. and Maintenance of Highways and Turnpike Roads*, H.C. 431 (1818); *Rep. Sel. Ctee. on Turnpike Trusts and Tolls*, H.C. 547 (1836); *Rep. Sel. Ctee. on Canals,* H.C. 252 (1883); *Rep. R. Comm on Canals*, Cd. 3183-4, H.C. (1906); *Rep. Sel. Ctee. on Railroads and Turnpike Trusts*, H.C 295 (1839); *Rep. Sel. Ctee. on Railways*, H.C. 50, 92 etc. (1840); *Railway Returns*, 1841 onwards, listed under different names. For other useful papers see list in W.R. Powell, *Local History From Blue Books: A Select List of the Sessional Papers of the House of Commons* (1962), pp.39-41.
17. H.S. Cobb, *The Local Port Book of Southampton for* 1439-40 (1961) is a good local example of the material to be found.
18. E. Welsh (ed.), *The Admiralty Court Book of Southampton,* 1566-1588 (1968).
19. See W.B. Stephens, *Sources*, pp.139-53 which is particularly useful for sea-going trade and shipping.
20. S. Fowler, *PRO Reader's Guide No 8: RAF Records In The PRO* (1994).
21. Royal Air Force Museum, Department of Research and Information Services, Aerodrome Road, Hendon, London, NW9 5LL.
22. Post Office Archives & Record Services, Freeling House, Mount Pleasant Complex, Phoenix Place, London, EC1A 1BB.

Chapter 5: Working Life, pp.48-65

1. J.E.T. Rogers, *A History of Agriculture and Prices in England*, 7 vols (1866-1902, repr. 1963); Thomas Tooke, *A History of Prices ... from 1793 to 1856*, 6 vols (1838-57, repr. 1928); Lord Beveridge, *Prices and Wages in England: Vol 1: The Mercantilist Era* (1939); E. Gilboy, *Wages in 18th Century England* (1934).
2. See Appendix 3/1, Parliamentary Papers.
3. Department of Employment, *British Labour Statistics: Historical Abstract,* 1886-1968 (1961); the quote is from British Labour Statistics, p.5.
4. R. Floud and D.N. McCloskey (eds.), *The Economic History of Britain Since* 1700, 2nd edn (1994).
5. For the 1911 census some women refused to be 'numbered' if they did not 'count' in terms of representation. See M. Turner, 'Women and the 1911 Census', *Ancestors*, 5 (2002), pp.62-4.
6. C.A. Crompton, 'An Exploration of the Craft and Trade Structure of Two Hertfordshire Villages, 1851-1891: An Application of Nominal Record Linkage to Directories and Census Enumerators' Books', *The Local Historian*, 28, 3 (1998), pp.130-44.
7. D. and J. Mills, 'Farms, Farmers and Farm Workers in the 19th-Century Census Enumerators' Books: A Lincolnshire Case Study', *The Local Historian*, 27, 3 (1997), p.143.
8. www.historicaldirectories.org/hd/index.asp 'Historical Directories is produced and owned by the University of Leicester. It is a digital library of local and trade directories for England and Wales, from 1750 to 1919. Within the digital library there are high quality reproductions of comparatively rare books, essential tools for research into local and genealogical history' – taken from the introductory pages of the website.
9. www.genuki.org.uk Launched as a website devoted to UK and Irish genealogy, Genuki drills down from its home page, through national and country pages to individual towns and parishes (although not every town or parish has its own page yet). See P. Christian, 'The Genius of Genuki', *Ancestors*, 31 (2005), pp.58-9.
10. See G. Shaw, 'The Content and Reliability of 19th Century Trade Directories', *The Local Historian*, 11 (1974), pp.85-8; G. Shaw and A. Alexander, 'Directories as Sources in Local History', *The Local History Magazine*, 46 (1994), pp.12-17.
11. N. Raven, 'Trade Directories and Business Size: Evidence from the Small Towns of North Essex, 1851', *The Local Historian*, 31, 2 (2001), pp.83-96.

12. J. Unwin, 'Apprenticeships and Freedoms: The Computer Analysis of the Records of the Cutler's Company in Sheffield', *The Local Historian*, 25, 4 (1995), pp.194-208.
13. A microfiche personal name index has been created by the Society of Genealogists.
14. See Appendix 3/2, National Register of Archives and Archives Network Links.
15. More specific examples would be the *Report from the Select Committee on Woollen Clothiers' Petition*, HC, 30 (1803), and the *Report into the Fishing Apprenticeship System*, Cd no. 7576 (1894).
16. TNA JUST 1, records of itinerant justices and other court records relating to the central control of justice at local level, 1198-1528; KB 9, Court of King's Bench Crown Side: Indictments Files, Oyer and Terminer Files and Informations Files, *c.*1294-1675.
17. *Some Sessions of the Peace in Lincolnshire,* 1360-75, Lincoln Record Society, XXX (1937); reprinted in R.B. Dobson, *The Peasants' Revolt of* 1831, Macmillan, 2nd edn (1983), p.70.
18. Simon A.C. Penn, 'Female Wage-earners in Late 14th Century England', *Agricultural History Review*, 35/1 (1987), p.5. [The Somerset roll is TNA JUST 1/773, mm 1-4.]
19. A still useful introduction to wage assessments (including a list of known wage assessments at the time of its publication) is W.W. Minchinton (ed.), *Wage Regulation in Pre-Industrial England* (1972).
20. See Appendix 3/1, Parliamentary Papers; and see also British Labour Statistics: Historical Abstract, 1886, 1968 (1971).
21. See in particular E.P. Thompson, *Customs in Common* (1991) and P. Linebaugh, *The London Hanged*, 2nd edn (2003).
22. See Appendix 3/2, National Register of Archives and Archives Network Links.
23. William Baird and Co., GB248/UGD 164/1, Glasgow University Archive Services.
24. *Historical Farm Records: a Summary Guide to Manuscripts and Other Material in the University Library Collected by the Institute of Agricultural History and the Museum of English Rural Life* (1973). This material (and any others collected since 1973) can be searched electronically on their online catalogue at www.ruralhistory.org/index.
25. J.M. Fletcher and C.A. Upton, 'The Domestic Accounts of Merton College, Oxford, 1482-1494', *The Local Historian*, 28, 1 (1998), pp.16-23.
26. TNA. CRES 2/127. Enclosure of Delamere Forest, 1796-1819.
27. London Metropolitan Archives, A Acc 262/42/28. Wood family at Littleton.
28. J.T. Smith, *English Gilds: the Original Ordinances* ... (1870). This volume transcribes several medieval guild ordinances from across the country.
29. For example, RAIL 410/1982: Alexandra Dock goods station, wages staff, covers the 52 years between 1877 and 1929.
30. D. Hawkins, *Railway Ancestors: A Guide to the Staff Records of the Railway Companies of England and Wales* 1822-1947 (1995); C. Edwards, *Railway Records: A Brief Guide to Sources* (2001).
31. Much of the MH 12 correspondence for the early 20th century has been lost or destroyed.
32. LMA MAB series, Metropolitan Asylum Board; and TNA MH 17 Poor Law Commission and successors: correspondence with Asylum Districts and Boards, 1845-1930.
33. BL. Add 61357, ff, 34-35b, 74-77b, 96, 111, 114.
34. Bodleian Library MSS, Top. Leics. c. 2-6.
35. NLW BROOMHALL, 190-2.
36. TNA PL 12/1-11; Palatinate of Lancaster: Chancery Court: Exhibits.
37. *Report from the Select Committee on Labourers Wages*, 392 (1824); *Report from the Select Committee on the State of the Coal Trade*, HC, 663 (1830); *Reports of Special Assistant Poor Law Commissioners on the Employment of Women and Children in Agriculture*, 510 (1843); *Return of Rates of Wages in the Minor Textile Trades of the United Kingdom with Report ThereonI*, 689 (1890), and the *Report of an Enquiry by the Board of Trade into Working-Class Rents and Retails Prices Together with the Rates of Wages in Certain Occupations in Industrial Towns of the United Kingdom in 1912*, Cd. 6955 (1913). See also Appendix 3/1, Parliamentary Papers for other PPs in this subject area.
38. See Appendix 3/2, National Register of Archives and Archives Network Links.
39. D. Tonks, *My Ancestor Was a Coalminer* (2004); C. and M. Watts, *My Ancestor was a Merchant Seaman*, repr. with addendum (2004); A. Sherman, *My Ancestor was a Policeman* (2004); D. Hawkins, *Railway Ancestors*; C. Young, 'Staying in Touch' [postal workers], *Ancestors*, 19 (2004), pp.35-40. In each case there are references to the location of material.
40. L. Snook, 'A Professional Occupation? The Training of Teachers in Liverpool, 1889-1901', *The Local Historian*, 34, 3 (2004), pp.132-9.
41. There are also two early 19th-century Bow Street Police registers in MEPO 2/25 and MEPO 4/508.
42. A. Bevan, *Tracing Your Ancestors*, 6th edn (2002). However, you should be aware that where these records survive in TNA they usually list the name and period of career.
43. See Appendix 3/3, Equity Courts.
44. There are a number of Parliamentary Papers relating to the 'sweating trades'; see BOPCRIS website.
45. See Appendix 3/2, National Register of Archives and Archives Network Links.
46. See www.oldbaileyonline.org and the crime and punishment section at www.llgc.org.uk.
47. See Appendix 3/1, Parliamentary Papers. One of the most well known and useful *Report of the Commission on the Labour of Women and Children in Mines*, 1842, xiii; see D. Tonks, 'Lost Children of the

Revolution', *Ancestors*, 26 (2004), pp.14-20.
48. J. Gibson and C. Rodgers, *Coroner's Records in England and Wales*, 2nd edn (1992).
49. R.F. Hunnisett (ed.), *Sussex Coroners' Inquests* 1485-1558 (1985); *Sussex Coroners' Inquests,* 1558-1603 (1996) and *Sussex Coroners' Inquests* (1998).
50. R.F. Hunnisett (ed.), *Sussex Coroners' Inquests,* 1558-1603, nos 16 and 158.
51. See Appendix 3/2, Parliamentary Papers.
52. D. Neave, 'The Local Records of Affiliated Friendly Societies', *The Local Historian*, 16 (1984), pp.161-7; see also D. Weinbren, 'Mutually Beneficial: Using the Records of Friendly Societies', *Ancestors*, 22 (2004), pp.57-62.
53. www.historyshelf.org/shelf/friend/index.php.
54. For transcripts of a selection of such material see A. Aspinall, *The Early Trade Unions: Documents from the Home Office Papers in the Public Record Office* (1949).
55. See Appendix 1, Parliamentary Papers.
56. Kirkintilloch Trades Council Records, 1930-75; includes minutes, 1949-1971, rough minutes, 1969-1972, and cash book, 1930-1975. GB1015/GD34, East Dunbartonshire Information and Archives.
57. For example Add Mss 57562–57635, Records of the Society of London Bookbinders, 1794-1919.
58. Bradford Tin-Plate Workers' Society, 1864-1913 (MSS.101/SM/BR), Birmingham and Midland Sheet Metal Workers' Society, 1825-1972 (MSS.101/SM/BIT, MSS.101/SM/BIM and MSS.101/SM/BIW) and London Society of Compositors, 1785-1955 (MSS.28/CO).
59. John Burnett, David Vincent and David Mayall, *The Autobiography of the Working Class* (1984-9).
60. A full electronic list of the material is available on the website, www.brunel.ac.uk; follow links to the library.
61. P. Bagwell, 'The Railway Service Gazette and the Railway Review', *The Bulletin of the Society for the Study of Labour History*, 28 (1974), pp.38-40.
62. For example John Martin's work on Northamptonshire enclosure sought to re-examine the view that enclosure in the 16th century was largely determined by the changing relative prices of wool and grain. J. Martin, 'Sheep and Enclosure in 16th Century Northamptonshire', *Agricultural History Review*, 36, 1 (1988), pp.39-54.
63. *Report on the High Price of Coals. Means to Lower and Prevent Excessive Prices for the Future*, 14 (1702-3), Journals of the House of Commons (1803 reprint) and the *Third Report from the House of Commons Select Committee on the State of Agriculture*, H.C., 465 (1836). See Appendix 3/1, Parliamentary Papers.
64. TNA, E 122/173/3. II James I. See T.S. Willan (ed.), *A Tudor Book of Rates* (1962) and R.C. Jarvis, 'Books of Rates', *Journal of the Society of Archivists*, V (1977).
65. Rev. David Davies, *The Case of Labourers in Husbandry Stated and Considered* (1795) and Sir F.M. Eden, *The State of the Poor* (1797).

Chapter 6: Religion, pp.66-75

1. For the Anglo-Saxons see P.H. Sawyer, *Anglo-Saxon Charters, an Annotated List and Bibliography* (1968); for the Normans see H.W.C. Davis and J. Whitwell (eds), *Regesta Regum Anglo-Normannorum*, vol. I, 1066-1154 (1913); C. Johnson and H.A. Cronne (eds), vol II, 1100-1135 (1956); H.A. Cronne and R.H.C. Davis (eds), vol. III, 1135-54 (1968). For Henry II (1154-89), see L. Delisle and E. Berger, *Recueil des Actes de Henri II,* 3 vols (1920) and for Richard I, L. Landon, *The Itinerary of Richard I* (1935). J.C. Holt and R. Mortimer, *Acta of Henry II and Richard I* (1986) gives a list of royal charters in British repositories.
2. For further information see TNA's guide, 'Sources for the History of Religious Houses and Their Lands, C.1000-1530'.
3. There is a fairly comprehensive list in G.R.C. Davis, *Medieval Cartularies in Great Britain* (1958).
4. See *Public Record Office Lists and Indexes, V, VI, VIII, XXXIV XXV.*
5. Printed in H. Hall (ed.), *The Red Book of the Exchequer,* Vol. I (1897), pp.186-445.
6. Printed as *The Book of Fees,* 3 vols (1921-31).
7. See TNA guide (footnote 2 above) for further details of record classes.
8. Printed in B.A. Lees, *Records of the Templars in England* (1935).
9. This is a complex subject which can only be summarised here, but the TNA guide already referred to on the History of Religous Houses is a mine of information.
10. See D. Robinson, 'Bishops' Registers', in K.M. Thompson (ed.), *Start Guides to Records: Second Series* (1997).
11. This has been demonstrated by Jack Howard-Drake with his ongoing publications on Oxford church court depositions. J. Howard-Drake, *Oxford Church Court Depositions, 1542-1622* (1991-2005) [some years missing].
12. Tarver, Anne, *Church Court Records* (1995), dust jacket; Record Office for Leicestershire, Leicester and Rutland; 1D41/11, 1D41/13, 1D41/21 and 1D41/26.
13. See, for example, Harley MSS 280, 594-5.
14. See David Shorney, *Protestant Nonconformity and Roman Catholicism* (1996) for further details of TNA sources; there is also a journal, *Recusant History.*
15. *Census of* 1851*: Religious Worship, England and Wales, Report and Tables* (1852-3) LXXXIX.
16. See W.B. Stephens, *Sources*, pp.270-1, for further information.

17. See also Stephens, *Sources*, pp.284-6, 295-6 for information on printed material.

Chapter 7: Education, pp.76-85

1. Report of the *Royal Commission on Revenues and Management of Certain Colleges and Schools*, xx, xxi (1864).
2. See case study in M. Turner, 'Grey Coats and Blue Coats: Life in an 18th-Century Charity School', *Ancestors*, 11 (2002-3), pp.12-17.
3. See Appendix 3/2, National Register of Archives and Archives Network Links.
4. At the Society's offices, 16 Kingston Road, London, SW19 1JZ; tel. 0845 3306033.
5. The British Schools in Queen Street, Hitchin, Hertfordshire include both a galleried and a monitorial classroom, which are open to the public.
6. British and Foreign School Society: www.bfss.org.uk/archive/index
7. Detailed reports of the archive's holdings are given in G.F. Bartle, 'The Records of the British and Foreign School Society at Borough Road', *Journal of Educational Administration and History*, July 1980; G.F. Bartle, 'The Records of the British and Foreign School Society', *The Local Historian*, 16, 4 (1984), pp.204-6.
8. St Mary's College, Twickenham; access to the records is by appointment only and you will need to contact The Archivist, St Mary's College, Strawberry Hill, Waldegrave Road, Twickenham, TW1 4SX. The catalogue can be searched remotely at www.libsys.smuc.ac.uk.
9. See Ann Morton, *Education and the State From 1833* (1997), which describes central government education records.
10. There are surviving papers of the Commission in TNA 7 74/1-2.
11. See W.B. Stephens, *Sources*, chapter 7, for more information and the TNA education research guides.
12. Memorandum no 414, at the Research Enquiries Desk at TNA, identifies Treasury Board Papers relating to education between 1839 and 1860.
13. www.ndad.ulcc.ac.uk.
14. *Report from the Select Committee on Public Libraries*, 1849, vol. xvii.

Chapter 8: Poverty, pp.86-101

1. For full text of 1601 *Act for the Relief of the Poor*: http://users.ox.ac.uk/~peter/workhouse
2. P. Slack, *The English Poor Law*, 1531-1782 (1990), p 26.
3. For full text of 1662 *Act for the better Relief of the Poor of this Kingdom* [Settlement and Removal Act]: http://users.ox.ac.uk/~peter/workhouse
4. For example see P. Lindley, *Settlement Certificates in the Archdeaconry of Doncaster* 1692-1846 (2000) [a published index] and Lindley, P., *From Pillar to Post: Settlement Examinations in the Archdeaconry of Doncaster* 1730-1846 (2001) [2 volumes].
5. For full text of 1722-3 *An Act for amending the Laws relating to the Settlement, Imployment, and Relief of the Poor* [Knatchbull's Act]: http://users.ox.ac.uk/~peter/workhouse.
6. For full text of 1782 *An Act for the better Relief and Employment of the Poor* [Gilbert's Act]: http://users.ox.ac.uk/~peter/workhouse.
7. L. Kent and S. King, 'Changing Patterns of Poor Relief in Some English Rural Parishes circa 1650-1750', *Rural History: Economy, Society, Culture*, 14, 2 (2003), pp.120, 148-9.
8. In particular for this period see two parliamentary reports: *Report of the Select Committee on ... Poor Laws*, H.C. ser I, ix (includes returns from overseers in 1776 and 1803-5); *Returns on Expense and Maintenance of Poor of the Poor in England*, XIII (1803-4). It is clear that published returns should always be compared with surviving overseers and other vestry records where they survive; see S. Wittering, 'How Reliable are the Government Poor Law Returns', *The Local Historian*, 30, 3 (2000), pp.160-4.
9. W.E. Tate, *The Parish Chest*, 3rd edn (1969), p 200.
10. F.M. Eden, *The State of the Poor Together with Parochial Reports* (1797, reprinted 1966) and Rev. D. Davies, *The case of Labourers in Husbandry, Stated and Considered* (1795) are the best known contemporary surveys.
11. *Report from His Majesty's Commissioners for Inquiring into ... The Poor Laws*, 44, XXVII (1834). However, see also M. Blaug, 'The Myth of the Old Poor Law and the Making of the New', *Journal of Economic History*, 23 (1963), pp.151-84.
12. A good example of the latter is E.M. Dance (ed.), *Wimbledon Vestry Minutes, 1747-1788* (1964).
13. F.G. Emmison and Irvine Gray, *County Records* (1967), p.20.
14. G.A. Chinnery, *Records of the Borough of Leicester. Volume VII: judicial and allied records* 1689-1835 (1974), pp.25-6, 29-30.
15. See Appendix 3/4, State Papers Domestic and Appendix 3/5, Home Office Correspondence, 1782-1959.
16. PPs: *Select Committee on the Poor Laws of this Kingdom*, IV (1816); *Select Committee on the Poor Laws*, VI (1817); H of L, *Select Committee on the Poor Laws*, V (1818); *Select Committee on the Poor Laws*, V, 1818; *Second Report from the Select Committee on the Poor Laws*, V (1818); *Third Report from the Select Committee on the Poor Laws*, V (1818); *Abstract of the Answers and Returns ... Relative to the Maintenance of the Poor in England*, 1813-15, XIX (1818); II, *Select Committee on the Poor Laws* (1819).
17. Board of Agriculture, *The Agricultural State of the Kingdom* (1816, repr. 1970, with an introduction by

G. Mingay).
18. J.R. Poynter, *Society and Pauperism: English Ideas on Poor Relief,* 1795-1834 (1969), pp.333-51.
19. A. Charlesworth (ed.), *An Atlas of Rural Protest in Britain* (1983), pp.142-54.
20. Largely based on A. Brundage, *The Making of the New Poor Law,* 1832-1839 (1978).
21. For full text of 1834 *An Act for the Amendment and Better Administration of the Laws Relating to the Poor in England and Wales:* http://users.ox.ac.uk/~peter/workhouse.
22. Earlier Gilbert Unions still in existance in the first half of the 1840s can be identified by the *Ninth Annual Report of the poor Law Commissioners* in 1843. *Ninth Annual Report of the Poor Law Commissioners* (468) xxi, 1843.
23. N.C. Edsall, *The Anti-Poor Law Movement,* 1834-44 (1971); J. Knot, *Popular Opposition to the* 1834, *Poor Law* (1986).
24. See Appendix 3/5, Home Office Correspondence, 1782-1959.
25. G. Howells, 'Emigration and the New Poor Law: The Norfolk Emigration Fever of 1836', *Rural History: Economy, Society, Culture,* 11, 2 (2003), pp.145-64.
26. E.T. Hurren, 'Labourers are Revolting: Penalising the Poor and a Political Reaction in the Brixworth Union, Northamptonshire, 1875-1885', *Rural History: Economy, Society, Culture,* 11, 1 (2000), pp.37-55; E.T. Hurren, 'Agricultural Trade Unionism and the Crusade against Outdoor Relief: Poor Law Politics in Brixworth Union, Northamptonshire, 1870-75, *Agricultural History Review,* 28, 2 (2000), pp.200-22.
27. S. Thomas, 'Power, Paternalism, Patronage and Philanthropy: The Wyndhams and the New Poor Law in Petworth', *The Local Historian,* 32, 2 (2002), pp.99-117. [1830s]; the records are held at Petworth House but can be consulted via the West Sussex Record Office.
28. D. Hunter, 'The Poor Law in Hackney a Century Ago', *The Local Historian,* 34, 4 (2004), especially pp.249-51.
29. PP. *Royal Commission on the Aged Poor: Minutes of Evidence, with Appendix and Index* (1895); *Select Committee Report, Minutes of Evidence etc. on the Aged Deserving Poor* (1899).
30. PP. *Report of the Royal Commission on the Poor Laws and Relief of Distress,* xxxvii (1909 – both majority and minority reports are included).
31. For an example of this see the transcription for MH 12/14720: P. Carter (ed.), *Bradford Poor Law Union: Papers and Correspondence with the Poor Law Commission, October 1834-January 1839* (2004).
32. Very few papers survive after 1900 due to war damage during the Second World War.
33. The master of the Barnet Union, then in Hertfordshire, kept a diary from 1836 to 1838, which was partly transcribed by Robert M. Gutchen in *Down and out in Hertfordshire* (1984); it will shortly appear in its entirety in a Hertfordshire Record Society volume.
34. One of the fullest sets of records is for the Leicester Union (ref 26D68), including three (out of four) sets of letter books. See K.M. Thompson, 'The Leicester Poor Law Union, 1836-1871', PhD, University of Leicester (1988).
35. The Workhouse, Upton Road, Southwell, Nottinghamshire, NG25 0PT.
36. There are examples all over the country, such as in Ware (Hertfordshire), Saffron Walden (Essex) and much of the old Middlesex Pauper Lunatic Asylum at Hanwell (which had been part of St Bernard's Wing, Ealing Health Authority, as late as the 1990s).
37. See Andy Reid, *The Union Workhouse. A Study Guide for Local Historians and Teachers* (1994, 1998).
38. For details of surviving workhouses (as well as much more on poor law, relief and workhouse history) see http://users.ox.ac.uk/~peter/workhouse
39. See also W. Hannington, *The Problem of the Distressed Areas,* 1937.
40. B. Swann and M. Turnbull, *Records of Interest to Social Scientists,* 1919 *to* 1939*: Introduction* (1971); B. Swann and M. Turnbull, *Records of Interest to Social Scientists, Unemployment Insurance,* 1911 *to* 1939 (1975); and B. Swann and M. Turnbull, *Records of Interest to Social Scientists,* 1919-1939*: Employment and Unemployment* (1978).
41. Swann and Turnbull, *Employment and Unemployment,* pp.290, 320-1.
42. Many VCHs have sections on charities. S.M. Dawson, *A History of Hobbayne's Charity: With Particular Reference to the Period* 1612-1878 (1964) is an example of an early charity being established in the 15th century; S. Fowler, '"One Hundred Years of Instant Help": The Richmond Philanthropic Society, 1870-1970', *The Local Historian,* 27, 3 (1997), pp.144-63. The records of the Peabody Trust are held at The London Metropolitan Archive, see K. Chater, 'Builder of the Poor', *Ancestors,* 31 (2005), pp.40-3.
43. On almshouses see R. Burlison, 'For the Sake of the Poor', *Ancestors,* 32 (2005), pp.36-40; and www.institutions.org.uk/almshouses (currently the coverage is patchy with a fair coverage for some counties but not for others; with a request for further details to be sent to the website author).
44. J.D. Martin, *Leicester Charity Organisation Society* 1869-1976 (1976).
45. B. and J. Hurley, 'Those in Whom We Trust', *Ancestors,* 31 (2005), pp.32-4.
46. NAS, *History at Source: Poor Relief in Scotland* (1995), covers the 15th to 20th centuries and includes facsimile copies of original records.
47. R. Mitchison, *The Old Poor Law in Scotland: The Experience of Poverty,* 1574–1845 (2000).
48. R.A. Cage, *The Scottish Poor Law* 1745-1845 (1981), pp.158-69.
49. For details of surviving workhouses (as well as much more of poor law, relief and workhouse history) see the Scottish pages at http://users.ox.ac.uk/~peter/workhouse

50. In the SCAN Virtual Vault you can see examples of poor relief records from Scottish archives.
51. J.A. Haythornthwaite (ed.), *Scotland in the Nineteenth Century: An Analytical Bibliography of Material Relating to Scotland in Parliamentary Papers,* 1800-1900 (1993).

Chapter 9: Sickness and Health, pp.102-12

1. R. Porter, *Disease, Medicine and Society in England* 1550-1860 (1987), pp.23-7.
2. Herefordshire Bishop's Registers are at the Herefordshire RO in record series AL 19.
3. Staffordshire RO, General Accounts, Lordship of Holderness D641/1/2/239, Accounts of lands in Holderness held as of Honour of Albemarle, escheated to crown: by death of tenants *[1349];* East Sussex Record Office: Additional Manuscripts AMSJ, Court roll of Crowham manor in Westfield, 1327-1375 (with gaps), the effects of the Black Death shown on mm 3-5.
4. TNA C 143/322/6, 30 EDWARD III.
5. TNA C 1/42/108. 1386-1486 [from the TNA catalogue] regarding a case brought by Nicholas Sax, a London surgeon.
6. See Appendix 3/6, records of the Privy Council; 3/4, State Papers Domestic and 3/5, Home Office Correspondence, 1782-1959.
7. www.british-history.ac.uk/source.asp?pubid=107 See also M. Pelling and F. White, *Medical Conflicts in Early Modern London: Patronage, Physicians and Irregular Practitioners* 1550-1640 (2003).
8. http://library.wellcome.ac.uk
9. A search on the A2A web site revealed references in London Metropolitan Archives, as might be expected, but also references to material elsewhere. See also copies of the *London Gazette.*
10. R. Barker, 'The Local Study of the Plague', *The Local Historian,* 14,6 (1981), pp.332-40.
11. See Appendix 3/2, The National Register of Archives and Archives Network Links.
12. E. Chadwick, *Report on the Sanitary Condition of the Labouring Population* (1842, repr. 1965).
13. *Report of the Royal Commission on the Health of Towns, HC* 1844 *xvii and* 1845 *xviii.*
14. For a useful short overview see J. Cassidy, 'Endangered Lives: Health and the Victorians', *Ancestors,* 17 (2003-4), pp.34-40.
15. B. Lancaster, '"The Croydon Case", Chadwicks' Model Town Under Siege', *The Local Historian,* 34, 1 (2004), pp.17-27.
16. Introduction to catalogue of LBH records in Hertfordshire Archives and Local Studies.
17. K.J. Dodds, 'Much ado About Nothing?: Cholera, Local Politics and Public Health In 19th-century Reading', *The Local Historian,* 21, 4 (1991), pp.168-76.
18. First report of the Royal Sanitary Commission with the Minutes of Evidence up to 5th August 1869, xxxii, 1868-9; PP, Royal Sanitary Commission: Second Report, Volume I, xxxv, 1871 and PP, Royal Sanitary Commission: Sanitary Laws: Second Report, Volume III, Part ii, xxxi, 1874.
19. Annual report of Joseph Dare, quoted in Malcolm Elliott, *Victorian Leicester* (1979), pp.74-5.
20. The first man to be designated a Medical Officer of Health was in Liverpool, in January 1847, but Malcolm Elliott argues in his book *Victorian Leicester* (1979) that the Leicester appointments preceded him; the local board was rebuked for making the appointments as the General Board had not yet prescribed the duties of such officers.
21. Elliott, *op. cit.*, p.88.
22. C. Charlton, 'The Fight Against Vaccination: The Leicester Demonstration of 1885', *Local Population Studies,* 30 (1983), pp.60-6.
23. J.T. Biggs, *Sanitation Versus Vaccination* (1912).
24. C. Booth, *Life and Labour of the People* (1889 – in 2 vols.; the title of Vol 2 reads *Labour and Life of the People*); *Labour and Life of the People,* 2nd edn (1889-1891); *Life and Labour of the People in London* (1892-1897); *Life and Labour of the People in London* (1902-1903).
25. www.booth.lse.ac.uk
26. St Bartholomew's Hospital Archives and Museum: St Bartholomew's Hospital; St Thomas material is at the London Metropolitan Archives.
27. See for example, E. Frizelle and J. Martin, *The Leicester Royal Infirmary,* 1771-1971 (1971).
28. The HOSPREC database is at www.nationalarchives.gov.uk/hospitalrecords
29. See Appendix 3/1, Parliamentary Papers.
30. PP. *Social Insurance and Allied Services Report* (1942-3), v, Cmd.6404, Cmd.6405.
31. For example, W.G. Hall, 'A Country General Practitioner at Work in Somerset, 1686-1706: John Westover of Wedmore', *The Local Historian,* 20, 4 (1990), pp.173-86; J. Douch, 'William Waylett (1728-1815): Surgeon and Man-Midwife of Lydd', *The Local Historian,* 23, 3 (1993), pp.163-9; A. Johnson, *The Diary of Thomas Giordani Wright: Newcastle Doctor,* 1826-1829 (2001).

Chapter 10: Housing, pp.113-24

1. W.E. Tate, *Domesday of English Enclosure Acts and Awards* (1978). The *Domesday* indicates whether or not a map and plan is part of the award.
2. N. Barratt, *Tracing the History of Your House: A Guide to Sources* (2001). This book is based on sources at TNA. It goes much further than tracing *a house* and really moves into sources which trace *housing.*
3. W.M. and F. Marcham (eds), *Court Rolls of the Bishop of London's Manor of Hornsey,* 1603-1701 (1929), pp.78, 82.

4. H. Richardson (ed.), *The Court Rolls of the Manor of Acomb* (1969), pp.9, 20.
5. J. Middleton, *View of the Agriculture of the County of Middlesex* (1798), p.103 [p.117 in the 2nd edn].
6. P. Carter, 'Poor Relief Strategies: Women, Children and Enclosure in Hanwell, Middlesex, 1780 to 1816'. *The Local Historian*, 25, 3 (1995), pp.164-77. [Using the Hanwell vestry minutes held at the Ealing Local Studies Library.]
7. For example J. Holman, *Index of Surrey Probate Inventories 16th-19th Centuries* (1986).
8. Hertfordshire Archives and Local Studies, D/EP F369-70, 1789.
9. Nancy Cox and Jeff Cox, 'Probate inventories: the legal background – Part I', *The Local Historian*, vol. 16, 3 (1984), p.136.
10. See, for example, Tom Arkell, 'Interpreting Probate Inventories' in Tom Arkell, Nesta Evans and Nigel Goose, *When Death Do us Part* (2000), pp.72-3.
11. David Hey, *Family History and Local History in England* (1987), p.54.
12. Lionel M. Munby (ed.), *Short Guides to Records. First series* (1994), p.31.
13. J. Stobart, 'The Economic and Social Worlds of Rural Craftsmen-Retailers in 18th-Century Cheshire', *Agricultural History Review*, 52, II pp.141-60.
14. David Hey, *The Oxford Companion to Local and Family History* (1996), pp.238-9; Nancy Cox and Jeff Cox, *The Local Historian*, vol. 16, 3, 4 and 8; vol. 17, 2 (1984-6).
15. J. Spavold, 'Using a Relational Database: The Example of the Church Gresley Inventories', *The Local Historian*, 26, 2 (1996), pp.89-101.
16. Herrick MSS, ref DG9/2409.
17. For further details on inventories see K. Grannum and N. Taylor, *Wills and Other Probate Records* (2004), pp.91-106.
18. M.W. Beresford, 'Building History from Fire Insurance Records', *Urban History Yearbook* (1976), pp.7-14; M.W. Beresford, 'Prometheus Insured: The Sun Fire Agency in Leeds During Urbanization, 1716-1826', *Economic History Review*, 35, 3 (1982), pp.373-89; L.D. Schwarz and L.J. Jones, 'Wealth, Occupations and Insurance in the Late Eighteenth Century: The Policy Registers of the Sun Fire Office', *Economic History Review*, 36, 3 (1983), pp.365-73; T.V. Jackson, 'The Sun Fire Office and the Local Historian', *The Local Historian*, 17, 3 (1986), pp.141-9; D. Hawkings, *Fire Insurance Records for Family and Local Historians 1696–1920* (2003).
19. For more details and information on the location of the maps see P.A. Neaverson, 'Fire Insurance Plans' in K.M. Thompson (ed.), *Short Guides to Records* (1997).
20. These sources are covered in detail in N.W. Alcock, *Documenting the History of Your House* (2003); an excellent guide for individual houses.
21. See W.B. Stephens, *Sources*, pp.312-13 for details on other periodicals. The first 10 volumes of *The Builder* are available at www.bodley.ox.ac.uk/ilej.
22. W.H.G. Armytage, 'The Chartist Land Colonies, 1846-1848', *Agricultural History*, 32, 2 (1958), pp.87-96; P. Searby, 'Great Dodford and the Later History of the Chartist Land Schemes', *Agricultural History Review*, 16, 1 (1968), pp.32-45; P. Searby, 'Creating Paradise: the Chartist Land Scheme and its Cottages 1843- 1849', *The Local Historian*, 34, 4 (2004), pp.214-226. [The last article refers to the National Trust scheme.]
23. E. Chadwick, *Report on the Sanitary Condition of the Labouring Population* (1842), reprinted with an introduction by M.W. Flinn (1965).
24. See www.booth.lse.ac.uk
25. Quoted in Malcolm Elliott, *Victorian Leicester* (1979), pp.102-3.
26. *Ibid.*, pp.119-21.
27. See Gillian Cookson, 'Building Plans', in K.M. Thompson (ed.), *Short Guides to Records* (1997), pp.79-82.
28. A. Cox, *Public Housing* (1984). [A guide to central and local government, newspaper, photographic, film, private and oral sources for public housing in London.]
29. C.G. Pooley and S. Irish, *The Development of Corporation Housing in Liverpool 1869-1945* (1984).
30. S. Durgan, 'Providing for "the Needs and Purses of the Poor": Council Housing in Chelmsford Before 1914', *The Local Historian*, 33, 3 (2003), pp.175-89.
31. For details of proposed working-class housing in Glasgow see: www.gdl.cdlr.stratch.ac.uk/redclyde/redclyo82
32. W. Hannington, *The Problem of the Distressed Areas* (1937); includes a series of photographs showing examples of slum housing.
33. Miller, Mervyn, *Letchworth. The First Garden City*, 2nd edn (2002).
34. Filler, Roger, *Welwyn Garden City* (1986).
35. The Town and Country Planning Association was founded by Sir Ebenezer Howard in 1899 and is the oldest charity concerned with planning and the environment; see its web site, www.tcpa.org.uk.
36. E.g. 3136; the accounts were published in A. Hamilton Thompson, 'The Building Accounts of Kirby Muxloe Castle, 1480-1484' in *Transactions of the Leicestershire Archaeological Society*, vol. xi (1919-20), pp.193-345.
37. There is a special web site devoted to Pevsner and his books: www.pevsner.co.uk.

Chapter 11: Radicalism and Unrest, pp.125-42

1. There are published calendars for the Close Rolls in C 54, Fine Rolls in C 60 and Patent Rolls in C 66.

2. R.B. Dobson (ed.), *The Peasants' Revolt of 1831*, 2nd edn (1983); for example Medieval Sourcebook: *Anonimalle Chronicle*: English Peasants' Revolt 1381 at www.fordham.edu/halsall/source/anon1381
3. A. Charlesworth (ed.), *An Atlas of Rural Protest in Britain,* 1548-1900 (1983), see chapter 2 for an overview of the events.
4. See Appendix 3/2, The National Register of Archives and Archives Network Links.
5. See Appendix 3/4, State Papers Domestic.
6. See Appendix 3/5, Records of the Privy Council.
7. See Appendix 3/7, Records of the Treasury Solicitor.
8. Brit Lib, Lansdowne, 2, 25; Brit Lib, Stowe 150 ff. 184, 186 and Bod Lib, MS. Eng. c. 3190, ff. 143-4.
9. See p.3.
10. We are thinking here of machine-breaking in general and not only the specific Luddite disturbances of *c.*1811-3. See in particular A. Randall, *Before the Luddites: Custom, Community and Machinery in the English Woollen Industry,* 1776-1809 (1991) and A. Charlesworth, D. Gilbert, A. Randall, H. Southall and C. Wrigley, *An Atlas of Industrial Protest in Britain* 1750-1990 (1996).
11. J. Neeson, *Commoners: Common Right, Enclosure and Social Change in England* (1993).
12. E.P. Thompson, 'The Moral Economy of the English Crowd in the Eighteenth Century', *Past and Present*, 50 (1971), pp.76-136; reprinted in E.P. Thompson, *Customs in Common* (1991), pp.185-258; you will also find in *Customs* his further reflections in *ibid.*, 'The Moral Economy Revisited', pp.259-351. For the spread and prevalence of food riots see A. Charlesworth (ed.), *An Atlas of Rural Protest in Britain,* 1548-1900 (1983), pp.63-118.
13. W. Brown (ed.), *Yorkshire Star Chamber Proceedings*, Yorkshire Archaeological Society (1908), pp.178-81 [no. LXXVIII].
14. TNA ASSI 35/21/9. From J.S. Cockburn, *Calendar of Assize Records, Hertfordshire Indictments, Elizabeth I* (1973), pp.28-9.
15. TNA. ASSI 35/45/3. From J.S. Cockburn, *Calendar of Assize Records, Hertfordshire Indictments, James I* (1975), p.6.
16. TNA ASSI 35/49/2. From J.S. Cockburn, *Calendar of Assize Records, Essex Indictments, James I* (1982), p.31 (no. 190).
17. TNA ASSI 35/52/1. From *ibid.*, p.81 (no. 521).
18. TNA PC 1/2/165.
19. TNA SP 36/50.
20. TNA HO 42/34.
21. TNA KB 1/30. Easter 40. Geo. III, no 2. For further information of the case and a reproduction of the 'portrait' see Thompson, *Customs*, plate VI between pp.276-7, 481-2.
22. www.oldbaileyonline.org
23. See Appendix 3/8, records of the Treasury Solicitor, Appendix 3/4, State Papers Domestic, Appendix 3/6, records of the Privy Council.
24. See Appendix 3/5, Home Office Correspondence.
25. See Appendix 3/4, State Papers Domestic.
26. E.g. *A relation of the cruelties and barbarous murthers and other misdemeanors done upon some of the inhabitants of Enfield, Edmonton, Southmyms, Hadley* (1659); *A Relation of the riotous insurrection of divers inhabitants of Enfield* (1659); *Bloudy News from Enfield* (1659). See D. Pam, *The Story of Enfield Chase* (1984).
27. Aylmer, G.E., *The Levellers in the English Revolution* (1975).
28. See the PRO Handbook 12, *Records of the Forfeited Estates Commission* (1968).
29. *A List of Persons Concerned in the Rebellion* (1890) and Dobson, D., *Directory of Scots Banished to the American Plantations* (1984); see also footnote below.
30. J. Oates, 'Sources for the Study of the Jacobite Rebellions of 1715 and 1745 in England', *The Local Historian*, 32, 3 (2002), pp.156-72. B. Lenman, *The Jacobite Risings in Britain* 1689-1746 (1980), gives references to a wide range of published material; R.C. Jarvis, *Collected Papers on the Jacobite Risings* (1971/2), in 2 vols, gives references to unpublished material at TNA and elsewhere; R.C. Jarvis, *The Jacobite Risings of* 1715 *and* 1745 (1954), extracts of Lieutenancy and Quarter Sessions records of Cumberland; B.G. Seton and J.G. Arnot (eds), *The Prisoners of the '45* (1928-9), has a tabular analysis of the careers and fates of most of the prisoners and references to the documents used; T.B. Howell, *A Complete Collection of State Trials* ... vols XV and XVIII (1816), includes the trial records of some of the more notable prisoners with some texts from reports of Sir Michael Foster (trial judge) who compiled *A Report of Some Proceedings on the Commission for the Trial of the Rebels in the Year* 1746 ... (1792).
31. M. Thale (ed.), *Selections from the Papers of the London Corresponding Society,* 1792-1799 (1983); M.T. Davis, *London Corresponding Society,* 1792-1799 (2002) [6-volume set of pamphlets, periodical and parliamentary reports].
32. J Gale Jones, *A Political Tour Through Rochester, Chatham, Maidstone, Gravesend, &c.* (1796, repr. 1997), with an introduction by P. MacDougall.
33. For some of the problems in evaluating the Home Office material see C. Emsley, 'The Home Office and its Sources of Information and Investigation, 1791-1801', *English Historical Review*, 1979, 94 (372) pp.532-61.
34. T. B. Howell, *A Complete Collection of State Trials* ... vols XXII-XXVIII covers the 1790s (1817-20).

35. National Maritime Museum: *Captain Alexander Hood* 1758-1798, *Official papers. Papers relating to Spithead Mutiny, including correspondence with Admiral Lord Bridport.* MKH/15; *Sir Edward William Campbell Richard Owen, Admiral* 1771-1849, *Official Papers. Reflections on the Mutiny at Spithead* 1797. COO/2/a; *Logbook of the Clyde, Captain Charles Cunningham, kept by John Smith,* 1796-1800. *With an account of the mutiny at the Nore.* BRK/15; *Journal of the mutiny at the Nore* 1797, *probably kept by Captain W.J. Gore, aide de camp to Sir Charles Grey.* HSR/B/12; *Memorandum from Sir Charles Grey to Mr Dundas on the mutiny at the Nore dated* 25 *June,* 1797. AGC/24/5.
36. J.V. Orth, *Combination and Conspiracy: A Legal History of Trade Unionism,* 1721-1906 (1992), p.27.
37. C.R. Dobson, *Masters and Journeymen: a Prehistory of Industrial Relations* 1717-1800 (1980). Dobson uses selected newspapers of the basis of the research to uncover much early trade union/combination activity and has listed these in his appendices.
38. See Appendix 3/2, The National Register of Archives and Archives Network Links.
39. See Appendix 3/4, State Papers Domestic; Appendix 3/6, Records of the Privy Council; Appendix 3/8, Records of the Treasury Solicitor; and Appendix 3/5, Home Office Correspondence.
40. A. Aspinall, *The Early English Trade Unions: Documents from the Home Office Papers in the Public Record Office* (1949). Aspinall includes transcriptions from HO 40, 41 42, 43, 44, 48, 49, 73, 79 and 102. However HO 42 is the most common class used. There is a general index at the end of the volume which enables a search by place. M. Thomis, *Luddism in Nottinghamshire* (1972).
41. See also P. Carter, 'The National Archive and English Working-Class Politics, 1790-1918: An Introduction to the Papers of the Home Office and Treasury Solicitor for Local Historians', *Local History Magazine*, 74 (1999), pp.12-24.
42. See W.H. Fraser, 'Letters From Lancashire, 1811-2', *Bulletin of the Society for the Study of Labour History*, 44 (1982), pp.15-17. Fraser was working on Scottish Weavers' Association papers (1808-12) held at NAS for a publication for the *Journal of the Scottish Labour History Society* when he came across the correspondence.
43. P. Keen, *The Popular Radical Press in Britain,* 1817-1821 (2003). This volume reproduces facsimiles of some of the rarer periodicals of the period; see also L. Nattrass, *William Cobbett: Selected Writings* (1998). Contains articles from the 1790s, extensive sections from *Cobbett's Weekly Political Register* through to his pamphlets in the 1830s.
44. Although dated, in some ways this is still the best place to start: E. Hobsbawm and G. Rudé, *Captain Swing* (1969). The place index on pp.374-82 is an excellent starting point for local researchers at TNA into the agricultural disturbances of 1830-1. However, essential now is the recent M. Holland (ed.), *Swing Unmasked: the Agricultural Riots of 1830 to 1832 and their Wider Implications* (2005). The additional CD of data is excellent for local historians.
45. A useful Parliamentary Papers list is provided in *Captain Swing* above.
46. Jill Chambers has produced (and is continuing to produce) a series of county volumes with day-by-day accounts of the riots and trials in each county. Complete at present is Essex Machine Breakers (2004); Wiltshire Machine Breakers, 2 vols. (1993); Hampshire Machine Breakers, 2nd edn (1996); Buckinghamshire Machine Breakers (1998); Berkshire Machine Breakers (1999); Berkshire Machine Breakers (1999); Gloucestershire Machine Breakers (2002) and Dorset Machine Breakers (2003).
47. R. Johnson, *Sentenced to Cross the Raging Sea: The Story of Sam Johnson, Victim of Oldham's Bankside Riot of* 1834 (2004). It is heavily footnoted and littered with practical pointers for similar pieces of research.
48. M.E. Rose, 'The Anti-Poor Law Movement in the North of England', *Northern History*, I (1966); N. Edsall, *The Anti-Poor Law Movement,* 1834-44 (1971); J. Knott, *Popular Opposition to the* 1834 *Poor Law* (1986); R. Wells, *Resistance to the New Poor Law in the Rural South* (1985).
49. See the various reports, letters and newspaper accounts of the riots in Bradford in 1837 in TNA MH 12/14720; this volume has been transcribed and published in P. Carter, *Bradford Poor Law Union: Papers and Correspondence with the Poor Law Commission, October* 1834 *to January* 1839 (2004).
50. For example, a source-based anthology of diaries and journals relating to the Great Reform Act etc: E.A. Smith, *Reform or Revolution? A Diary of Reform in England,* 1830-32 (1992); a near contemporary account of factory reform in Alfred Kydd, *The History of the Factory Movement* (1857, reprinted 1966). Examples of Parliamentary Papers include: *Report from the Select Committee on the Petitions for Reform in Parliament*, 263 (1830-31); *Reports Upon the Boundaries of the Several Cities Burghs and Towns in Scotland, in Respect to the Election of Members to Serve in Parliament; with Plans*, 408 (1831-32); *Report of the Royal Commission on the Administration and Practical Operation of Poor Law*, 44, xxvii-xxxviii (1834); *Dorchester unionists: Indictment and Record of Conviction, in Prosecution Against G. Loveless and others*, 1834, 205 (1835)
51. TNA. MH 32/57. Assistant Poor Law Commissioners and Inspectors, Charles Mott's correspondence, 1838-1843.
52. MH 32/3. Assistant Poor Law Commissioners and Inspectors, Colonel A. C. a'Court's correspondence, 1836.
53. C. Godfrey and J. Epstein, 'Interviews of Chartist Prisoners, 1840-1841', *Bulletin of the Society for the Study of Labour History*, 34 (1977), pp.27-34; for details of the prisoners see www.chartists.net/political-prisoners-1840. There is also some useful Chartist material at www.curl.ac.uk/rslpguide/guidehp, which is a guide to 19th-century pamphlets.

54. Further material from this period onwards is explained and illustrated in S. Folwer, *Sources for Labour History* (1995) [guide to PRO/TNA records].
55. British Library, ADD 54512. Sir C.J. Napier Papers, Vol. III (f. 259).
56. NAS, GD1/1045/6. Letter from Rev. Forrest Frew to his daughter, Catherine, 28 May 1841.
57. J.F.C. Harrison and D. Thompson, *Bibliography of the Chartist Movement* (1978).
58. D.J.V. Jones, *The Last Rising: The Newport Insurrection of* 1839 (1985), pp.230-1.
59. For example www.chartism.com contains lists of manuscript sources, newspapers, reference and collected works etc. for the later Chartist phase.
60. *Report of the Commissioners of Inquiry for South Wales*, 531, xvi (1844).
61. Trades Union Commission, *The Sheffield Outrages* (1867, repr. 1971), with an introduction by Sidney Pollard.
62. See Appendix 3/2, The National Register of Archives and Archives Network Links.
63. John Saville, *The Labour Archive at the University of Hull* (1989).
64. See also I. MacDougall, *Catalogue of Some Labour Records in Scotland and Some Scots Records Outside Scotland* (1978).
65. A. Marsh and V. Ryan, *Historical Directory of Trade Unions*, 3 vols. (1980-94); very useful for tracing the various different names of unions as they change/merge.
66. www.genesis.ac.uk
67. The Labour Party and Communist Party of Great Britain material can be found on www.nmlhweb.org and for ILP records see www.lse.ac.uk
68. www.unionhistory.info
69. www.history.ac.uk/hop
70. J.R. Vincent, *Pollbooks: How Victorians Voted* (1967); J. Sims, *A Handlist of British Parliamentary Poll Books* (1984); R.H.A. Cheffins, *Parliamentary Constituencies and Their Registers Since* 1832*: a List of Constituencies from the Great Reform Act with the British Library's Holdings of Electoral Registers Together with the Library's Holdings of Burgess Rolls, Poll Books and Other Registers* (1998); Society of Genealogists, *Directories and Poll Books Including Almanacs and Electoral Rolls in the Library of the Society of Genealogists,* 6th edn (1995); J. Gibson and C. Rogers, *Poll Books c.*1696-1872*: A Directory to Holdings in Great Britain*, 3rd edn (1994); J. Gibson and C. Rogers, *Electoral Registers Since* 1832, 2nd edn (1990).
71. F.W.S. Craig, *British Parliamentary Election Results* 1832-85, 2nd edn (1989); *British Parliamentary Election Results* 1885-1918, 2nd edn (1989); *British Parliamentary Election Results* 1918-49, 3rd edn (1983); *British Parliamentary Election Results* 1950-73, 2nd edn (1989); *British Parliamentary Election Results* 1974-83 (1984); and C. Rallings and M. Thrasher, *British Parliamentary Election Results* 1983-97 (1999).

Chapter 12: Law and Order, pp.143-60

1. J.H. Baker, *An Introduction to English Legal History* (4th edn, 2002) traces the development of the main features of English legal institutions from Anglo-Saxon times to the present; it is a standard work.
2. W.J. King, 'Untapped Resources for Social Historians: Court Leet Records', *Journal of Social History*, 15 (1982), quoted in J.A. Sharpe, *Crime in Early Modern England,* 1550-1750 (1984), p.26.
3. C.M. Fraser and K. Emsley, *The Court Rolls of the Manor of Wakefield, October* 1639 *to September* 1640 (1977), p.68 [12 October 1639], p.107 [16 October 1639] and p.135 [13 April 1640].
4. Many of these have been published as record society volumes and should be checked before attempting to look through the originals, as they will contain further information on the records and their arrangement; for example C.A.F. Meekings and D. Crook, *The* 1235 *Surrey Eyre* (1979). See also D. Crook, *Records of the General Eyre* (1982).
5. J. Sharpe, *Crime in Early Modern England* (1984), p.24; Sharpe states there are very few for the reign of Charles I and refers to a very late hanging case at the North Yorkshire Quarter Sessions in 1654.
6. See J.S. Cockburn, *A History of English Assizes,* 1558-1714 (1972); for discussions on the problems associated with the records. L. Knafla, *Kent at Law,* 1602 (1994) and D.T. Hawkings, *Criminal Ancestors* (1992); also covers assizes and related records.
7. See J.S. Cockburn, *A History of English Assizes*, 1558-1714 (1972) and his *Calendars of Assize Records* for the Home Circuit (1975-97) [Essex, Hertfordshire, Kent, Surrey and Sussex for 1558-1625, continued to 1688 for Kent]. These are calendars of indictments.
8. www.oldbaileyonline.org.
9. P. Linebaugh, 'The Ordinary of Newgate and His Account', in J.S. Cockburn (ed.), *Crime in England,* 1550-1800 (1977).
10. A database of cases taken from the Welsh Gaol Files for 1730 to 1830 is fully searchable online at the NLW web.
11. See R. Paley and S. Stark, 'Quarter Sessions Focus', *Ancestors*, 17 (2003-4), pp.16-18; R. Radcliffe, 'Keeping the Peace', *Ancestors*, 17 (2003-4), pp.19-25; G. Redmonds, 'Scenes from an Ordinary Life', *Ancestors*, 17 (2003-4), pp.26-32.
12. The 18th-century Denbighshire Quarter Sessions Rolls have been published on a CD-ROM; *Unrolling the Past: Denbighshire Quarter Sessions Rolls,* 1706-1800, Denbighshire Archives Service (2003).
13. G. Lamoine, *Charges to the Grand Jury,* 1689-1803 (1992).
14. E. Crittall (ed.), *The Justicing Notebook of William Hunt,* 1744-49 (1982); E. Silverthorne (ed.), *Deposition Book of Richard Wyatt, JP,* 1767-1776 (1978) and R. Paley (ed.), *Justice in* 18*th Century Hackney: The*

Justicing Notebook of Henry Norris and the Hackney Petty Sessions Book [1730-53] (1991). See also *Summary Convictions: Minor Offences in Wiltshire 1693-1903* CD produced by the Wiltshire Family History Society.

15. See Cecil Sinclair, *Tracing your Scottish Ancestors* (1990), pp.89-90.
16. Some trials have been printed in Pitcairns Criminal Trials in Scotland, 1498-1624, 1829-31; records of the Proceedings of the Justiciary Court, Edinburgh, 1661-1678, 1905 (also now available in CDROM version). Others were published in the Notable Scottish Trials series which began in 1905. These volumes included transcript of the trials and an introduction by the various editors. In 1911 a series of Notable English Trials was introduced and eventually these were combined as Notable British Trials.
17. *Acta Curiae Almirallatus Scotiae,* 1557-1561/2 (1937).
18. P. Rayner, B. Lenman and G. Parker, *Handlist of Records for the Study of Crime in Early Modern Scotland (to 1747)* (1982).
19. A. Collinson, 'The Implementation of Change in the Nottinghamshire House of Correction at Southwell, 1775-1840' (unpublished certificate thesis, 2000).
20. A still first-rate starting place is S. and B. Webb, *English Prisons Under Local Government* (1922, repr. 1963). More up-to-date general surveys are by S. McConville, *A History of English Penal Administration* 1750-1877 (1981) and *English Local Prisons* 1860-1900*: Next Only to Death* (1995). M. De Lacy, *Prison Reform in Lancashire,* 1700-1850*: A Study in Local Administration* (1986) is an excellent local study with a useful note on general and specific sources for the study of prisons.
21. A card index of people in debtors' prisons in London from 1775 can be consulted at the Corporation of London Records Office.
22. D.T. Hawkings, *Criminal Ancestors: A Guide to Historical Criminal Records in England and Wales* (1992), especially appendices 2, 4, 5, and 6.
23. See appendices in *ibid.*
24. British Library. E.g. 3802.
25. W. Smith, *State of the Gaols in London, Westminster and Borough of Southwark* (1776), Howard, J., *State of the Prisons* (1777) and J. Neild, *The State of the Prisons* (1812).
26. See Powell, *Local History from Blue Books*, p.26; see Appendix 3/1, Parliamentary Papers.
27. *Royal Commission ... to Inquire into the Condition and Treatment of the Prisoners Confined to Birmingham Borough Prison*, 1809 (1854); *Report ... on the Present State of Discipline in Gaols and House of Correction*, 499 (1863).
28. P. Priestley, *Victorian Prison Lives* (1985). It includes over 200 biographies of prisoners, governors, wardens, chaplains and hangmen.
29. Some of the entries from the Edinburgh Tolbooth Warding and Liberation Books, 1657 to 1817 have been published in J. Fairley (ed.), *Book of the Old Edinburgh Club*, vols 4-6, 8, 9, 11 and 12 (see National Archives of Scotland fact sheet on crime and criminals).
30. See Appendix 3/7, Treasury Board Letters and Papers.
31. W. Le Hardy (ed.), *Calendar to the Sessions Books ...* [Hertfordshire] ... 1752-1799 (1935), p.371.
32. See Appendix 3/4, State Papers Domestic.
33. P. Carter, 'Home Office 47: Judges' Reports on Criminals, 1783-1830', *Archives*, XXIX, 110 (2004), pp.50-5; and P. Carter, 'Home Office 47 (judges' reports on criminals 1783-1830): the work of The National Archives Local History Research Group', *The Local Historian*, 34, 2 (2004), pp.80-8. The first set of this material to be listed has been published as *Pardons and Punishments: Judges' Reports on Criminals,* 1783-1830*: HO (Home Office)* 47 (2004). Calendared by the National Archives Local History Research Group, with an introduction by Paul Carter.
34. P. Carter, 'Early Nineteenth-Century Criminal Petitions: An Introduction for Local Historians', *The Local Historian*, 31, 3 (2001), pp.130-53.
35. P. King, *Crime, Justice, and Discretion in England,* 1740-1820 (2000).
36. See Appendix 3/5, Home Office Correspondence.
37. For a detailed guide to modern sources see M. Cale, *Law and Society: An Introduction to Sources for Criminal and Legal History From* 1800 (1996).
38. See Martyn Bennett, 'Constables' Accounts' in K.M. Thompson (ed.), *Short Guides to Records. Second Series* (1997), p.20.
39. Parish Constables Accounts, DE 2559/24, April 4 1663. Record Office for Leicestershire, Leicester and Rutland.
40. T. Palmer, *Tudor Churchwardens' Accounts* (1985), p.196.
41. According to Bennett (see note 38 above), constables' accounts do not survive very often and many of them were destroyed or re-used after they had been audited.
42. J. Kent, *The English Village Constable,* 1580-1642*: A Social and Administrative Study* (1986); Keith Wrightson, 'Two Concepts of Order: Justices, Constables and Jurymen in 17th Century England', in J. Brewer and J. Styles (eds), *An Ungovernable People: The English and Their Law in the Seventeenth and Eighteenth Centuries* (1980).
43. See D. Philips, 'Good Men to Associate and Bad Men to Conspire: Associations for the Prosecution of Felons in England, 1760-1860', in D. Hay and F. Snyder, *Policing and Prosecution in Britain,* 1750-1850 (1989). Philips provides a list of English associations and their known dates of establishments (drawn

from his own research). In the same volume see also the county study by King, P.J.R., 'Prosecution Associations and Their Impact in 18th Century Essex'.

44. H. Fielding, *An Inquiring into the Cause of the Late Increase of Robberies*, 2nd edn (1757); P. Colquhoun, *Treatise on the Functions and Duties of a Constable* (1803); P. Colquhoun, *Treatise on the Police of the Metropolis ...* (1795).
45. Papers used by the Royal Commission Appointed to Inquire as to the Best Means of Establishing an Efficient Constabulary Force PP 1839 XIX [169].
46. I. Bridgeman and C. Emsley, *A Guide to the Archives of the Police Forces of England and Wales* (1989).
47. www.policehistorysociety.co.uk.
48. www.open.ac.uk/Arts/history/policing/index.
49. See also Powell, *Local History from Blue Books*, p.26 and see Appendix 3/1, Parliamentary Papers.

Chapter 13: National and Local Administration, pp.161-74

1. Taken from the Parliament Website: www.parliament.uk/works/parliament.cfm
2. For example, R. Butt, *The History of Parliament: the Middle Ages* (1989); M.A.R. Graves, *The Tudor Parliament* (1985).
3. See also M.F. Bond, *Guide to the Records of Parliament* (1971).
4. The Parliamentary Archives are made up of the Records of the Houses of Lords and Commons, other official collections relating to Parliament, private papers of politicians, political bodies and pressure groups, and records relating to the Palace of Westminster.
5. All are listed on the A2A catalogue.
6. To search the catalogue of the Parliamentary Archives see the Parliamentary Archives at www.parliament.uk/parliamentary_publications_and_archives/parliamentary_archives.cfm and then see the catalogue option: *Portcullis.*
7. House of Lords Record Office Memoranda, No. 85, *Witnesses before Parliament: A Guide to the Database of Witnesses in Committees on Opposed Private Bills* 1771-1917 (1997)
8. House of Lords Record Office Memoranda, No. 75, *The Papers of 'Britain in Europe': the campaign for a positive vote in the* 1975 *referendum about Britain's continued membership of the European Community* (1988).
9. All of these papers are on the National Register of Archives (NRA).
10. Copies of Hansard can of course be consulted at the House of Lords Record Office as well as being widely available in public libraries.
11. www.history.ac.uk/hop
12. These are mainly held at CROs and this is the recommended route to track down material. However, TNA may hold particular copies of local authority byelaws confirmed by the Local Government Board, Ministry of Health and the Ministry of Housing and Local Government, only for England and Wales; see records series HLG 25. See TNA's Byelaws research guide.
13. Although the records of borough administration will be held locally there is much to be found in Home Office correspondence (including some unlisted material in HO 52). See 3/5, Home Office correspondence: 1782-1959.
14. See K.M. Thompson, 'Power and authority in Leicester, 1820-1870', MA thesis, University of Nottingham (1985).
15. See M. Bailey, 'Trade and Towns in Medieval England: New Insights from Familiar Sources', *The Local Historian*, 29, 4 (1999), pp.194-211.
16. Record Office for Leicestershire, Leicester and Rutland: BRII/17.
17. F.G. Emmison and Irvine Gray, *County Records* (1948, repr. 1967).
18. Surviving Land Tax records are held at CROs although a selection of records centring on the late 18th and early 19th centuries is at TNA in record series IR 8, IR 20, IR 21, IR 22, IR 23, IR 24 and IR 25.
19. For listings of coroners' material see J. Gibson and C. Rogers, *Coroners' Records in England and Wales* (1997).
20. David Dean (ed.), *St Albans Quarter Sessions Rolls* 1784-1820 (1991), pp.25-6.

Chapter 14: Family and Social Life, pp.175-85

1. See David Hey, *The Oxford Companion to Local and Family History* (1996), pp.162-3.
2. Alan MacFarlane, *Marriage and Love in England* 1300-1840 (1986); Houlbrooke, Ralph, *The English Family*, 1450-1700 (1984); and Michael Anderson, *Approaches to the History of the Western Family*, 1500-1914 (1980).
3. See R.B. Outhwaite, 'Age at Marriage in England from the Late Seventeenth to the Nineteenth Century', *Transactions of the Royal Historical Society*, 5th series, no. 23 (1973); Colin D. Rogers and John H. Smith, *Local Family History in England* (1991), pp.30-60.
4. Rogers and Smith, *op. cit.*, p.74.
5. See E.P. Thompson, 'The Sale of Wives', *Customs in Common* (1991), pp.404-66.
6. Rogers and Smith, *op. cit.*, p.37.
7. See, for example, Janet Kennish, 'Rough Music in Black Datchet', *The Local Historian*, vol. 31, no. 3, August 2001, pp.154-67.

8. Rogers and Smith, *op. cit.*, p.61.
9. *Ibid.*, pp.60-4.
10. D. Annal, 'The Secret Life of the Death Duty Register', *Ancestors*, 20 (2004), pp.16-9; S. Colwell, 'Pay as You Go', *Ancestors*, 25 (2004), pp.49-55. See also TNA research guide to wills and death duty records after 1858 for further information.
11. See, for example, Kathryn M. Thompson (ed.), *Rothley in* 1851 (1994), based on work done in a WEA class.
12. It is for this reason that soccer matches traditionally kick off at 3.00 pm; it enabled workers to go home for lunch and get to the match in time.
13. Palmer, Roy, *The Folklore of Leicestershire and Rutland* (1985), p.109.
14. See www.folklore-society.com.
15. R. Palmer, *The Sound of History* (1996).
16. Stephen S. Doree, *Early churchwardens' accounts of Bishops Stortford* 1431-1558 (1994), p.183.
17. See, for example, A. Eyles, F. Gray and A. Readman, *Cinema West Sussex: the First Hundred Years* (1996).
18. See D.M. Owen and S.W. Woodward (eds), *The Minute Book of the Spalding Gentlemen's Society*, 1712-1755 (1981); the society met in a local coffee house to support mutual benevolence and their improvement in the liberal sciences and polite learning and discussed antiquities, art, astronomy, health matters, water engines and much more.
19. For example, the Grand Tour diary of the 3rd Earl Cowper as Lord Fordwich, 1757-60, and associated letters, in Hertfordshire Archives and Local Studies, refs D/P F308, DE/Na F8, 57, 69.
20. Wisbech museum in Cambridgeshire, for example, is the Diocesan Record Office for a part of west Norfolk and holds parish records for the area, as well as other material.
21. A list of charters conferring rights over markets and fairs in the period 1 John to 22 Edward IV (1199-1483) was published as Appendix XIX to *The First Report of the Royal Commission on Market Rights and Tolls* (1889), from which a card index has been compiled by TNA giving the precise modern references to the grants cited. Summaries of these grants (but not complete translations) can be found in the printed *Calendars of Charter Rolls, Close Rolls* and *Patent Rolls*, which are available in major reference libraries as well as at TNA. This list, however, omits grants made by special jurisdictions (notably the Duchy of Lancaster and the Palatinates of Chester, Durham and Lancaster). For the period since 1483 there is no comprehensive list of grants. Enrolments noted in the Calendars of Charter Rolls (to 1516), Close Rolls (to 1509) and Patent Rolls (to 1575) have been included in TNA card index. Grants that could be traced through lists of Inquisitions *ad quod damnum* and the *Brevia Regia* and verified from the indexes to the patent rolls, were tabulated in the Appendix to the *Final Report of the Royal Commission* (1891), and these are also in the card index. See also the online Gazetteer of Markets and Fairs in England and Wales to 1516 at www.history.ac.uk/cmh/gaz/gazweb2.
22. See V. Toulmin, 'The National Fairground Archives: Its Origins, Development and Holdings', *The Local Historian*, 33, 2 (2003), pp.74-82. This is an explanatory article on the archive and where material may be found.

Appendices, pp.186-202

1. For further details see Horwitz, H., *Chancery Equity Records and Proceedings*, 1600-1800, 1998. The various record series mentioned here are listed to varying degrees of adequacy. See the Chancery Research Guides at TNA website for updates on how the records can be searched.
2. For further details see Horwitz, H., *Exchequer Equity Records and Proceedings*, 1649-1841, 2001; Bryson, W.H., *The Equity Side of the Exchequer*, Cambridge, 1975 and D.B. Fowler, *The Practice of the Court of Exchequer* (1975, in two volumes). The various record series mentioned here are listed to varying degrees of adequacy. See the Exchequer Research Guides at TNA website for updates on how the records can be searched.
3. There is a manuscript list in ZBOX 2/7 for 1803. Not all Treasury papers are recorded in the *Calendars* and all of the records in T 98 are omitted.

Bibliography

The number of books on local history and particular sources has grown enormously in the last couple of decades; the list below can therefore only touch the surface. There are two national specialist publishers of local history: Phillimore & Co. Ltd, Shopwyke Manor Barn, Chichester, PO20 2BG and Sutton Publishing, Phoenix Mill, Thrupp, Stroud, GL5 2BU. In addition many small publishers produce books on a particular locality or subject. The British Association for Local History has also published relevant titles and its books are distributed by Phillimore. Many counties have a Record Society which edits and publishes material of interest to local historians.

Chapter 1: Introduction to Sources

Bristow, J., *The Local Historian's Glossary of Words and Terms* (2001)
Cannon, J. (ed.), *The Oxford Companion to British History* (1997)
Cheney, C.R. (ed.), *A Handbook of Dates For Students of British History* (1945, 2000)
Crosby, A.G. (compiler), *Unlocking the Past: the Local Historian Index and Abstracts* 1952-1999 (2001)
Currie, C.R.J. and Lewis, C.P., *A Guide to English County Histories* (1994, 1997)
Dymond, D., *Researching and Writing history: a practical guide for local historians* (1999)
Emmison, F.G., *Archives and Local History* (1966, 1974)
Emmison, F.G. and Gray, I., *County Records* (1967)
Friar, S., *The Local History Companion* (2001)
Friar, S., *The Sutton Companion to Local History* (2004)
Gooder, E.A., *Latin for Local History* (1961)
Hey, D., *Family History and Local History in England* (1987)
Hey, D., *The Oxford Companion to Local and Family History* (1996)
Hoskins, W.G., *Local History in England* (1959, 1984)
Hoskins, W.G., *Fieldwork in Local History* (1967)
Hoskins, W.G., *The Making of the English Landscape* (1955)
Latham, R.E., *Revised Medieval Latin Word-list* (1965)
Lord, E., *Investigating the Twentieth Century* (1999)
Marshall, H., *Palaeography for Family and Local Historians* (2004)
Mullins, E.L.C., *Texts and Calendars: An Analytical Guide to Serial Publications* (1958)
Mullins, E.L.C., *Texts and Calendars II: An Analytical Guide to Serial Publications,* 1957-1982 (1983)
Munby, L.M. (ed.), *Short Guides to Record: First Series* (1972, 1994)
Munby, L.M., *Dates and Time* (1997)
Murphy, M., *Newspapers and Local History* (1991)
National Library of Wales (ed.), *Guide to the Department of Manuscripts and Records* (1995)
Perks, R., *Oral History: Talking About the Past* (1992, 1995)
Porter, S., *Exploring Urban History* (1990)
Rogers, A., *Approaches to Local History* (1972, 1978)
Sheppard, J. and Foster, J., *British Archives* (4th edn 2002)
Sinclair, C., *Tracing Your Scottish Ancestors: A Guide to Ancestry Research in the Scottish Record Office* (2nd edn 1997)
Sinclair, C., *Tracing Scottish Local History: a Guide to Local History Research in the Scottish Record Office* (1994)
Stephens, W.B., *Sources for English Local History* (1981)
Stuart, D., *Latin for Local and Family Historians* (2000)
Thompson, K.M. (ed.), *Short Guides to Records: Second Series* (1997)
Thompson, P., *The Voice of the Past* (1978, 1988)

Tiller, K., *English Local History* (1992, 2001)
Waller, P. (ed.), *The English Urban Landscape* (2000)
Williams, M.A., *Researching Local History: The Human Journey* (1996)

Chapter 2: The Land

For England and Wales the *Agrarian History* series is a natural starting place (details immediately below in chronological order):

Piggot, S. (ed.), *The Agrarian History of England and Wales: Volume I/i: Prehistory* (1981)
Finberg, H.P.R. (ed.), *The Agrarian History of England and Wales: Volume I/ii: A.D. 43-1042* (1972)
Hallam, H.E. (ed.), *The Agrarian History of England and Wales: Volume II:* 1042-1350 (1999)
Miller, E. (ed.), *The Agrarian History of England and Wales: Volume III:* 1350-1500 (1991)
Thirsk, J. (ed.), *The Agrarian History of England and Wales: Volume IV:* 1500-1640 (1967)
Thirsk, J. (ed.), *The Agrarian History of England and Wales: Volume V/i,* 1640-1750 *Regional Farming Systems* (1984)
Thirsk, J. (ed.), *The Agrarian History of England and Wales: Volume V/ii,* 1640-1750 (1985)
Mingay, G.E. (ed.), *The Agrarian History of England and Wales: Volume VI,* 1750-1850 (1989)
Collins, E.J.T. (ed.), *The Agrarian History of England and Wales: Volume VII/i and VII/ii,* 1850-1914 (1999)
Whetham, E.H. (ed.), *The Agrarian History of England and Wales: Volume VIII,* 1915-1939 (1978)

Alcock, N.W., *Old Title Deeds* (1986)
Ault, W.O., *Open-Field Farming in Medieval England* (1972)
Beddard, P., 'Website Tells the Story of Where we Live in Maps, Statistics and Travellers' Tales', *Local History News*, no.73 (2004), pp.9-10
Beresford, M.W., *History on the Ground* (1957)
Board of Agriculture, *The Agricultural State of the Kingdom* (1816) repr. with an introduction by Mingay, G.E.
Cobbett, W., *Rural Rides* (2001 ed.), edited by Dyck, I.
Dibben, A.A., *Title Deeds* (1971)
Evans, E.J. and Crosby, A.G., *Tithes, Maps, Apportionments and the* 1836 *Act: A Guide for Local Historians* (1978, 1993, 1997)
Harley, J.B., *Ordnance Survey Maps: A Descriptive Manual* (1975)
Harley, J.B. and Phillips, C.W., *The Historian's Guide to Ordnance Survey Maps* (1984)
Hindle, B.P., *Maps for Local History* (1988)
Hindle, P., *Maps for Historians* (1998)
Hollowell, S., *Enclosure Records for Historians* (2000)
Gaskell, S.M., *Building Control: National Legislation and the Introduction of Local Bye-Laws in Victorian England* (1983)
Gelling, M., *Signposts to the Past* (2000)
James, D., 'Building Plans' in Reeder, D. (ed.), *Archives and the Historian* (1989)
Kain, R.J.P. and Prince, H.C., *Tithe Surveys for Historians* (2000)
Muir. R., *The New Reading the Landscape: Fieldwork in Landscape History* (2000)
National Library of Wales (ed.), *Estate Maps of Wales,* 1600-1836 (1982)
Oliver, R., *Ordnance Survey Maps: A Concise Guide for Historians* (1993)
Owen, D.H., *Early Printed Maps for Wales* (1996)
Razi, Z. and Smith, R. (eds.), *Medieval Society and the Manor Court* (1996)
Short, B., *Land and Society in Edwardian Britain* (1997)
Smith, D., *Maps and Plans for the Local Historian and Collector* (1988)
Wallis, H. (ed.), *Historian's Guide to Early British Maps* (1994)

Chapter 3: The People

Arkell, T., Evans, N. and Goose, N. (eds.), *When Death do us Part: Understanding and Interpreting the Probate Records of Early Modern England* (2000)
Camp, A.J., *Wills and Their Whereabouts* (4th ed., 1974)
Gibson, J.S.W., *Wills and Where to Find Them* (4th ed., 1994)
Grannum, K. and Taylor, N., *Wills and Other Probate Records: A Practical Guide to Researching Your Ancestors' Last Documents* (2004)
Higgs, E., *Making Sense of the Census* (1989)
Higgs, E., *A Clearer Sense of the Census* (1996)
Higgs, E., *Making Sense of the Census Revisited* (2005)
Mills, D. and Schürer, K., *Local Communities in the Victorian Census Enumerators' Books* (1996)
Schürer, K. and Arkell, T. (eds.), *Surveying the People* (1992)

Shaw, G. (ed.), *Directing the Past. Directories and the Local Historian* (2004)
Woods, R., *The Population of Britain in the Nineteenth Century* (1992, 1995)

Chapter 4: Transport, Communications and Trade

Albert, W., *The Turnpike Road System in England, 1663-1840* (1972)
Aldcroft, D.H. and Freeman, M.J. (eds.), *Transport in the Industrial Revolution* (1983)
British Railways Pre-Grouping Atlas and Gazetteer (1976, 1988)
Edwards, J.E. and Hindle, B.P., 'The Transportation System of Medieval England and Wales', *Journal of Historical Geography*, 17 (1991), pp.123-34
Hutchinson, G., *Medieval Ships and Shipping* (1994)
Jones, E.T., 'River Navigation in Medieval England', *Journal of Historical Geography*, 26 (2000), pp.60-82
Langdon, J., 'Inland Water Transport in Medieval England', *Journal of Historical Geography*, 19 (1993), pp.1-11
Szostak, R., *The Role of Transportation in the Industrial Revolution* (1991)
Turnbull, G., 'Canals, Coal and Regional Growth in the Industrial Revolution', *Economic History Review*, 40, 4 (1987), pp.537-60
Webb, S. and Webb, B., *The King's Highway* (1913)

Chapter 5: Working Life

Berg, M., *The Age of Manufacturers, 1700-1820: Industry, Innovation and Work in Britain* (2nd edn 1994)
Burnett, J., *Idle Hands: The Experience of Unemployment, 1790-1990* (1994)
Campbell, R.H., *The Rise and Fall of Scottish Industry, 1707-1939* (1980)
Cockerell, H.A.L. and Green, E., *The British Insurance Business, 1547-1970* (2nd edn 1994)
Edwards, P., *Rural Life: Guide to Local Records* (1993)
Fraser, W.H., *The Rise and Fall of British Trade Unionism, 1700-1998* (1999)
Hammond, J.L. and Hammond, B., *The Village Labourer, 1760-1832* (1911)
Hammond, J.L. and Hammond, B., *The Town Labourer, 1760-1832* (1917)
Hammond, J.L. and Hammond, B., *The Skilled Labourer, 1760-1832* (1919)
Harvey, P.D.A., *Manorial Records* (1984, 1999)
Hopkins, E., *A Social History of the English Working Classes 1815-1945* (1979)
John, A. (ed.), *Unequal Opportunities: Women's Employment in England, 1800-1918* (1985)
Munby, L., *How Much is That Worth?* (1989)
Neeson, J.M., *Commoners: Common Right, Enclosure and Social Change in England, 1700-1820* (1992)
Pinchbeck, I., *Women Workers and the Industrial Revolution, 1750-1850* (1930); Virago edn 1981 with an introduction by Hamilton, K.
Roberts, E., *Women's Work 1840-1940* (1988)
Robson, C.R., *Masters and Journeymen: A Prehistory of Industrial Relations, 1717-1800* (1980)
Rule, J. (ed.), *British Trade Unionism, 1750-1850: The Formative Years* (1988)
Snell, K.D.M., *The Annals of the Labouring Poor, 1660-1900* (1985)
Thompson, E.P., *Customs in Common* (1991)

Chapter 6: Religion

Green, S.J.D., *Religion and the Decline of Christianity in Modern Britain* (1994)
Ifans, D., *Nonconformist Registers of Wales* (1994)
Jones, G., *The Descent of Dissent* (1989)
McLead, H., *Religion and Society in England, 1850-1914* (1996)
McLead, H., *Religion and The Working Class in Nineteenth-Century Britain* (1984)
Rawlins, B.J., *The Parish Churches and Nonconformist Chapels of Wales, Their Records and Where to Find Them; vol.1: Cardigan, Carmarthen, Pembroke* (1987)
Shorney, D., *Protestant Nonconformity and Roman Catholicism* (1996)
Tate, W.E., *The Parish Chest* (3rd ed., 1969)
Tarver, A., *Church Court Records* (1995)
Williams, C.J. and Watts-Williams, J., *Parish Registers of Wales* (1986)

Chapter 7: Education

History of Education Society, *Studies in the Government and Control of Education Since 1860* (1970)
Morton, A., *Education and the State From 1833* (1997)
Sanderson, M., *Education, Economic Change and Society in England* (2nd edn 1995)
Simon, B., *Education and the Social Order, 1940-1990* (1991)
Vincent, D., *Literacy and Popular Culture: England 1750-1914* (1989)

Chapter 8: Poverty

Brundage, A., *The English Poor Laws, 1700-1930* (2002)

Brundage, A., *The Making of the New Poor Law, 1832-39* (1978)
Cage, R.A., *The Scottish Poor Law 1745-1845* (1981)
Checkland, S.G. and Checkland, E.O.A. (eds.), *The Poor Law Report of 1834* (1974)
Crowther, M.A., *The Workhouse System, 1834-1929: The History of an English Social Institution* (1981)
Driver, F., *Power and Pauperism: The Workhouse System, 1834-1884* (1993)
Fraser, D. (ed.), *The New Poor Law in the Nineteenth Century* (1976)
Lees, L.H., *The Solidarities of Strangers: The English Poor Laws and the People, 1700-1948* (1998)
Mitchison, R., *The Old Poor Law in Scotland: the Experience of Poverty, 1574-1845* (2000)
Poynter, J.R., *Society and Pauperism: English Ideas on Poor Relief, 1795-1834* (1969)
Rose, M.E., *The English Poor Law, 1780-1930* (1971)
Slack, P., *The English Poor Laws, 1531-1782* (1990)
Slack, P., *Poverty and Policy in Tudor and Stuart England* (1988)
Timmins, N., *The Five Giants: A Biography of the Welfare State* (1996)
Webb, S. and Webb, B., *English Poor Law History, Part 1: The Old Poor Law* (1906)
Webb, S. and Webb, B., *English Poor Law History, Part 2: The Last Hundred Years* (1929)
Webb, S. and Webb, B., *English Poor Law History Policy* (1910)
Wells, R., *Wretched Faces: Famine in Wartime England, 1795-1801* (1988)
Wood, P., *Poverty and the Workhouse in Victorian Britain* (1991)

Chapter 9: Sickness and Health
Cartwright, F.F., *A Social History of Medicine* (1977)
Chadwick, E., *Report of the Sanitary Condition of the Labouring Population of Great Britain* (1842 repr. 1965)
Digby, A., *Making a Medical Living: Doctors and Patients in the English Market for Medicine, 1720-1911* (1994)
Getz, F., *Medicine in the English Middle Ages* (1998)
Hamlin, C., *Public Health and Social Justice in the Age of Chadwick: Britain, 1800-1854* (1998)
Hardy, A., *Health and Medicine in Britain since 1860* (2001)
Henriques, U.R.Q., *Before the Welfare State: Social Administration in Early Industrial Britain* (1979)
Laybourn, K., *The Evolution of British Welfare Policy and the Welfare State, c.1800-1993* (1995)
Laybourn, K., *Social Conditions, Status and Community, 1860-c.1920* (1997)
Platt, C., *King Death: the Black Death and its Aftermath in Late Medieval England* (1996)
Porter, R., *Disease, Medicine and Society in England 1550-1860* (2nd edn 1993)

Chapter 10: Housing
Barratt, N., *Tracing the History of Your House* (2001)
Burnett, J., *A Social History of Housing, 1815-1970* (1978)
Chapman, S.D., *The History of Working-Class Housing: A Symposium* (1971)
Grenville, J., *Medieval Housing* (1999)
Greysmith, B., *Tracing the History of Your House* (1994)
Melling, J. (ed.), *Housing, Social Policy and the State* (1980)
Milward, R., *A Glossary of Household, Farming and Trade Terms from Probate Inventories* (1977, 1986)
Pooley, C.G., *Local Authority Housing Origins and Development* (1996)
Rodger, R., *Housing in Urban Britain 1780-1914* (1989)
Upton, C., *Living Back-to-Back* (2005)

Chapter 11: Radicalism and Unrest
Belchem, J., *Popular Radicalism in Nineteenth Century Britain* (1996)
Charlton, J., *The Chartists: The First National Workers Movement* (1997)
Charlesworth, A. (ed.), *An Atlas of Rural Protest in Britain* (1983)
Edsall, N.C., *The Anti-Poor Law Movement, 1834-44* (1971)
Epstein, J. and Thompson, D. (eds.), *The Chartist Experience. Studies in Working-Class Radicalism and Culture, 1830-1860* (1982)
Fagan, H. and Hilton, R.H., *The English Rising of 1381* (1950)
Hill, C., *The World Turned Upside Down: Radical Ideas During the English Revolution* (1972)
Hilton, R., *Class Conflict and the Crisis of Feudalism: Essays in Medieval Social History* (1985)
Hobsbawm, E. and Rudé, G., *Captain Swing* (1969)
Holland, M. (ed.), *Swing Unmasked: the Agricultural Riots of 1830 to 1832 and Their Wider Implications* (2005)
Jones, D.V.D., *The Last Rising: The Newport Insurrection of 1839* (1985)
Knott, J., *Popular Opposition to the 1834 Poor Law* (1986)
Manning, B., *The English People and the English Revolution* (2nd edn 1991)
Randall, A., Charlesworth, A., Gilbert, D., Southall, H. and Wrigley, C., *An Atlas of Industrial Protest in Britain, 1750-1984* (1996)
Royle, E., *Chartism* (2nd edn 1986)
Thompson, D., *The Chartists: Popular Politics in the Industrial Revolution* (1984)

Thompson, E.P., *The Making of the English Working Class* (2nd edn 1968)
Underdown, D., *Revel, Riot and Rebellion: Popular Politics and Culture in England, 1603-1660* (1985)
Williams, G.A., *The Merthyr Rising* (1978)
Wood, E.M. and Wood, N., *A Trumpet of Sedition: Political Theory and the Rise of Capitalism, 1509-1688* (1997)
Wright, D.G., *Popular Radicalism: Working Class Experience, 1780-1880* (1988)

Chapter 12: Law and Order

Baker, J.H., *An Introduction to English Legal History* (3rd edn 1990)
Beattie, J.M., *Crime and the Courts in England, 1600-1800* (1986)
Cockburn, J.S., *A History of English Assizes, 1558-1714* (1972)
Cockburn, J.S. and Green, T.A., *Twelve Good Men and True: The Criminal Trial Jury in England, 1200-1800* (1988)
Emsley, B., *Crime and Society in England, 1750-1900* (2nd edn 1996)
Gatrell, V.A.C., *The Hanging Tree: Execution and the English People, 1770-1868* (1994)
Hay, D., Linebaugh, P. and Thompson, E.P. (eds.), *Albion's Fatal Tree: Crime and Society in Eighteenth Century England* (1975)
Ignatieff, M., *A Just Measure of Pain: The Penitentiary in the Industrial Revolution, 1750-1850* (1978)
Kent, J.R., *The English Village Constable, 1580-1642: A Social and Administrative History* (1986)
King, R., *Crime, Justice and Discretion in England, 1740-1820* (2000)
Linebaugh, P., *The London Hanged: Crime and Civil Society in the Eighteenth Century* (2nd edn 2003)
Parry, G., *A Guide to the Records of the Great Sessions in Wales* (1995)
Philips, D. and Storch, R.D., *Policing Provincial England, 1829-1856: The Politics of Reform* (1999)
Radzinowicz, L., *History of English Criminal Law and its Administration from 1750*; 5 volumes (1948-86)
Randall, A. and Charlesworth, A. (eds.), *Moral Economy and Popular Protest: Crowds, Conflict and Authority* (2000)
Webb, S. and Webb, B., *The Prisons Under Local Government* (1922)

Chapter 13: National and Local Administration

Black, J., *Robert Walpole and the Nature of Politics in Early Eighteenth-Century Britain* (1990)
Eastwood, D., *Government and Community in the English Provinces, 1700-1870* (1997)
Hollis, P., *Ladies Elect: Women in English Local Government, 1865-1914* (1987)
Lubenow, W.C., *The Politics of Government Growth: Early Victorian Attitudes Toward State Intervention, 1833-1848* (1971)
Pugh, M., *The March of the Women, A Revisionist Analysis of the Campaign for Women's Suffrage, 1866-1914* (2000)
Turner, M.J., *The Age of Unease: Government and Reform in Britain, 1782-1832* (2000)
Ward, R., City-State and Nation: Birmingham's Political History, 1830-1940
Webb, S. and Webb, B., *The Parish and the County* (1906)
Webb, S. and Webb, B., *The Manor and the Borough* (1908)

Chapter 14: Family and Social Life

Houlbrooke, R.A., *The English Family, 1450-1700* (1984, 1990)
Malcolmson, R.W., *Popular Recreations in English Society 1700-1850* (1973)
Rogers, C.D. and Smith, J.H., *Local Family History in England* (1991)
Stone, L., *The Family, Sex and Marriage in England 1500-1800* (1977)
Walton, J.K. and Walvin, J. (eds.), *Leisure in Britain 1780-1939* (1983)

Index

References which relate to illustrations only are given in **bold**.